BY ANTHONY EVERITT

Alexander the Great

The Rise of Athens

The Rise of Rome

Hadrian and the Triumph of Rome

Augustus

Cicero

SPQR: A Roman Miscellany

ALEXANDER THE GREAT

ALEXANDER THE GREAT

HIS LIFE AND HIS MYSTERIOUS DEATH

ANTHONY EVERITT

RANDOM HOUSE

NEW YORK

Published in the United States by Random House, an imprint and
division of Penguin Random House LLC, New York.

RANDOM HOUSE and the HOUSE colophon are
registered trademarks of Penguin Random House LLC.

Illustration Credits: Alexander, Carole Raddato/Wikimedia Commons; shrine of
the nymphs, Mieza, Jean Housen; Hephaestion, unknown; lion of Chaeronea,
Odysses; theater at Aegae, CJD (Jim) Roberts; royal crown and *larnax,*
Sarah Murray/Wikimedia Commons; Philip II, Manolis Andronikos;
Artaxerxes III, Bruce Allardice/Wikimedia Commons; bringers of tribute,
A. Davey; Cyrus's tomb, Soheil Callage; Issus, https://upload.wikimedia.org/
wikipedia/commons/a/ae/Battle_of_Issus.jpg; Alexander sarcophagus,
CC-BY-SA-2.5; hunting scene, Carole Raddato/Wikimedia Commons;
Tachar palace, Persepolis, Darafsh Kaviyani; marriage of Alexander and
Rhoxane, Web Gallery of Art; tetradrachm, ancientcoincollector;
Gedrosian desert, Marsyas.

LIBRARY OF CONGRESS CATALOGING-IN-PUBLICATION DATA
NAMES: Everitt, Anthony, author.
TITLE: Alexander the Great: His Life and His
Mysterious Death / Anthony Everitt.
DESCRIPTION: New York: Random House, 2019. | Includes
bibliographical references and index.
IDENTIFIERS: LCCN 2018059885| ISBN 9780425286524 (hardback) |
ISBN 9780425286548 (ebook)
SUBJECTS: LCSH: Alexander, the Great, 356 B.C.–323 B.C. | Greece—
History—Macedonian Expansion, 359–323 B.C. | Generals—Greece—
Biography. | Greece—Kings and rulers—Biography. | BISAC: HISTORY /
Ancient / General. | BIOGRAPHY & AUTOBIOGRAPHY / Historical. |
HISTORY / Military / General.
CLASSIFICATION: LCC DF234.E84 2019 | DDC 938/.07092 [B]—dc23
LC record available at https://lccn.loc.gov/2018059885

Printed in the United States of America on acid-free paper

randomhousebooks.com

246897531

First Edition

Book design by Barbara M. Bachman

For Daphne and Jeremy
with much love

PREFACE:
THE KING TAKES
A HOLIDAY

———

MORE THAN TWO MILLENNIA HAVE ELAPSED, BUT ALEXANDER the Great is still a household name. His life was an adventure story and took him to every corner of the known world. Good looks burnished his image. His memory and his glamour persist.

MODERN SCHOLARS HAVE TRIED their best to tell the truth about the young Macedonian, but their accounts reflect the concerns of their own age as much as they do of his. In the first half of the twentieth century, he was the model of an English gentleman and an idealistic believer in the unity of mankind. After the Second World War, he became for many a prototype of the totalitarian dictator, a classical Hitler or Stalin.

It is time for a new look. Naturally this biography reflects our own twenty-first-century hopes and fears, most particularly about the nature of power and the fascination—and impermanence—of military success. It could hardly do otherwise. But I aim to evoke the realities of life in the ancient world, the beliefs Alexander might have held. In many ways, he was a typical Macedonian king and was nothing like a modern statesman. He deserves to be measured against the values of his own time and not of ours.

My intention is to understand rather than to praise or to condemn.

———

AN UNTRIED KING OF Macedonia hardly out of his teens at the outset of his campaigns, Alexander conquered the vast Persian empire and never lost a battle. He was one of the world's great commanders.

His somewhat ambiguous private life has attracted more than its fair share of attention and he has become a gay icon (although he was not much interested in sex with any gender).

Alexander was naturally inquisitive and was intrigued by science and exploration. He enjoyed athletics and the arts, and used the poet Homer's great epic about the Trojan War, the *Iliad,* as a bible.

His life ended when he was only thirty-three, but, paradoxically, this has kept him evergreen in our imaginations. However, his personality had a dark side. He glorified war and the fame it conferred on the valiant, as did many of his contemporaries. He enjoyed violence and was suicidally brave, appearing to see fighting in battle as a form of healthy physical exercise.

From time to time he committed acts of great cruelty, but he was also chivalrous, kind, and loyal.

ALEXANDER'S DEATH IS AN unsolved mystery. Was he a victim of natural causes, felled by some kind of fever, or did his marshals assassinate him, angered by his tyrannical ways? An autopsy would decide the question, but it is too late for that.

The trail is long cold. All who recalled the terrible fortnight of his dying had their own reputations to protect and they were not under oath when publishing their memoirs. The secret of Alexander's end will not be discovered by poring over disputed narratives, but by assessing his interaction with others. Who were the men and women he knew, and who his friends and enemies? What did they think of him and he of them? Where lay their loyalties, and where the imperatives of self-interest?

This book follows Alexander's spectacular career, and its sudden conclusion, as if it traced the trajectory of an arrow. It will lead us eventually to an unraveling of the riddle.

IN THE YEAR 323 B.C. Alexander enjoyed an overdue vacation in the deluxe metropolis of Babylon in Mesopotamia. This was one of the great cities of the Persian empire and over the centuries had grown accustomed to looking after the needs of invaders. Its Hanging Gardens were one of the Seven Wonders of the ancient world. A few weeks there of uninterrupted leisure and pleasure were just what Alexander and his careworn soldiers needed. The youthful Macedonian monarch had spent a good ten years fighting his way nonstop through the Persian empire to its Indian frontier, deposing the Great King and seizing power himself. After winning victories in the Punjab and along the Indus River, he marched back to civilization through a searing desert, losing thousands of his men for lack of water before reaching the safety and the comforts of Mesopotamia.

Alexander was still a handsome man in his prime whose triumphant past augured a shining future. His next and imminent project was to establish commercially viable townships along the Arabian coast. A port had been specially built near Babylon to house a new fleet. Meanwhile the army prepared to march south by land. Victory was taken for granted, but after that, who knew what?

For now, in late May, as the unrelenting heat of summer approached, he needed a good rest. Babylon had all the necessary facilities. There was water everywhere; the river Euphrates on its way to the Persian Gulf passed through the center of the city and poured into the moats that lay alongside the lofty defensive walls of baked mud brick. And beyond the walls lay swamps and lagoons bursting with wildlife, irrigation channels, and reservoirs.

Two colossal palaces stood in the north of Babylon, with offices and workshops. One of them functioned, at least in part, as among the world's earliest museums, housing treasured artifacts from earlier times, and was probably where kings and their families lived in grand but private seclusion. The other, which modern archaeologists have named the Southern Palace, was set aside mainly for administration and for ceremonial functions. Offices and workshops surrounded five courtyards, one of which opened onto a vast throne room whose walls were glazed in blue and yellow tiles and decorated with floral reliefs, lions, and fan-shaped designs suggesting the fronds of a palm tree.

On the river's edge beside the palace, the Hanging Gardens astounded visitors. A set of ascending terraces, angled back one above the other, rested on great brick vaults. Each terrace contained a deep bed of earth and was planted with trees and shrubs. The effect was of a wooded hillside. A staircase led up to all the floors, and water drawn from the river by mechanical pumps irrigated each tier. The story was told that Babylon's most successful king, Nebuchadnezzar II, constructed the Hanging Gardens for his wife, who missed the mountains of her childhood.

In principle, there was nothing so very unusual about them, for they were a condensed urban version of the large walled garden or park much favored by the wealthy and the powerful, who sought refreshing green relief from the parched landscapes of the east. The Greek word for such a garden was *paradeisos,* from which we derive our "paradise."

As the design of the Hanging Gardens goes to show, the people of Babylon and other Mesopotamians were skillful managers of water. They built canals and irrigation systems, and just to the north of the Southern Palace they constructed what seems to have been a large reservoir.

On the eastern side of Babylon, an outer wall formed a first defense against attack and enclosed large areas of less populated ground. It led to a so-called summer palace, two thousand meters north of the main city. Here ventilation shafts counteracted the heat of the day and, away from the crowded city center, afforded some relief to the ruling family. The palace may also have functioned as a military headquarters; there was certainly plenty of space for an army encampment nearby. Alexander preferred being with his men to living in the city, and spent time in the royal tent or aboard ships on the river. So whether there or in the palace, he oversaw the preparations for his Arabian expedition and relaxed.

THE NAVY WAS APPROACHING a state of high readiness and an intensive training program was under way. Different classes of warship raced against one another and the winners were awarded golden wreaths. Alexander decided to organize a banquet for the army on the evening of May 29 (according to the Greek calendar, Daesius 18). It was held to celebrate the end of one campaign, the invasion of India, and the imminent onset of a new one, the invasion of Arabia.

But in the interval there was time for a good time. Wine was sent round to every unit in the encampment, as were animals for sacrifice to the gods—that is, for roasting on an altar and then, as was the way in the ancient world, for eating. The guest of honor at the king's table was his admiral of the fleet, a Greek called Nearchus, a loyal if not especially talented follower, who had been a boyhood friend.

Alexander knew well his Euripides, the Athenian tragic poet of the late fifth century, and recited verses from his play *Andromeda*. The plot concerned a beautiful young princess who was chained to a rock and awaited death from a sea monster. At the last minute the hero, Perseus, arrives on his flying horse, Pegasus, and rescues her. Only fragments of the drama have survived and we do not know what lines the king spoke, but one certainly fits his high opinion of himself.

> I gained glory, not without many trials.

The convention among civilized partygoers was that serious drinking only began once the meal was over. Wine was a little syrupy and could have a high alcohol content compared with vintages today. It was usually served diluted with water. A large two-handled bowl, or *crater,* containing wine (it could hold as many as six quarts of liquid), was brought into the dining room where guests reclined on shared couches. The host, or a master of ceremonies chosen by those present, decided how much water should be mixed with the wine and how many top-ups should be allowed. Guests had individual cups, and servants used ladles to fill them.

The Macedonians and their monarchs had a proud tradition of heavy alcohol consumption. It was not at all uncommon for a session to end with drinkers passing out. In a play performed in Athens earlier in the fourth century, Dionysus, the god of wine, sets out the stages of inebriation:

For sensible men I prepare only three *craters:* one for health (which they drink first), the second for love and pleasure, and the third for sleep. After the third mixing bowl is drained, sensible men go home. The fourth *crater* is nothing to do with me—it belongs to bad behavior; the fifth is for shouting; the sixth is for rudeness and insults; the seventh is for fights; the eighth is for breaking the furniture; the ninth is for depression; the tenth is for madness and unconsciousness.

Alexander had experience of the higher numbers of the scale and drank a toast to each of the twenty men present in the room. Then he decided to leave the party early and get some sleep. This was unusual behavior for him; he may have been feeling a little off-color. As was his habit, he took a bath before sleeping, but then a Thessalian friend of his, Medius, invited him to join a late-night party. "You'll enjoy yourself," he promised. The king agreed and continued drinking. Eventually he left and turned in.

On the following day, he felt feverish and spent much of his time in bed. He played dice with Medius and dined with him. Alcohol was on the menu again. According to one version of events, Alexander challenged a fellow guest to down a *crater* of wine in one go. After he had done so, the man counterchallenged the king to repeat the trick. Alexander tried, but failed. He felt a stabbing pain in his back "as if he had been pierced by a spear," gave a loud cry, and slumped back onto his cushion. He left the party, ate a little food, and took a bath. He now definitely had a fever and fell asleep on the spot in the bathhouse.

By the morning of the third day, Alexander was no better. He was carried out on a couch to conduct the usual daily sacrifice to persuade the gods to watch over him and his army. His indisposition was an annoying setback, but no more than that. He issued instructions to his officers for the imminent Arabian campaign and amused himself by listening to Nearchus reminisce about his adventures at sea.

Then the king was carried on his bed to a waiting boat and taken downstream to the palaces in Babylon. Here he was installed in the *paradeisos* or, in other words, the Hanging Gardens, doubtless because of their calm, quiet, and coolness. He lay in a vaulted chamber beside a large bathing pool. He discussed vacant posts in the army with his commanders and spent time chatting with Medius.

Days passed; Alexander's condition gradually worsened. There seems to have been a variety of pools and bathhouses in the vicinity, and the king was transferred to at least one of them and finally to a lodge beside the reservoir. These constant removals suggest growing panic among the king's staff.

It was increasingly obvious that he was gravely ill; his commanders and high officials were warned to stay within reach. Generals waited in the courtyard. Company and regimental officers were to gather outside the gates. On June 5 Alexander was ferried back to the Summer Palace. He stayed either there or in the royal tent in the nearby army encampment.

The fever did not abate. By the next evening it was obvious that the king was dying. He had lost the power of speech and he handed his signet ring to his senior general, Perdiccas. In this way he dramatized an at least temporary handover of power.

A rumor spread that Alexander was already dead. Soldiers crowded round the palace entrance, shouting and threatening to riot. A second doorway was knocked through the bedroom wall so that they could walk more easily past their dying leader. They were let in, wearing neither cloak nor armor. Alexander's historian Arrian writes:

> I imagine some suspected that his death was being covered up by the king's intimates, the eight Bodyguards, but for most their insistent demand to see Alexander was an expression of their grief and longing for the king they were about to lose. They say that Alexander could no longer speak as the army filed past him, but he struggled to raise his head and gave each man a greeting with his eyes.

Seven of his commanders undertook a ritual of incubation. They spent the night in the temple of a Babylonian deity, hoping for an omen-bearing vision or dream. They inquired whether the king should be moved there, but were told, discouragingly, that they should leave him where he was.

On June 11, between three and six o'clock in the afternoon, Alexander died, a month or so short of his thirty-third birthday. What was to happen next? everyone wondered uneasily. Nobody knew. If the stories are correct, the king himself had been no wiser. While still able to speak, he turned his disenchanted attention to the succession. When someone asked him: "To whom do you leave the kingdom?" he replied: "To the strongest." He is said to have added: "I foresee great funeral games after my death."

Perdiccas asked when he wished divine honors paid to him. He replied: "When you yourselves are happy." It is reported that these were Alexander's last words.

WHAT KILLED THE KING was as uncertain as the future from which he was now excluded. Natural causes were assumed. However, after a while, circumstantial details of a plot to poison him emerged into the light of day. So the real question may have been *who* killed the king.

We have two explanations of Alexander's death, both decorated with data, opaque with cross-my-heart-and-hope-to-die verisimilitude. One gives a verdict of murder, and the other of a complicated natural death. Which are we to believe?

To tease out the truth, let us begin the story of this brief, incandescent life at the beginning. A little prince arrives at the raucous, dangerous court of Macedonia.

CONTENTS

——

LIST OF MAPS

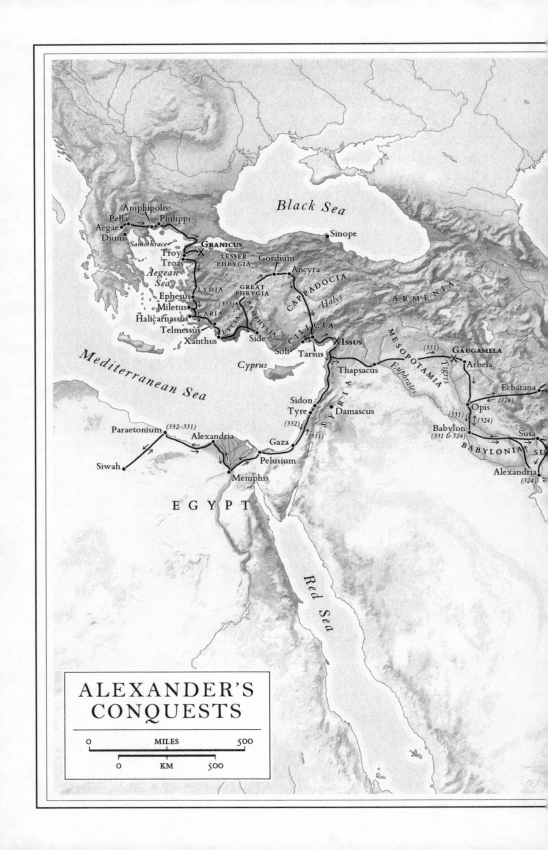

Black Sea

Amphipolis
Pella
Aegae
Dium
Philippi
Samothrace
Troy
Troas
Aegean Sea
GRANICUS
LESSER PHRYGIA
Gordium
Ancyra
Sinope

LYDIA
(331)
GREAT PHRYGIA
CAPPADOCIA
Halys
ARMENIA

Ephesus
Miletus
Halicarnassus
CARIA
LYCIA
PAMPHYLIA
CILICIA
Issus
MESOPOTAMIA
(331)
GAUGAMELA
Arbela

Telmessus
Xanthus
Side
Soli
Tarsus

Cyprus
Thapsacus
Tigris
Ecbatana
(324)

Mediterranean Sea
Sidon
Tyre
(332)
SYRIA
Damascus
(331)
Opis
(324)
(331)
(324)

Paraetonium
(332–331)
Alexandria
Gaza
Babylon
(331 & 324)
Susa
SU

Siwah
Pelusium
Memphis
BABYLONIA

E G Y P T
Alexandria
(324)

Euphrates

Red Sea

ALEXANDER'S
CONQUESTS

| 0 | MILES | 500 |

| 0 | KM | 500 |

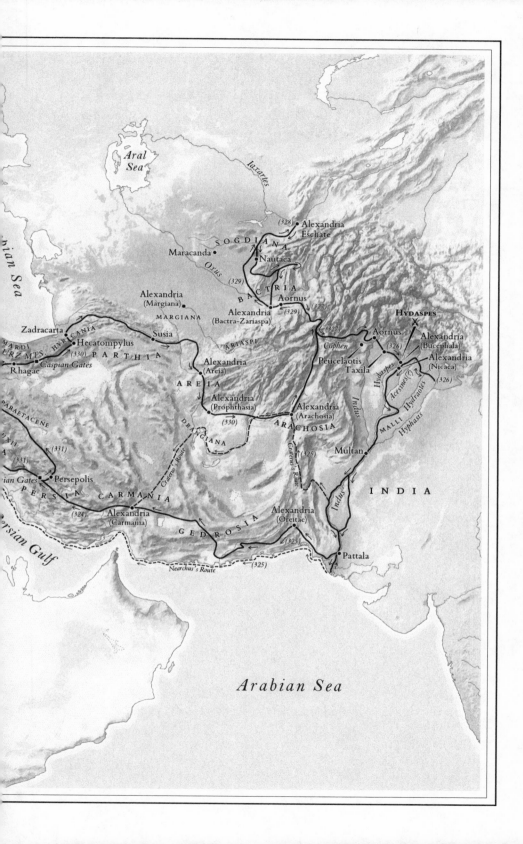

ALEXANDER THE GREAT

CHAPTER 1

GOAT KINGS

―――――

JULY 20 IN THE YEAR 356 B.C. WAS A GREAT DAY FOR PHILIP, AND it marked a high point in his life so far.

An intelligent and charismatic young man in his midtwenties, he had been king of Macedonia for the past two years. This was no sinecure, for he was surrounded by enemies. On the day in question, he was with his army on campaign; three messengers arrived one after another at his camp, each bearing wonderful news.

The first rider brought a report from his trusty and talented general Parmenion, who had scored a victory against Macedonia's hereditary foes, the fierce, wild Illyrians. Then came a dispatch from southern Greece, where the Olympic Games were being held. Philip had entered a horse in one of the equestrian events. Only the very wealthy could afford the training and upkeep of two- or four-horse chariots, but financing a competitor in a four-and-a-half-mile horse race was costly enough. Philip's investment had paid off, for his mount came in first. The publicity would give a shine to his embattled reputation.

But the last messenger arrived from Pella, his capital city. His wife Olympias had given birth to a healthy boy. The official seers or soothsayers said that the arrival of a son timed to coincide with these other successes augured well. When he grew up he would surely be invincible. For his father, there was the prospect of continuing the dynasty.

The infant's name was to be Alexander.

The baby crown prince faced the prospect of a daunting inheritance. He soon came to understand the realities of life and death as a member of the royal family. Being a clever and observant child, he remembered what he saw, and early lessons set the pattern of his adult attitudes.

Here are some of the things he must have learned.

THE ROCKY AND VERTIGINOUS geography of Macedon was hostile to good governance. The kingdom lay to the north of Mount Olympus, traditional home of Zeus and the other anthropomorphic divinities of the Hellenic pantheon. Its center was a fertile alluvial plain bordered by the wooded mountains of northern Macedonia. Its coastline was interrupted by the three-fingered peninsula of Chalcidice, which was peppered with Greek trading settlements.

Macedonia was inhabited by unruly tribes which devoted their time and energy to stock-raising and hunting. They regularly moved sheep to and from grazing grounds—the lowlands in winter and the highlands in summer. They paid as little attention as possible to central authority. There was a myriad of villages and very few settled urban communities.

The kingdom had one important raw material in almost limitless amounts—high-quality timber. Trade increased around the Aegean Sea, for travel or transport by sea was easier by far than to go by land. There was growing demand for merchant ships and war galleys and, it followed, for planking and oars. The tall trees of Macedonia were ideal for the purpose, unlike the stunted products of the Greek landscape. Pitch was also exported for caulking boats.

Life, even for despots, was basic. The "father of history," Herodotus, who flourished in the fifth century B.C., writes of the primitive Macedonian monarchy. His contemporaries would have recognized the simplicity of the royal lifestyle, which had changed little over the centuries. The king lived in a farmhouse with a smoke hole in the roof, and the queen did the cooking. Herodotus, who probably visited Macedonia, commented: "In the old days ruling houses were poor, just like ordinary people."

Up to Philip's day and beyond, the monarch adopted an informal way of life. At home he hunted and drank with his masculine Companions, or *hetairoi*. In the field he fought at the head of his army and was surrounded by a select bodyguard of seven noblemen, the *somatophylaxes*. His magnificent armor inevitably attracted enemy attacks.

He mingled easily with his subjects and eschewed titles, being addressed only by his given name or "King." He had to put up with impertinence from the rank and file, just as Agamemnon, commander-in-chief at Troy, was obliged to hear out Homer's Thersites, a bow-legged and lame troublemaker, whose head was filled "with a store of disorderly words."

In effect, a king like Philip was not an autocrat but a tribal leader, and his success or failure would largely depend on his performance in war and his magnanimity in peace. It was important that he be generous with personal favors, together with gifts of estates, money, and loot on campaign.

Like Agamemnon, he was wise to consult his senior officers. Philip suited the role very well, ruling with a relaxed sense of humor on the surface and adamantine determination underneath. An anecdote epitomizes his style. At the end of one campaign, he was superintending the sale of prisoners into slavery. His tunic had ridden up, exposing his private parts. One of the prisoners claimed to be a friend of his father and asked for a private word. He was brought forward to the king and whispered in his ear: "Lower your tunic a little, for you are exposing too much of yourself the way you are sitting." And Philip said, "Let him go free, for I'd forgotten he is a true friend indeed."

Little is known about a king's constitutional rights, but it seems that he was appointed by acclamation, at an assembly of citizens or of the army. Capital punishment of a Macedonian had to be endorsed by an assembly. But even if his powers were limited, a canny ruler could almost invariably get his way. The eldest son usually—but by no means always, as we shall see—inherited the throne.

The philosopher Aristotle, whose father was official physician at the Macedonian court, was thinking about Philip when he observed that "kingship . . . is organized on the same basis as aristocracy: [by] merit—either individual virtue, or birth, or distinguished service, or all these together with a capacity for doing things."

Successive rulers tried again and again, without conspicuous success, to impose their will on their untamable subjects. Then, toward the end of the sixth century B.C., the outside world intervened in the shape of Darius I, absolute lord of the vast, sprawling Persian empire, which stretched from the shores of the eastern Mediterranean to the gates of India, from Egypt to Anatolia. It has been well described as a desert punctuated by oases. There were well-watered plains, often more abundant than today, and arid wastes. Rugged mountain ranges and broad rivers made travel—and for that matter warfare—complicated and challenging.

The empire was founded by Cyrus the Great in the middle of the fifth century B.C. The Persians were originally nomads, and even in their heyday as an imperial power, their rulers were always on the move between one or other of their capital cities, Susa, Persepolis, and Ecbatana. Their great throne halls were versions of the royal traveling tent in stone. Like all nomads, they were enthusiastic horsemen and their mounted archers were ferocious in battle.

It has been estimated that the empire was home to about fifty million inhabitants. They came from a variety of cultures, spoke a medley of languages, and practiced a wide array of religions; wisely, they were governed with a light touch. However, if they rebelled against the central authority, they could only expect fire, rapine, and slaughter. In the last resort, the empire was a military monarchy.

The Great King, as he was usually called, wanted to secure the northwestern corner of his wide domains by establishing an invulnerable frontier, the river Danube. This would entail subjugating Thrace, the large extent of land between the Balkan mountains, the Black Sea, and the Sea of Marmara. On today's political map, it includes portions of Greece, Bulgaria, and Turkey.

About 512 B.C., a vast Persian army invaded Thrace and then marched on beyond the Danube, but here Scythian nomads outplayed Darius by refusing engagement. They knew perfectly well that his forces would run out of time and supplies and would be forced to withdraw.

The Great King saw that his gains were at risk from the mountain tribes in the west and he decided to annex Macedonia. He commissioned one of his generals to deal with the matter. Envoys were sent to the king of the day, Amyntas I, demanding earth and water, the symbols of submission and allegiance. Amyntas accepted his role as a vassal and married his daughter to a Persian high official, for he saw many advantages in allowing Macedonia to become an imperial province (or, to adopt the Persian word, satrapy). With Darius's backing he knew he would have a good chance of enlarging his kingdom and beating down his independent-minded subjects.

His teenaged son, who was to succeed him as Alexander I, saw things differently and, according to Herodotus, took violent measures at a state banquet in honor of the envoys. As the evening wore on, the guests became more and more drunk. Respectable women did not usually attend such events, but were brought in at the Persians' express request. Amyntas was deeply offended and, doubtless pressed by his furious son, laid a plot. He told the Persians they could have sex with any of the women they liked. He added: "Perhaps you will let me send them away to have a bath. After that they will come back again."

The women were exchanged for beardless male teenagers, armed with daggers, who lay down beside the envoys in the dining room and made short work of them. Their retinue, carriages, and so forth were disposed of, and it was as if they had never existed. The Great King tried to have them traced, but without success. Any inquiry was received with a blank face.

The mature Alexander was probably Herodotus's source for this story, and it may be a boastful fabrication, but it illustrates the humiliation felt in leading Macedonian circles by the Persian occupation, which was to last thirty years.

It was this humiliation, though, that laid the foundations of Macedonian power, for it did not prevent Alexander I, once he had succeeded to the throne, from using Persian support to make substantial territorial gains. It is a painful irony that without the Great King's armed intervention Macedonia would never have become a great power.

SOUTH OF MACEDONIA LAY the isles of Greece, populated by small, fierce, ambitious, and inventive republics, chief among them Athens, the *ville lumière* of the ancient world, and, in the Peloponnese, the military state of Sparta.

Although the Greeks, or Hellenes as they called themselves, disagreed with one another about almost everything, they were unanimous in the opinion that they were a cut above their foreign neighbors. Anyone who was not Greek was a barbarian, or *barbaros:* that is, he spoke a strange language which sounded like "bar bar." He was not to be respected or trusted.

If the Greeks were members of an exclusive club, in other respects they were energetically outgoing. They were traveling traders and from the eighth century onward their ships sailed up and down the Mediterranean. They founded permanent settlements along the coasts and islands of the Aegean Sea as well as in Sicily and southern Italy. These were partly designed to protect and develop mercantile routes and partly to absorb excess citizens in an age when a rising population outstripped local food production.

As Plato put it, these new communities sat like "frogs around a pond" and greatly expanded the influence of the Hellenic world. They were proudly independent. Unluckily, many of them, the city-states of Ionia, lined the littoral of Anatolia. This marked the western edge of the Persian empire and, unsurprisingly, the Ionian city-states fell under the Great King's control.

Few mainland Greeks were bothered by the annexation of Macedonia, but many deeply resented the fate of their counterparts across the Aegean. In 499 B.C. the Ionians raised the standard of revolt, throwing out the despots whom the Great King had appointed to govern them. Democratic Athens incautiously dispatched a small flotilla to assist the rebels. They helped burn down the great and wealthy city of Sardis, capital of Lydia, although they soon afterward sailed home. By 493 the rebels threw in the towel.

Darius was unused to opposition. According to Herodotus, "He strung an arrow and shot it in the air, shouting: 'Lord God, grant me vengeance on the Athenians!' Then he ordered one of his attendants to say to him three times whenever he sat down to dinner: 'Sire, remember the Athenians.'"

In 490, after an abortive attempt two years previously, the Great King sent a fleet directly across the Aegean on a punitive mission. It landed at the bay of Marathon in Attica, the territory of Athens, where

it was surprisingly but decisively defeated by an Athenian army. This was only a minor setback, but the Persians sailed home smarting, and Darius vowed a return match. However, other business, not to mention his own death in 486, led to a ten-year delay.

HIS SON XERXES PICKED up the baton. He assembled an army of more than 200,000 men and about six hundred triremes, or war galleys. He marched along the Thracian coastline, shadowed at sea by the fleet, and in 480 came to Macedonia and northern Greece.

Since his accession, the new Great King had great expectations of Alexander I, whom circumstances had trained into a practiced dissembler. The historian Justin observed:

> When that monarch overspread Greece like a thunderstorm, he presented Alexander with the sovereignty of the whole region between Mount Olympus and the Haemus mountain range in the north. Alexander enlarged his dominions not so much by his own aggressiveness as through the generosity of the Persians.

The Macedonian acted as the Great King's emissary to Athens and we may surmise that, like the rest of the ancient world, he assumed that Xerxes would be victorious. And indeed that appeared to be the case. The population of Athens was evacuated en masse to a nearby island and the Persians took the empty city without difficulty and sacked it. They burnt its temples, the same fate that had been meted out to the citizens of Sardis. Athens was devastated, its broken columns smeared black with smoke. Modern archaeologists have found clear evidence of the flames. Darius's revenge, if delayed, was complete.

However, the allied Greek fleet, dominated by Athenian triremes, defeated the armada of Xerxes at the island of Salamis, to everyone's astonishment. The Great King withdrew hastily to his own realm, leaving a large army in central Greece to turn his fortunes around.

Alexander read the writing on the wall and his latent philhellenism began to revive. He was obliged to take part in the military campaign. He and a contingent of Macedonian cavalry stood loyally, it would seem, in the Persian ranks and faced a disputatious allied force on the field of Plataea in Boeotia.

The king decided to hedge his bets. During the middle of the night before the battle, when both armies were deeply asleep, he rode up to a Greek guard post and asked to speak to the allied commanders. Herodotus gives the details:

> The greater part of the sentries remained where they were, but the rest ran to their generals and told them that a horseman had ridden in from the Persian camp, refusing to say anything except that he wanted to speak to the generals and identified them by their names. Hearing that, the generals straightaway went with the men to the outposts. When they had come, Alexander said to them: "Men of Athens, I give you this message in trust as a secret which you must reveal to no one but Pausanias, the supreme commander, or you will ruin me."

He went on to advise the Greeks to expect the enemy, who had been inactive for some days, to attack on the morrow. This was invaluable information, and the Macedonian added: "Should you bring this war to a successful conclusion, remember me and help me to freedom. I have taken a huge risk for the sake of Hellas by revealing the Persian plans and preserving you from a surprise attack. I am Alexander of Macedonia."

We may forgive the king a touch of exaggeration. He had simply bought an insurance policy: however the day went, he would be on the winning side. As we shall see, this double game of treachery and shifting loyalties was played by a long line of Macedonian kings. They had little alternative to deceit when trying to make the most of a weak hand.

The following day, as forecast, the Persians attacked, and were routed. Their commander was killed. Xerxes' great invasion was over. Alexander did not wait long to turn his coat. We know that he attacked some Persian contingents on their gloomy way home, to considerable effect, for he dedicated gold statues of himself at the oracle of Delphi and at Olympia, headquarters of the Olympic Games, as a "first fruit of spoils from captive Medes." A little later he grabbed land in western

Thrace. Overall, Macedonia had quadrupled in size. The king was entitled to be pleased with himself.

Before the battle at Plataea, every Athenian soldier had made a vow: "I will not rebuild a single one of the temples which the barbarians have burned and razed to the ground, but will let them remain for future generations as a memorial to their impiety." For many years the blackened ruins on the city's citadel, the Acropolis, stood as a bitter reminder of Greek suffering.

Sooner or later, patriots believed, the hour would arrive for revenge, for a rerun of the Trojan War, when Agamemnon, Achilles, and their expeditionary force crossed the sea and destroyed a great Asian power.

THE QUESTION AROSE—WERE THE Macedonians Greek or of barbarian stock? Most proud Hellenes saw them as rough, vulgar, and simple-minded folk who fitted comfortably into the category of barbarian, but in fact their language, incomprehensible though it seemed to outsiders, was a dialect of Greek. The royal family claimed to trace its origins to Argos, a city-state in southern Greece, hence its name— the Argead dynasty. So they at least were sure of their identity.

But that was not enough. One Macedonian king after another worked hard to win over hostile opinion. The Olympic Games, then as now a festival of amateur athletics, were a Hellenic institution par excellence and only Hellenes were allowed to compete. When a young man, the wily Alexander I had trouble qualifying for the footrace and the pentathlon. According to Herodotus,

> The Greeks who were to run against him wanted to bar him from the race, saying that the contest should be for Greeks and not for foreigners. Alexander, however, proving himself to be an Argive, was judged to be a Greek. He accordingly competed in the furlong race and tied for first place.

The greatest poet of the age, Pindar, specialized in odes that celebrated Olympic victors; he addressed Alexander as the "bold-scheming son of Amyntas" who fully deserved the praise he showered on his head.

> It is right for the good to be hymned . . .
> with the most beautiful songs
> For this is the only tribute that comes near to the honors
> Due to the gods, but every noble act dies, if passed over in
> silence.

Alexander's efforts to erase his barbarian identity had some success, and even if he was not fully accepted, he acquired the complimentary sobriquet of "Philhellene."

AFTER HIS DEATH IN 452, some low, dishonest decades ensued. His successor, the equally wily Perdiccas II, lost many of Macedonia's recent territorial gains. The kingdom's once-tamed tribes kicked over the traces and became again more or less autonomous. When the Greek world led by Athens and Sparta entered into a long and exhausting civil war in the last third of the fifth century, the king sold them wood for triremes. He made and broke deals on the sidelines and played one side against the other. Unluckily, his duplicity did not always work to his advantage.

Then in 412 another outward-looking monarch assumed the throne. Called Archelaus, he instituted important economic and military reforms at home and was even more of a lover of all things Greek than his grandfather Alexander. He placed a special value on cultural production and invited leading Hellenic writers and artists to settle in Macedonia at public expense.

Apparently, the king was an effeminate homosexual and ran a relaxed and open court. The aged Euripides, the most popular and radical of the great Athenian tragedians, came to stay; he was accompanied by a younger playwright, Agathon, then about forty, who played a starring role in the philosopher Plato's *Symposium,* a semi-fictional account of a dinner party in Athens. They were rumored to be lovers— rather daring if true, for many Greeks disliked permanent adult same-sex relationships. (They did value liaisons between teenaged boys and young adult males; these were partly educational and partly erotic in character, but were temporary and usually gave way after a few years to close friendships and heterosexual marriage—see pages 42 to 43 for more details). The king challenged Euripides for kissing the middle-aged Agathon at a public banquet, but the old man replied, perhaps with a wintry smile: "Springtime isn't the only beautiful season; so is autumn."

Archelaus tempted the fashionable painter Zeuxis to decorate his house in the new Greek-style capital, Pella, to which he had moved his administration. However, he had no luck with Socrates. The philosopher turned down the king's invitation to visit, saying that he never accepted favors he could not repay.

The king instituted and oversaw a nine-day festival beneath Mount Olympus, home of the gods. It featured athletic and dramatic competitions in honor of Zeus and the Muses. He may well have hoped, unrealistically, that his festival would outshine the Olympic Games, also dedicated to the king of the gods. Like his predecessor Alexander, he competed at Olympia, in his case winning the chariot race (he did the same during the Pythian Games at Delphi).

The tone of the court became increasingly Hellenic, and little ruffians from the Macedonian aristocracy were polished with a Greek education. How far did the king's efforts succeed? The results were mixed. Royals and aristocrats were won over by the propaganda, but international snobbery was harder to overcome.

Thrasymachus was a noted philosopher and an educational and political consultant (what the Greeks called a sophist) who appears as a character in Plato's masterpiece, *The Republic*. He asked: "Shall we, who are Greeks, be slaves to Archelaus, a barbarian?"

He was not alone in being immune to blandishment. Archelaus's successors maintained the uphill struggle for acceptance, and Philip was no exception. When Plato died in 347, he went out of his way to "honor" the great philosopher's passing. But a cultured Athenian like Demosthenes regarded Philip not only as a political opponent but also as a boor. The king, he said dismissively, was "not only not Greek and unrelated to Greeks . . . but a wretched Macedonian, from a land where once you couldn't even buy a decent slave."

IF ARCHELAUS ENCOURAGED THE appurtenances of civilization, there were barbarian aspects of his public personality and of court culture at large that proved too ingrained to erase. The palace was a viper's nest of ambition, and members of the royal family were often at risk of extermination, especially at moments of transition between one reign and the next.

The king was no slouch in this regard. According to Plato, he was Perdiccas's illegitimate son by a slave and "had no claim to the throne he now occupies." However, he clambered up to it through a blood-bath. He invited a leading contender, his uncle (in whose household he seems to have lived), and the uncle's son to dinner. He got them drunk, packed them into a carriage, and drove them away by night; out of sight out of mind, they were then put to death.

The seven-year-old son of the late king, although far too young to rule, had a just title to the throne. He was thrown down a well and drowned. His surely incredulous mother was told that he had fallen in while chasing a goose.

Archelaus was a clever and farsighted ruler, but he should have known that those who live by the sword have a way of dying by it too. In 399, he was assassinated. The sources are confused and differ. According to one account, a boyfriend called Craterus killed him and seized power. Within four days he himself was murdered, the biter bit. Aristotle noted dryly: "At the bottom of the coolness between them was Craterus's disgust with granting sexual favors."

The king's son, Orestes, succeeded his father, but, fatally for him, was another small boy. His guardian promptly put him to death and took his place. He lasted only a few years himself. Three more short-lived kings came and went, and finally in 393 a great-grandson of Alexander, lover of Greeks, took charge. This was Amyntas III—it is something of a surprise that any members of the dynasty were left standing after all the bloodletting—who stayed in place (barring a brief deposition) for two decades. He maintained the traditional Macedonian policy of routinely switching alliances, although he seems always to have had a soft spot for Athens.

On the domestic front, life was busy. Amyntas appears to have been a bigamist (not unusual among Macedonian royalty) and fathered at least seven children. One of his wives, Eurydice, has been presented as almost completely out of control. If we can believe the sources, she plotted the assassination of her husband, intending marriage to her son-in-law, Ptolemy. Her daughter, justifiably outraged, informed Amyntas of her intentions. He courageously forgave his wife and, against the odds, died in his bed in 370 at an advanced age.

Once again the royal family imploded, with Eurydice (it appears) at the sanguinary heart of events. Alexander II, a young man, ascended the throne, but was assassinated a couple of years later at the instigation of Ptolemy. The dowager queen's lover then set himself up as regent for her second son, Perdiccas III, who was still in his teens. The young king was energetic and daring; in 365 he had Ptolemy put to death and seized the reins of power.

History does not record Eurydice's fate, although she sought to retrieve her maternal reputation by encouraging her own education and that of her sons (not without some success, for Perdiccas developed a serious interest in philosophy). She dedicated an inscription to the Muses, in which she claimed that "by her diligence she succeeded in becoming literate."

Perdiccas fell afoul not of palace conspiracies, but of a military disaster. In 359, he attempted to wrest northern Macedonia from the permanently pugnacious Illyrians, but was struck down in a great battle. All the gains of the previous century or so were lost and the kingdom's neighbors gathered gleefully round to tear meat from the carcass.

The lost leader was survived by his son, Amyntas IV, yet another child heir who was obviously of no use in this emergency. Luckily, there was one final adult brother left alive. Old enough to show promise if too young to guarantee achievement, he was called Philip.

PHILIP WAS LUCKY TO have avoided the machinations of his mother. This was because he had spent the last few years as a hostage among the Illyrians and then in Thebes, the capital of Boeotia and, for the time being, the leading state in Greece. Absence from Pella had kept him in good health and he learned a great deal from his hosts.

He was a young and attractive teenager and his Theban host, a distinguished but amorous commander called Pammenes, is reported to have seduced him. This was a routine adolescent experience at the

Macedonian court and there is no evidence that the prince demurred. The episode is better understood as a rite of passage than as sexual abuse.

More importantly, Philip was introduced to a military genius, Epaminondas, whose mastery of tactics, discipline, and training had enabled Thebes to destroy forever the power of Sparta, the dominant military state of the age. He also encountered the three-hundred-strong Sacred Band, a crack regiment of male lovers. Its members were devoted couples, recruited on the principle that neither would want to disgrace himself in the presence of the other. This elite corps probably had its origin in the heroic age of solo champions and their chariot drivers.

Epaminondas was a cultivated man and employed a personal philosopher under whom Philip studied and was fascinated by, the thinker and scientist Pythagoras.

The two or three years the prince spent in Thebes showed him what it was like to live in one of the myriad Greek-speaking mini-states and be a fully paid-up Hellene. For, despite the best efforts of kings such as Alexander II and Archelaus, the Macedonian court was rough at the edges, still more than a little barbarian. Philip was impressed. There is little doubt that, as his historian Justin writes, his time at Thebes "gave Philip fine opportunities to improve his extraordinary abilities."

The prince probably returned to Pella about 365, soon after the accession of his sibling, the doomed Perdiccas. The new king trusted his little brother, whom he placed in charge of territory somewhere near the Thermaic Gulf on the eastern end of Macedonia and gave command of cavalry and infantry. There Philip was able to put into practice the military lessons learned in Thebes, as Perdiccas may have intended. It proved to be an essential apprenticeship.

The great Illyrian battle in 359 was a terrible moment in Macedonia's history. Philip almost certainly fought in it and witnessed the catastrophe. The king and four thousand of his men lay dead on the battlefield. There was widespread disillusion in Macedonia with the war. Enemies approached from every quarter: the tribes of Paeonia raided the kingdom, the Illyrians were planning a wholescale invasion, a pretender to the throne was backed by the Thracians, and the Athenians were helping another one with a fleet and a not insubstantial army.

Philip was appointed regent to his nephew, Perdiccas's infant son. Immediately he gave a master class of coolness under fire and tactical brilliance. Realizing that he could not defeat all his enemies at once, he placed them in a line and dealt with them one at a time. He married the daughter of Bardylis, the Illyrian king, bribed the Paeonians not to invade his kingdom, and suborned the Thracians not merely to abandon the Macedonian pretender, but to put him to death.

Philip then tricked the Athenians into holding back their expeditionary force by promising to hand over to them a prosperous coastal port, then ambushed their now isolated claimant and had him killed. The energetic regent soon persuaded the Macedonian assembly to advance him to the kingship. He was not cruel, but he *was* ruthless, and undeviatingly so, when his own survival was at stake. Learning from Archelaus and other royal ancestors that safety called for bloody hands, he eliminated his three stepbrothers, although he only caught up with two of them some years later. Seeing no threat from the infant cidevant king, he did not touch him and brought him up at court: a rare case of a royal child surviving.

Philip had not the slightest intention of keeping any of his promises. After a year had passed, he invaded Paeonia, inflicted a terminal defeat, and annexed it. Turning almost at once to Illyria, he won a stunning victory. His father-in-law, Bardylis, now over ninety years old, met his death in the field and seven thousand enemy soldiers also lost their lives. Perdiccas was avenged. More to the point, Philip had wrested back control of Upper Macedonia. His kingdom was united again.

He now ruled over a large and settled territory. Like his recent predecessors, he faced the challenge of transforming his role from that of the Homeric leader of an unruly war band to that of a head of government.

HOW WERE PHILIP'S TRIUMPHANT feats of arms achieved? He had been able to look back into the past for inspiration.

On the plain that lay between the city and the sea, two armies faced each other. It was the ninth year of a long and bitter struggle as a Greek expeditionary force attempted to capture the legendary city of Troy on the coast of Asia Minor. The origin of the war lay in the greatest sex scandal of the ancient world; the beautiful Helen had abandoned her husband, Menelaus, king of Sparta, and eloped with the handsome Paris, prince of Troy.

Homer, author of the great epic poem about the war, evokes the scene.

> In their swift advance across the plain, their marching feet had raised a cloud of dust, dense as the mist that the South Wind wraps round the mountaintops, when a man can see no further than he can heave a rock.

Mingling among the rank and file, kings and aristocrats stood on chariots. Once one of them had identified an enemy, who would also be riding a chariot, he jumped down onto the ground and challenged him to a duel. Each warrior carried two light throwing spears and a sword. For protection he had a round shield, which he could hang on his back if retreating. While the warriors fought, their poorly armed retainers cheered them along. They advanced or retreated in a mêlée, as the fortunes of their leaders ebbed and flowed, and seem not to have played a decisive role in the battle.

On the present occasion Paris, the cause of all the trouble, stepped out from the Trojan ranks to challenge any Greek to a duel. The cuckolded husband, Menelaus of Sparta, enthusiastically responded and leaped from his chariot. Paris was a coward and was whisked away by his divine patron, Aphrodite, goddess of love.

Archers were unpopular, for they killed unfairly from a safe distance. Later on in the siege, Paris loosed a shaft at the greatest warrior of all, the hot-tempered, beautiful Achilles, and killed him. Bows and arrows were evidence of bad character.

Greeks in later centuries agreed with Homer's (almost certainly) fictional heroes that war brought glory and that individual courage marked a man out for praise and fame. In that way he became almost godlike, *isotheos*.

By the eighth century B.C., the age of kings and lords in mainland Greece had passed. What is more, we have no idea whether the war at Troy ever took place. It may have been a literary invention. The Homeric description of warfare is implausible. Simply to use the chariot as a taxi service to the front line is odd behavior at a time when the Hittites in Asia Minor and the Egyptians deployed massed chariots in battle.

However, most people were convinced that this distant Hellenic conflict was historical. It inspired a belief in military glory. Philip knew it behooved a brave leader like Achilles to risk his life in the thick of the fighting, to fight hand-to-hand and to lead from the front. No skulking in the rear.

The Macedonian king fought by this rule and, unsurprisingly, was frequently wounded on his many campaigns. When one of his fiercest critics conceded that "he was ready to sacrifice to the fortune of war any and every part of his body," he was not exaggerating. A hand and a leg were maimed, a collarbone broken, and, worst of all, Philip lost an eye during the siege of a city. His doctor succeeded in extricating the arrow and the king survived. Despite being in great pain, he remained in command. When he took the city, he did not punish the defenders for their resistance. This was a sign of magnanimity, a virtue expected of a great monarch.

According to Plutarch, "he did not cover over or hide his scars, but displayed them openly as symbolic representations, cut into his body, of virtue and courage."

CITY-STATES DOMINATED BY MIDDLE-CLASS farmers and traders succeeded the feudal realms. The style of battle changed to match the new politics. This was the age of the citizen militia. In place of well-born charioteers hurling spears at individual opponents came disciplined troops of hoplites. These were heavily armed soldiers who marched in a tight formation called the phalanx.

The hoplite wore a metal helmet, a breastplate, greaves, and thigh pieces. He carried two thrusting spears and swords for hand-to-hand fighting, and protected himself with a large round shield, which also helped to cover his neighbor on the left and presented a shield wall to the enemy. The main strength of the phalanx lay in its momentum. Its function was to be a human battering ram and crash through the enemy's line. It pushed and it shoved. Most casualties were incurred once there had been a decision: the losers were slaughtered in flight.

Provided it held together and remained strictly in formation, the phalanx was hard to beat. However, it had some distinct disadvantages. It could not change front rapidly or keep up an orderly pursuit. It needed flat ground; bumps, holes, ditches, streams, and trees and bushes made it hard for men to keep their dressing. Once gaps appeared, they were vulnerable and could be broken up.

Because hoplites held their shields on their left arms, those who stood in the last file on the right were unprotected if outflanked, so they had a tendency to drift defensively rightward. This would stretch and thin the line, creating yet more dangerous gaps.

A further difficulty was that when each side in a battle presented a phalanx, the outcome could be a stalemate and a draw. The Thebans were the first to recognize this flaw and to find a solution. They tried it out on a summer's day in 371, outside a village called Leuctra in Boeotia. They faced the Spartans, whose army was generally held to be the finest of the day, and their allies.

As was usual, the Spartan phalanx took up the place of honor on the right of the battle line. Facing it on the Theban left, Epaminondas massed a column of infantry that was a phenomenal fifty ranks deep. The rest of his army was much weaker and was echeloned back so that it would not be tested in fighting. After a cavalry engagement, his mega-phalanx smashed the enemy's right wing by brute force. The result was a total victory for the Thebans, and Spartan power was broken for good.

Young Philip absorbed the military reforms of Epaminondas and the Theban's great friend Pelopidas with red-hot interest. We may imagine him listening to talk of tactics at Pammenes's dinner table and taking mental notes about the revolutionary new strategy of battle.

SOME YEARS LATER, when Philip became king, he remodeled the remains of the Macedonian army. What he had at his disposal was a strong cavalry force, called the Companions, which was recruited from the aristocracy (who could afford the upkeep of horses), and an undis-

ciplined and untrained peasant infantry militia, always anxious to return home and look after their farms and harvests. He developed it into
a well-trained standing army, capable of taking on all comers.

First of all, he stole the idea of the deep Theban phalanx, with an
important addition. Its weakness was that it would tend to crumble at
the point of impact like a rugby football scrum. So he replaced the
throwing spears with long pikes or sarissas. These were about eighteen
feet long and had to be held two-handed. In a charge the sarissas of the
first four or five ranks projected well forward beyond the front of the
phalanx, which usually consisted of sixteen ranks. The remainder held
their pikes up in the air to disrupt the impact of missiles. Hoplites who
were used to hand-to-hand combat found it very hard to cope with this
lethal outsized porcupine.

That said, the overwhelming phalanx shock could not always be
repeated if other armies also deployed similar deep infantry formations. For victory Philip depended on his heavily armed cavalry,
which was probably the best in the Hellenic world. Horsemen had
the obvious advantage of mobility. While the phalanx was holding
its ground and fully occupying the enemy infantry's attention, his
aggressive and fast-moving cavalry could gallop about the battlefield,
slashing and stabbing foot soldiers from above, sway the balance of
advantage, and win the day.

The Greek city-states, often democracies, paid little attention to
cavalry because horses were expensive to run and associated with dis-
credited aristocratic elites. Such Greek cavalry as there was usually
formed into a square, sixteen horsemen wide and sixteen deep. The
excellent Thessalian horsemen deployed in a diamond configuration,
which Philip modified into a triangle. The commander would occupy
the tip or point nearest the enemy. The cavalrymen behind him followed his galloping horse and shifted direction as and when he did.
This unique flexibility came at a serious risk of injury or death to the
commander if he was surrounded by the enemy. At every moment
during a charge, men had to be ready to come to his rescue. As Asclepiodotus, a military strategist of the first century B.C., observed: "Wheeling was thus easier than in the square formation, since all have their
eyes fixed on the single squadron-commander, as is the case also in the
flight of cranes."

In many armies of the day, civilians approached the number of combatants. Philip cut back the number of support staff and banned wives and children, prostitutes, small-time traders, and other camp followers. Carts were forbidden.

With the passage of time, Philip enlarged his army. When he assumed the throne he commanded about 10,000 infantry and 600 cavalry. By his death this had risen to 24,000 infantry and 3,000 cavalry. The wage for a foot soldier was one drachma a day; for a horseman, three drachmas. No Greek city-state could afford to keep a standing army of this size, but nobody drew the obvious conclusion that the balance of power in the eastern Mediterranean had been transformed. The change in degree was so great that it had insensibly become a change in kind.

AT THE HEART OF Philip's approach were training, discipline, and the maintenance of group morale. He held constant maneuvers and forced marches. He made his men carry their own provisions (including a thirty-day ration of flour) and equipment. He taught them to forage for food.

His objective was to make individual soldiers, and indeed the army itself, as nimble and self-sufficient as possible. The king mingled among his men, but he was no soft touch. Officers were disciplined as severely as other ranks. When Philip found one of them taking warm baths, he stripped him of his command. "In Macedonia," he said tartly, "we don't even allow a woman in childbirth to use warm water." He beat another man for breaking ranks when thirsty and going for a drink in a tavern.

Off duty, though, Philip was very much more relaxed. If we are to believe a contemporary, the fourth-century historian Theopompus, who spent considerable time as the king's guest, that would be to put it mildly. He wrote:

> Philip's court in Macedonia was the rendez-vous of all the most debauched and shameless characters in Greece or elsewhere. They were styled the king's Companions. As a rule, Philip showed no favor to respectable men who took care of their

property, but those he honored and promoted were high spend-
ers who passed their time drinking and gambling. In consequence, he not only encouraged them in their vices, but made
them past masters in every kind of wickedness and lewdness. . . .
Some of them used to shave their bodies and make them smooth
despite the fact that they were men not women, and others actually had sex with each other though old enough to be bearded.
They took two or three male prostitutes around with them and
themselves offered the same service to others. In effect, they
were not courtiers but courtesans, not soldiers but strumpets.
They were natural man-killers, but their behavior turned them
into man-whores.

We do not need to take this invective too literally, but throughout
the ages soldiers at leisure have been known to binge drink and to hunt
for sexual conquests. What is perhaps unusual is the impression given
of an open and dominant homosexual subculture. We know Philip admired that brigade of lovers, the Theban Band. The deep phalanx may
not have been the only innovation the young hostage thought worthy
of imitation.

PHILIP'S BABY SON, ALEXANDER, grew up in the court at Pella. If the
boy fashions the man, the experiences of his early years must have cast
a long shadow forward across his maturity.

As time passed and he moved from infancy through childhood and
into his teens, he learned about the world he was growing up in. He
was a bright little boy and stored the data in his mind for future use.

Alexander lived in a tough, bizarre environment. That palace conspiracies were toxic and bloody was one of the bitter lessons that history taught him. The only way forward was to react quickly and
decisively to perceived threats. The gory fate of ancestral kings in general, and his father's ruthless actions at the outset of his reign in particular, made the point very clearly.

The thrilling story of the two Persian invasions will have excited
Alexander. It identified an enemy—defeated, but powerful and malevolent for all that. Revenge is a tasty dish for the young imagination,

and the shame of Macedonia's subjection to the Great King still rankled.

The victories at Marathon and Salamis underlined the superiority of the Greek civilization which his father and the Macedonians sought to emulate and to which they claimed brassily to belong.

He was introduced to the rudiments of warfare and understood that fighting was to be his destiny. He must also have taken on board as normal the rough-and-ready Macedonian court. He admired his often absent father, and his father loved and was proud of his clever and fearless son. Philip unwarily trained him for high command at the first possible moment.

Alexander inhabited a violently masculine society—with one exception, his terrifying mother. She was Olympias, a princess from Epirus. From the moment of his birth her only care was to advance her son's interest with fiery ferocity. Even when he was a married adult, she was to remain the most important woman in his life.

CHAPTER 2

THE APPRENTICE

———

THE YOUNG GIRL WAS HELPED DOWN FROM THE SHIP ONTO THE open shore.

She was Polyxena, a princess of the Molossians, the leading tribe of the small realm of Epirus in northwestern Greece. She had just landed on the rocky island of Samothrace, some miles south of the coastline of Thrace.

The island looked as if a colossal boulder of granite and basalt had been tossed into the sea. Here and there, white foaming waterfalls streamed down precipitous cliffs. There was no cultivable earth and the few inhabitants eked out a living, as they do now, from fishing and tourism. In Polyxena's day, visitors stayed in the island's only urban settlement, which was guarded by cyclopean walls built from trimmed granite rocks. They came as pilgrims, for not far from the town stood the Sanctuary of the Great Gods in a wooded gorge.

Here arcane rites, or Mysteries, took place in honor of deities of the underworld, among them the fertility goddess the Great Mother. Others have enigmatic non-Greek names—Axieros, Axiokersa, Axiokersos, and Kasmilos. The nature of the ceremonies was a deep secret and adepts were silent about them, so that little information has come down to us; but their main attraction will have been the promise of an afterlife. Anyone could take part, free or slave, man or woman, adults or children, and people came from across the eastern Mediterranean.

It seems that prayers were offered up and pigs and sheep were sacrificed on rock altars. Libations were poured into ritual pits. Initiates underwent two stages. There were ritual dances in a large hall followed by a showing of sacred symbols in a smaller room. We may imagine torches in the darkness. Successful participants were probably given a purple belt and an iron ring to mark their sacred status and to symbolize the protection that initiation would confer.

Every summer, perhaps in July, a festival was staged, which centered on the performance of a sacred play featuring a ritual wedding. Although the island remained open for spiritual business all the year round, it may have been for this annual event that Polyxena and her family came to Samothrace.

During the ceremonies she met for the first time a dashing young prince, Philip of Macedonia. She was perhaps ten years old and the date was probably 365. This was soon after Philip had returned to his homeland following his spell as a hostage in Thebes. The trip to Samothrace may have been a celebration to mark his release.

We are told that the prince fell for Polyxena, whom we can suppose to have been a pretty and lively girl, and the couple were engaged. Presumably this was not an erotic infatuation, but a cool assessment of her likely future attractiveness. Rather more to the point, Epirus was of strategic importance, lying as it did on Macedonia's northern frontier. A marriage alliance would cement friendly relations between the two countries. It is perfectly possible that the encounter in a famous religious setting was planned in advance. This would enhance the authority or distinction of a betrothal that was as much a business proposition as a romantic affair.

At some point Polyxena acquired another name, Myrtale, after the Greek word for myrtle. The plant was sacred to the goddess of love, Aphrodite, who may have had a connection with the Mysteries at Samothrace. This suggests that the name was conferred on the girl to mark her engagement to Philip. Alternatively, she adopted it a little later at a coming-of-age ceremony.

The wedding was solemnized about 358 or 357 when Polyxena or Myrtale was of childbearing age. It must have been on this auspicious occasion that the young princess name-shifted again. Doubtless inspired by the Macedonian festival of Olympian Zeus, she was addressed from now on as Olympias, the name by which she is known to history.

ELITE WOMEN IN ANCIENT Greece were expected to spend their lives indoors and to concern themselves exclusively with household matters. They did not attend dinner parties even in their own homes. They might be briefly seen shopping in the marketplace under the watchful eyes of a domestic slave, or participating in religious festivals. Apart from their close male relatives, they met men only at weddings and funerals. The ideal female was one whom nobody talked about.

But in the northern kingdoms, such as Macedonia and Epirus, the situation was very different. A noblewoman or female member of a royal family played a far more prominent religious, social, and, in some circumstances, political role. She could hold and dispose of her own property and act as guardian for her children when minors. She engaged in diplomacy and corresponded with her relatives abroad; it is likely that she was literate. Throughout her life Olympias was a fervent letter-writer.

The career of Queen Eurydice, as reported, offered a ruthless role model for ambitious princesses such as Olympias. The nearest comparators to the Macedonian woman were to be found in the heroic pages of Homer and the great Athenian tragedies. These queens and princesses are ferociously independent.

Among them, Clytemnestra, queen of Mycenae in the Peloponnese, the peninsula that makes up southern Greece, ruled her kingdom without trouble during her husband Agamemnon's ten-year absence at the siege of Troy. When he returned home she stabbed him to death in the bath after trapping him inside a voluminous purple robe. The murder was payback for the sacrificial death of their daughter, Iphigenia, at her father's hands.

> Here where I struck I stand and see my task achieved.
> Yes, this is my work and I claim it.

Another fictional woman with agency was the witch Medea, who set up house in the Greek city of Corinth with Jason of the Argonauts.

A weak but ambitious man, he decided to marry the king's daughter. Medea, enraged, sent the bride a splendid but poisoned wedding dress and slaughtered her own two sons by Jason.

She admitted to no regrets. "It was not for you or your princess to trample on my love and live a life of pleasure, laughing at me," she said. "So call me lioness, yes, if you wish to, for I have my claws in your heart as you deserve."

We have no evidence that Olympias was a student of Greek tragedy, but her character and career betray a remarkable family resemblance to these women of legend. Few laughed at her with impunity—not even her husband.

SOME TIME AFTER THEIR MARRIAGE, Philip visited his wife's bedroom to have sex with her. He was disconcerted to find a snake stretched out alongside her in her bed as she slept. Plutarch tells us this had the effect of cooling the king's ardor and that he seldom came to sleep with the queen thereafter.

This would appear to have all the markings of a tall story. However, Olympias was a spiritual woman. An initiate of the transcendental Orphic religion, she took part, as did many Macedonian women, in the Bacchic rites of Dionysus. He was the god of transcendence through the wine harvest, theater, and out-of-body experiences.

Worshippers, mainly women but also men, flocked out into wooded mountains. They became delirious with excitement and began to rave. Exactly what took place during these nocturnal observances was a deep secret accessed only by initiates, but it seems that the climax involved the eating of raw goat flesh. This may have restaged the fate of Dionysus himself, who in his babyhood was ripped to pieces and eaten before being born again at the command of Zeus, king of the gods. The deep secret must have centered on the magical cycle of life, death, and rebirth. This gave new hope to adepts, desperate to ensure futurity.

We shall not go far wrong if we regard these rites as orgies both in the original and the contemporary senses of the word—namely, a frenzied mystical trance and sexual license.

Half a century or so earlier, during his stay at Pella under King Archelaus, the aged Euripides wrote his last play and masterpiece, *The Bacchae,* which tells a tragic story of the lethal power Dionysus exerts over his followers. A chorus of female devotees sings,

> What sweetness is in the mountains!
> Whenever the Bacchant, wearing the sacred fawn skin,
> Falls to the ground after the running dance,
> He hunts the blood of the slaughtered goat,
> A raw-eaten delight.

Stupefied by the god, the worshipper sees a transformed paradisal landscape:

> The plain flows with milk, it flows with wine,
> It flows with the nectar of bees.
> The air is thick with the smoke of Syrian myrrh.

As a member of the royal family, the queen probably played a leadership role in the Bacchic revels. Plutarch writes that Olympias used

> to enter into these states of possession and surrender herself to
> the inspiration of the god with even wilder abandon than the
> others. She would introduce into the festal procession numbers
> of large snakes, hand-tamed. They terrified the male spectators
> as they raised their heads from the wreaths of ivy and the sacred
> winnowing-baskets, or twined themselves around the wands
> and garlands of the women.

Snakes were associated in ancient times with religious cults, representative, or at least suggestive of, the phallus. The god of medicine, Asclepius, used them as healers. The dead were sometimes believed to return as serpentine revenants.

Many years later when Pella had dwindled into a village, the stories about the Macedonian queen received some surprising confirmation. The Greek author Lucian reported in the second century A.D. that

snakes were still to be found there, perhaps descended from those belonging to Olympias. They were

> great serpents, quite tame and gentle, so that they were kept by
> women, slept with children, let themselves be stepped upon,
> were not angry when they were stroked, and took milk from the
> breast just like babies.

Whichever way one looked at the matter, Olympias was a formidable agent in a man's world.

THE CHILDHOOD OF HER SON, Alexander, is encrusted with legends
invented after he had grown up and indeed postmortem, but they are
worth noting because they reflect authentic insights of his contemporaries into his personality. They show him to have been as much of a
handful as his mother.

From about the age of seven the boy left the care of women and
received schooling in the Greek manner. He was provided with a *paedogogus* called Leonidas, a relative of Olympias. A *paedogogus* was usually a trustworthy slave who accompanied a boy to his classes. He made
sure his charge behaved politely and obediently and was protected
from unwelcome sexual advances. But in this case Leonidas acted as a
kind of headmaster and supervised a range of specialist teachers. He
became, in effect, the boy's moral tutor.

Leonidas was a severe disciplinarian. The young Alexander accepted, but never forgot, a reprimand. Once the frugal and austere *paedogogus* caught him throwing an excessive amount of frankincense onto
an altar while sacrificing. He told the boy: "Once you have conquered
the lands that produce this spice you can be as extravagant as you like.
Till then, don't waste what you've got."

Years later, at the siege of Gaza, when he could access as much
frankincense as he liked, Alexander sent Leonidas half a ton of it together with a large quantity of myrrh, with the message "I have sent
you plenty of myrrh and frankincense so that from now on you don't
need to be mean to the gods any longer." This was generosity so crush-

ing as to qualify as revenge. Alexander had an excellent memory and he watered his grudges.

It appears that in due course a tutor took over Alexander's education, a boorish (but also well-born) personality called Lysimachus. He understood the art of flattery and apparently got the job by emphasizing the royal family's fine Homeric family tree. He referred to Alexander as Achilles, a much appreciated compliment. He called Philip by the name of Achilles' father, Peleus, and spoke of himself as Phoenix, the trusty warrior who had helped raise Achilles as a child and looked after him as if he were his son.

A FAMOUS STORY ABOUT ALEXANDER, perceptive if perhaps apocryphal, throws light on his ability to notice a telling detail, however slight, and use it to his advantage.

Thessaly with its broad plains in northern Greece was well-known for the high quality of its horses. Then one day, perhaps in 347 when the little crown prince was about eight or nine, a tall, finely bred stallion was presented to Philip for sale by a Thessalian dealer. He was a beautiful animal, in his prime, black with a white blaze on his forehead. He had been branded with the mark of his owner, a bull's head, and was named by the Greek word for bull's head, Bucephalas. The king showed some interest, despite the extraordinarily high asking price of thirteen talents, and went down to the plain to watch the horse's trials.

The animal proved to be unmanageable and evidently had not yet been broken in. He was upset by the shouting of the grooms and refused to allow anyone to mount him. Philip was angry and ordered that Bucephalas be taken away.

A small voice piped up. "What a horse they are losing," said Alexander. "And all because they've no idea how to handle him, or don't dare try." He repeated his complaint several times and his father realized the child was upset.

"Are you criticizing your elders and betters?" Philip asked. "Do you think you know more than them or could handle a horse better?"

"Well, I could handle this one better."

"If you can't, what punishment will you deserve for being so cheeky?"

"I'll pay for the horse!"

Everyone laughed, but Alexander was being serious. He agreed to the bet with his father.

Alexander walked briskly up to Bucephalas and took hold of his bridle and turned him to face the sun. This was crucial, for he alone had noticed that the horse shied at the sight of his shadow as it fell in front of him and moved whenever he did.

He ran alongside Bucephalas, stroking him to calm him down. Once the horse had recovered his spirits, Alexander threw aside his cloak and vaulted onto his back. He used the bit cautiously and then gave him his head. Bucephalas, his confidence fully restored, broke into a gallop.

The king and his court were on tenterhooks, but once they saw that the boy had mastered the horse, broke into spontaneous applause. Philip, we are told, wept for joy. He kissed Alexander when he had dismounted and is supposed to have remarked: "My boy, we'll have to find a suitable kingdom for you. Macedonia is too small."

A Corinthian merchant and aristocrat called Demaratus was a strongly pro-Macedonian statesman and a guest-friend of Philip. To be a "guest-friend" was to be protected by the iron taboos of ancient Greek hospitality. A traveler on political and commercial missions, Demaratus was present at the incident with the horse and immediately volunteered its selling price. He gave Bucephalas to Alexander.

Just as he had an indelible memory for an insult, so the boy never forgot a favor. Loyalty was his watchword. The Corinthian will reappear in this long story.

ALEXANDER WAS OBLIGED TO grow up quickly. He was introduced to the alcoholic world of Macedonian diplomacy when still only a child. In 346, the year after his acquisition of Bucephalas, a political delegation from the city of Athens, the most formidable sea power of the age, arrived in Pella and was treated to the usual boisterous banquet. As the wine went round after the meal, the ten-year-old crown prince played music on the cithara (a kind of lyre). Doubtless he acquitted himself admirably—perhaps too admirably, for it may have been on this occasion that Philip asked drily: "Aren't you ashamed to pluck the strings so well?" It was enough if a ruler could find time to listen while others played. That was the point and the boy took it. We hear no more of the cithara.

The presence of foreign embassies in Pella gave Alexander an opportunity to soak up detail about the world beyond Macedonia. He was especially interested in the great, mysterious empire of the Persians, which in the unforgotten past had conquered and annexed his father's kingdom. In the same year as his performance at the feast for the Athenian envoys, a famous public intellectual, Isocrates, issued a much read and much debated pamphlet inviting Philip to lead all the Greeks on a military expedition that would pay the Great King back for his predecessors' invasions not only of their homelands, but also of the Ionian cities of Asia. The king had not taken up the offer, but his son could dream of leading a crusade.

One day envoys from the Great King in faraway Susa, the Persian capital, arrived in Macedonia. Philip happened to be away, so Alexander, still a boy, received them in his place. According to Plutarch, he cross-examined them carefully, showing no interest in the famous Hanging Gardens of Babylon nor in how the Great King was dressed, but only in matters of substance.

What especially won his attention was the system of roads the Persians had established. Old caravan routes had been transformed into military highways, and bridges or fords were installed at river crossings. This enabled imperial troops to move fast to trouble spots. At intervals, state rest houses provided accommodation and a change of horses: this allowed official messengers to communicate speedily with the provinces, and state dignitaries to travel easily around the empire.

The incident gives us an Alexander who was a greedy consumer of data. He seems already to have grasped the fact that a military victory required competent logistics and organization. A good general—and we may be sure that he already imagined himself as one—found out all he could about the land in which he intended to campaign before marching into it.

———

PHILIP AND OLYMPIAS WERE very proud of their son, but two aspects of his personality worried them—his violently impulsive nature and, after the arrival of puberty, his surprising lack of interest in sex.

Alexander resented and resisted direct orders, although he could be persuaded by an appeal to reason. His parents took the view that he needed, in the words of the great Athenian tragedian, Sophocles, "the rudder's guidance and the bit's restraint." The task of training him could not be left to the common run of teachers and the routine curriculum of poetry, music, and rhetoric, or the art of public speaking.

So who in the civilized Greek world was the leading spokesman for rationality? There was no competition. At the age of forty, Aristotle was a well-known philosopher with a high reputation. He had studied for twenty years at Plato's informal university, the Academy in Athens. He conducted groundbreaking zoological research in the eastern Mediterranean, for in the ancient world there was little distinction drawn between philosophical thought and practical research. He also wrote and taught.

Aristotle spoke with a lisp; he had skinny calves and small eyes. He dressed well, wore rings, and had his hair cut short. His smart appearance contradicted the example of Socrates, the very model of a Greek philosopher, who seldom washed either his clothes or himself.

In 343 Philip decided to hire Aristotle as tutor to his thirteen-year-old son. Recruiting him was made all the easier because his father had been an official physician at the Macedonian court during the reign of Philip's father, Amyntas III. In their late teens they had met at Pella and so were already acquainted. The philosopher understood Macedonian culture in general and the exotic ways of the Macedonian royal family in particular.

Aristotle was a tough bargainer and only accepted the king's invitation on the condition that he rebuild Aristotle's native city, Stageira, a long-established city-state in the three-pronged peninsula of Chalcidice. Philip had sacked it five years previously in one of his many wars, but, ever the dealmaker, he seldom objected to changing his mind. He agreed to the condition: the inhabitants, who had been sold into slavery, were bought back, and the city rose from the ground again and was repopulated. A new aqueduct was constructed and two shrines to Demeter, goddess of the harvest, were built.

It was wisely decided that Alexander and a group of pupils of his own age should be removed from the temptations of a capital city and a busy court. Aristotle held his classes at Mieza, a pastoral retreat, also called the Gardens of Midas after its rich orchards and vineyards. Here a shrine sacred to the Nymphs was linked to two natural caves. Part of the complex was protected from the sun by a portico. Plutarch writes that in his day, around the turn of the first century A.D., guides still

> show you Aristotle's stone seats, and the shady walks where he used to spend time. It appears that Alexander learned from him not only the principles of ethics and politics, but also something of those more abstruse and esoteric studies which philosophers do not impart to the general run of students, but reserve for spoken communication with the initiated.

Like every Greek boy, Alexander will have practiced gymnastics and competitive sports throughout his childhood and teen years and presumably undergone some form of military training, although the ancient sources are silent. An anecdote has come down to us which shows him in a priggish light. He was the fastest runner among the boys of his own age, but when they suggested he enter the Olympic Games, he demurred. The contest would be unfair, he claimed. If he won, it would merely be over commoners, and if he lost it would be the defeat of a prince.

On the academic front, little is known in detail of what Aristotle taught him, although it will have included elements of the regular Greek syllabus, the study of poetry, and the art of public speaking. His royal student seems to have shown an interest in a branch of rhetoric called eristics. This is the art of arguing a case from opposing points of view. Isocrates came to hear of this and was displeased. He wrote to Alexander, warning him to take care: kings command rather than debate.

Aristotle's career shows an abiding emphasis on information gathering in many fields of research—literary, scientific, medical, biological, political, and philosophical. He collected maps (surely of special interest to the crown prince) and manuscripts. He revised and continued a list of winners at the Olympic Games and he commissioned reports on the constitutions of Greek states. These concerns must have been reflected in his curriculum.

Aristotle, who had an opinion about everything, pronounced on the geography of the world. The earth was a globe at the center of the universe and was "far smaller than some of the stars." A long habitable band of land lay in each of the two hemispheres. They were separated by an impassably hot zone and were surrounded by endless water, the outer Ocean. There was not the slightest suggestion of a New World somewhere beyond the seas and awaiting discovery.

The band in the northern hemisphere began at the Atlantic coast of Africa (which the Greeks called Libya) and the Pillars of Heracles, and stretched as far as to the Punjab. Beyond the Pillars of Heracles and India lay nothing except sea, which severed the habitable land and prevented it forming a continuous belt around the earth. This caught Alexander's imagination and to reach India and the shores of Ocean became one of his dreams.

Presumably Aristotle discussed politics with his pupils. This must have led to some tricky moments, for the general direction of Greek thought was toward republics, and more particularly the most appropriate constitutions for the small city-states that dominated the Hellenic political landscape. None of this will have pleased either king or crown prince. However, the philosopher saw a way round the difficulty: monarchy could qualify as an ideal constitution, provided the king possessed a high level of virtue (in Greek, *aretē*). In the *Politics,* he writes:

> When therefore either a whole family or a single individual among people at large can be found, whose virtue is so outstanding as to outstrip all the rest, then it becomes just that this family should become royal and sovereign over all things, and that this one man should become king.

Aristotle was not free from the vices of his age. Slavery was widespread throughout the ancient world and he endorsed it as a social institution. He believed that "by nature some are free, others slaves, and that for these it is both just and expedient that they should serve as slaves." He took a similarly dim view of foreigners. It was only right and proper that Greeks should rule non-Greeks; indeed, "non-Greeks and slaves are identical."

Alexander was greatly impressed by Aristotle, whom he saw as a surrogate father (Philip being frequently absent on campaign), and by the practical bent of his ideas. He was evidently an industrious student, even though he applied his studies strictly to his own personal interests. He developed a fascination for the practical sciences and was much taken by the diagnosis and treatment of disease. As an adult, he set himself up as an amateur doctor, looking after his friends when they were sick and prescribing therapies and diets. Years later, one of his generals, Craterus, fell sick, and Alexander was alarmed to hear that he was to be given hellebore, a toxic plant used as a purgative. He wrote to the general's doctor expressing his anxiety and prescribing the correct dosage.

Aristotle encouraged his charge's passion for Homer. He is reported to have prepared a special, annotated edition of the *Iliad,* which his pupil regarded less as a work of art than as a manual on the art of war. This was the so-called "casket copy," which in later times Alexander carried about with him everywhere on his travels, almost as a holy relic.

He prided himself on knowing the *Iliad* by heart as well as most of the *Odyssey.* When at leisure or at an evening meal, he liked to involve those around him in a literary game, asking them to quote favorite lines from Homer. He always insisted that the following line from the *Iliad* was the finest of them all.

He is two things: a good king and a mighty spearman too.

IT WAS A FINE spring day in the year 401, more than half a century previously, and a great battle was about to be fought on the left bank of the Euphrates.

And now it was noon, and the enemy were not yet in sight; but when afternoon was coming on, there was seen a rising dust, which appeared at first like a white cloud, but sometime later like a kind of blackness in the plain, extending over a great distance. As the enemy came nearer and nearer, there were presently flashes of bronze here and there, and spears and the hostile ranks came into sight. There were horsemen in white cuirasses on the left wing of the enemy. . . . Next to them were troops with wicker shields and, farther on, hoplites with wooden shields which reached to their feet, these latter being Egyptians, people said; and then more horsemen and more bowmen.

This evocation of the prelude to battle is justly famous. It is taken from the *Anabasis* (or Journey Up-country), one of the great adventure stories of world literature. The author was a young Athenian, Xenophon, who was an officer in a force of ten thousand Greek mercenaries. These were hoplites (those heavily armed infantrymen who deployed in a tightly disciplined phalanx). They had been hired by a royal prince, Cyrus, namesake of the empire's founder, to spearhead a revolt against his brother, Artaxerxes II.

The Great King's army so outnumbered the enemy that Cyrus's left wing did not extend beyond his brother's center. It was here that, as was the practice of Persian monarchs, Artaxerxes was standing in his chariot and surrounded by elite troops and bodyguards.

The rebel mercenaries were stationed by the river, on Cyrus's right wing. When their phalanx charged, the opposing troops lost no time in running away. The Greeks chased after them and, so far as they were concerned, victory was theirs. Then Cyrus, young and passionate, led a small cavalry force straight at his brother. Xenophon writes:

He caught sight of the Great King and the compact body of men around him, and immediately he lost control of himself and, shouting "I see the man," rushed upon him and struck him on the breast and wounded him through his breastplate.

Artaxerxes fell from his horse and was brought out of the mêlée by some of his guardsmen. Cyrus's bold maneuver had succeeded and many of the Great King's people submitted to him. But he impetuously went on charging deep into the enemy ranks. By this time darkness was falling and all was confusion. Cyrus was wounded above the temple and then killed by a common foot soldier.

The battle was won, but the rebellion was over. Artaxerxes recovered and reigned for nearly half a century.

The victorious Greek mercenaries were dismayed by the turn of events. How would they be treated now? The Persians lured their generals to a conference and executed them. Their places were filled by new elected leaders, including Xenophon. The "ten thousand" resolved not to surrender, but to fight their way back to the Hellenic world. After great hardships and much fighting, they at last reached the coast of the Black Sea and safety. "The sea, the sea," the men shouted joyfully as they crested rising ground and saw below them the wide expanse of blue water.

There were few Greek boys who were not told of this astonishing feat of endurance and survival and for the literate it was a best seller. Serious politicians and soldiers studied the episode—and so, we may be sure, did the Macedonian crown prince, inquisitive as he was about the military strength of the Persians.

So far as Alexander was concerned, Xenophon taught an essential truth. He observed:

> An intelligent observer could see at a glance that while the King's empire was strong in terms of lands and men, it was weak on account of its lengthened communications and the dispersal of its forces, if someone were to launch a quick military strike against it.

We have seen that the Great King governed through a system of provincial governors or satraps, but before modern technology information could not travel faster than a horse. It took ninety days to reach Sardis, on the Mediterranean coast, from Susa, the Persian capital. The satraps were almost impossible to control at such distances. Some were even allowed to establish hereditary dynasties. They had their own military capabilities, even if they exercised no control over garrison commanders, who acted as policing officials and reported directly to the Great King. As a further check on good behavior, a government inspector called the Eye of the King informed faraway Susa of what was going on in the empire.

But these precautions did not always work. In the middle of the fourth century, a number of satraps rebelled. When the insurgency, or more precisely a sequence of insurgencies, eventually collapsed, many were given back their old jobs. This was a clear sign—a tacit acknowledgment—that the center could not hold the periphery to its will.

The empire looked fierce, but in fact was frail. Its vast armies wore attractive and exotic uniforms, but were mostly ill-trained levies. The performance of the Greek regiment at Cunaxa and afterward demonstrated beyond any doubt the superiority of the hoplite and the phalanx. Xenophon was exaggerating when he wrote, "If any man makes war on Persia, whoever he may be, he can roam up and down the country to his heart's content without striking a blow," but he had a point. Most agreed with Aristotle when he asserted the natural superiority of the Hellenes.

Cyrus's decision to hurl a collective spearhead of cavalry at his brother's person was a brilliant, albeit risky, tactic. It eliminated the enemy's numerical superiority by ending the battle before numbers could be brought fully into play. Once his hordes knew their master was dead, they had nothing left to fight for and would abandon the struggle. It was only Cyrus's foolhardiness that transformed victory into defeat.

Alexander digested Xenophon's book. He took from it two lessons: first, a determined invader could survive, even thrive, in the heart of the Persian empire; and, second, in battle it made tactical sense to seek to kill the Great King. A late Roman writer was not far wrong when he observed: "Alexander the Great would not have become great if Xenophon had never existed."

SO FAR AS HAVING sex was concerned, Alexander was incurious. He showed no signs of attraction to women. This does not necessarily imply a particular orientation. Terms such as homosexuality or heterosexuality had not yet been invented. For him and his contemporaries, sex was what you did, not what you were.

Perhaps the general air of license at Pella put the boy off. Perhaps he simply had a low sex drive.

Alternatively, a psychoanalyst might point to his closeness to his mother, and how he would do anything to please her. They both had their life projects—and for each of them *he* was that project. Her love may have been embarrassingly smothering, but he could completely trust her.

Alexander was an eligible youth, not simply because of his high birth but also because of his good looks (or so we are told). He was short and muscular; his hair was blond "like a lion's mane." A straight nose rose to his forehead, which bulged slightly above the eyes; he had fair skin, and his chest and face would redden during exercise or under emotion; his eyes were heterochromatic, one being gray-blue and the other dark brown; his teeth were like small sharp pegs or nails. His voice was harsh and high-pitched, and early sculptural portraits give him a girlish air.

Plutarch writes of his "neck which was tilted slightly to the left" and of "a certain melting look." A less friendly interpretation of the same evidence speaks of a lopsided face and watery eyes.

Alexander's favorite sculptor, Lysippus, who worked in bronze, knew him from when he was a boy and was able to produce a convincing, and at the same time attractive, likeness. He was the only artist allowed to make three-dimensional representations of Alexander. This was not just a question of personal taste or a reward for flattery: sculpture and coins were among the best means a ruler had in those days of communicating his authority to large publics. Lysippus can be said to have invented, or at least to have asserted, the Alexander brand.

Although we cannot be absolutely sure today where the young Macedonian stood on the scale between beauty and ugliness, he seems to have been personable enough.

Olympias and Philip were worried about their son. They feared that he would grow up into an effeminate man, in our terms a queen, someone like King Archelaus. They decided to hire the services of an attractive prostitute from Thessaly called Callixeina. They paid her to go to bed with Alexander and take his virginity. His refusal to cooperate may be ascribed to a weak libido, but it is just as likely to have been due to irritation. Few boys like parents to choose their first date. But Olympias was nothing if not persistent and often begged her son to sleep with the girl, albeit without success.

For the simplest explanation of his behavior we could do worse than consider Alexander's sexual orientation. He studied under Aristotle with a small class of contemporaries drawn from Philip's inner circle, the sons of aristocrats and generals. One of these was a boy called Hephaestion, who had attracted Alexander by "his looks and boyishness." The two fell for each other and were inseparable for the rest of their lives. It is hard to believe that there was not a sexual component in the relationship. But if there was, it will have been short-lived, for Plutarch reports that Alexander "used to say that sleep and sex, more than anything else, reminded him of his mortality. By this he meant that tiredness and pleasure both proceed from the same human weakness."

We have already seen that homosexual activity was widespread among the Macedonian elite. But there was more to this than rough fun. Royal and aristocratic Macedonians looked southward, to Greece, for the conventions of male sexual behavior among the upper class.

These were highly specialized. Young male adults were expected to enter into love affairs with prepubertal teenaged boys. These affairs were a form of higher education. The senior partner, the lover or (in Greek) *erastes,* was expected to train the loved one, or *eromenos,* in the cultural norms of Hellenic society. By imitation the *eromenos* would learn from his *erastes* how to be a good citizen, how to compete physically in the gymnasium, and, in the long run, how to be brave on the battlefield (exemplified, most notably, by that regiment of lovers, the Theban Sacred Band). Once the *eromenos* became an adult, the relationship was expected to cool into a lifelong friendship.

Sex between the couples was allowable, but not compulsory, and many straight young Greeks doubtless heaved a sigh of relief when they were able to graduate to marriage and heterosexuality. However, there were conventions to be observed. The *eromenos* must never be buggered. The most widely approved sex act was intercrural (that is, the *erastes* frotted his erect penis between the legs of his beloved).

The boy was not expected to show any signs of arousal; he was offering himself as a free gift to his mentor rather than satisfying his own desire.

The most famous pederastic pair were Alexander's hero Achilles, the protagonist of the *Iliad,* and Patroclus. They were widely recognized as lovers, but there was some doubt in ancient times as to which of them was the *erastes* and which the *eromenos.* Plato has one of the speakers in his dialogue *The Symposium* (or *The Drinking Party*), clear the matter up.

> Aeschylus [the tragic playwright], by the way, is quite wrong when he says [in his play *The Myrmidons*] that Achilles was the *erastes* of Patroclus. Achilles was the more beautiful of the two— indeed he was the most beautiful of all the heroes—and he was still beardless and, according to Homer, much younger than Patroclus.

Achilles may indeed have been beautiful and beardless, but when we first meet him in the *Iliad,* he is certainly not prepubertal. We must assume that the lovers had graduated some while previously into an adult friendship.

Alexander saw himself as a latter-day Achilles not only for his bravery and skill as a warrior, but also because he and Hephaestion were *eromenos* and *erastes* on the model of Achilles and Patroclus. It is a reasonable supposition that his schoolfellow was the older of the two, albeit only by a small margin. It appears that the liaison merely mimicked pederasty while being closer to a modern conjunction of more or less coeval partners.

THE EMERGENCIES OF REAL life interrupted the calm rural seminars at Mieza. In 340 Philip appointed his son, only aged sixteen, to be regent of the kingdom and keeper of the royal seal during his absence on a major campaign in the Thracian Chersonese. His education was over. This very remarkable promotion was not just a product of paternal love, but also a recognition of Alexander's precocious maturity and ability.

A senior general, Antipater, was appointed as his adviser, with the task of preventing any foolish mistakes. Philip trusted him completely; once on a campaign he slept for an unusually long time and when he woke up remarked: "I slept safely for Antipater was awake."

He seems to have thought well of his charge and allowed him latitude. In any case, the ambitious teenager seized the opportunity of power like a man offered water in a desert. He put down a rebellion by a Thracian tribe, capturing its city and replacing its inhabitants, whom he drove out, with a body of Greek settlers.

He renamed the place Alexandropolis, or City of Alexander, which may have caused the king to raise his eyebrows; Philippolis would have been rather more appropriate. The boy was getting too big for his boots and, when he clumsily tried to bribe some Macedonians to win their allegiance, his father, grandmaster of the backhander, gave him a firm dressing-down. For all that, Philip thought the world of Alexander and kept up a regular correspondence with him.

By contrast, the crown prince's filial devotion was coming under strain. He wanted to become a great warrior and had been watching his father's victorious progress in war after war with rising resentment. The greater his paternal inheritance, the less there would be for him to conquer. He used to say bitterly to his friends: "My father will get in before me in everything."

And indeed Philip had been doing extraordinarily well since his first astonishing year on the throne, when he had defeated a ring of enemies by a judicious combination of force, deceit, and diplomacy. He overcame the little principalities that made up northern Macedonia and recruited their clan leaders as courtiers in Pella and as commanders in the field. These were the Companions we have previously seen. As Macedonian power grew, some of them were non-Macedonians who saw exciting career prospects under Philip (Nearchus of Crete, for example, and Eumenes his Greek secretary, whom we will meet later). These men were the poet Hesiod's "gift-devouring lords," who expected munificence from their monarchs. They were lavishly rewarded with land and cash for their loyalty and their labors. Their young sons were recruited as Royal Pages.

In a word, Macedonia had become a united and populous state. It was no longer a backwater that could safely be ignored.

——

THE KING'S MILITARY REFORMS were leading, as he intended, to the establishment of a substantial but expensive standing army and here he was caught in a complicated vicious circle. The more soldiers he employed, the more resources he needed to cover their cost. As a result he was obliged to go on enlarging the territories he controlled, for their tax revenues and their gold or silver mines. And then he needed even more conscripts to defend these new possessions and fight his endless wars.

Over more than twenty years, Philip massively expanded his kingdom. At its greatest extent it may have boasted a population of 500,000, far larger than that of any Greek city-state. Perhaps as early as 352, he was appointed archon (Greek for ruler) for life of Thessaly. The Thessalian plain stretches down to the famous pass of Thermopylae and lies alongside Epirus in the west, Olympias's homeland and a close Macedonian ally. He invaded the tribal lands of Thrace and after hard-fought campaigns became their overlord. His army threatened the Bosporus. The Athenians, who had already lost their traditional influence in Chalcidice to the Macedonian king, depended on grain imports from the Black Sea and felt threatened.

They were right to worry. Philip cast his roving eye on the city-states of southern Greece, looking out for opportunity (in the historian Justin's words) "as from a watch-tower." A ruinous war between a small *polis* called Phocis and the Thebans, who were declining from their brief zenith after the battle at Leuctra but were still easily provoked, gave the king his entrée. The Phocians were responsible for guarding the oracle at Delphi, a township in its territory, perched precariously on the steep lower slopes of Mount Parnassus.

They raised large mercenary armies, which they paid for by raiding the national treasuries that stood around the shrine of Apollo. These were packed with gold and silver thank-offerings to the god of prophecy from all over the Hellenic world. The Phocians promised, hand on heart but fingers crossed behind their backs, to reimburse him.

The conflict was called the Sacred War because of the link to Delphi. The Thebans were soon on the run, suffering (in the words of a contemporary) "an *Iliad* of woes." The Macedonian king decided it was his convenient duty to punish the desecrators of the holy site. To begin with Phocis did well, even beating Philip in battle on one occasion, in 353. He withdrew, but promised to return "like a ram, which next time would butt harder."

He was as good as his word. The following year, 352 or 353, he won a decisive victory at the charmingly named Battle of the Crocus Field. The king made his men wear wreaths of laurel, Apollo's tutelary plant, but his motive was of course strategic rather than religious. He was using the opportunity to strengthen his hold as a defender of Greek values. Hostilities persisted, but by 346 Philip had destroyed the final remnants of Phocian resistance. He was appointed president of the Amphictyony of Delphi, an association of local states charged with ensuring the oracle's independence. Philip's power now touched the frontier of Thebes and was within striking distance of Athens.

No one now could safely say the king was not a Greek.

PHILIP'S FOREIGN POLICY DID not depend simply on military force. The income from the gold and silver mines of Macedonia and Thrace brought in an enormous annual income of a thousand talents. The king began to manufacture coins, including his famous gold staters, or "philips," as they were nicknamed. Much of this newfound wealth helped to finance his costly standing army, which included mercenaries as well as native Macedonians, but the remainder was dedicated to buying the goodwill and guest-friendship of leading Greek statesmen, even ones hostile to him. He used to admit that "I enlarged my kingdom far more by the use of gold than of weapons."

An unfriendly critic, the contemporary historian Theopompus, thought Philip was profligate and incompetent. "He was the worst manager in the world—not only himself but also his entourage. He did not merely spend money, he threw it away." But this was entirely to miss the point. True, Philip's generosity was on a Homeric scale and he often found himself short of ready cash, but spraying philips around foreign governments had the intended effect. It made friends and influenced people.

Unlike his son, Philip thoroughly enjoyed sex and had affairs with young men and women. But that was entertainment; when it came to marriage, the criterion was *raison d'état*. Olympias was his chief spouse but by no means his only one. His contemporaries used to joke: "With every campaign, Philip married a new wife." These unions were politically driven, perhaps temporary, and they tended to be with the daughters of rulers with whom he had been at war. The brides included Audata, an Illyrian princess; Phila, daughter of a tricky Upper Macedonian ruler; and Meda, daughter of a contumacious Thracian king. Wives sealed deals.

Philip seems to have married two women from Thessaly, which may show the importance he placed on bringing it under his control and of the complexity of its politics. Olympias was a difficult wife, but she was not at all jealous of her husband's philandering and became friends with Nicesipolis, one of the pair from Thessaly. Nicesipolis had the reputation of being a witch; Olympias, an acknowledged expert in such matters, was asked to check her out before Philip slept with her. She met the woman and took an instant liking to her. "No more of these slanders," she said. "You are your own best magic." When Nicesipolis died in childbirth, the queen took her daughter into her household and brought her up.

PHILIP ADMIRED ATHENS, the "violet-crowned" city, its history and its culture. It epitomized the Greekness to which he and his predecessors on the Macedonian throne aspired. That did not prevent him from tricking the Athenians whenever it was in his interest to do so, nor them from obstructing his path whenever they could.

To the outside observer, the city had recovered from its total defeat, in 404, after its long war with the militaristic state of Sparta in the Peloponnese. Athens was a maritime power. After a period of quiescence it reestablished a league of island and coastal city-states in the Aegean Sea and its fleet once again ruled the waves as it had done in the fifth century. It suppressed pirates, protected its essential grain supplies from the Black Sea, and guarded against a resurgence of Persian aggression.

But first impressions can deceive. The population of adult male citizens had been devastated by the conflict, falling from an estimated 40,000 to between 14,000 and 16,250—in other words, a 60 percent collapse. There was simply not the personnel with which to restore the great Athenian empire of yore.

Also, the city had lost much of its wealth and never fully made up the deficit. From its great port at Piraeus, it could still afford to send out a fleet of one hundred warships, but not for long. What was worse, Athenians had (unsurprisingly) lost their appetite for warfare. Survivors usually opted for a quiet life and Athenians preferred to see their taxes spent at home on public works and citizens' grants than on military adventures.

That excitable historian Theopompus may have exaggerated Athenian decadence, but he had a point when he wrote:

> It is an Athenian, [who] . . . even on military expeditions surrounded himself with flute players and whores and harpists and grossly misused the funds appropriated for the war. However, the Athenians never gave him any trouble. On the contrary . . . they held him in higher regard than any other citizen. And justly so, for they themselves lived a life that tempted young men to while away their time among flute players and with prostitutes. Those who were a little older spent their days drinking and gambling and that sort of dissipation. The Athenian people as a whole spent more on public banquets and the consumption of meat than on the administration of the city.

The Macedonians knew little about the sea; from Philip's perspective Athens, for all its flaws, still posed a threat to his growing ambition to be master of all Greece. Once his dominance was undoubted, he intended to launch a military expedition against the Great King, avenge the invasions of Darius and Xerxes, and free the Ionian city-states along the Asian littoral from Persian oppression. He aimed to march in the footsteps of Xenophon.

In 340, without many expectations, the king tried one last time to come to terms with the Athenians. He took a two-pronged approach. As we have seen, he appointed Alexander as regent and led his army to the Chersonese, his aim being to control the Bosporus. In this way he threatened the merchant shipping from grain-rich Scythia (today's

Ukraine) and denied the Athenian war fleet access to coastal ports. Then, with his sword in one hand, he picked up a pen with the other.

Philip sent Athens a long letter of complaints about the city's unreasonable behavior. Many of these were justified, even though its author was no innocent abroad. The tone of voice was that of a reasonable man much put upon, who hoped his readers would change their minds about him.

However, the document concluded with a very firm statement of likely consequences:

> These then are the complaints I have to make. You were the aggressors and, thanks to my patience, are still making further attacks on my interests and doing me all the harm in your power. So I shall defend myself, with justice on my side, and, calling the gods to witness, I shall bring my dispute with you to an issue.

The Athenians, in a jumpy frame of mind, decided to take this as a declaration of war.

Philip had allowed for the worst and was ready to react, although he was delayed by a severe thigh wound incurred during a campaign against the irrepressible Thracians. Another small war had broken out in the Amphictyony of Delphi. As its president, the king was entitled to bring his army down from Macedonia to settle the dispute, and that was what he did. But, once he was in central Greece, he laid aside pretense and marched south along the high road to Thebes and Athens. These two neighbors had loathed each other for generations, but the threat to them was palpable and immediate. They agreed to an instant entente and sent out a call for other Greek *poleis* to come to their aid. Within days an allied force set out to confront the Macedonian king.

THE PLAIN RUNS NORTHWEST to southeast and is bounded by two lines of high ground and foothills. On the south stands the acropolis of the small town of Chaeronea. From that vantage point one can look across open country and make out the river Cephisus with its mountainous backdrop a couple of miles away.

It was here that the allied Greek army chose to stand and fight the Macedonians. After Philip had tricked his way through a heavily defended pass, this was the only obstacle that prevented him from invading the homelands of his enemies. The allies had assembled some 35,000 foot soldiers and 2,000 cavalry, whereas Philip had about the same number of cavalry, but only 30,000 infantry, probably the full strength of his field army.

The king commanded a force of elite Macedonian infantry on his right wing. It faced an Athenian phalanx of ten thousand hoplites. Alexander, only eighteen, was given the crucial task of leading the Macedonian horse on the left beside the Cephisus. Four centuries later, Plutarch recalled that an oak tree by the river used to be called Alexander's oak, because he had pitched his tent beside it on the night before the battle. Opposing him stood the Theban hoplites, headed by the Sacred Band. We do not know where the allied cavalry was placed. Perhaps they were held in reserve. In any event, they played no part in the fighting. Lightly armed troops protected both Philip's and the Athenians' flanks.

The allied advantage was only theoretical, for the Macedonian soldiers belonged to a full-time professional army and had years of battle experience. On the other hand, the Athenian hoplites had had only one month of regular fighting in the previous quarter of a century.

Each side had a well-thought-out battle plan. The allied line was echeloned back, or (to use the technical term, "refused"), from the Athenians on the left near Chaeronea to the right where it touched the Cephisus. This meant that the fighting would start when the Athenians and Philip's troops on the Macedonian right engaged. If the allies succeeded in pushing the king back, their line could then swing round and attack the enemy's center and right like a closing fan. If the Macedonians prevailed, many allied soldiers would have a good chance of being able either to run away into the southern hills or flee along the plain.

Philip's plan was even cleverer. It depended on indiscipline among the brave but inexpert Athenians. Technically it was ambitious: it would involve the entire Macedonian line swivelling as if on a pivot. Philip would stage a managed withdrawal up some rising ground. This would stretch the Greek line, which would presumably be advancing across open ground toward the refused enemy line. At some point a gap or a thinning of the ranks would appear. Alexander on the Macedonian left would then lead a cavalry charge through the gap and the battle would, to all intents and purposes, be over.

Hostilities opened at dawn, probably on August 2, 338. As both armies were echeloned, only the Athenians and Philip's elite troops made contact at first. In the event, Philip's intuition about the Athenians was correct. They rushed impetuously forward and their general, one Stratocles, shouted: "On, on, on, to Macedonia!" Philip, contracting his phalanx as it pulled back behind its wall of spears, remarked: "The Athenians haven't a clue how to win a battle."

The gap the king had foreseen opened between the Greek center and the Sacred Band as the men shuffled leftward in order to keep in touch with the rampaging Athenian hoplites. Alexander saw it and knew his moment had come. Leading a wedge-shaped formation of cavalry, he thundered across the plain. The Thebans were soon surrounded and fighting for their lives on the riverside. The Sacred Band was destroyed where it stood.

Two miles away the king reversed his retreat and attacked the astonished Athenians. He drove them into the hills; one thousand were killed and two thousand taken prisoner. The rout soon became general.

Many centuries later, archaeologists excavated an enclosure near where the Sacred Band had fought and which was now their grave. Two hundred and fifty-four skeletons lay in seven neat rows. Out of the three hundred lovers, only forty-six had survived. Even Philip was moved. Inspecting the battlefield after the fighting was done, he came upon the corpses of the Sacred Band and is reported to have said: "Death to those who suspect these men to have done anything dishonorable."

ALEXANDER WAS THE BOY of the hour, as his father generously acknowledged. It was his charge, with himself riding in the most dangerous position at the pointed apex of the cavalry wedge, that had delivered the decisive blow during the battle and precipitated the rout of the Greeks. His friends were tempted to argue that he, rather than his father, had gained the victory.

But to do so would have been a mistake. The cunning Philip deserves the credit, for he was the one who designed the plan of action—the false retreat creating the gap in the Greek line, which in turn set loose the Macedonian horse. Alexander had been no more than a piece, a high-value piece certainly, on the game board.

His father became "extravagantly fond" of him, Plutarch observed, so much so that he enjoyed hearing the Macedonians speak of Alexander as their king and Philip as their general. It was universally understood that the years of apprenticeship were over. Nobody needed to spell it out, but Alexander was heir to the throne not simply by virtue of blood, but on merit. Our sources voice no criticism of him, and evidently the royal family were united.

How then did it come to pass that within a month or two of Chaeronea, Alexander's legitimacy was placed in question and his mother, Olympias, repudiated as an adulteress?

CHAPTER 3

"THE BULL IS WREATHED"

EVERY FOUR YEARS, OLYMPIA, A SMALL TOWN IN ELIS IN THE NORTH-ern Peloponnese, became an international, or at least a Panhellenic, city. Wars were suspended and, under the protection of a general truce, anyone who could prove he was a Greek was welcome to attend the Olympic Games. Crowds poured in to watch the athletic races and matches or, indeed, to take part as competitors. Unmarried women could be spectators, but married women were barred on pain of death.

Arts and sports festivals always had a religious origin and purpose in the Hellenic world, and Olympia was no exception. The town stood between a river and rising ground; a stadium, gymnasium, baths, and the athletes' sleeping quarters provided essential facilities for the games, but at Olympia's heart was a large sacred enclosure called the Altis. Here two temples stood, dedicated to the king and queen of heaven, Zeus and his consort, Hera. It was in honor of Zeus that the games were held (Hera had her own separate festival, at which unmarried women competed). Along the northern edge of the enclosure was a line of treasuries, looking like tiny temples, where grateful city-states housed valuable gifts to their divine patron.

It was in this enclosure that Philip, victor of Chaeronea, had the nerve to commission a remarkable building. Called the Philippeum after the king, it was a round structure, made of burnt brick. It was circled by marble columns. These carried the roof whose beams were held together by a large bronze poppy. Inside stood a life-size group of statues made from gilded marble by the fashionable Athenian sculptor Leochares. They depicted the senior members of the Macedonian royal family: Philip, Olympias, and Alexander were accompanied by the king's parents, Amyntas IV and his murderous spouse, Eurydice. Other wives and brothers were deemed superfluous and were omitted.

What are we to make of this? The first and most obvious point is that all was harmony in the palace at Pella. Olympias was confirmed as number one wife and Alexander as the much-loved crown prince.

Second, the Philippeum appears to give notice that the Macedonian royals were edging toward "hero" or semi-divine status. In ancient Greece, the boundary between gods and humans was porous. Remarkable men were recognized to have something sacred about them. To quote the great first-century-B.C. Roman orator, Cicero, ordinary people might confer "the deification of renown and gratitude upon distinguished benefactors to whom they paid their respects and sacrificed at their shrines."

A few outstanding legendary personalities might actually be transformed into full-on gods. One notable example was the strongman Heracles, from whom Philip proudly claimed ancestry. He was born a mortal but endowed with immortality.

However, in historical times, full apotheosis was unheard of, and Philip did not aspire so high. Ever the creative experimenter, he was among the first monarchs of a large realm or empire to found a ruler cult. From the fourth century onward this became a popular means by which a king could win consent to, even approval of, his rule. Through religious spectacle he could dramatize his subjects' loyalty. Philip must have hoped that his newly acquired divine status would differentiate him from the quarrelsome politicians of the Greek city-states. It would give him authority without entangling him in their savage internecine politics.

For the average Hellene, though, unused as he was to this innovative political idea, the Philippeum was an instance of overweening pride that leads a man to ignore the divinely fixed limits of human action. Alexander's opinion is unknown, but as with all his father's projects, we can safely assume that he gave it some serious thought.

AT A BANQUET ON the evening after the Battle of Chaeronea, Philip drank too much and behaved badly. He toured the battlefield and jeered at the corpses. He went on to insult his prisoners of war. One of them, a brave (or at least cocky) Athenian politician called Demades, made a witty allusion to the Greek commander-in-chief during the siege of Troy and the notorious lame troublemaker serving in his army: "King, when fate has cast you in the role of Agamemnon, aren't you ashamed to play the part of Thersites?"

Philip pulled himself together and as an apparent token of apology freed the Athenian captives without ransom. He even gave them clothes to wear when going home. In fact, he knew very well that he needed to conciliate Athens. Its massive fortifications made the city impregnable. Its fleets ruled the waves. Despite the decision at Chaeronea, Athens was still a force to be reckoned with. Alexander and Antipater, who had advised him during his regency, were sent to Athens to hand over the dead and negotiate a peace. A nervous city commissioned an equestrian statue of the king and gave the two Macedonians honorary citizenship.

The king artfully avoided triumphalism, refusing to hold victory sacrifices, to wear garlands, or to use perfumes. He let it be known that he did not want to be addressed as King, preferring the less autocratic title of General. He was "careful to manage Greek affairs rather than rule openly." According to the Greek historian Polybius, "By his kindness and moderation he brought all the Athenians and their city under his control, not letting emotion push him on to further success."

Philip ensured that no Macedonian soldiers should set foot in Attica and raised no objection to an epitaph in honor of the Athenian fallen, carved in marble and erected on the battlefield. It read:

STRIVING TO SAVE THE SACRED LAND OF GREECE
WE DIED ON THE FAMOUS PLAINS OF THE BOEOTIANS.

Negotiations were conducted with an enemy who had been defeated, not conquered, and Philip made no attempt to interfere with the Athenian democracy. Hostile politicians, such as the great orator Demosthenes, were not pursued.

There was, of course, a price to be paid for friendliness. Athens had to accept the loss of her interests in the Chersonese and the winding up of her maritime league, although she was allowed to keep some of her overseas possessions (Delos, for example, and some other islands). The city's lifeline to the Black Sea and Scythian grain supplies remained intact, but was vulnerable, for Philip was now in a position to close the Hellespont whenever he wanted. The Athenians would think twice before annoying him again.

Many Greeks were quite pleased with the new Macedonian ascendancy. Not only had their leaders been showered with golden philips, but also the king guaranteed their security without interfering in their domestic affairs. There were to be no punitive garrisons (except for unreconciled Thebes and a couple of other places). The constant quarreling between hot-tempered ministates would now be a thing of the past. In the Peloponnese, Sparta was still furious at having lost its status as a superpower (at Leuctra) and, in its efforts to regain that stature, was a constant threat to its neighbors. In the autumn of 338 Philip toured the region, announcing, to great acclaim, that he would seek redress of grievances against Sparta. When Sparta refused to cooperate, he simply confiscated its frontier lands and gave them to the complainants. The once all-powerful Hellenic superpower was too weak to react militarily.

Philip's generosity was not disinterested. He wanted to see a formal "common peace" incorporating all the Greek states, not only the recent belligerents. Naturally, it would be agreed and implemented under his guidance. So in addition to bilateral accords, he summoned a general peace congress at Corinth in late 338. A treaty was negotiated, or perhaps dictated, which established a supranational political institution, the League of Corinth. Each member had a seat on a governing council, and a league leader was to be elected.

All the delegates swore a solemn oath:

I swear by Zeus, by Ge [the earth], by Helios, by Poseidon, by Athena, by Ares and by all gods and goddesses I shall abide by the treaty and shall not break its terms, nor shall I bear arms against any of those who abide by their oaths . . . nor shall I overthrow the kingdom of Philip nor the constitutions that were in existence in each city, when they swore the oaths concerning the peace. . . . I shall make war upon the one who transgresses the common peace, in accordance with whatever is resolved by the common council and whatever the *hegemon,* or leader, orders and I shall not desert the cause.

This is a telling document. Practical, clear, and decisive, it bears all the hallmarks of Philip's authorship. It forbade constitutional change; a democracy was to remain a democracy, an oligarchy an oligarchy, a monarchy a monarchy. This was a policy designed to encourage cooperation and loyalty. All the oath-givers swore to take military action against transgressors, but it was implicit that the Macedonian army was the one to be feared and to keep order. The league council had executive powers, but was most unlikely to test the patience of the Macedonian king. He was happy to risk opposition, in the reasonable belief that most Greeks favored peace and would give him a majority of votes at meetings. The identity of the "leader" was left unstated, but hardly needed to be spelled out. Philip was elected as *hegemon,* and the isles of Greece looked forward to a long period of tranquillity.

In Athens the oath was inscribed on a marble stele, but, to remind Philip that the city was not altogether a pushover, it passed a law against tyranny, also displayed on two inscriptions surmounted by a personification of Democracy about to crown the People of Athens. It decreed that "if anyone revolts against the people for the purpose of setting up a tyranny . . . whoever kills him shall be free from prosecution."

Philip had no intention of governing Greece directly; that would have been too much trouble for no reward. His military superiority guaranteed good behavior, and the pretense of self-government smoothed over the bitter truth of defeat. If the Greeks kept their heads down, he would not interfere in their affairs. The league was a clever invention to assert his power with the minimum effort and expense. Another telling lesson in statecraft for the crown prince.

Some months later, in 337, the king summoned a second congress at Corinth. This time he had a new project to announce. He was at last taking the advice of old Isocrates. His plan was nothing less than to invade the Persian empire. It seems that the supreme leader, the *hege-mon,* had the right to convene a Panhellenic army and to lead it on campaign as supreme commander (*strategos autokrator*). He required military contributions from member states, calculated according to the size of their populations.

How long had the king been mulling over this ambitious scheme? And what exactly were his war aims? These are important questions and very hard to answer. Philip guarded his secrets. To exact revenge for the humiliations of Macedonia when it was a province of the Persian empire may have been a dreamy adolescent's fantasy, especially after he had digested Xenophon's *Anabasis.* Every young Greek boy— everyone who aspired to acceptance as a genuine Hellene—recalled with rage the expeditions of Darius and Xerxes. It was time for Philip to get his own back.

Are we to take the rhetoric of revenge seriously? It incorporated a large quantum of propaganda, which veiled true motives such as greed, ambition, and a growing sense of Persian weakness. That said, the memory of past wrongs has often enough infused the language of political debate with true feeling.

We can be sure that the adult Philip did not regard a crusade as a practical proposition until he had transformed Macedonia from a gory backwater into a great power. Perhaps Isocrates' pamphlet of 346 marks a turning point, but even so years would pass before the idea of a Hellenic crusade became a settled policy. The Macedonian army could not possibly leave for Asia until Greece had been made safe— until Chaeronea had been fought and the League of Corinth created.

THE CONDITIONS WERE NOW right for an invasion and there was a good practical reason for moving fast. Philip seldom had much cash in hand. His bribery and corruption budget was heavily oversubscribed and his large professional army consumed money. If his empire did not continue expanding, it would have no alternative but to contract.

We have no precise idea what the Macedonian war aims were to be, but Isocrates has left helpful clues. His pamphlet discusses the available options as offered by an intelligent and well-informed contemporary.

A minimum objective would be to free the chain of Greek city-states along the Asian littoral. The catch was that, although their liberation would be easy, they would be difficult to defend. The infuriated Persians would do all they could to regain what they had lost. There would be endless trouble.

Philip was not so frivolous as to suppose he could overthrow the vast Persian empire, but there was a halfway option at which the Macedonians could tilt. This was the conquest of Asia Minor up to a defensible frontier in Cilicia and the Taurus Mountains. Isocrates recommended that permanent Hellenic settlements be founded to create buffers between the newly acquired Greek lands and the remainder of the Persian empire. This may well have been the king's intention.

Before taking any important decisions, the Greeks were careful to discover the will of the gods. One way of doing this was to consult the oracle at Delphi. The Greeks were afraid of their regiment of gods and goddesses, who lived in human shape and, like humans, could be fierce and unpredictable. The main purpose of religion was to please them. An oracle was a divine institution where the pious could ask for guidance about the future. The most famous was the one at Delphi, and leading men of the age often asked for its opinion before taking any major step, such as declaring war. It was administered by priests, but the prophecies were announced by the Pythia, a local peasant woman of blameless life. Entranced, she uttered frenzied cries, which officials translated into comprehensible verse. Apollo spoke through her.

The oracle was well-informed about current affairs and its advice was often astute, although it had a reputation for giving dangerously ambiguous responses. It appears occasionally to have taken bribes. However, the Greeks were a religious people and there is little reason to suppose that the priests at Delphi were regularly guilty of conscious deceit or fakery.

Philip sent a delegation to ask the Pythia whether he would conquer the Great King. She prophesied:

> The bull is wreathed. All is done. There is also the one who will smite him.

The king was puzzled, but took the view that this was a favorable response, signifying the sacrificial slaughter of the Persians. He gave the go-ahead for the invasion.

The expedition was set to take place in the spring of 335 and, in the meantime, an advance force was dispatched to cross the Hellespont and enter Anatolia. It was to be led by his father's foremost general, Parmenion. Philip said of him: "The Athenians elect ten generals every year, but in many years I have only found one general—Parmenion." The veteran commander was joined by Amyntas, son of Arrhabaeus, one of three princeling brothers from Lyncestis in up-country Macedonia, and, later, by Attalus, a leading Macedonian close to the king. They were probably friends of that other Amyntas, son of King Perdiccas, who (readers will recall) had been supplanted as monarch by Philip on the grounds that he was a child and not competent to rule.

THEN SOMETHING WENT TERRIBLY WRONG. Philip, now in his mid-forties, fell in love. His new object of desire was a pretty young noblewoman called Cleopatra (also Eurydice), whom he chose to be a new wife, the first for some years. Apparently, he forced Olympias, his chief queen, to share the palace with her. Relations at court became strained. Olympias took mortal offense and incited Alexander to oppose his father.

During a celebratory banquet on the wedding day, matters came to a head. It was an occasion in the Greek style: guests lay on couches and food was served to them. After the meal, large quantities of alcohol were consumed. Cleopatra's uncle, Philip's general Attalus, who had not yet left for the east, was present. He became very drunk and shouted out: "Now, for sure, we'll have legitimate kings, not just bastards." By this he meant either that Olympias was promiscuous or, perhaps, that Alexander was born of a foreign mother and so not fully Macedonian.

In any event, the crown prince was enraged. He jumped up from his couch, yelled back, "Cretin, do you take me for a bastard, then?" and hurled a drinking cup at Attalus's head.

The king, also drunk, heard the exchange and lost control of himself. He lurched to his feet and drew his sword against his son. But he was so overcome with wine and fury that he tripped and fell flat on his face. Alexander jeered at him: "Look at the man who was preparing to cross from Europe to Asia, and who can't even keep his balance when crossing from one couch to another."

He stormed off, collected his mother, and galloped out of the country. He left Olympias at her native Epirus, where her brother Alexander was king. He then rode north to Paeonia, ancient foe of Macedonia, where he may have stayed with King Langarus of the Agrianians, a Paeonian tribe.

One ancient source claims that Philip now announced, "Alexander is not my son," and divorced Olympias for alleged adultery. Whether or not the story was true, the unity of the royal family was irretrievably broken.

HOW CAN THINGS HAVE arrived at such a disastrous pass, and so suddenly? Philip, usually a wily and astute politician, had managed to destroy harmony in his family at a single stroke. It was now next to impossible for him to leave for Persia while his embittered son was at large and doubtless plotting against him.

According to Plutarch, the king's motives were purely personal. His love for Cleopatra trumped all other concerns. But this does not sound like the Philip we knew, who was used to slaking his lust whenever he felt like it and whose polygamy was regulated by *raison d'état*. We may allow him to have been attracted by his new wife, but there must have been some weightier rationale for his behavior.

One possibility is that the marriage was an insurance policy. We have seen how dangerous warfare was for Macedonian kings. They were expected to be in the thick of the battle, as Philip's tally of wounds goes to show. Both father and son could well lose their lives in the impending clash of arms, as Philip's elder brother, Perdiccas, had done. The union with Cleopatra was intended to produce an additional male heir. Although it would be many years before the infant was old enough to rule, he could at least represent the Argead dynasty and be a focus for loyalty. As it happened, Cleopatra gave birth to a girl, called Europa.

The incident at the banquet suggests that relations between Alexander and the king were cooling. Attalus was unlikely to have made his provocative remark unless he believed that Philip would appreciate it. Inaccurate gossip had it that the crown prince deserved the credit for victory at Chaeronea. Philip claimed to be delighted when people spoke jokingly of Alexander as their king and himself as their general. But it was the kind of remark that could have rankled. History is strewn with quarrels between rulers and their underemployed offspring, suddenly grown-up and eager for action.

It has even been argued that Philip believed that Alexander and the impossible Olympias were plotting his overthrow. It is true that a monarch's heir was often a magnet for a regime's critics, but in this case there is no evidence, not even the whisper of a rumor.

The simplest explanation for the quarrel may be the best one: namely, two male lions cannot coexist in a single pride. Alexander was energetic, glamorous, and talented, with a mind and temper of his own. It stands to reason that he would clash with his father, who was unaccustomed to competition in his own home. Very probably, irresponsible courtiers such as Attalus pursued their own interests by egging one or the other of them on.

As we know, Alexander liked to compare himself with Achilles, and never more so than now. His father stood for Agamemnon, the Greek commander-in-chief, with whom Homer has Achilles quarrel over a pretty young female captive. Metaphorically, the Macedonian prince now sulked in his tent much as his Homeric hero had done long ago, and literally, outside the walls of Troy.

Philip recognized that he was at a dead end. Obviously he could not launch his Persian expedition with so much confusion and hostility at home. He can have had little doubt that his son was inflaming the surprised and delighted Illyrians.

He did not know how to fill the breach. Fortunately, a man trusted on both sides made an appearance and tendered his good offices. This was Demaratus, the wealthy Corinthian who had bought Bucephalas for Alexander. It was the best present the boy had ever received in his childhood, and years later horse and owner were still inseparable.

Demaratus was pro-Macedonian and an old friend of the king. According to the Athenian orator Demosthenes, he was among those leading Greeks who sold their native cities for Philip's money. Demosthenes said: "These men flung away national prosperity for private and selfish gain; they cajoled and corrupted all the citizens within their grasp, until they had reduced them to slavery." Demaratus would doubtless have responded, not without reason, that he was a political realist who had to make the best of the Macedonian hegemony.

He paid a visit to Pella, and after formal greetings had been exchanged the king asked him whether the Greek states were in harmony with one another. The Corinthian was privileged to speak freely, and took the opportunity do so. He replied, with heavy sarcasm: "Good for you to ask how well the Greeks are getting on together, Philip, when you are getting on so well with your close relatives."

This sobered the king. He understood that he would have to make peace with his son—and Demaratus was the obvious go-between. Alexander was as difficult to tame as his horse and it took some time to persuade him to come back home. We do not know the terms the two men agreed upon, but his position as Philip's heir was confirmed. Presumably he was given guarantees of his personal safety. He gathered round him a number of trusty friends.

Olympias was very probably reluctant to move back to Pella and remained in Epirus. But therein lay a danger. Who knew what mischief she would get up to if unsupervised? The ever creative mind of the king devised a plan that would control his wife (or former wife) on the one hand, and on the other create the opportunity for a magnificent ceremony that would embody and dramatize the triumphant unity of the Macedonian state and its royal family.

He gave his daughter by Olympias, called Cleopatra (not to be confused with the king's new wife), in marriage to the king of Epirus, Alexander. Personal relations in Philip's vicinity were complicated. This was the handsome Alexander who himself had had an affair with Philip and was Olympias's brother; so Cleopatra was his niece. Consanguinity was no bar when political necessity called, and the wedding was fixed for October 336 in the old capital and religious center of Aegae.

The only disadvantage was that it would be difficult to avoid inviting the mother of the bride.

———

IT WAS PROBABLY AT this point that Attalus, who had caused all the trouble, was dispatched to share command with Parmenion in the east. To put him out of the way showed a sensitivity to Alexander's feelings.

Before his departure (we do not know how long before, but presumably not very long), he intervened in one of Philip's complicated amours. A handsome Royal Page named Pausanias was the king's *eromenos*. He was supplanted by another lad, also inconveniently called Pausanias. The spurned youth was so distressed that he made a scene, accusing his successful rival of being a hermaphrodite and ready to accept the advances of anyone who was interested. By "hermaphrodite," he implied that the rival allowed himself to be penetrated by his partner—the one thing no respectable boy would ever permit, even in a society that accepted homosexual relations.

The accusations struck home and the second Pausanias committed suicide in spectacular fashion. A few days later, when Philip was on campaign and fighting in a battle, he stepped in front of him and received on his body all the blows aimed at the king.

We are not told of Philip's reaction, but the boy had been a friend of Attalus, who was greatly vexed by his death. Never a man to manage his feelings, he invited the first Pausanias to dinner and got him drunk. He and his other guests raped him and he was then handed to his stable boys, who subjected him to the same ordeal.

When Pausanias came round, he realized what had been done to him and went to the king to lay a complaint. Philip was sympathetic, but felt he could not afford to offend Attalus, the new queen's uncle and one of his military commanders. He tried to buy Pausanias off with presents and a promotion among the Royal Pages, who acted as the king's bodyguards.

Pausanias refused to be mollified and nursed his wrath.

WITH THE CROWN PRINCE'S return, we may guess that the atmosphere in the palace at Pella was icy.

This was exemplified by a curious incident. The king was still busy negotiating marriages. As part of advance planning for the invasion of

Persia, he was in touch with Pixodarus, the provincial governor, or satrap, of Caria (in western Anatolia), who was preparing to abandon the Great King and take Macedonia's side in the forthcoming war. To cement their alliance, the satrap proposed that his daughter marry Philip's son Arrhidaeus, by his Thessalian wife, Philinna. Although he was the king's eldest male child, Arrhidaeus suffered from some kind of mental illness, or perhaps epilepsy. He was unable to play a full part in political life, but, like his sister, he could still be a useful power pawn.

Alexander got wind of the scheme and, acting completely out of character, panicked. Prompted by his mother and friends, he felt sure that the planned marriage signified that his father intended to disinherit him in favor of his half-brother. The suspicion was irrational, for Philip was not the kind of man to hand over his hard-won gains to an incompetent.

Nevertheless, Alexander was determined to head off the threat. He asked a well-known tragic actor, Thessalus, who had won top drama prizes at Athens, to go to Pixodarus as his envoy and throw in a spanner. (Because performers traveled from festival to festival around the Mediterranean, governments often hired them as emissaries or agents.) Thessalus informed the satrap that the proposed bridegroom was weak-minded (a fact the Macedonian king had evidently kept to himself) and suggested that instead he mark down his daughter for Alexander.

Philip soon learned what had happened and lost his temper. He stormed into Alexander's room, taking with him one of the young man's friends, Philotas, son of his favorite general, Parmenion. It is a reasonable guess that this youth had been the one who informed the king of what was going on. If so, we can be sure that Alexander stored the betrayal in the back of his mind for future action.

According to Plutarch, Philip gave his son a piece of his mind, but was careful to avoid another irrevocable split. He simply "reproached him for behaving so ignobly and so unworthily of his position as to wish to marry the daughter of a mere Carian, who was no more than the slave of a barbarian king."

Presumably Alexander would be needed on campaign. The king would want to keep him under his eye and it seems most unlikely that he would be appointed as regent of Macedonia again.

Thessalus did not fare so well. He was put in chains and sent back to

Macedonia to await punishment. The prince's group of youthful followers were banished from court. They included Ptolemy, son of Lagus, but rumored to have been sired by the king; Harpalus, probably the nephew of Phila, one of Philip's seven wives; and Nearchus, a Cretan by birth who lived in Amphipolis in the Chalcidice. Alexander was fiercely loyal to these early supporters, and in later years promoted them and overlooked their peccadilloes. For the moment, though, they vanished from view, leaving their charismatic chief alone in a bleak world.

Ostensibly peaceful relations resumed, but Philip looked to shore up his dynasty by reaching out yet again to matrimony. He decided to marry off Cynane, his daughter by Audata, his Illyrian queen. She was a remarkable young woman, well known for her "unfeminine" enthusiasm for military affairs. She accompanied her father on an Illyrian campaign and, despite her mother's origin, killed with her own hand an Illyrian queen on the battlefield.

Her husband was to be her first cousin Amyntas, son of King Perdiccas. As we have seen, he had been supplanted as king during his infancy but was living unharmed at the Macedonian court. We do not have a window into Philip's soul, but it looks as if he was preparing (once again) for a day when Alexander was no longer available, for whatever reason, to succeed him.

Amyntas may not have had the ambition for kingship, but he was an adult and in his right mind. Above all, the blood royal flowed through his veins.

With all these marriages, it is decidedly odd that Philip showed no interest in finding a wife for his son. Perhaps in truth he had given up on him.

THE WEDDING OF THE KING of Epirus to Philip's daughter Cleopatra was to be the most splendid event. The object was to display the king as a civilized, generous, and friendly Hellene, who deserved his new role as *hegemon*.

The venue was the kingdom's old capital, Aegae, where Macedonia's kings were interred. A monumental palace, built during Philip's reign, was a landmark visible for miles. Two or three stories were or-

ganized around a large, columned courtyard. The building was sump-
tuously decorated with mosaic floors and frescoed walls. The external
walls were covered with a lustrous marble stucco. A large gallery overlooked an open-air theater; this was constructed from banked earth
and only the stage and the front row were made of stone. An altar
dedicated to Dionysus, god of theater, stood in the middle of the orchestra, a circular space between the audience and the players, from
which a chorus commented on the action.

The guest list was international. Anybody who was anybody in the
Greek world was expected to be present. Philip's guest-friends were
summoned and members of his court were expected to bring along as
many foreign acquaintances as they could. Musical contests, athletic
games, and lavish banquets were programmed. Crowds flocked to
Aegae. Representatives of important city-states presented the king
with golden wreaths. Athens was among the donors despite its traditional hostility to Macedonia; after handing over its wreath, the city's
herald announced a new law that if anyone plotted against King Philip
and fled to Athens for refuge, he would be "delivered up."

At the wedding banquet a hugely popular Athenian actor, Neoptolemus, gave a recital. He was "matchless in the power of his voice," and
many years ago had trained the young orator Demosthenes how to
speak long sentences in a single breath. One of the pieces he performed
was a melancholy ode on the vanity of human wishes. He was refer-
ring to the disaster that struck the Persian invaders of Greece in 490
and 480, and the king was delighted. But superstitious listeners feared
it was a bad omen for the future.

> Your thoughts reach higher than the air.
> . . .
> But there is one who'll catch the swift,
> Who goes away obscured in gloom,
> And sudden, unseen, overtakes
> And robs us of our distant hopes—
> Death, human beings' source of many woes.

At last late drinkers went to bed. Games were scheduled for the following day. While it was still dark, a multitude of spectators poured

into the theater where performances and contests were to be held, and soon every space in the theater and presumably on the gallery above was taken.

Outside, a splendid ceremonial procession was formed. Statues of the twelve Olympian gods on their thrones were carried into the theater. According to the historian Diodorus, these were "worked with great artistry and decorated with a dazzling show of wealth to strike awe in the beholder." Joining them was a thirteenth statue of Philip. It was set down with the others as if he, too, were divine. The Philippeum will have come to many people's minds. Evidently the king was determined to set himself apart from and above ordinary mortals.

Then Philip himself arrived. Unusually, he ordered the Royal Pages to walk behind him at a distance. Contradicting the impression of arrogance created by the statues, he wished to be seen as someone guarded by the goodwill of all Hellenes. He had no need of spearmen. He told some friends in the procession to go on ahead. Wearing a white cloak, he walked along a narrow passageway into the theater, a vulnerable figure with only the two Alexanders at his side, his son and his new son-in-law.

THE EMBITTERED PAUSANIAS WAS among the pages on duty that morning. He had continued to feed his rage. The absent Attalus was beyond reach in Asia, but if he could not punish the man who had wronged him, he could at least strike down the one who had failed to avenge him. Carrying a Celtic dagger under his cloak, the young man took up a position at the entrance to the theater. As he was a member of the court, his presence attracted no particular attention.

The young man darted forward without warning as the king emerged onto the orchestra and plunged the dagger inbetween his ribs. Shock and awe among the packed spectators. Philip died at once, his white cloak stained with blood. He was forty-six. His murderer rushed out by another exit from the theater.

Some of the bodyguard ran to the king to try and help him; others, who may have been among Alexander's entourage, chased after Pausanias. Three of them were close friends and contemporaries of the crown prince. They were Perdiccas, an aristocrat from Upper Macedonia who may have been of Argead descent, and Leonnatus, who was related to Queen Eurydice, Philip's mother, and had been brought up with Alexander; so too, probably, was another follower, Attalus (no connection with Philip's general).

Pausanias had posted horses at the city gate for his getaway and enjoyed a good start. He would have reached them if his boot hadn't been trapped in a vine root. Perdiccas and the guards caught up with him and speared him to death.

All was confusion.

MACEDONIA DID NOT HAVE robust institutions that could cope with sudden vacuums of power. For a short time, perhaps a day or so, there might be no certain authority. It looked as if Macedonia was reverting to type with palace coups and lethal purges in the royal family. The distinguished guests decided to wait on events at Aegae.

Antipater realized there was not a moment to lose. The army was in an uneasy frame of mind: they were upset by Philip's death, and were worried by the prospect of a long foreign campaign under an inexperienced leader. Alexander was not a particularly popular figure; with his foreign mother, perhaps he was not a true Macedonian. His quarrel with Philip had isolated him, and many leading personalities had set their faces against him.

However, he had long been groomed, at least implicitly, as his father's successor. The wily old general immediately presented the prince, wearing a breastplate, to an army assembly, which seems to have had the power to elect or confirm a new king. It at once acclaimed him. Diodorus writes that Alexander rose to the challenge and

established his authority far more firmly than anyone thought possible, for he was quite young and so not universally respected. First, he promptly won over the Macedonians by tactful statements. The king was changed only in name and the state would be run on principles no less effective than those of his father's administration. Then he addressed himself to the embassies which were present and good-naturedly asked the Greeks to remain as loyal to him as they had been to his father.

One of his first regnal acts was to deal with Attalus, whose charge of illegitimacy still affronted him. The tricky general, not unnaturally alarmed for his safety after Philip's demise, had begun plotting with the Athenians. He then changed his mind and betrayed them to Alexander as proof of his undying loyalty. The king was not deceived and sent a *hetairos,* or Companion, with a small band of men to the advance force in Asia with instructions either to bring him back alive or put him to death there. In the event Attalus was executed in situ. Parmenion had little choice but to allow this to happen despite the fact that his fellow commander was his son-in-law. His complaisance came at a price for Alexander, in that many of the key commands in the army were held by Parmenion's sons, brothers, or other relatives. This was tolerable, though, for they were capable and obedient officers.

The removal of Attalus was not enough to make Alexander secure. Philip had been something of a confidence trickster and his legacy was dispersing like the morning mist. Both at home and abroad, the situation suddenly deteriorated. According to Plutarch,

> Greece was still gasping over Philip's wars. Thebes was staggering to her feet after her fall and shaking the dust of Chaeronea from her arms. Athens was stretching out a helping hand to join with Thebes. All Macedonia was festering with revolt and looking toward Amyntas and the sons of Aeropus. The Illyrians were again rebelling, and trouble with the Scythians was impending for their Macedonian neighbors. Persian gold flowed freely through the hands of popular leaders everywhere.

The Amyntas to whom Plutarch refers was the son of Perdiccas, who had an irreproachable if theoretical claim to the throne. The sons of Aeropus were Arrhabaeus and his two brothers from Lyncestis who were close to Amyntas and whose father had quarreled with Philip.

Alexander acted at once to stifle domestic opposition. In particular, he sensed conspirators in the background who were implicated in the assassination. Two of Aeropus's sons were immediately put to death, so far as we can tell without trial. At some unknown date in 336 or 335 the supposed pretender, Amyntas, was also killed. The brother left alive was Alexander Lyncestes, husband of one of Antipater's four daughters. Recognizing the danger he was in as soon as Philip was struck down, he ran to his namesake's side and was among the first to rally to his cause. He was armed and he guarded the prince as he left the theater and made his way to the palace next door.

This demonstration of instant loyalty, combined (no doubt) with his wife's family connection, saved his life. We do not know how he reacted to his brothers' fate, but he made sure not to complain in public. It was enough to be high in favor, for now.

BUT WERE THESE MEN guilty as accused?

One of Alexander's first tasks was to arrange his father's funeral. He was interred in a two-room tomb at Aegae. In the main chamber was a fresco of the rape of Persephone, queen of the Underworld. It was here that Philip lay for more than two millennia until benignly disturbed by twentieth-century archaeologists.

It is suggestive that Alexander had the Lyncestian brothers ceremonially executed at the burial place, convinced (we have to presume) of their culpability. We may recall that Achilles sacrificed twelve Trojans at the funeral pyre of his lover Patroclus; perhaps Homer's royal student had this bloodstained precedent in mind.

However, no certain evidence has ever been adduced and the new king may simply have been eliminating a possible competitor for the throne whether or not he really wanted the job. Perhaps Amyntas did not. For many years he had lived a quiet life at court and never caused any trouble. But ambition for the throne, latent during Philip's reign, may now have been ignited. We simply do not know, and perhaps the new king did not either. From his point of view, though, security came first.

Pausanias had a powerful enough motive to have acted alone, and could have done so. But gossip swirled around Aegae and implicated very senior personalities. If anyone were to ask who benefited from Philip's demise (in other words, were we to apply the Roman orator Cicero's famous test, *Cui bono?*), the answer was obvious. The clear winners were Alexander himself, a crown prince without a future whose only role would have been forever to follow a few steps behind his father, and his ferocious mother, Olympias, who would do anything to advance his interests.

Contemporaries guessed at their involvement and there is some evidence to confirm it, although not necessarily trustworthy. The Argead dynasty's history is peppered with regicides, and both mother and son were known to be ambitious and decisive. We are told that Pausanias went to Alexander and complained about his treatment. Alexander gave him an enigmatic reply. He simply quoted a line from Euripides' tragedy *Medea,* which refers to the accusation that the witch from Colchis was planning the murders of her faithless lover, Jason; his wife-to-be; and her father:

The father, bride and bridegroom all at once.

By this Alexander was understood to have meant Attalus, his daughter Cleopatra, and Philip. He was signaling his tacit encouragement of Pausanias should he decide to resort to violence.

The fact that the murderer was killed by his pursuers rather than captured alive for questioning aroused suspicion. The captors were all known to be close associates of Alexander. Perhaps they had acted to stop Pausanias from revealing the names of conspirators.

Olympias made no attempt to disguise her joy at her husband's demise. It was alleged that she arranged for the getaway horses. En route to the king's funeral she is reported to have placed a golden wreath on Pausanias's corpse, which was hanging on a cross. A few days later she had the body taken down and cremated. The queen then turned her attention to Philip's widow, whom she made watch her baby daughter being grilled to death on a brazier. After that she forced the hapless young woman to hang herself. Alexander was furious at this cruel behavior, which reinforced the Macedonian reputation for barbarousness. However, he was too close to his mother, too much in her thrall, to punish her. We may suppose that it was he who found a place in Philip's tomb for the two tragic corpses.

It is perfectly possible that Olympias and Alexander encouraged or even commissioned Pausanias to kill the king. Alternatively, they may

have been accessories to the deed, catching wind of his intentions, but not informing Philip.

It is also conceivable that they had no idea of what Pausanias had in mind and were taken by surprise like everybody else. After all, it seems improbable that two such politically aware personalities would choose an international festival attended by many VIPs as the moment for an outrage that would seriously damage the Macedonian "brand" and that risked throwing the realm into terminal crisis.

In summary, we know too little to convict, and there are other equally plausible scenarios.

THE GREAT KING, for example (or one of his satraps), had every motive to remove the man who was planning to destroy him.

Palace plots were not exclusive to Macedonia and the Persian succession had always been a problem. The current ruler was Darius III, who had recently emerged from a short but turbulent crisis.

According to Herodotus, the Persians, like other Middle Eastern peoples, valued eunuchs highly for their fidelity. The mercenary soldier and writer Xenophon agreed. He observed that the founder of the Achaemenid empire, Cyrus, had recognized that a ruler is at greatest personal risk "when at meals or at wine, in the bath, or in bed and asleep." He needed servants who were trustworthy. The advantage of eunuchs was that, being unable to procreate, they usually had no family members to promote and as a group were despised by society at large: consequently they were completely dependent on their masters.

THERE WERE EXCEPTIONS TO the rule, though, as the career of the chiliarch, or grand vizier, Bagoas went to show. "A eunuch in physical fact but a militant rogue in disposition," as Diodorus nicely put it, he poisoned his employer, Artaxerxes III Ochus, and replaced him with his son Arses. He put to death the new king's brothers, doubtless to avoid any challenges to the regime and to isolate his protégé. Arses unwisely put it about that he was displeased with Bagoas for his outrageous behavior and intended to punish him. The vizier struck first, murdering Arses and his family. Having now disposed of most of the dynasty, he was hard put to find a replacement, eventually in 336 choosing a member of the royal house's cadet branch called Codomannus. Codomannus took the regnal name of Darius III.

A man of considerable courage, Darius once accepted a challenge to single combat during a campaign against a fierce Iranian tribe. He killed his opponent. He was also no dupe: he took care to give Bagoas a dose of his own medicine. When offered a poisoned cup, the Great King passed it to the eunuch, who had no alternative but to drink and die.

The threat from Macedonia was imminent and will have been at the top of Darius's agenda. He could well have attempted to eliminate Philip, just as he later tried to suborn Greek soldiers and a senior Macedonian to kill Alexander. That said, we will be hard pressed to imagine a plausible intermediary or link between Persepolis and Pella, between the Great King and a maddened youth.

Guilt might also attach to Athens, with its long tradition of anti-Macedonian politicians, headed by the orator Demosthenes. He seems to have heard of the assassination suspiciously early, which has led some to suppose that he was an accessory before the fact; more likely, he had a fast messenger in his pay. He was happy to collaborate with the young monarch's enemy, Attalus, although nothing came of this. He also willingly accepted large bribes from the Great King. According to Plutarch, Demosthenes was "overwhelmed by Persian gold." He gave himself "prodigious airs" and had a shrine dedicated to the killer. He persuaded the *boule,* or state council, to offer a thanksgiving sacrifice, as if for good news. In his speeches, he gave Alexander the insulting nickname of Margites after the stupid hero of a mock epic on the Trojan War.

Once more, although many Athenians hated the Macedonian monarch and might well have plotted to put an end to him, there is no supporting evidence. Terrorism was not the Athenian style. In any case, a noisy democracy was not well suited to keep a secret, and we do not even hear of rumors.

PHILIP II OF MACEDONIA was a very great man indeed. He transformed his country from a barbaric backwater into the leading power in Greece. He was hard to resist, for access to gold and silver mines and a deep reservoir of human capital enabled him to recruit and pay a large standing army. The Hellenic city-states did not have the resources to counter the threat he posed.

The king had an acute sense of timing. Ruthlessness went alongside a sense of humor. He was not naturally cruel, but was violent when occasion called for it. He endured great pain without complaint. On the battlefield he led from the front, as his many scars testified. But he preferred to get his way through the diplomatic tools of bribery and marriages. Military conflict was a last resort, with the standout exception of the invasion of Persia.

Is it going too far, though, to argue that Philip's death was not quite so untimely as has been claimed? A case can be made that he was past his best. His mishandling of his wife and the crown prince, the provocative marriage to Cleopatra, the hubristic monument at Olympia, the Philippeum, the even more hubristic statues carried into the theater at Aegae all suggest a coarsening of his political instincts and a surprising insensitivity.

Nevertheless, Alexander's inheritance was his father's towering achievement. Thanks to Philip, Hellas had become, in effect, an adjunct of Macedonia, and his army was a finely tuned instrument of war. The new king was a lucky man.

HOWEVER, THE BEGINNING OF his reign echoed that of Philip. Suddenly, Macedonia looked as if it were falling apart again with a callow youth at the helm. The opportunity for old enemies was too good to lose. As before, the neighboring tribal kingdoms in the north rose in arms and the subdued Greeks threw off the Macedonian yoke.

No one gave the boy a chance.

CHAPTER 4

THE LONE WOLF

———

ALEXANDER WAS DEAD. THERE WAS NO DOUBT ABOUT IT.

He had wandered off into darkest Thrace, where he had fallen victim to the barbarians who lived there. His army had been wiped out and the young king had fallen. The civilized world heard reports to this effect in political circles, believed them, and breathed easily again. It recovered its balance and forgot about Macedonian bullies.

But this is how the future actually played itself out.

FOR ALL HIS QUARREL with Philip, Alexander ought to have been grateful for his inheritance. He now presided over a highly disciplined and effective army and a large and wealthy empire. But without its tricky founder, it appeared to be breaking up. There would be no simple handover. The boy king would have to fight for what he had been given.

On his accession in June 336, Alexander's advisers urged caution. He should leave the Greek city-states to their devices and, above all, refrain from using force against them. As for the restless tribes on the Macedonian border, he should treat them gently and negotiate deals before they opted for war. The king totally disagreed. Safety lay in speed and risk.

The Greek city-states were thrilled by Philip's assassination, which their leading citizens had witnessed in person in the theater at Aegae. All across Hellas they moved to recover their independence. The Thebans voted to expel a Macedonian garrison and to deny Alexander overall leadership of the grand anti-Persian coalition. Despite the fact that they had given Philip citizenship rights, the Athenians and their leading orator, Demosthenes, could hardly restrain themselves. Plutarch writes that they

> immediately offered up sacrifices for the good news and voted a crown for Pausanias, the king's assassin, while Demosthenes appeared in public dressed in magnificent clothing and wearing a garland on his head, even though his daughter had died only six days before.

Demosthenes sneered that Alexander would never set foot out of Macedonia, for he was perfectly happy to saunter around Pella and "keep watch over the omens."

Meanwhile the young king took action. He marched south, persuading the Thessalian confederation and the Amphictyonic League to vote resolutions that he succeed his father as *hegemon* of the Greeks.

Envoys from Ambracia, an ancient city in southern Epirus, apologized for declaring independence; Alexander politely replied that "they had been only a little premature in grasping the freedom that he was on the point of giving them voluntarily."

He continued down through the undefended pass of Thermopylae. One day the citizens of Thebes were amazed to see a large Macedonian army standing outside their walls. The Athenians were sure that their turn would be next. But Alexander only had time for clemency. He simply insisted that the two cities accept him as *hegemon*. Offering profuse apologies, they immediately capitulated and he proceeded to convene a meeting of the Panhellenic League of Corinth.

Demosthenes was appointed to an embassy that made its way north to grovel before the king, but at Mount Cithaeron he lost his nerve and went back to Athens. Perhaps he was worried that his compromising correspondence with Attalus had fallen into the king's hands. Also, he needed to give Darius something for all the Persian gold he had received.

League members fell over themselves to please their new master. Alexander made fun of the tiny city-state of Megara when it offered him honorary citizenship, but he accepted the honor when he was told that the only other person to have been granted it was the demigod Heracles (the king's alleged ancestor). When the League duly gathered again at Corinth, its members were reconfirmed as free and independent—a status contradicted for the open-eyed by the ever-present threat of military force. The League members elected him as their leader in succession to Philip and appointed him as general plenipotentiary in the great war of liberation against Persia. An inscription of the oath they took has survived:

> I swear by Zeus, Earth, Sun, Poseidon, Athena, and Ares, by all the gods and goddesses, I shall abide by the peace and I shall not break the agreement with Alexander the Macedonian. . . . I shall fight against the breaker of the common peace in whatever way seems good to the general council and may be prescribed by the *hegemon*.

During his brief stopover in Corinth, Alexander is said to have made arrangements to meet Diogenes, one of the most celebrated thinkers of the day. He had acquired a taste for philosophy thanks to Aristotle's tutorials in the Gardens of Midas and liked to reward those of whom he approved with his patronage.

Diogenes made a point of living as simply and "naturally" as possible. He begged for his necessities. He wore only a loincloth and slept wherever he chose, sometimes (apparently) in a large ceramic jar. He defecated and masturbated in public. In his austerity and poverty, Diogenes bore some resemblance to the near-naked religious ascetics, or holy men, of India, the Brahmins.

He acted in this way to draw attention to the luxury and corruption of the present age, and is reported to have said: "Humans have complicated every simple gift of the gods." He was a founder of the Cynic (Greek for "doglike," hence without shame) school of philosophy. Virtue was realized by action, Cynics believed, not in theory. The greatest of Greek philosophers, Plato, thought little of Diogenes' ideas and is said to have called him "a Socrates gone mad." None of his writings have survived.

Diogenes was extremely independent-minded. He spent his days in a suburb of Corinth and declined to go to the city center to meet Alexander. The Macedonian king, not at all put out, made his way to where Diogenes was lying on the ground and basking in the sun.

When the philosopher saw Alexander and his entourage approach, he raised himself a little on his elbow and stared at him.

"Can I do anything for you?" asked the king.

"Yes, you can stand a little to one side out of my sun."

This putdown ended the interview. However, Alexander was not at all displeased, as he could well have been. This was because he recognized in Diogenes a fellow spirit. One of them had withdrawn from the world and the other meant to subjugate it, but both were stubborn, implacable, and self-absorbed.

Later, his courtiers laughed at the philosopher, but the king simply remarked: "You can say what you like, but if I were not Alexander, I should have liked to be Diogenes."

ALEXANDER AND HIS ARMY promptly vanished. He was in a hurry to deal with the revolts in the north.

But first of all he called by at Delphi, home of the oracle of Apollo. Like his father before him, Alexander sought a consultation about his chances of success in Persia, but he was determined neither to be misled nor to mislead himself when assessing the divine hexameters. The discussions at Corinth had been lengthy and by the time Alexander reached the oracle it was late November. Unfortunately, the temple of Apollo was closed between mid-November and mid-February. The god was taking a rest.

The king was not used to being denied. He summoned the Pythia to explain herself. She refused to officiate, saying that to do so would be against the law. So he went up to her himself and tried to drag her by force to the temple where she held her seances. She cried out: "You are invincible, my son!" No ambiguity there.

The quick-witted Alexander immediately withdrew his request.

He needed no other prophecy, he declared, for he had extracted from her exactly the prediction he was looking for. Thoroughly satisfied, he resumed his journey.

A MOMENT OF CRISIS was at hand. Tribal kingdoms along Macedonia's borders were on a war footing and threatened Macedonia's very existence. Not only did Alexander need to pacify them thoroughly if he was to be able to leave safely for a long absence in the east, but he also had to win his soldiers' loyalty, not to mention the broader approval of Macedonia's body politic. At present, these were only on loan.

How was Alexander to handle the uprising of Triballians and Illyrians? They occupied parts of Thrace, the wide-ranging territory which, as we have seen, lay south of the Danube (the Ister, to the Greeks) and north of Macedonia and the Aegean Sea. Thracian tribesmen were fierce and warlike, although in the heat of the moment they could be unruly and disorganized.

They had resisted foreign conquerors such as the Persians and the Macedonians. They were regarded as rather primitive, lived in large open villages rather than cities, and had few civic institutions, but had they managed to unite their forces they could have been more than a match for the Greeks, who founded colonies on the coast but left the hinterland to its own devices, or for that matter Philip's invincible phalanx. In 339 the Triballians had inflicted a defeat on Alexander's father as well as a serious wound that left him with a bad limp.

A war of outright conquest and annexation such as Darius the Great had conducted was out of the question. It would take too long and require a large army of occupation. Alexander had at his disposal perhaps no more than fifteen thousand highly trained Macedonians—which included a phalanx of foot soldiers, cavalry from Upper Macedonia, lightly armed troops, slingers, and archers. Of special value were the Agrianians, a Thracian tribe, who were crack javelin throwers and whose king, Langarus, was a personal friend; as already noted, he probably gave Alexander shelter during his brief exile from Macedonia. A force of that size could be supplied without too much difficulty and, above all, would be able to move fast. This was exactly what Alexander needed.

Alexander's aim was to demonstrate complete military superiority in a brief but theatrically impressive campaign. He intended to fight his way to the natural frontier of the Danube. He arranged for a squadron of warships to sail up the river where they would rendezvous with the army at a predetermined place and time. This impressive maneuver would be an assertion of overwhelming power, after which Alexander would feel safe to march on Persia without risking insurgencies in his rear.

In the spring of 335, the king led his army into Thrace from the Greek port of Amphipolis on the Aegean Sea. After ten days in friendly territory, he reached the Haemus mountain range (in today's Balkans), where he found the enemy, Free Thracians (that is, Thracians independent of foreign rule), holding a high mountain pass (perhaps the Shipka Pass) and blocking his advance. They had assembled wagons in front of their line as a defensive stockade.

Alexander decided to storm the pass frontally, but guessed that the Free Thracians intended to allow the wagons to roll down the steep but even contour of the hill and crash into his infantry. The tribesmen would follow this up by a general charge. Somehow the king had to neutralize such a plan. Should the wagons be released, he ordered his hoplites either to open ranks if there was room and let them through, or to stoop or lie down under linked shields so that the wagons would roll over them.

Extraordinarily enough, Alexander's plan worked and not one of his men was killed, although we may suppose some bruises and broken bones. The Macedonians then stood up and charged uphill in close formation. At the same time, archers on the left and the king on the right, with some elite troops and Agrianian javelin throwers, threatened the enemy's flanks should they advance down the hill.

In fact, the poorly equipped tribesmen were so daunted by the failure of the wagons and by the discipline of the Macedonian infantry that they fled down the mountainside, every man for himself. Fifteen hundred of them were killed and all the women and children who accompanied them were captured.

———

HAVING CROSSED THE BALKANS, Alexander now entered the territory of the Triballians.

Their king was no fool. He understood the implications of Alexander's victory and decided to avoid a full-scale battle. He sent a large
number of his warriors together with the women and children to a
place of safety, a large island on the Danube. Then as the Macedonians
approached the river a force of Triballians countermarched in a bid to
cut off his rear. If the enemy succeeded in garrisoning the Balkan
passes, Alexander's position would become very difficult. So he turned
around his army and went in hot pursuit of the Triballians. He caught
up with them as they were making camp in a densely forested glen.
The trees were so closely grouped together that direct attack would
certainly fail. Aware that tribal hordes were undisciplined and liable to
react violently to provocation, the king devised a stratagem. He sent
his archers and slingers to the edge of the wood where they discharged
their missiles at the enemy. Meanwhile he formed up his phalanx out
of view but ready for action.

As Alexander had calculated, he so irritated the Triballians that they
rushed out of the wood and drove back the archers and slingers. The
trap snapped shut when they were suddenly faced with the Macedonian phalanx and cavalry. It was too late to regain the safety of the trees
and defeat was total; three thousand Triballians fell, as against Macedonian losses of eleven horsemen and forty foot soldiers.

Three days after the battle, Alexander arrived at the Danube, where
he met the squadron of warships as prearranged. His next task was to
land on the island and round up all the tribespeople who had taken
refuge there. However, he soon saw that the water ran too fast and the
banks were too steep for a landing to be practicable. So he was forced
to come up with a new idea.

It would have to communicate shock and awe, to strike the enemy
as an almost miraculous achievement. Otherwise the king would fail to
achieve his strategic objective—namely, so to cow the insurgent tribes
that they would create no trouble in the future.

Then inspiration came. Fortuitously, another tribe, the Getae, who
lived on the far side of the Danube, arrived at its banks en masse with

four thousand horse and ten thousand infantry. They were determined to prevent the Macedonians from coming over.

At this point, the historian Arrian applies to Alexander the ancient Greek word *pothos*. This means a desire or yearning for what one does not have. It was a notable feature of Alexander's personality. He was not subject to personal ambition as ordinarily conceived so much as to a need to achieve the impossible. *That* was true glory, he believed.

On seeing the Getae, Alexander conceived a *pothos* to cross the wide river. Once again he improvised. He gathered together a number of dugout canoes, which the locals used for fishing, and ordered his men to make rafts out of their leather tent covers by stuffing them with hay. During the course of one night fifteen hundred cavalry and four thousand infantry were ferried across. This was an astonishing feat and our sources leave unexplained the transit of the horses; perhaps they swam supported by rafts.

The Macedonians reached the far bank while it was still dark and marched smartly to the Getae encampment, which they stormed while the tribesmen were still asleep. Survivors fled to a permanent but poorly fortified settlement three and a half miles away, which Alexander also attacked. The Getae abandoned it, put as many women and children as possible on horses, and set out for empty country as far away from the river as they could get.

Alexander called a halt to the fighting. Not one of his men had been lost. The settlement was razed and sacrifices were offered to Zeus, Heracles, and the benevolent god of the Danube. The king led his men back across the river in daylight and they returned to their camp.

The Triballians on the island looked on aghast. What they had witnessed was superhuman. Alexander was too good for them, they concluded, and immediately capitulated. A spate of shocked embassies from Thracian tribes arrived to make peace with the Macedonian king.

BAD NEWS SOURED THE savor of victory. The following day, Alexander learned that Macedonia itself was under attack. Illyrians governed by Cleitus, the ruler of a fierce tribe called the Dardani, had launched an invasion of the northwest frontier. He was the son of the old battler Bardylis, who had devoted his long life to transforming Illyria into a great power. As we have seen, Philip had destroyed him and his army in 358. Now his unforgetting offspring was pressing for another round of conflict.

Cleitus was occupying Pelium, a fortified settlement that commanded a mountain pass between Illyria and Macedonia. Before he launched his invasion he was awaiting another insurgent leader, Glaucias of the Taulantii, a cluster of Illyrian tribes on the Adriatic coast (roughly in today's Albania). Alexander realized he had to move fast if he was to prevent the two monarchs from joining forces. He made for Pelium with all speed, determined to deal with Cleitus before Glaucias appeared on the scene.

As if he did not have enough enemies already, Alexander learned that his progress would be delayed, perhaps fatally, by another dissident tribe, the Autariates, which planned to intercept him en route.

Threatened by three hostile armies, the king had his back to the wall. He was to be rescued by his friend Langarus.

It is only between those who are good, and resemble one another in their goodness, that friendship is perfect. Such friends are both good in themselves and, so far as they are good, desire the good of one another. But it is those who desire the good of their friends for their friends' sake who are most completely friends, since each loves the other for what the other is in himself and not for something he has about him that he does not need to have.

This was Aristotle, Alexander's onetime tutor, asserting the high importance of friendship or *philia*—and, more particularly, of male friendship. It was a topic of great interest to the ancient Greeks, and the philosophers Socrates and Plato had devoted much thought to it.

So too, we may guess, had the young king. He derived his idea of self-worth from Homer's epics, the *Iliad* and *Odyssey*. His lordly warriors owed their personal glory, their honor, not only to courage and victory on the battlefield, although that was a large part of it, but also to the conventions of friendship.

Aristocrats traveled around the Mediterranean and developed a network of equals on whose hospitality they could depend. These relationships had a basis in affection, but from a practical point of view they functioned as alternatives to the institutions of modern life—banks, travel agencies, passports, legal services, hotels.

When that great but god-bullied hero, Odysseus, is washed up on the shores of the legendary land of Phaeacia, he is offered food and drink and a bed for the night before he is even asked to identify himself. Only when all his needs have been satisfied is he invited to tell the story of his life and trials. He is laden with valuable gifts and sent on his way without cost in a Phaeacian ship.

Guest-friendship survived into the age of the Hellenic city-state. The underlying principle was that a favor given created a moral obligation to reciprocate. *Philia*'s mutually profitable courtesies facilitated the comings and goings of the merchant and the sailor. It also enabled politicians to explore foreign-policy issues with international counterparts or to deploy personal alliances against the interests of regimes in power. The interdependence of friends was supported by arranged marriages, homosexual pairings, and partnership in commercial enterprises.

Alexander pursued friendship with enthusiasm. Many of his fellow-pupils in the shady walks at Mieza reappeared in Alexander's circle as adults. Those who committed crimes or misdemeanors were easily forgiven. Affection promoted the not-so-talented, and anyone who betrayed personal loyalty lived to regret it.

Alexander had gotten to know Langarus during his teen years, when Philip had appointed him regent at the age of sixteen. Langarus had been an open supporter of the young prince and the two had developed a strong relationship.

In 335 Langarus, accompanied by a crack troop of foot guards, was in attendance during the Thracian expedition and must have been pleased to see the confidence that Alexander placed in his fellow tribesmen. Arrian writes:

> When he heard that Alexander wanted to know who the Autariates were, and how numerous, he told him not to give them another thought. They were the least military of the tribes in the region. He himself would invade their land, then they would have something of their own to worry about.

The Agrianian king was as good as his word. Fire and the sword silenced the hapless tribe.

Alexander was so pleased with his friend that, in addition to generous gifts, he offered him the hand of his half-sister, the redoubtable Cynane. She had been the wife of Amyntas, son of his uncle King Perdiccas, but seeing that Alexander had recently executed him she was on the market again. This was, to put it mildly, a good marriage. But nothing came of the project, for Langarus unexpectedly fell ill and died after his return from ravaging the Autariates. Had he survived, he would surely have played a considerable role in Alexander's life.

THE FORTIFIED SETTLEMENT OF Pelium stood on a rise in the center of a small plain, inside a bend of the river Eordaicus. To the north, south, and west thickly wooded heights overlooked the plain. The river itself flowed westward through the narrow Wolf's Pass. Here, between the river and some precipitous cliffs, there was room only for four men abreast, although there was more space on the other side, across a ford.

When Alexander's weary army arrived at the plain, he was taking a considerable risk and he was relieved to find that Cleitus was still alone. The tribal chief was occupying Pelium and the surrounding heights. The Macedonians made camp in the vicinity. Relying on the superior fighting quality of his men, Alexander decided to launch a frontal attack on the fortified settlement, thus tempting the enemy to come down from the hills and take the Macedonians on their flanks and in the rear. Alexander was ready, of course. He smartly about-turned his army and routed Cleitus's warriors. He then hemmed in the enemy inside Pelium with a contravallation. The corpses of three boys, three girls, and three black rams were found in the enemy's deserted positions. In an act of futile cruelty that offended Hellenic sensibilities, they had been sacrificed for victory.

On the following day, the military situation was transformed, negatively. Glaucias and his army arrived and occupied the hills Cleitus had abandoned. From holding the initiative, Alexander was now outnumbered and surrounded. From every eminence enemies gazed threateningly down on him and his men.

What was worse, Alexander was desperately short of supplies. He ordered Parmenion's son, the competent but conceited Philotas, to take the baggage vehicles and as many cavalrymen as he needed to guard them, and gather foodstuffs from nearby fields. When Glaucias learned of this foraging expedition he set out to attack it. Scouts reported the danger to Alexander, who marched off as fast as he could to the rescue. He took with him his elite foot guards, the hypaspists or "shield carriers," the archers and his favorites, the Agrianians, along with four hundred cavalry. The rest of his army he left in front of Pelium to keep Cleitus boxed in. Glaucias preferred discretion to valor and after a skirmish allowed the Macedonian king to lead his foragers safely back to camp.

The supply problem had been solved, but otherwise Alexander's situation remained desperate. How could he extricate himself from the trap he had so incautiously entered? To retreat in the face of two hostile armies was too dangerous, so he took the bold decision to advance between them to the Wolf's Pass; in that way he would keep them divided and his own force united. Once beyond the pass he would be free from encirclement.

The following morning the king staged a coup de théâtre unique in military history. He arranged his phalanx as a solid block, 100 men wide and 120 men deep, with a squadron of 200 horsemen on each flank. Arrian describes what happened next.

> He commanded total silence and an instant obedience to commands. He first ordered "spears upright" to the foot soldiers, then at another order he had them lower their spears to the ready and simultaneously swing the massed points to the right and the left. After this he advanced the entire phalanx at a quick march, executing wheels on each wing in succession.

The enemy watched with growing amazement the speed and precision of the drill. Glaucias's Taulantians came down from the high ground to have a better look. Suddenly the left half of the phalanx formed itself into a wedge and charged Cleitus's Dardani. They panicked and fell back. Then the Macedonians shouted out their battle cry, *alala,* and beat their spears on their shields. Glaucias's men were the target this time and, petrified by the din, hastily sought refuge inside the fortress.

By this extraordinary means Alexander had bought himself enough time to move his phalanx unopposed along the river to the Wolf's Pass, where it could be forded. He and his bodyguards and Companion cavalry stormed a ridge from where he was able to guard his army as it crossed over.

Once the infantry had reached the other side it re-formed into a long thin rectangle. Presumably the baggage train followed. Before moving out from the pass, it waited for Alexander's cavalry to descend the ridge. By this time the enemy had understood what was happening and did its best to impede the Macedonians.

Arrian takes up the story.

> Alexander let them get close, then rushed them with his own company while the main phalanx shouted the war-cry and got ready to attack them through the river. Faced by this concerted onslaught, the enemy broke away and fell back. In the ensuing interval, Alexander brought the Agrianians and the archers down to the river at the double. He himself got across ahead of them, and when he saw the enemy closing in on the hindmost he had the catapults set up on the far bank and ordered fire at maximum range of all the missiles they could discharge: the archers had begun to cross, and he ordered them too to shoot from midstream. Glaucias's troops would not venture within range.

The army then cheerfully marched off to safety. Although we do not know how long the whole operation had taken, we can assume that the shadows cast by the circumscribing hills were lengthening. Not a single Macedonian had lost his life.

Meanwhile, Cleitus and Glaucias took the view that they had soundly beaten the Macedonians—or at least driven them off. They saw no need to chase after them on the far side of the pass. Alexander had evidently taken fright and they would not be troubled by him again. Their armies bivouacked carelessly around Pelium and they did not trouble to build defenses or mount guards. This was unwise. Alexander had been given a fright, but had not taken fright. Presumably using excellent scouting methods once again, Alexander learned of these careless dispositions and launched a night attack. He assembled a strike force of hypaspists, Agrianians (as ever), and two infantry brigades—in all, some seven thousand men—silently reentered the Wolf Pass, and crossed the river undetected. The rest of the army followed on behind.

The king fell on the still sleeping enemy. Many were dispatched in their beds and others taken alive. The rest fled in an uncontrolled rout. Alexander pursued them for miles. Cleitus took refuge in Pelium. Then he set fire to the place and escaped to the land of the Taulantians. He and Glaucias had plenty of time to discuss what went wrong with their campaign, but one thing was certain—Thrace and Illyria would be quiet for many years.

Alexander had achieved his strategic goal and could safely follow his dreams eastward.

BUT ALTHOUGH ALEXANDER'S FIRST serious military outing under his own command had *ended* in victory, in truth it had not gone very well.

His impetuosity landed him in serious, nearly terminal, trouble, although his ready admission, however painful, of a setback helped him to win through. He never lost his delight in danger. We need to remember that he and his generals were very young men, mostly in their early twenties. Many of them had grown up with Alexander and gone to school with him. They were high-spirited and audacious. They were living out a boys' own adventure.

There were two adults to lend a restraining hand—Antipater and Parmenion—although neither was present for this campaign. They knew better than to oppose the king's will, but they contributed stability and sensible advice—which was sometimes taken. As the years passed Alexander and the others matured, but at heart he remained the kid who never grew up.

He enjoyed one huge advantage: he had inherited Philip's army. His father had spent years drilling and disciplining it. It was now a flexible and highly efficient organism. The young king managed it with the firmness, sensitivity, and affection with which he rode his horse Bucephalas, and he found it instantly responsive to command.

Both Philip and Alexander were personally brave, led from the front, and risked life and limb in every battle. In one respect, though, the son was very different from the father. Both faced a similar challenge when they assumed the throne—attacks from old foes on every side. Philip preferred diplomacy and its subset, wholesale corruption, to war, although he resorted to war enthusiastically when necessary. In 358 he decided to act with caution. He dealt with his opponents one at a time, negotiating or paying for temporary cessations of conflict with some of them while facing the most pressing threats on the battlefield.

In 336, Alexander was much more impatient. One of his qualities was intelligent rapidity. He reacted instantly to events and combined this with a taste for subterfuge and surprise. He always sent scouts out ahead of his army so that he was well informed about the enemy and unlikely to become a victim of ambush. The speed with which he managed his campaigns constantly caught enemies on the back foot. Confronted with emergencies in mainland Greece and in northern Macedonia and Thrace, he made war precede, not follow, diplomacy. He took on everybody at once, marching his exhausted men at a hectic pace from hotspot to hotspot, and invariably arrived on the scene sooner than expected. To his opponents the effect was almost magical. It gave an impression of focused energy and invincible force. Resistance often collapsed without a fight.

Once the enemy had conceded, Alexander was inclined to clemency. The defeated chieftains Cleitus and Glaucias were left alone and, as we have seen, a treaty with Thebes and Athens was soon agreed. If obliged to run for a second time around the course, he could be violent and cruel. As at Pelium he refused to accept defeat, but insisted on returning to the fray until he obtained his bloodbath.

Alexander watched the enemy with close attention. He had an uncanny talent for noticing small changes or movements and correctly interpreting them. So he guessed the secret purpose of the stockade of carts. Once he had identified a problem he would instantly improvise a solution, however eccentric; to win an encounter by a consummate display of drill was a remarkable example of his imagination at work.

He knew the importance of small casualty lists to the morale of his soldiers. He learned a bitter lesson at Pelium when his logistics failed and the army ran out of food. It was a failure that he never allowed to occur again.

IN THE AUTUMN OF 335, news arrived in Athens that the young king was no more. Demosthenes produced a man before the *ecclesia,* or citizens' assembly, who had been wounded in a battle with the Triballi a long way away in darkest Thrace. He had witnessed the destruction of the Macedonian army and seen the king fall. The account was plausible and was widely accepted. The outcome of this report was, as Justin observed, that "the feelings of all the cities were changed and the garrisons of the Macedonians besieged."

Some exiles slipped into Thebes from Athens one night to stir up the people. They spoke at the assembly, "making play with the fine old words 'liberty' and 'free speech,'" and persuaded the Thebans to shake off the Macedonian yoke. Two officers of a Macedonian force occupying the Cadmea, the city's citadel, were assassinated. The Thebans were playing with fire, for they were signed-up members of the League of Corinth and the common peace. To abrogate unilaterally an international treaty was to break an oath sworn before the gods. This was sacrilege and could be punished by the destruction of one's city, the killing of all adult males, and the selling of all women and children into slavery.

But the Thebans felt safe to launch their rebellion because, they argued, Alexander's death freed them of their allegiance. They took comfort from a growing mood of resistance throughout Greece. The Athenian *ecclesia* voted for an immediate alliance with Thebes and planned to send troops in support. Armed contingents were on their way from the Peloponnese. Demosthenes, well funded by the Great King, scattered gold throughout Greece to win over uncertain consciences.

Alexander, undead, was informed of these developments and saw that he could not ignore them. He immediately abandoned any plans he had for mopping up in Thrace and ordered his expeditionary force to proceed south with all speed (presumably the baggage train followed at its own slower pace). The first stage of the journey was through an inhospitable and mountainous landscape with few inhabitants. He must have sent ahead for supplies of food and, after covering a distance of 120 miles as the crow flies, arrived on the seventh day in Thessaly. We may assume a brief pause for eating, drinking, and resting. Then the march resumed. After another 120 miles the Macedonians rushed through the unguarded Hot Gates, or Thermopylae, and six days after leaving Thessaly arrived in Boeotia.

This was a remarkable achievement. The Greeks had no idea that Alexander had passed through Thermopylae until he was in Boeotia with his army at the town of Onchestus, only a day's march from Thebes. He showed that the gibes of Demosthenes had got under his skin. He remarked: "Demosthenes called me a boy while I was in Illyria and among the Triballi, and a youth when I was marching through Thessaly. I will show him I am a man by the time I reach the walls of Athens."

The shocked Theban leaders made the best of a bad job by insisting on Alexander's death and arguing that it had to be another Alexander who commanded the Macedonian force. Few were convinced and the heart went out of the rebellion. The Peloponnesians halted at Corinth and then went home. Athens had second thoughts about sending military assistance.

The trusted eyewitness packed away his bandages and vial of pig's blood.

IT MAY HAVE BEEN at about this time that the king sent top-secret messages to the regent Antipater and possibly to his mother, Olympias. The last thing he needed was for a palace conspiracy to erupt, adding domestic to foreign troubles. It was too dangerous to allow Amyntas, son of Perdiccas, to continue as a potential pretender to the throne and a rallying point for his opponents, however innocent he was of intention. So he was put to death.

Olympias had killed Philip's last queen, Cleopatra, and her little girl, Europa. As usual she overdid things. The exotic cruelty of their deaths (the mother forced to hang herself after watching her child incinerated) attracted adverse comment.

We do not know for certain that Olympias was acting under her son's orders, but she may have been. As we have seen, though, he was reported to have been furious with her for acting so barbarically. One way or another, the historical record suggests that no holds were barred when it came to a dispute inside the Macedonian royal family. Cruelty to kith and kin was a popular tradition.

Children were regarded as an extension of their father and mother, and their murder when politics destroyed their parents was almost automatic. It occurred in drama as well as during real-life dynastic struggles and is a central theme of Euripides' masterpiece, *The Trojan Women*. The plot echoes the horrors of the Macedonian court: Troy has fallen and a Trojan princess's daughter has been sacrificed at the tomb of Achilles. Her little son has to die too, because the Greek leaders are afraid that the boy will grow up to avenge his father, the great warrior Hector. Realpolitik trumps decency and mercy.

The queen mother's intervention was perfectly understandable, contemporary observers will have felt. Maybe she had acted a little roughly, but within the conventions of the age.

THE DAY AFTER HIS ARRIVAL at Onchestus, Alexander made his way to Thebes and encamped in front of the walls.

On the way he halted at the shrine of Iolaus, a guardian demigod of Thebes and nephew of Heracles. He was the great man's charioteer and companion of his Labors (some said his *eromenos*). The shrine was a place where male lovers worshipped and exchanged vows. We may assume that Alexander paid his respects (doubtless accompanied by Hephaestion).

Having rushed to the seat of the revolt, the king now waited patiently. It would be much more convenient if the Thebans submitted without a fight, just as they had done the previous year. However, during this interval, Alexander did not waste his time. He contacted city-states hostile to Thebes, all of them league members, and persuaded them to join him. They would give him useful cover if he captured the city and decided to punish it.

Over the preceding centuries Thebes had made itself unpopular with its neighbors. It had never succeeded in winning permanent control of the smaller city-states inside Boeotia, the territory it claimed as its own. The Thebans had infuriated the entire Greek community by siding with the Persians when King Xerxes invaded mainland Hellas in 480, and had made a name for themselves as traitors or Medisers (from the Medes, who were an ancient Iranian people; their name was used as a synonym for Persians). In the fourth century they became the greatest military power in Hellas, but only for an arrogant but brief decade, during which time they won no friends.

Alexander hoped for reconciliation, but enemy skirmishers made life difficult for his men and he decided to move camp to a better position. He settled outside the Electra Gate, near the Cadmea where the Macedonian garrison was holed up. He straddled the road from Athens up which a relief force might be expected to come.

The citadel was close to the city wall; to improve the wall's defensive strength, the Thebans built two wooden palisades in front of it. Alexander agreed to a plan of attack with Perdiccas, the commander of two Macedonian battalions (which as the camp guard were in a forward position). He was among the king's most loyal friends, and had been one of those who had pursued and killed Philip's assassin. The men were growing impatient and were worried about their friends on the Cadmea. Perdiccas launched an assault before receiving orders to do so.

They broke through the first palisade and charged the defending troops. Their success forced the king's hand. To avoid the battalions being cut off, he was obliged to send in the archers and Agrianians to occupy the space between the palisades. Perdiccas now forced his way through the second palisade, but was severely wounded and had to be evacuated (he survived).

The desperate Thebans turned on their pursuers and pushed them back. Alexander had foreseen this eventuality and had assembled his infantry in full battle array on open ground. As at Pelium, the Thebans lost formation as they chased the Macedonians away from the city's defenses. They suddenly found themselves confronted by a phalanx bristling with long pikes. Routed, they ran into the city, so panic-stricken that they failed to shut the gates.

The Macedonians poured in behind them and the garrison in the

Cadmea joined their victorious comrades. Bitter street fighting ensued. Alexander was to be seen here, there, and everywhere. Organized resistance lasted for only a short time and the Macedonians advanced to the city center. The Theban cavalry broke out and rode off in flight across the plain.

It was at this point that the embittered neighbors of Thebes took their long-awaited revenge. Arrian notes:

> There followed a furious slaughter. It was not so much the Macedonians as the Phocians, Plataeans, and other Boeotians who began the indiscriminate killing of the now defenseless Thebans. They broke into houses and killed the occupants; they killed any who attempted to fight back; they killed even the suppliants at the altars; they spared neither women nor children.

Corpses were piled high in the streets. The number of the Theban dead was estimated at six thousand, and thirty thousand prisoners were counted. Five hundred Macedonians lost their lives, by Alexander's standards quite a high number.

WHAT WAS TO BE done with Thebes, that ancient city of legend and history? This was where Oedipus had ruled, killed his father, married his mother, and blinded himself in expiation. Here too the man-woman seer, Tiresias, had prophesied. Alexander was in two minds, or possibly three. At heart, he favored a severe penalty. This would deter the Greeks from rising again during his absence in Persia and so support the overriding strategic aim which he had also pursued in Thrace. However, he preferred not to take the blame, so he handed the decision to the council of the League of Corinth. They should judge. He was well aware that there were scores to settle and that he could depend on council members to be harsh. Finally, he made a mental note to be magnanimous to individual Thebans, as occasion arose.

The council, convened in special session, behaved as he guessed it would. Among other witnesses, a Plataean reminded his audience that in 373 Thebes had attacked his tiny town on the edge of Boeotia and driven out all the inhabitants. That universal moralist, Isocrates, had denounced the crime and its perpetrator. Memories were long. An eye for an eye and a tooth for a tooth.

There were precedents for the execution of all adult males and the enslavement of the women and children. It was the convention when a city resisted a siege, and some argued for this ancient prototype of genocide. However, the council finally recommended that the king and *hegemon* take no more lives, but sell the entire population on the slave market and raze the city. Alexander will have recalled that it was the same penalty his father had imposed on the thriving city of Olynthus in 348. He accepted the judgment and put it into effect. It would be as if Thebes had never existed.

The final profit from the sale was the considerable sum of 440 silver talents (a talent was a measurement of weight and amounted to about 26 kilograms, or 57 pounds). It will have been some time before the cash became available and presumably it was added to the king's war chest.

The king took steps that would, he must have hoped, sweeten his now blood-soaked reputation. The morning after the city's capture, he restored order and called off his men. A decree forbidding any further butchery was proclaimed, and a large number of Thebans—guest-friends, pro-Macedonian politicians, priests, and any who could show that they had opposed the uprising—were set free together with their families. Of the thirty thousand prisoners it appears that only twenty thousand were sold. The Macedonian soldiery turned their energies to pulling down the city's buildings, except for its temples and sacred places. These were spared to avoid offending the gods. It is said that Alexander compelled the Theban musician Ismenias to play his pipes while the city was being demolished.

One of the greatest poets of Hellas was Pindar. He flourished in the fifth century and most of his poems are celebrations of young athletes, victorious at the four-yearly Panhellenic games of Olympia, Delphi, Corinth, and Nemea. He has a deep sense not only of the tragedy of life, but also of the glory, however fleeting, of human achievement. This famous coda from one of his victory odes evokes the character of his work.

Creatures for a day! What is a man?
What is he not? A dream of a shadow
Is our mortal being. But when there comes to men
A gleam of splendor given of heaven,
Then rests on them a light of glory
And blessed are their days.

Pindar was a Theban and Alexander took good care to ensure that amid all the mayhem his house was left untouched and all his descendants were spared.

A troop of Thracians broke into the home of a noblewoman called Timocleia. While they were plundering everything they could find, their commander took the opportunity to rape her. When he had finished, he asked Timocleia whether she had any gold or silver hidden. She was a person of great presence of mind, and replied that indeed she had. If he came into the garden she would show him where it was. She led the man to a well and told him that when the city had been stormed she had dropped in it all her most valuable possessions. He leaned over and peered down the shaft, whereupon she gave him a firm push so that he fell in. She threw stone after stone onto him until he was dead.

The Thracians grabbed Timocleia, tied her hands, and brought her before the king for him to judge her fate. He was impressed by her calm demeanor and asked her to identify herself. She replied: "I am the sister of Theagenes who commanded our army against your father, Philip, and fell at Chaeronea fighting for the liberty of Greece."

Alexander thoroughly approved of what she had just done and set her and her children free. The world should know that this was royal justice.

SOME WOLVES WERE TRYING to surprise a flock of sheep. Unable to reach the peaceable animals because of the dogs that were guarding them, they decided to use a trick to get what they wanted.

They sent some delegates to ask the sheep to give up their dogs. It was the dogs, they said, who created the bad blood between them. If only the sheep would get rid of *them,* peace would reign between sheep and wolves. The sheep did not foresee what was going to happen and gave up the dogs. The wolves could now follow their instincts: they made supper of the unguarded sheep.

Demosthenes told this fable to the Athenian *ecclesia*. Alexander had indicated that he was willing to overlook its support of Thebes provided that it hand over to him eight anti-Macedonian politicians, including the great orator himself. They were the guard dogs and Alexander was a lone wolf, worse than those who run together. According to Aristotle, "Wolves tend to be man-eaters when they hunt singly rather than in a pack." Demosthenes strongly advised his fellow citizens not to surrender him and his colleagues if they did not want to be eaten up.

The statesman Demades had been on good terms with King Philip and had criticized his boorish behavior after the Battle of Chaeronea; he was also friendly with Alexander. For a handsome consideration, he volunteered to plead with the king on their behalf. Plutarch comments sardonically that the Athenian "may have trusted in his personal relationship with Alexander, or he may have counted on finding him sated with blood, like a lion that has been glutted with slaughter."

At any rate, Demades persuaded the king to pardon all but one of the eight men, including Demosthenes, and arranged terms of peace for the city.

BUT ALEXANDER'S ATTEMPTS AT magnanimity failed to win over public opinion. The Greeks were horrified by the destruction of Thebes and were not deceived by his delegation of judgment to the League of Corinth. It was *his* will that had prevailed. Nor were they persuaded by the clemency he showed to individuals. Over time, he also came to regret what he had done, being too clearheaded to believe his own propaganda, and acted kindly toward Thebans who crossed his path in the years to come.

It was Alexander's *pothos,* as it had been his father's, to be received as a Greek and not as a barbarian. But even when he wore sheep's clothing, the commander-in-chief of Hellas was still a wolf.

CHAPTER 5

FIRST BLOOD

———

As HIS SHIPS APPROACHED THE COAST OF ASIA MINOR, THE NEW Achilles—as Alexander saw himself—relived the experience of making landfall where legend had it that King Agamemnon and his Greek fleet had arrived many centuries before. Now as then, their destination was holy Ilium or, as we call it today, Troy. Here the Greeks had besieged the city, and after ten long years the city had fallen.

For the young Macedonian this was not just a story, but true history. He found only a mound of ruins, but, for all that the windy plain of Troy, as the ancient poets liked to call it, was holy ground. The war marked the first round in a catalogue of clashes between the west and east. By invading Persia he was following an ancient tradition.

SOMETIME IN MAY 334, the king left his general Parmenion to ferry the Macedonian army across the Hellespont (today's Dardanelles). Meanwhile he set out with a flotilla of sixty warships on a brief but deeply felt pilgrimage to the site of Ilium. He was determined to be first to disembark, and before setting sail from the European shore he sacrificed at the grave of Protesilaus. A daring Thessalian, he had been the first to jump onto the beach, but had been cut down by a Trojan "while leaping foremost of the Achaeans upon the soil of Troy."

Halfway across the narrows, Alexander propitiated the god of the sea, Poseidon, friend of Troy, who had obstructed the Greek invaders. To avoid a repetition, he sacrificed a bull in honor of the god, his wife Amphitrite, sea nymph and queen of the sea, and the Nereids, their fishy female companions. He poured a drink offering into the sea from a golden bowl.

Then, when his ship ran up the beach, Alexander sprang ashore in full armor and hurled his spear into the ground, in this way laying a claim to the ownership of Asia. He cried: "From the gods I accept Asia, won by the spear." This took some nerve. The young pretender had not won even a single battle.

He then went up to the city four miles or so inland. It was now a somewhat dilapidated tourist destination and little more than a village. Passing through the ancient walls on top of a tumulus, he dedicated a complete set of armor to the goddess Athena, protector of the Greeks, and in return took from her "small and cheap" shrine some of the consecrated arms that were said (implausibly, but he believed it) to date from the Trojan War. He also sacrificed to Troy's old king Priam; he wanted to turn away Priam's anger at having been put to the sword by Achilles' son Neoptolemus, from whom Alexander was descended. Usually he enjoyed boasting about his pedigree.

ONCE THE FORMALITIES WERE over, the king wandered among the ruins. Someone came up to him and asked if he would like to see a lyre that had once belonged to Paris.

"I don't care a jot for that lyre," came the dismissive reply. "Where is the one Achilles played when singing of glorious deeds?"

Alexander and Hephaestion stripped off and oiled their bodies, as if they were athletes, and ran a race with their comrades. Alexander placed a wreath on a column that was supposed to be Achilles' tomb, remarking that he wished he had as great a poet as Homer to celebrate *his* deeds, and Hephaestion placed another on the grave of Achilles' *erastes,* Patroclus.

To the modern eye these are exotic goings-on, but they made sense to Alexander. He was sincere, but he also had a keen eye for publicity. He was seeking to express in dramatic terms the legitimacy of his expedition in the eyes of the Greeks. Everyone could remember the two

Persian invasions and believed in the justice of revenge. But Alexander wanted to go beyond a mere branding exercise, and to create a religious justification. He asserted his supernatural ancestry and saw his place in history as reflecting a divine circularity. He was truly an echo of a heroic past and that was how he meant to be understood.

Finally, it is clear that these rituals at Troy meant something personal to him together with Hephaestion. He had listened to his tutor Aristotle, for whom *philia* was a great good. Whatever his reservations were about sex, he seemed determined to live his life as one of a loving and inseparable male couple.

ALEXANDER ENJOYED A PARTY. Back in November or December of 335, at the outset of his campaign and a few months before his arrival at Troy, he held a splendid one, which marked the culmination of months of military preparation.

As a matter of policy, he looked after his soldiers well; he made sure that they regularly enjoyed periods of rest and he mounted festivals for their pleasure. He assembled his expeditionary force at Dium, one of the kingdom's holiest sanctuaries. Here, beneath Mount Olympus, home of the gods, he conducted the traditional sacrifice to Zeus, tutelary deity of the Macedonians.

Then in the theater at Aegae he presented a nine-day drama competition in honor of the nine Muses, which his Hellenophile ancestor King Archelaus had founded seventy years previously. For his guests he commissioned a vast marquee capable of accommodating a hundred diners, with a couch for each one to recline on. The layout probably entailed a central lobby flanked by eleven-couch dining spaces—in descending order of grandeur to match each guest to his perceived importance. The king arranged for a similar marquee to be the royal headquarters when he was on campaign. He did not forget the common soldiers, to whom he distributed sacrificial animals and "everything else suitable for a festive occasion, and put them into a fine humor."

This was the first time that Alexander had attended a public event at the scene of his father's assassination in June of the previous year. Among those he invited to the celebrations were ambassadors from the

Greek cities who had also been there as shocked witnesses. The pomp and circumstance were designed to allay the memory and to assert his mastery.

ALEXANDER HAD UNDER ARMS a large number of men. Many Macedonians among them had served a long time with Philip and, if some were a little long in the tooth, they were tough and experienced. The army consisted of some 32,000 infantry and 5,100 cavalry (mostly Macedonian Companions and Thessalian horsemen). These totals included the 12,000-strong Macedonian phalanx and the same number of Greek allied and mercenary infantry (supplied under the terms of the League of Corinth or simply attracted by the money); in principle the latter were good fighters, but their loyalty might be suspect when they faced the Greek mercenary regiments whom the Great King hired. Also, Alexander recruited nearly eight thousand Thracian foot soldiers and horsemen, one thousand archers and Agrianian javelin-throwers—a small but invaluable elite team.

When added to Parmenion's advance force of ten thousand infantry and one thousand cavalry, the grant total under Alexander's command may have been about fifty thousand. (There may have been a further eight thousand infantry, mainly Greeks, who were responsible for guarding land already won.)

Of an armada of 182 triremes, or war galleys, 160 were provided by the Greek allies and mostly by Athens. Triremes were very labor-intensive. Each one required 200 oarsmen, or a total complement of 36,400 men.

This was not all, for many technical and military experts were needed for a variety of different purposes—a siege train, a baggage train, engineers (to build roads and tunnels), surveyors (to collect information on routes, camping grounds, and possible battlefields), secretaries and administrators, surgeons and physicians, grooms and muleteers. In a remarkable innovation, Alexander was the first commander in antiquity (so far as we know) to establish a public relations department.

A former student of Aristotle called Callisthenes was invited to join the expedition as its official historian—or, more accurately, propaganda chief.

The entire invasion force, both by land and sea, amounted to about 90,000 men, of whom more than half were Greek. This was of the same order of magnitude as the expeditionary force that the Great King Darius had sent across from Asia to punish the city of Athens, whose sailors had burned the great city of Sardis.

Alexander gave his men strict instructions not to plunder the territory they were to pass through. He told them: "You should spare your own property, and not destroy what you are going to own."

The king left behind a substantial garrison in Europe, including a twelve-thousand-strong phalanx, under the command of the experienced and trustworthy Antipater, whom Alexander appointed regent in his absence. For all his remarkable recent victories, there remained a risk that the Greeks or the Illyrians might stir up trouble if they felt they could get away with it. What was more, the Persian fleet, which greatly outnumbered his own, might intervene in Greece and set up a second front.

THE PHILOSOPHER AND SCIENTIST Aristotle expected his students to help him assemble and publish all kinds of data, for only through observation and experiment could human knowledge be advanced. Alexander was not just interested in conquest. He was determined to outdo all his old tutor's other pupils and collect a vast store of information about botany, biology, geography, and zoology.

Alexander appointed a team of experts including architects, geographers, botanists, astronomers, mathematicians, ethnographers, and zoologists. We are told that they sent back to Aristotle regular accounts of their discoveries together with samples of fauna and flora. These probably contributed to his celebrated *Enquiries into Animals* and the many accurate eyewitness reports it contains.

The king took a special interest in animals, especially those he could watch and make use of (horses, for example, and hunting dogs). Bucephalas was an inseparable companion and he owned a dog called Peritas whom he brought up from a puppy. When he saw peacocks for the first time in his life, he was so impressed that he wanted to prevent by law any attack on them.

According to the Roman encyclopedist Pliny the Elder,

he gave orders to some thousands of persons throughout the whole Asia and Greece, all those who made their living by hunting, fowling, and fishing and those who were in charge of warrens, herds, apiaries, fishponds and aviaries, to obey his instructions, so that he might not fail to be informed about any creature born in any region.

In the long run, this ambitious and well-funded research program had a profound influence on the development of the sciences and ultimately opened up awareness of the Indian subcontinent to the west. At a personal level, his thoughtfulness toward animals casts an attractive light on Alexander's nature.

WHAT WAS IT LIKE to be a soldier marching in Alexander's army and, more particularly, what was the experience of battle?

Most of a soldier's time was spent marching, often across rough ground, and he could in an emergency cover more than twenty miles a day. Alexander demonstrated this with his rapid descent on Greece and did so again when he followed Xerxes' invasion route along the Thracian coast to the Hellespont.

Formations varied according to the terrain, but out in front were scouts, after whom might come the cavalry, then the baggage, and finally the infantry. When advancing through a defile the army would as a rule divide into two columns with the baggage between them. Curiously, nightly camps were not dug in and fortified.

A number of factors slowed the army down, chief of which was the baggage train; this included heavy equipment such as siege catapults; camp followers of all sorts; carts and pack animals carrying every kind of goods including loot accumulated on campaign; and traders selling wares. Both Philip and Alexander did their best to exert control. The former banned the use of wagons and refused to allow wives and prostitutes to accompany the army. He fixed the number of civilian servants to one for every ten men. Soldiers carried their armor and weapons together with utensils and some food.

Another factor holding up a soldier was his need to eat. On a lengthy expedition he could not carry enough staples such as grain or wine for more than a few days. Water was required in huge quantities, for the animals as well as the men. Horses and pack animals required regular rest periods and time to graze.

A large army was a curse to the lands it passed through, for few places had enough surplus to satisfy it. Most days it needed to spend time foraging, either buying or stealing everything edible in fields and farmhouses. Hungry soldiers could strip a countryside bare. An army could not remain stationary for extended periods when distant from sea or river transport, because it would rapidly consume the food and forage surpluses of the surrounding territory. It was obliged to move on and pillage somewhere else if it was to survive.

Cavalry played a crucial part in Alexander's battle plans, but horse riding was a much trickier business than it became in modern times. Horseshoes were unknown and care had to be taken, if horses were ridden for long distances on rough ground, not to wear down their hooves. They needed periods of respite and could not safely canter or gallop for very long. Moreover, the stirrup had not been invented and only a basic saddle was used (perhaps a folded cloth or pad held in place by a strap around the horse). This reduced not only the rider's stability but also his leverage when thrusting or throwing his javelin. Horses were small, not much larger than a sturdy pony nowadays, and riders mounted by vaulting. In sum, the main challenge facing a rider was not to fall off—especially in the mêlée of a battle.

Large-scale battles were rare but terrifying. They could take place only on a large, flat or flattish area of ground. They usually took place in the summer. Men would fight in a fog of blinding dust raised by feet and hooves (or less frequently in a storm of rain and mud, which was almost as bad). The noise was earsplitting.

A soldier in a phalanx, eight or sixteen rows deep, was part of a fixed formation and had no freedom of maneuver. He could not easily hear commands by trumpet or see flags raised and lowered once an engagement had started. Even orders from a junior officer nearby were hard to interpret, and in fact once the fighting had begun there was little a Philip or an Alexander could do, except by prearrangement, to react to events in the field. Both commander and other-rankers must have felt very alone and vulnerable.

When the phalanx, bristling with sarissas, charged, it raised a deafening *paean,* or war song. Only men in the front two or perhaps three rows of infantry were likely to have direct contact with the enemy, and then only at spear's length. A phalanx's chief task was not to fight hand-to-hand but to keep in tight formation and shove forward. Only if they broke up were they lost.

Troopers faced many more dangers than foot soldiers. When the battle had reached its crisis, their function was to charge on Alexander's orders at a weak point in the enemy's front line. This was the only time as commander that he was able to influence the course of the fighting. It was why he personally led his cavalry into the jaws of death. They could see him and followed wherever he chose to ride.

THE AFTERMATH OF BATTLE was as pain-rich as the fighting itself. Hellenic armies as far back as those in Homer employed physicians to tend the wounded. At Troy the Greeks enjoyed the services of two sons of the god of healing, Asclepius. One of these was called Machaon. When a king was struck down by an iron-tipped arrow, Machaon extracted it

> though the pointed barbs broke off as the head was pulled out. . . . When he found the place where the sharp point had pierced the flesh, he sucked out the blood and skillfully applied a soothing ointment with which the friendly centaur Cheiron had equipped his father.

As a word-perfect lover of Homer and a daring fighter in the field, Alexander will have understood the need for an efficient medical service in his own army. He also learned about medicine from Aristotle, son as he was of Philip's personal physician, whose groundbreaking treatises on human anatomy (sadly lost) helped develop the healing art. We may guess that the Macedonian expeditionary force was well supplied with the most up-to-date medical expertise.

Most injuries were inflicted during a rout and those on the losing side were usually slaughtered by victorious cavalry. Military doctors worked on many kinds of wounds. Through practice they became skillful bone surgeons, and amputations were common. A skeleton dating from about 300 B.C. has been found in Campania with an artificial leg, realistically modeled in bronze sheeting over a wooden core.

The main problem with surgical operations was the lack of anesthetics, which meant that they had to be brief. The agony could only be dulled with alcohol or concentrated liquors from the opium poppy and henbane. A draft of white mandrake (*Mandragora officinarum,* a highly poisonous hallucinogen and soporific) was recommended before procedures. It could induce unconsciousness and, if patient and surgeon were unlucky, death.

While serious internal injuries were usually fatal, men often recovered from flesh wounds, whether caused by cutting weapons or projectiles. A special forceps was devised to extract arrowheads. In the absence of modern antiseptics, septicemia was common and lethal. The disinfectant properties of honey, salt, and (in Egypt) saltpeter seem to have been well known. Some doctors understood the value of pitch, especially useful for coating amputees' stumps, and of turpentine. Sulfides of arsenic seem to have been used to clean wounds.

According to one modern estimate, as little as 20 percent of prescribed medication was of any value, so it is remarkable that Philip and his son recovered from the many serious wounds they sustained in battle.

RELATIONS BETWEEN OLYMPIAS AND Alexander did not suffer permanent damage because of her cruel treatment of Philip's last wife, Cleopatra, and her daughter.

Mother and son remained close. According to a story told by Plutarch, Olympias "confided to him, and to him alone, the secret of his conception." The obvious implication was that he was the son of a divine father, probably Zeus, adulterous ruler of the Olympian gods and husband of touchy Hera. The idea attracted Alexander's passionate interest and evidently he talked about it. Embarrassed, she is said to have repudiated the claim with a witty remark. "Will Alexander never stop slandering me to Hera?"

People around the young king were worried for the future if he left Macedonia without marrying. Both Antipater at home and Parmenion with the advance force in Asia were keen that he first find a wife and procreate. The fact they had nubile daughters may have played a part in their thinking, but they were making a more serious point. They knew that the young king was a reckless risk-taker on the battlefield and the chances were high that he would not survive the forthcoming campaign. There was no obvious heir and the kingdom would face a period of upheaval, and as in past centuries very probably sink back to its old status as a second-rate power.

The anxiety was understandable. Everyone could remember that Philip had married at the first opportunity—years before he became king—and then frequently thereafter. This was how a bachelor leader on whose life many people's fate depended was expected to behave.

Alexander was having none of it. He was eager for action and spoke vigorously against his generals. "It would be a disgrace," he pointed out, "for one who has been appointed by Greece to command the war, and who had inherited his father's unconquerable army, to sit around at home enjoying a marriage and waiting for children to be born."

Mothers had no formal or legal role in the marriage of their sons, but we have seen that Olympias did not hesitate to interfere in Alexander's sex life and she must have had a view on the generals' advice. She was the chief woman in his life, and a wife would have been an obstacle between her and Alexander. To judge by what is known about Olympias's character, their close one-to-one relationship would be damaged if a third person were allowed to join it. If she was asked for her opinion, we can safely guess that she told Antipater, whom she loathed, and Parmenion to mind their own business.

MEMNON AND HIS BROTHER Mentor were crafty Greeks from the island of Rhodes. They made a good living as mercenaries and were excellent military tacticians. They were also skilled at changing sides while remaining masters of their fate. Their employers got the best out of them by not being too unsuspicious.

The brothers were close to a high-ranking Persian, Artabazus, the satrap of Hellespontine Phrygia in northwestern Anatolia. He fathered a very large number of children (eleven boys and twelve girls, startlingly by the same woman). One of his daughters, a beauty, was called

Barsine; Mentor married her. He died and Memnon stepped into his shoes.

Artabazus turned his coat and joined a satraps' revolt against the Great King. He found himself on the losing side and in 352 he and the brothers took refuge at the Macedonian court. It was here that Alexander, still a small boy, first met Barsine, who was some years older—probably in her late teens. (Their paths were to cross again in future years.) However, the exiles made their peace with the Great King and returned to the fold. Artabazus became one of Darius III's most loyal supporters, and Memnon was sent with five thousand mercenaries to deal with Parmenion and his advance force.

Originally dispatched by Philip with ten thousand men, the old Macedonian general had enjoyed mixed fortunes. In 336 he had pushed down the coast and many Greek cities along the seaboard rose against their Persian master. Altars were erected to Philip and in Ephesus a statue of the king was placed inside the temple of Artemis. But then the offensive had faltered. In the following year, while Alexander was scoring victories in Greece and Thrace, Memnon campaigned with great effectiveness and drove Parmenion back into the Troad (now the Biga Peninsula, in northwestern Anatolia) and the Hellespont.

MEANWHILE DARIUS WAS READY to deal with the Macedonian king once and for all. Since seizing the throne in 336, he had put down native revolts in Egypt and probably in Babylonia. He emerged as a tough and competent ruler. By the summer of 334 he had mobilized a fleet of some four hundred war galleys and ordered the gradual mobilization of the western satrapies. He sent some cavalry reinforcements, but otherwise saw no reason to involve himself personally in the campaign. Alexander was a menace, but a local one. In total, the Persians mustered an estimated force of fifteen thousand cavalry and five thousand or six thousand Greek mercenaries.

The Persian command debated whether it would be sensible to station their forces along an east–west mountain range. This would have the advantage of restricting the Macedonian intruders to the northwestern corner of Asia Minor, but the greater disadvantage of risking an attack in the rear by insurgent Greek cities at the same time as they attempted to destroy Alexander or at least to push him back into Europe. To avoid being sandwiched, it was decided to move eastward and establish a headquarters at Zelea, a town near Cyzicus on the Black Sea.

On hearing that the Macedonian army had crossed into Asia, a war council debated what to do next. Present were four commanders and two satraps, Spithridates of Lydia and Arsites of Hellespontine Phrygia. Memnon was also in attendance. He strongly advised the Persians not to risk taking on the Macedonians. They outnumbered the Persian infantry, were far superior in fighting quality, and had Alexander with them in person, whereas the Great King, hundreds of miles away in Susa, was a conspicuous absentee.

According to Arrian, Memnon spelled out the action they should take: "Instead, they should march on, destroy fodder by getting the cavalry to trample it down, burn the crops in the ground, and not even spare the towns in their path. Alexander will not stay in the country if he is denied provisions." This was good counsel, for a large army could not survive without a continuous supply of food for its soldiers and hay or grass for its animals. However, Arsites, whose province would have to bear the brunt of this scorched-earth policy, vehemently disagreed.

He said he would not permit the burning of even a single house belonging to the people in his charge. Others at the meeting feared that Memnon, being a wily and untrustworthy Hellene, was deliberately delaying hostilities to persuade Darius to keep him in employment. Their suspicions seemed to be justified when the enemy left Memnon's Phrygian estate unharmed (in fact, Alexander did not mean to show friendship, but to feed misgivings). Memnon's track record as a former rebel against the Great King made it hard for him to defend himself, although on this occasion his advice was correct.

Eventually, it was decided that the Persians should seek battle on ground of their choosing.

ALEXANDER WAS BROKE, as he admitted ruefully in a speech Arrian has him give to his troops years later:

My inheritance from my father consisted of a few gold and silver drinking cups and less than sixty talents in the treasury [a silver talent was worth about 6,000 drachmas]. There was also about 500 talents' worth of debt contracted by Philip. I myself borrowed another 800 in addition to this.

Philip had consistently overspent, despite an estimated income of a thousand talents a year from his Thracian mines. To all the stated reasons for the Persian expedition, we must add a financial one.

Alexander admitted that neither he nor Philip could afford *not* to mount an invasion. (Even if they had decided to stay at home, they would still have been driving on fumes.) We do not know whether the Greeks paid for their military and naval contributions, but, even if they did, the daily payroll for the expeditionary force was punishingly large. On the reasonable assumption that an infantryman's daily wage was one drachma a day and a cavalryman's two drachmas, it probably added up to some seven talents.

Alexander probably paid for his Balkan campaign by looting and slave-market sales. When he left Pella for Phrygia in west central Anatolia in the spring of 334, he had enough money to maintain his army for no more than a month. Financial pressure argued for a decisive battle as soon as possible, as Memnon very well knew or guessed. Only then would Alexander be able to amass booty after a victory, levy taxes from the liberated Ionian cities, and raid provincial Persian exchequers.

He was open with his officers about his impending bankruptcy. Plutarch reports that Alexander would not board ship at the Hellespont until he had inquired into all his Companions' financial circumstances. He gave an estate to one, a village to another, and the revenues of some port or community to a third.

When he had shared out or given away all the royal property, Perdiccas asked him, "But, king, what are you leaving for yourself?" "My hopes!" replied Alexander. "In that case, then," said Perdiccas, "those who serve with you will have a share of them too." With this, he declined to accept the property that had been allotted to him, and several of Alexander's other friends did the same.

If one reads between the lines of this famous anecdote, it is evident what was really happening: the king was borrowing from his entourage and putting up the collateral. If he was not immediately victorious, his ambitious plan would dwindle into a humiliating demobilization.

HIS OMNIPRESENT SCOUTS WARNED Alexander that they had located the enemy on the far side of the river Granicus, a mountain stream originating at Mount Ida. He at once marched in battle order toward it. He formed his heavy infantry into two phalanxes and posted the cavalry on either side. He ordered the baggage train to follow behind. These dispositions meant that he could defend himself if harried by cavalry (the rear phalanx could about-turn and face the rear if necessary). More to the point, he would be able to spread out speedily into his actual line of battle with cavalry on the wings and infantry in the center.

It was the afternoon of an early spring day in 334 and, if possible, the king wanted to wrong-foot the Persians by moving at once to an engagement. A short sharp attack before evening fell would cause astonishment and so enhance his chances of winning.

When the Granicus came into view, Alexander gave it a hard stare. It was a shallow, fordable stream, about thirty or so meters wide, which ran across a flat alluvial plain. The water did not fill the bed but meandered to and fro over a clay floor covered with rounded stones. At most it would reach a man's knees. On either side there were steep banks up to three meters high. These would have been a serious obstacle except for the fact that here and there were gentle gravel slopes leading up from the riverbed to the plain.

On the far side of the Granicus, set back a little from the riverbank, stood some 20,000 enemy cavalry about sixteen troopers deep and extending for some two and a half kilometers. On a ridge farther behind them, twenty thousand infantry kept watch; perhaps some eight deep, they were mainly Greek mercenaries.

If the Persians were expecting to fight that day, they had no plans for the infantry to enter the action. This is very odd and can perhaps be put down to incompetence (but let us not forget that the capable Mem-

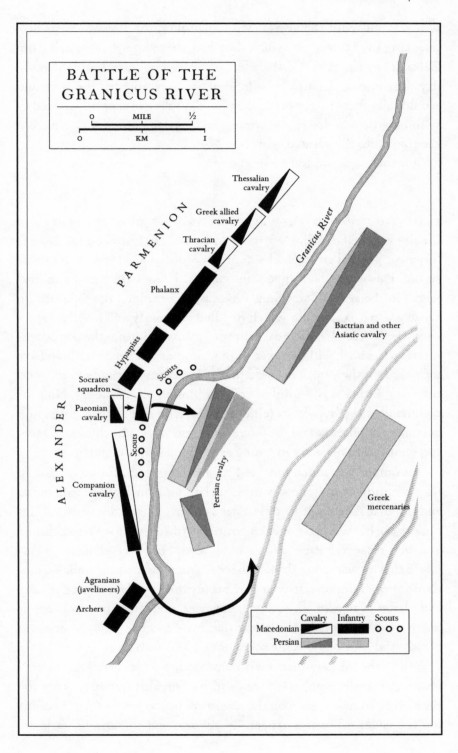

BATTLE OF THE
GRANICUS RIVER

O   MILE   ½

O   KM   I

Thessalian
cavalry

Greek allied
cavalry

Thracian
cavalry

Phalanx

Hypaspists

Socrates'
squadron

Scouts

Paeonian
cavalry

Scouts

Companion
cavalry

Agranians
(javelineers)

Archers

P A R M E N I O N

A L E X A N D E R

Granicus River

Bactrian and other
Asiatic cavalry

Persian cavalry

Greek
mercenaries

	Cavalry	Infantry	Scouts
Macedonian			○ ○ ○
Persian			

non was still with the army). More plausibly, the Persians were biv-
ouacking in the order in which they had arrived on their march from
Zelea. They thought the Macedonians would not attack so late in the
day. Just in case the attack came, though, they guarded the river and
would only form up for battle the next day; they probably intended to
withdraw the cavalry to the wings and bring the infantry down from
the ridge into the vacated center.

But there was not to be a next day.

PARMENION WAS EFFECTIVELY ALEXANDER'S military deputy and
usually commanded the left wing in battle. He had been his father's
foremost general from the beginning of the reign. Now in his mid-
sixties, Parmenion had three sons, two of whom held senior appointments in the army. The eldest, Philotas, commanded the Companion
cavalry, a crucial posting which he filled efficiently and loyally. However, if we recall Alexander's dressing-down during the Pixodarus
marriage scandal, Philotas was in the room at the time and may have
informed on the prince or perhaps was held up as a paradigm of good
behavior. Either way, he did not endear himself to Alexander. Nicanor
commanded the hypaspists (elite infantry who acted as a flexible link
between the phalanx and the Companion cavalry). The third son, Hector, seems to have been too young as yet for a major command.

Alexander was much indebted to the old general for conniving in
the execution of his fellow commander and son-in-law, the influential
and popular Attalus. It is sometimes said that Alexander resented this
obligation, but was in too weak a position to dismiss the well-established
and well-respected Parmenion and his sons. However, there is no evidence that he wanted to do so. The three men served him well. Parmenion's alleged unpopularity at court is justified by claims that the king
had a habit of rejecting his advice; however, there were other occasions
when it was accepted. The worst that can be said is that the one was
elderly and cautious and the other young and audacious.

While the Macedonian high command was deliberating its next
move, Parmenion spoke. "It seems to me, sir, that our plan is for the
time being to make camp on the riverbank just as we are." In his opinion the riverbank was a dangerous obstacle and the army should at-

tempt an unopposed crossing early next morning. He warned that "a failure at the very beginning . . . would threaten the outcome of the entire campaign." Alexander abruptly dismissed the recommendation. He ordered Parmenion to take up his position on the left while he made his way to the right (the traditional post of honor for a commanding general).

For a while the two armies took no action, standing behind each riverbank. There was a deep silence.

LIKE A BOXER, THE KING intended to deliver a left jab followed by a right punch. He drew up his army along the front for the same length as the Persian line. He placed the Thessalian, Greek, and Thracian horse under Parmenion. The center was occupied by the infantry: the phalanx and then the hypaspists. Next to them was a special assault force comprising the scouts and Paeonian light cavalry from Thrace together with a squadron of Companion heavy cavalry that was to lead the way.

The right wing was dominated by the Companion cavalry under Philotas; finally, the line was completed by the small but deadly contingents of Agrianian javelin throwers and Cretan archers.

We can deduce Alexander's plan from what happened. It was to weaken the cavalry "wall" along the Persians' left wing so that when the king led the Companions to crash against the wall it would crumble.

First, the Agrianians and Cretans moved to their right, seeking to outflank the Persians. The effect was to draw the enemy along upstream, eventually thinning its line. Then the assault force advanced across the river up a gravelly slope. This was an almost suicidal act of bravery, but its highly trained members were expendable. They were, in effect, a loss leader or (to use the imagery of chess) a pawn sacrifice. Their task, no doubt understated in the pre-battle briefing, was to soak up the Persian defense at whatever cost. The Persian cavalry were tempted to the bank of the Granicus and showered their javelins down on the attackers, who responded as best they could with thrusting spears. A few defenders, led by Memnon and his sons, rode down onto the riverbed.

Macedonian lives were being lost. It must have been hard holding back, but the king waited. At last, when the mauled survivors of the assault force were retreating, he judged the right moment to have come. To the sound of trumpets he led the Companions in a wedge-shaped formation, supported by some hypaspists, and delivered the coup de grâce. He had little difficulty in pushing his way up another of the gravelly slopes, for the Persians had already delivered most of their missiles and now, being at the river's edge, they were in no position to build the necessary momentum for a charge. Alexander and some Companions reached the top of the bank, but in disorder.

From the beginning, the Persian high command had been able to see Alexander because of the attention shown him by his awed entourage and because of the magnificence of his armor. He wore tall white feathers on either side of the crest of his helmet and was carrying the antique shield he had obtained at Troy. The Persians gathered opposite him, for their simple battle aim was to kill the king. Apparently, they pulled back from the river until they had a clear sight of him on level ground and then rode pell-mell in his direction.

From the Macedonian viewpoint, this was the most dangerous moment of the battle. Alexander, at the heart of the mélée, received two blows on his breastplate and three on his shield. Arrian describes the scene:

> A fierce fight developed around him, and in this time brigade after brigade of the Macedonians made the crossing with little difficulty now. The fighting was from horseback, but in some respects it was more like an infantry battle, a tangled mass of horse against horse and man against man.

This was a struggle worthy of the *Iliad*.

The Macedonians were beginning to make headway when Alexander's lance broke. He asked a groom for his, but that too had snapped. Luckily old Demaratus of Corinth, who had bought the horse Bucephalas for Alexander when he was a child, was among the crowd of Companions and volunteered his lance.

The king saw Darius's son-in-law Mithridates riding out far in front of the others and bringing a body of cavalry with him. He charged ahead and knocked Mithridates off his horse with a thrust in his face.

A Persian nobleman brought down his ax with all his strength upon Alexander's head. He sheared off part of Alexander's helmet and one of its plumes, but failed to wound him. Alexander knocked him off his horse and drove his lance into his chest. Meanwhile, another of Darius's sons-in-law had raised his scimitar against Alexander from behind. Cleitus, the grizzled commander of the Royal Squadron (and brother of the king's long-ago wet nurse), sliced off the Persian's arm with a single swipe of his sword. Alexander only avoided death by one man's fast reaction.

A turning point had been reached. All the Companions were now fully engaged. Under their pressure, the Persian center collapsed, and the left was disintegrating as the archers and javelin throwers, mingling with the cavalry, outflanked it and rolled it up. It was now late afternoon, and low sunlight half-blinded the Persians, while it shone from behind the Macedonians.

At some stage, Parmenion ordered the Thessalian horse and the Macedonian phalanx to destroy the disheartened—albeit till now disengaged—enemy in front of them.

Whatever they did and whenever they did it, the Thessalians performed well: according to Diodorus, next to the king they "won a great reputation for valor because of the skillful handling of their squadrons and their unmatched fighting quality."

TWO HOURS OR LESS had passed since the fighting started. The Greek mercenaries on the ridge watched stunned by the pace of events. What should they do now? Because Alexander was leading a Panhellenic crusade, they would inevitably be regarded as traitors. They faced a bleak future, if they had a future at all.

They asked the king for quarter, but after the dangers of the battle he was in no mood to grant it. In a rage he charged at them and lost his horse (not Bucephalas on this occasion), which was pierced through the ribs by a sword thrust.

This did not improve Alexander's temper. He sent the phalanx against the Greeks and ordered the cavalry to surround them. Perhaps they would have been wiser to follow Xenophon's example after the Battle of Cunaxa and march away at once. It took some time to massacre them. Few escaped, among them those who shammed death among the corpses. Two thousand were taken prisoner and sent in chains to Macedonia and forced labor.

Although they had no hope, the mercenaries gave a good account of themselves, Plutarch writes: "It was here that most of the Macedonians who were killed or wounded, fought or fell, since they were battling at close quarters with men who were expert soldiers and had been rendered desperate."

It is said that the Persians lost twenty thousand infantry, most of them presumably Greek mercenaries, and twenty-five hundred cavalry; these are plausible numbers, if a little on the high side. From Darius's point of view the loss of eight senior commanders, mainly in the confused fighting around Alexander, was a more serious blow. Luckily for his cause, that great survivor Memnon lived to fight another day. The local satrap, Arsites, fled the field to Phrygia. It was his advice that had led to the debacle, and from shame he committed suicide.

As for Macedonian casualties, twenty-five Companions died in the first attack. Alexander had sacrificed them to clear the path for him, and he may have felt a little guilty on their account. He commissioned his favorite sculptor, Lysippus, to make bronze statues of them, which were erected in the sanctuary to Zeus at Dium, Macedonia's "sacred space."

Of the rest of the cavalry, more than sixty died; so did about thirty foot soldiers. Alexander gave them magnificent funerals on the next day, with their arms and other equipment. He exempted their parents and children from land taxes and all other forms of personal state service and property levies. (He also buried the Persian commanders and, now that the blood mist had cleared, the slaughtered Greeks, in an astute gesture of goodwill and of respect for heroism.)

Arrian writes that, with typical attention to his men and their morale, Alexander "showed great care for the wounded, personally visiting every one of them, inspecting their wounds, asking how they came by them and giving them the opportunity to boast about their exploits." Later in the year, recently married officers and men were given leave to spend the winter in Macedonia with their wives. This hugely popular gesture was not accompanied by any softening of discipline: pillaging was still forbidden, camps were set up in the countryside, and men were not billeted in towns. The king's generosity had a practical aspect, for the soldiers were told to bring back fresh Macedonian recruits.

Spoils from the enemy headquarters—drinking vessels, purple hangings, and other such luxury goods—were customarily awarded to an army's commander; Alexander sent most of them to Olympias.

The king also paid attention to public opinion in Hellas. He wanted to reemphasize the war's official purpose—revenge for the invasions of Darius I and Xerxes. He sent to Athens three hundred Persian panoplies to be dedicated to the goddess Athena in her temple on the Acropolis with the inscription: "Alexander the son of Philip and the Greeks except the Spartans dedicated these spoils from the barbarians living in Asia."

WHAT DO WE LEARN of Alexander's feelings and intentions at this juncture? Did he have a firm idea of what he was doing?

He looked around the detritus of struggle as night fell on his victorious army, and his first emotion must have been one of unalloyed joy. He had fought gloriously; Achilles in the Elysian Fields was proud of him, he knew for sure. If there had ever been any doubt about his claim to be Greek and about his descent from gods and demigods, Granicus had dispelled it. He had inherited the leadership of the Hellenes; now he had earned it. At last Philip's army was truly his.

But courage was not the only quality that decided the day. The Macedonians were more disciplined than their opponents and the quality of their weaponry superior. Their cornel-wood spears gave them a decided advantage over the Persians' flimsy javelins.

Granicus was the moment Alexander took wing. He had displayed his talent as a field commander. With his eye for detail and his swift determination of tactics, first demonstrated in the Balkans, he had won the confidence both of his commanders and of the rank and file. He won battles. His men trusted him for his lunatic courage; he would himself do anything he asked of them, and more. Thanks to his devotion to their interests, the bond between them grew strong and stronger. They would follow wherever he led. In fact, it is hardly an exaggeration to speak of a collective love affair.

But if Alexander's performance in the field impressed his men, it aroused anxiety among his generals and courtiers. His performance at the Granicus was that of an immature and rash youth. He would have won the admiration of the warrior heroes of the *Iliad,* and he surely had this in mind. But the fact is that he had nearly died in the blood-soaked scrum on the riverside. A childless bachelor, he had refused to take the advice of Antipater and Parmenion and find a wife. The battle confirmed their worst fears that one sword thrust, one flying arrow, would put an end to the expedition. Had it not been for Cleitus, Alexander's reign would already have been over. Being the new Achilles was a perilous and irresponsible enterprise.

Maybe there was something of the sociopath in the king's nature, excessively self-absorbed as he was and seemingly unable to enter into, or at least imagine, the feelings of others. We can only guess at this, though; we will never know it.

As for his aims, some of Alexander's remarks indicate that he expected to stay and govern, rather than score victories and go home. But how much territory did he expect to conquer? And how was conquest to be consistent with liberation, so far as the Ionian city-states were concerned?

We must not forget his fathomless capacity for *pothos*. He harbored the dream of empire, but had to keep quiet about it. For his expeditionary force, freeing the Ionian cities and maybe acting as their guarantor and overlord was sufficient. The men would have strongly objected to an outsize project that kept them from home and family for many years.

More likely, Alexander did not know what his *precise* intentions were. He was following his star. As the adage has it, no one rises so high as he who knows not where he is going.

He awaited his moment.

CHAPTER 6

UNDOING THE KNOT

———

O NCE UPON A TIME IN PHRYGIA, A REGION OF CENTRAL ANATOLIA, there lived a poor old man called Gordius, who scraped a simple living from a smallholding. He owned an inexpensive cart and two pairs of oxen, one for the plow and the other to pull the cart.

One day an extraordinary thing happened. As he was plowing his field, an eagle flew down and perched on the yoke of his cart and stayed there all day. Awestruck, Gordius decided to ask for an explanation from the seers or clairvoyants of Telmessus, a town in Caria where lived a number of families with prophetic gifts. Whether men, women, or children they were skilled in the interpretation of omens. One of these foretellers was the famous Aristander, Alexander's personal divination expert.

The old man approached a village in the Telmessian area and met a young woman drawing water from a well. They fell into conversation and he told his story. It turned out that she had the gift, and she advised him to return to the site of the omen and sacrifice to Zeus.

She agreed to come back with him and manage the ceremony. They married and a son was born, Midas. When he had grown into a handsome young man, Phrygia was involved in a bitter civil war, and an oracle asserted that a cart would bring peace. A people's assembly was discussing the matter when Midas drove up with his parents. They immediately decided he was their designated king.

Midas was the king who famously asked a god that anything he touched should turn into gold. But once the gift had been granted, he found that he could no longer eat or drink. Bread and wine became metal in his hand or on his lips. As the old proverb says, he should have been careful what he wished for, lest it came true.

One of Midas's first regnal acts was to dedicate his father's old cart on the city's acropolis as a thanks offering to the king of the gods for sending him the eagle.

AT THIS POINT LEGEND shifts gear into history.

The cart existed. A yoke was attached to it by a complicated knot of cornel bark. It was prophesied that whoever could undo it was destined to rule Asia. This was too much of a challenge for Alexander to resist. In the spring of 333 he led his army to Gordium, the impressive capital of Phrygia, with massive fortifications and grand palace buildings. He insisted on climbing up to the acropolis, where the cart was on display in the temple of Zeus, and trying his luck with the knot.

The bark was so tightly entangled that it was impossible to see how it was fastened. The king could find no way of undoing it. He was surrounded by a crowd of Phrygians and Macedonians and would lose face if he admitted defeat. He could not allow that to happen. So he drew his sword and with a single blow cut through the knot. "It's undone *now*," he growled.

Some might call this cheating, but so far as Alexander and his entourage were concerned the prophecy had been fulfilled. That night a storm blew up, with thunder and lightning, confirmation of Zeus's approval.

The incident had great publicity value. It will have encouraged the Macedonians to believe that the gods were on their side, but more importantly it helped to justify their presence in Asia and may have shaken the loyalty of Darius's subjects.

BY THE TIME OF his visit to Gordium in 333, Alexander was already well on his way to conquering Asia Minor (that is, Anatolia, or our modern Turkey). The prophecy was approaching fulfillment.

After the victory at the Granicus in May the previous year, the king's first task had been to secure the Mediterranean coastline and deny it to the powerful Persian fleet, which dominated the Aegean Sea. After sending Parmenion off to secure the capital of Hellespontine Phrygia, the king marched his army south to the great Lydian city of Sardis. Many of the Ionian city-states were fearful of being liberated, in case the Persians were to return, and kept their heads down for the time being, but the commander of Sardis's acropolis, a Persian nobleman called Mithrenes, came out some miles to meet the king. He surrendered the city and, even more helpfully, its treasure, for Alexander was running out of cash.

Greeks and Macedonians had no time for barbarians and most of the army will have expected him to be treated harshly. However, Alexander was no racist and was willing to make use of men from any ethnic background provided they were able and experienced. He kept Mithrenes with him "in a position of honor" and two years later appointed him to be satrap of Armenia.

Reluctant ever to give an individual too much power, the king appointed a Macedonian to the satrapy of Lydia, and another one to command the Sardis garrison. A Greek treasurer handled the financial affairs of this wealthy province and reported directly to the king.

Alexander, a tireless tourist, spent time looking around Sardis. He was particularly impressed by the strength of the citadel—very precipitous and fortified with a triple wall. Somewhere on the summit he decided to build a temple to Olympian Zeus and an altar for sacrifices. He was looking around for a suitable site when the god signified his choice by letting off peals of thunder and soaking the royal palace (and only the royal palace) in a downpour of rain.

THE KING MOVED ON to the prosperous city of Ephesus on the Ionian coast (in today's Turkey). Before he arrived, the garrison of Greek mercenaries requisitioned two triremes and vanished: no doubt they had heard of the fate meted out to Memnon's Greek regiment at the Granicus and were disinclined to share it. The citizens welcomed Alexander's arrival. Two years previously, as reported, Parmenion's advance force had briefly taken Ephesus, where they had erected a statue of

Philip in the celebrated temple of the mother-goddess Artemis and established a semi-divine cult in his honor. But the Macedonians had faced serious opposition from the Persians under Memnon and were forced to withdraw. In their absence the statue was pulled down.

Now they were back, and led by a new young king. Most of the Ionian cities were governed by pro-Persian upper-class elites, or oligarchies, and Ephesus was no exception. Alexander, having cast himself as liberator of the Greeks, favored democracies, and the city's rulers were thrown out of office. The leading oligarch, his son, and his nephew sought sanctuary in the temple, but were dragged out and stoned to death.

Alexander immediately put a stop to this settling of scores, typical of the quarrelsome Hellenic city-states. Arrian writes that he "prevented any further inquisitions and vengeance, knowing that, if given license to do so, along with the guilty the people would kill innocent men out of personal enmity or designs on their property. No other action won Alexander as much credit as his handling of Ephesus at this time."

The temple of Artemis had been badly damaged by fire on the day of Alexander's birth and had never been restored. The geographer and historian Strabo, writing three centuries later, recounts that the king offered to pay for the rebuilding on condition that the gift was recorded on a marble inscription. The proud Ephesians felt that this would be too high a price and declined the offer on the ground that it was "inappropriate for a god to dedicate offerings to gods." Any possible offense was cleverly masked by sycophancy.

While at Ephesus the king met the famous artist Apelles, who had painted his father many times. Apelles had an international reputation and his pictures "sold for the price of a whole town." His work was remarkable for its elegance, he could catch a likeness, and, unlike many of his fellows, he knew when he had put enough work into a painting, when to put down his brush. He restricted his palette to white, yellow, red-brown, and black.

Alexander commissioned a full-length portrait of himself as Zeus wielding a thunderbolt. This was touching on the sacrilegious and suggests that Alexander, proud of his descent from the hero Heracles, was following his father's self-presentation as godlike, *isotheos*.

Apelles found his sitter to be a know-it-all, who liked to pontificate about art, although he had no specialist knowledge. He had a word in Alexander's ear: "Sir, please keep quiet, for the lads who grind the colors are laughing at you."

Alexander took the reprimand in good part. He was so impressed by the artist's work that he awarded him a generous fee of twenty talents and exclusive rights to his painted image.

After sending out two military detachments, one of them led by Parmenion, to receive the surrenders of towns in the region, the king set off for his next destination, the great port of Miletus. This time resistance was expected and the Macedonians prepared for a siege.

ONE FINE MORNING A thousand years earlier, the Trojans woke up to find that their Greek enemy had left. The shore where they had beached their fleet was deserted. The siege, which had lasted ten years, was finally over. It was time to celebrate.

There was nothing to be seen except for a giant wooden horse. What could its purpose be? A man claiming to be a Greek deserter explained to a wondering crowd that the colossus was intended as a religious offering that would assure the enemy of a safe passage home. It was too large to be taken into the city, so the happy Trojans widened a gate by demolishing part of the city wall and dragged it inside. They then settled down to an evening's serious drinking.

It was a trick, of course, invented by the wily Odysseus. Inside the horse's belly, warriors awaited their moment. The Greek ships had not set sail across the Aegean Sea, but were moored out of sight behind the nearby island of Tenedos. Once the city was asleep (stupefied, in many cases), the armed men slipped out of the horse and were joined by the main army after the fleet had returned to the beaches.

The city was fired and sacked.

For the Greeks, the Trojan War was a momentous event and is evidence of the trouble they had always had with sieges. Their main method for capturing cities was deceit and bribery. It was only to be expected that Troy should fall, not to attack, but to subterfuge.

Centuries later, the Greeks lagged far behind Persia, which mined tunnels, built mounds to the height of defensive walls, and used battering rams. Philip, Alexander's father, recognized that a well-defended city was a challenge to his forces and he had no objection to duplicity. A wooden horse was fit only for myth, and anyway he had another more likely animal in mind. He confessed: "There is no citadel to which one cannot send up a little donkey laden with gold."

However, both Philip and Alexander were determined to improve the art of siegecraft. They borrowed many of their techniques from the Carthaginians and the Syracusans, who regularly clashed in Sicily where both held substantial territories.

The main problem was that city walls, which used to consist of masonry rubble or even mud, were getting stronger. During the fifth century B.C., wealthy states began building them from accurately cut rectangular or polygonal stone blocks, surmounted by mud-brick battlements. Narrow sallyports allowed defenders to launch sorties. Athens was a maritime power and boasted the most powerful fleet in the Mediterranean. She made herself impregnable from land assault by building massive stone walls around her port, Piraeus, and linking it to the city by means of a "corridor" of two high stone walls punctuated at regular intervals by two-story towers. In effect, Athens became an island.

So the question facing the Macedonians was how to counter stone. Philip and Alexander invested heavily in imaginative engineers. One of these was a Thessalian called Diades. He claimed to have invented, but probably only improved, wheeled towers constructed from wood and hides. These would have up to ten floors with windows on each side, protected from arrows by leather curtains. They could bring the besiegers level with the top of a fortification and enabled them to fight guards on the battlements on equal terms. An assault bridge allowed soldiers to cross over onto a wall, a fortification, or a building. The tallest tower Diades ever built was more than fifty meters high.

The other solution to the problem of lofty stone walls was artillery. Sicilian engineers invented the arrow-shooting catapult. To begin with this was no more than an outsize crossbow, but in Philip's day the more deadly torsion catapult was invented, powered by twisted sinew or hair. It was soon adapted for stone-throwing, and a large one could hurl heavy rocks as far as 100 meters.

Battering rams developed rapidly at this time. The most important innovation was to house them in a covered vehicle called a tortoise. This could be sixteen feet long; a small tower stood on its pitched roof, which held pots of water for extinguishing fires. The ram itself could be pulled back and forth by ropes, like a pendulum; these gave way to rams on rollers, which had a constant momentum and greater penetration. A specialist form of ram was the drill, twenty feet long with a sharp metal point that could pierce walls.

Defenders, no longer able to sit comfortably behind their stone walls, countered the new siege devices with developments of their own. Above all, they needed to be active with countermeasures. Towers were built that accommodated heavy artillery, for the higher a catapult was from the ground, the greater its range. Ditches were dug in front of walls to make it difficult for mobile siege towers to approach. Crenellated battlements were replaced by screen walls with shuttered openings and loopholes.

Thanks to the technological advances of men like Diades, the balance of advantage now lay with the besieger, provided that he was determined, not pressed for time, and able to endure high casualties. A victorious general was liable to lose more men in a siege than on the battlefield. However, the besieged could win the day if they had strong defenses, plentiful food supplies and running water, and could boast loyal citizens and brave soldiers.

MILETUS WAS ONE OF the wealthiest Greek city-states on the coastline of Asia Minor. Founded by Athens, it was perched on a headland at the foot of the rocky, jagged Mount Latmos and looked across a bay at the mouth of the river Maeander. It became a center for philosophical and scientific studies. Its greatest citizen was the sixth-century-B.C. thinker and political consultant Thales, who devoted much of his time to the cause of Milesian independence. It was an era of political upheaval, dominated by Cyrus the Great and culminating in the creation of the Persian empire.

Thales rejected the use of mythology to explain the nature of the universe in favor of hypotheses that could be tested—in other words, he pioneered the scientific method. Philosophers of his era often supposed that all material things were modifications of one eternal substance. According to Thales, this substance was water.

Thales is credited with inventing geometry by generalizing from Egyptian land measurement. He was also an astronomer and is reputed to have predicted a solar eclipse. Aristotle regarded him as the first philosopher in the Hellenic tradition.

As we have seen, for a few brief years at the close of the fifth century, Miletus joined other Greek city-states in the Ionian revolt against Persian rule. Their navy lost a decisive battle off the small island of Lade near the harbor entrance. The city itself was besieged and captured. The Great King was back in control.

Now, in the autumn of 334, more than a century and a half later, the empire was again being challenged. Miletus was a rich prize, as the Persians well knew. They sent their fleet of 400 warships to reach the city before the Macedonians. However, Alexander's one hundred and sixty ships arrived there first and anchored at Lade. From this position they could intercept any Persian ships that tried to enter the port, and the enemy was forced to moor some distance away, under Mount Mycale.

Parmenion advised the king to fight at sea, arguing that although the Macedonian fleet was half the size of the enemy's, a naval battle was worth the risk—and a defeat would not have serious consequences. Alexander strongly disagreed. It made no sense, he said, to pit their own inexperienced sailors against the better-trained Cypriots and Phoenicians who made up the Persian fleet. A defeat would be a blow to his reputation for invincibility and would encourage revolt in Greece.

So the king let the fleets look after themselves and prepared for a siege. He dismissed some envoys from Miletus, who offered equal access to the walls and harbor for both sides. "Go back at once inside the city," he told them, "and warn your compatriots to be ready for battle tomorrow."

Alexander's engineers got down to work, under his supervision, and proved their worth. Siege engines (presumably battering rams and catapults) were brought up and soon demolished a section of wall. The soldiers worked in relays. A longer stretch of wall was weakened; once it had been broken down, the army prepared to launch a major assault. The Persians at Mycale were powerless and could only watch over the fate of their friends and allies.

The admiral of the Macedonian fleet at Lade observed this early success and feared that the desperate Persians might risk running the gauntlet into the port and smuggling in aid. So he rowed along the coast to the harbor mouth, where he lined up his triremes and packed them close together like sardines with their prows facing outward. Miletus was now completely blockaded by sea.

The garrison of Greek mercenaries lost hope. Some of them jumped into the sea and paddled on their upturned shields to an uninhabited islet. Others tried to slip away in small boats, but were caught by the triremes at the harbor mouth. Most of the defenders were killed in the city itself. The Rhodian general Memnon and other high officials had made their escape from the battlefield at the Granicus and taken refuge in Miletus; they went on their travels again.

The Milesians made it clear that the Persian garrison had been responsible for the resistance to the siege. Leading citizens carrying suppliant olive boughs prostrated themselves before the king and placed their city in his hands. Alexander was a little skeptical. He noticed many statues of athletes who had won victories in the Olympic and the Pythian Games and asked, "Where were the men with bodies like these when the barbarians took over your city?" However, he took the Milesians at their word and treated them with kindness. All other adult males were sold into slavery.

With the siege now over, Alexander sailed some triremes to the islet. They were equipped with ladders on their prows for scaling the sheer cliffs. However, when he realized that the mercenaries were prepared to fight to the death, the king was moved by their courage. He pardoned them on condition that they sign up in his army. The story is very probably true, for he had a soft spot for brave enemies. He may also have wanted to make a show of reconciliation with Greek mercenaries. The massacre at the Granicus had been counterproductive. Thousands of embittered Greeks were in the Great King's pay; believing they could expect no mercy from Alexander, they remained his most obdurate enemies. It was in his interest to win them over to his side.

It was now time to deal with the Persian fleet marooned at Mount Mycale. Alexander sent Philotas with a small mixed force of cavalry and infantry to prevent the sailors from leaving their ships. Finding supplies in this barren spot was already difficult; Philotas made it impossible. After a perfunctory attempt to entice the Macedonian fleet out of the harbor, the Persians, half starved and thirsty, sailed away.

The siege showed that the Macedonians could defeat the Persian navy from dry land, or at least render it harmless. What was the point, Alexander mused, of maintaining a fleet of his own, especially when it was too small, too inadequate, and too expensive to be of practical use. He decided to disband it altogether, except for a few transports for carrying the siege equipment. His army was well on its way to capturing Asia Minor. He would make do without ships.

At the time it seemed like an excellent idea.

MILESIANS MIGHT DISAGREE, but Halicarnassus was the greatest of the Ionian city-ports.

The capital of Caria, it stood on a barren peninsula that extended into the Aegean Sea and commanded a fine harbor. Its most famous son was Herodotus, who wrote a prose epic about the Persian invasions of Greece in the fifth century B.C.

The city had been governed for many years by members of the same family: Hecatomnus, who founded the regime, and his three sons and two daughters. Although they were officially only satraps, the Great King was content to let them settle into dynasties and, in effect, become monarchs themselves. There were pros and cons to this arrangement. It conferred stability, continuity, and in-depth local knowledge; on the other hand, overmighty subjects might be tempted to bid for complete independence.

The most successful Hecatomnid was Mausolus, the eldest of three brothers, who reigned between 377 and 353 and expanded his sphere of influence to include Rhodes and other islands. He moved his capital to Halicarnassus and invested in an ambitious program of public works. He was a Hellenophile, and the best Greek architects, artists, and engineers were hired. The harbor was deepened and a fine city wall was built, with watchtowers, three fortified citadels, and deep protective ditches. Streets and squares were paved, statues erected and temples dedicated. Halicarnassus became one of the most spectacular cities in the ancient world.

Its inhabitants acquired a reputation for decadent living. Some fantasists blamed a city fountain for making "effeminate" all who drank from it. Strabo disagreed: "It seems that the effeminacy of man is laid to the charge of the air or of the water; yet it is not these, but rather riches and wanton living, that are the cause of effeminacy."

Like the pharaohs in Egypt, male Hecatomnids married their female siblings, perhaps to keep the ruling family to a manageable size and limit the number of potential claimants to the throne. Mausolus married his sister Artemisia, who acted as his co-ruler. The union was, or became, a love match. On her brother's death, the grief-stricken queen supposedly swallowed his ashes, mixed in a drink. She commissioned an elaborate tomb, the Mausoleum (whence our "mausoleum"), on a hill overlooking the city. Within three years she, too, was dead.

The Hecatomnid clan held on to power. Artemisia was followed by a brother, who died and left his sister-wife, Ada, as queen regnant. She was displaced by the youngest of the brothers, Pixodarus (the man whose plan to marry his daughter to Alexander's half-brother Arridhaeus had caused so much grief). He in turn was succeeded by his son-in-law, a prominent Persian called Orontobates.

Halicarnassus was the next siege on Alexander's list, after which he would have realized his immediate strategic aim, the conquest of Asia Minor. He marched south and received surrenders from towns en route. He made a detour to the fortified town of Alinda, where the deposed widow Ada lived in exile. She petitioned the king to reinstate her as queen of Caria, which he immediately promised to do.

He had a taste for ladies of a certain age, and he fell if not in love then in warm friendship with her. He allowed her to adopt him and gave her the official title of Mother. Every day she used to send him cakes and sweets from her kitchen. Finally, Ada offered to send him her finest bakers and cooks. These little tokens of her affection began to be embarrassing and, according to Plutarch, he politely reprimanded her:

> I do not need your chefs, because my tutor Leonidas provided me with better ones—a night march for breakfast and a light

breakfast to give me an appetite for supper. This same Leonidas would often come and open my chests of bedding and clothes, to see if my mother hadn't hidden some titbits inside.

One can only wonder what Olympias made of all this. Alexander frequently corresponded with her, but perhaps he took care not to draw this new relationship to her attention.

HALICARNASSUS PROMISED TO BE a challenge. Memnon and many Persians, together with several thousand Greek mercenaries, had concentrated their forces there after leaving Miletus. The Great King's navy, still smarting from its failure there, rode at anchor inside the harbor. Now that the Macedonian fleet had been disbanded, nothing could be done to prevent supplies from being brought into the city.

Alexander pitched camp on the eastern side of Halicarnassus; siege engines and provisions arrived by sea. The king reconnoitered the walls. A body of defenders suddenly stormed out of a nearby gate to the accompaniment of long-range artillery fire. The Macedonians had little difficulty driving them back inside, but after a few days the king decided to assess the western fortifications near a gate that led to the town of Myndus twelve miles away.

He was briefly distracted by some traitors inside Myndus who promised to hand it over to him. One day he went in person up to the town wall around midnight, but the agreed signal was not given and the Macedonians returned empty-handed.

The siege now began in earnest. It was decided to demolish a section of wall in the north of the city. Sappers began by filling in a part of the ditch so that the wheeled towers and battering rams could be pushed close to the wall. Penthouses were placed against it to protect diggers who were undermining its foundations. A surprise nighttime sally was repulsed: about 170 defenders lost their lives against sixteen of Alexander's troops (although 300 were injured because they had not had enough time to put on their armor).

One piece of good news was that the Halicarnassian fatalities included Neoptolemus. He was the son of Arrabhaeus, the Macedonian nobleman who had been executed for his (alleged) involvement in

Philip's assassination. This provoked his desertion to the Persians. By contrast, his brother Amyntas was an officer of high standing and ability and remained loyal and trusted. Neoptolemus was not long dead when the king confirmed his confidence in Amyntas by appointing him to an important command.

A few days later, two towers and connecting walls were destroyed and a third tower badly shaken. That evening two men from Perdiccas's infantry battalion, who were tent-mates, drank too much wine and quarreled about their exploits. To prove their virility they ran up to the piles of collapsed masonry. Soldiers from the city came out to confront them and a fight started. More men from both sides joined the mêlée and soon a fierce battle was underway. This was the second time that Perdiccas and his men had endangered Alexander's career by their foolhardiness (the first time had been at the siege of Thebes).

He and his staff appeared in person; the Macedonians drove back the enemy and, writes Arrian, Halicarnassus "came near to being captured." That may be so, but it looks as though the struggle was more even than the historian suggests. According to Diodorus, the king asked the enemy through a herald for a truce to recover the bodies of his men who had fallen during the engagement. Evidently, he did not control the area where they lay. The clear implication is that the Macedonians had had the worst of it.

Ephialtes and Thrasybulus, Athenians fighting on the Persian side, advised Memnon not to give up the dead bodies for burial, but chivalrously he granted the request.

The defenders rapidly plugged the gap in their defenses by constructing a crescent-shaped brick wall behind the debris. On the next day, the king brought up his siege engines against it, but one of his towers and some wickerwork shelters for the sappers were destroyed when enemy soldiers with torches set light to them. They were chased back inside, but the damage had been done.

A DAY OR TWO'S pause ensued. Memnon and his staff met in council to discuss the situation. Despite their successes, they realized that unless the besieged took some sort of aggressive action their future was bleak. Ephialtes devised a clever plan. One thousand mercenaries were to emerge with torches and once again set light to the siege engines. The Macedonians would react by sending in troops. Once they were fully engaged, a second troop of mercenaries, led by Ephialtes, would issue from a nearby city gate and take the Macedonians in the flank. If this tactic showed any sign of succeeding, Memnon and his full army would arrive to deliver the coup de grâce.

The plan very nearly worked. At an agreed time the first column burst out of the city and set fire to new siege engines. There was a tremendous conflagration. Missiles rained down on the Macedonians from the top of the replacement wall and from a mobile tower that had been specially built for the occasion. The king went forward and took personal command. Then Ephialtes emerged from the gate at the head of a second column, a deep, close-knit phalanx, and charged. He happened to crash into young and inexperienced troops, who flinched. Memnon then arrived on the scene in force.

The Macedonians were facing defeat, and Diodorus claims that "Alexander did not really know what to do." There was in fact nothing that he could do; the day was only saved by some battle-hardened warriors—Philip's old soldiers—who launched a counterattack against the enemy phalanx.

Fortune had beckoned to Memnon—and then changed her mind. Ephialtes was killed in the fray and his mercenaries were driven back inside Halicarnassus. They pushed toward the open gate, but a bridge that led to it over the ditch broke under their weight. Some were trampled to death or shot down from above. In the panic of the moment, the gates were closed too soon and many were left outside. They were slaughtered at the foot of the city wall.

It was now evening and Alexander called back his troops. Some argue that if he had persevered, Halicarnassus would have fallen there and then. But battles in the dark can have unpredictable outcomes and his men were exhausted. It is probable that he was in touch with leading citizens and did not wish to initiate a sack.

Memnon was a realist. He conferred urgently that night with his commanders and the Carian satrap, Ada's usurping son-in-law, Orontobates. They decided that they could not hold out for much longer, for many of their best soldiers had lost their lives or been wounded, and the city's fortifications were being battered down by the Macedonian artillery. They may also have feared a popular uprising. They acted at once while it was still dark, firing the city and burning their wooden tower and the arsenal where they kept their artillery. They withdrew their best troops into two of Halicarnassus's three more or less impregnable fortress citadels and left the city itself to the Macedonians. All remaining personnel—Memnon and Orontobates among them—stores, and equipment were evacuated by the Persian navy to the island of Cos.

Alexander was informed of exactly what was happening by some turncoats and immediately marched his army into Halicarnassus. He ordered all fire-raisers to be put to death. Civilians were to be treated with respect.

Dawn was now breaking and it was possible to see the destruction wrought during the night. The king surveyed the occupied fortresses and decided it was not worth the time and energy to besiege them. With the city in his hands, there would have been little point. Ada was proclaimed queen and a garrison was installed of three thousand mercenary infantry and some two hundred horse, under the command of Ptolemy.

HALICARNASSUS SHOWED THE DECISION to disband the Macedonian fleet to have been a mistake.

As a Greek, Memnon had never been fully trusted by the Persian court. Now he sent his wife and children to Darius as hostages for his good behavior and, as he had hoped, he was appointed commander-in-chief of operations in Asia Minor. He allocated money to pay for the fleet and a sizable body of mercenaries. His plan was to force Alexander to abandon his Asian campaign by taking the war to mainland Greece. In the absence of opposition, Memnon and the Persian fleet captured island after island. Soon the entire Aegean Sea would belong to the Great King. Diodorus writes:

> News of the general's activity spread like wildfire and most of the Cyclades sent missions to him. As word came to Greece that Memnon was about to sail to Euboea with his fleet, the cities of that island became alarmed, while those Greeks who were

friendly to Persia, notably Sparta, began to have high hopes of a change in the political situation.

Having no warships, Alexander was powerless to intervene. Unless there was a material change for the better in the military outlook, he would be obliged to go back to Europe. Then his luck turned. In early spring 333, while campaigning on the island of Lesbos, Memnon suddenly died; no diagnosis has come down to us, but perhaps the cause was a heart attack. His nephew Pharnabazus inherited his command and acted energetically, but he was no Memnon. The grand plan expired with its deviser.

(The Fates had a dry sense of humor, for Pharnabazus was the brother of the beautiful Barsine, soon to become Alexander's mistress.)

Alexander recognized his error and commissioned a new fleet. This was a hugely expensive project and took some time to implement. Pharnabazus remained free to career around the Aegean, but only for some months. Two admirals were appointed and were given five hundred talents for their costs; for his part, Antipater received six hundred talents, presumably to assist with recruitment. The League of Corinth was instructed under its treaty obligations to send a naval contribution.

Alexander needed to assure himself that Asia Minor was fully pacified. He set out eastward along the southern littoral. Meanwhile Parmenion was instructed to retrace his steps northward to Sardis, after which he would strike inland, assert Macedonian power, and challenge the Persian satrap of Phrygia. They would meet again at Gordium in the center of Anatolia.

AT ABOUT THIS TIME an unnerving incident took place. A Persian nobleman called Sisines, who was a member of Darius's intimate circle, was arrested by Parmenion's men. His cover story, which ultimately he did not use, was that the Great King had sent him to visit the satrap of Phrygia, but in fact his real mission was to corrupt Alexander of Lyncestis, who commanded an elite cavalry squadron in Parmenion's service.

This namesake of the king was one of the various noblemen who had been caught up, innocently or otherwise, in the assassination of Philip II. As we have seen, his two brothers had been executed for their alleged complicity in the crime, but he had been spared because he was the first to hail the new king in the theater at Aegae. More to the point, perhaps, Antipater, Alexander's leading backer, who had stage-managed his accession, was the other Alexander's father-in-law and may have protected him. Ostensibly loyal, the Lyncestian had served in the army as an able commander of the Thessalian cavalry.

Having been caged, Sisines sang. Sometime previously, a Macedonian defector had brought a (presumably) treasonous letter from this Alexander to the Great King. In response, Sisines was to give the Lyncestian a confidential message that, if he were to kill Alexander the king, he, Darius, would install the Lyncestian on the Macedonian throne and present him with a thousand gold talents.

Sisines was sent under guard to Alexander, to whom he repeated the story. What was to be made of it? It was possible that this was an example of ancient psyops, a trick to confuse the enemy, discredit a valued officer, and damage morale. Alternatively, Sisines was telling the truth and the Lyncestian had been a traitor all along. The evidence was circumstantial and rested on a single, uncorroborated, and probably untrustworthy source.

Alexander asked his Companions for advice. Their opinion was that it had been a mistake to give the best of the cavalry to a man of dubious loyalty. He should rid himself of the traitor before he could suborn the Thessalians "to some revolutionary purpose."

They reminded the king of a recent omen, which was obviously a refence to Sisines' revelation. During the siege, he had been taking a midday nap when a swallow flew about over his head chirping noisily. The sound bothered him in his sleep and he brushed the bird away with his hand. Instead of flying off, the swallow perched on his head and stayed there till he was fully awake.

Alexander took the incident seriously and consulted his seer, Aristander, who said that it signified a plot against his life. However, seeing that the swallow was a friendly, talkative bird, he predicted that the plot would come to light.

The king was uncertain of the Lyncestian's guilt, and did not have him charged and brought to trial. He ordered Parmenion to arrest him and keep him under guard. And so Alexander the Lyncestian remained for the next three years.

———

ALEXANDER NOW HAD TO decide whether to await the arrival of Darius and his host and do battle with him in Asia Minor, or to confront the Great King in his own heartland. Of course, he chose the latter, more aggressive option. Time was short, for the mustering of the vast Persian army was proceeding apace. He needed to conclude his business in Asia Minor as soon as possible.

His choice came at a high price. The farther he and his invasion force moved away from Asia Minor the more likely it was that Pharnabazus would exploit his naval monopoly and recover some of his gains. It would not be long before Miletus and Halicarnassus went back under Persian rule. Alexander will have told himself that this would not matter greatly. His new fleet would soon be ready, he expected. Assuming that he won his showdown with the Great King, and he did assume it, the Ionian cities would drop into his hands again.

The Macedonian army moved fast through Lycia (on the southern coast of Turkey) and its largest city, Telmissus, Aristander's hometown of fellow prophets, capitulated without fuss. Envoys from the important port of Phaselis, with its two harbors, offered their surrender and awarded him a golden crown. As a friendly gesture, the king helped the inhabitants demolish a fort built by hostile Pisidians. He then continued to the fertile lands of Pamphylia, leaving his main army briefly to make its own way while he rode along a coastal path. This path was submerged when a southerly blew, but luckily a north wind got up and the way opened to Alexander and his troop.

The citizens of Aspendus surrendered, promising to hand over the horses they bred as tribute to the Great King and to make a fifty-talent contribution to his army's costs. They changed their minds and then, seeing Alexander arrive in person outside their walls, nervously changed their minds again. The king was not amused and raised the payment to one hundred talents. He was lucky, for if Aspendus with its high, sheer acropolis overlooking the river Eurymedon had decided to resist, a siege could have lasted for months.

The king continued north. One town looked too difficult to capture quickly, so he simply bypassed it and went on to mop up various others. He then passed into Phrygia and reached Celaenae, a green oasis in the barren landscape of Anatolia and, more significantly, a city of strategic importance. It stood at the headwaters of two rivers, the Maeander and the Marsyas, and was a junction of major highways.

The citadel perched on high cliffs and was garrisoned by Carian and Greek mercenaries. When the king sent a herald up to them demanding their immediate capitulation, they simply showed the man around the substantial fortifications before sending him on his way. For once Alexander opted for discretion rather than valor. Instead of a direct assault, he blockaded the citadel with his army and waited. After ten days, supplies were running short and the defenders' resolve was wavering.

They put a remarkable proposition to the king. If they were not relieved within sixty days, they promised to hand over the citadel. Even more remarkably, Alexander agreed to the terms, left a modest force to police the deal, and hurried on.

After accepting fistfuls of surrenders, Alexander and Parmenion met, as arranged, at Gordium. Having done their philoprogenitive duty, the newly married husbands arrived from Macedon together with three thousand newly levied foot soldiers and three hundred horse.

The slicing of the knot and the thundering approval of the king of the gods marked a symbolic turning point. The new lord of Asia was ready to march east to fulfill the prophecy and claim his inheritance.

WHAT CAN WE SAY of Alexander's post-Granicus performance, especially so far as the sieges are concerned? Long-term investment in his engineers, up-to-date siege equipment, and long-range artillery had paid off handsomely. Even the most solid fortifications collapsed under the bombardment of his torsion catapults. This was to his credit.

However, the incident of Perdiccas's drunk soldiers suggests a problem with control of his men under the mental and physical strain of a siege. Worse than that, to have had to parley for a truce was a profound humiliation for a man whose stock-in-trade was invincibility. And he had been outmaneuvered by Ephialtes in front of the walls of Halicarnassus. For once, this most quick-thinking of commanders could not think how to turn the tables on his enemy. His career could have come to an abrupt end had it not been for Philip's grizzled warriors—and the luck for which he was justly famous.

Gratitude was not Alexander's strong suit (he preferred people being grateful to *him*) and years later an old soldier reminded him of this episode, the memory of which the king did his best to suppress. We are told that he said: "You have no time for Philip's men, but you are forgetting that if old Atarrhias here had not called back the younger fellows when they shrank from fighting, we would still be hanging out at Halicarnassus."

Nevertheless, mischance and mistakes apart, the king had more or less achieved his goal of conquering Asia Minor. As we have seen, his father would probably have halted at this point and followed the advice of Isocrates, who had died in 338, the year of Chaeronea, fatal to liberty. As already reported, he had argued that a chain of newly founded Greek city-states running south from Sinope on the Black Sea coast to Cilicia on the Mediterranean would create a barrier between a much enlarged Macedonian empire and the diminished but still extensive lands of the Great King.

Intellectuals are often impractical; the notion that an aggrieved Persian empire, thirsting for revenge, would be deterred by a line of puny statelets was absurd. Alexander knew he would only be secure once he had put an end to the rule of the Achaemenids. When did he reject Isocrates' "halfway house"? He seems not to have broadcast his inward thoughts, and little evidence about them has come down to us. He may have dreamed of total conquest as a teenaged boy, as crown prince and then king, or only during his campaign in Asia Minor. But his long-term intentions can be deduced from his actions. He may not have told anybody, but he fully intended to take over as Great King from Darius.

His tactics were as clear-cut as his strategy. Everything he did was aimed at forcing Darius to stake his empire and his life on one great battle, which he and his Macedonians expected to win outright. With Asia Minor lost, the Great King's honor required him to take the field himself.

CHAPTER 7

THE EMPIRE
STRIKES BACK

Alexander was dying. It looked very much as if his campaign was drawing to a premature close. Officers and men held their breath.

By the time he and Parmenion met at Gordium in early summer of 333, the whole territory of Asia Minor was more or less under their control, although the Persian fleet was still making mischief in the Aegean. Now it was time to pursue the Great King and confront the numberless horde he was assembling. After a quick expedition against tribes in Cappadocia, Alexander marched south. His plan was to reach Cilicia: this fertile coastal province was entirely enclosed on its landward side by inhospitable mountains. Once the Macedonians had reached the sea they would then turn eastward and march toward the river Euphrates and Mesopotamia.

The first obstacle they encountered was the Cilician Gates, a pass through the Taurus range, which separated the Anatolian plateau from the coastal plain of Cilicia. It was long, cliff-bound, at its narrowest point had room only for four soldiers marching abreast, and was heavily guarded. Alexander assembled a crack assault force of his foot guards, the hypaspists. Under cover of darkness they made their way to the defile. Unfortunately, they were detected, but it was evidence of

Alexander's growing reputation as a bogeyman, which he sedulously cultivated, that when the defenders learned he was leading the operation in person they abandoned their posts and ran away. When dawn broke, the king led his army through the pass without incident.

His destination was Tarsus, no mean city. It was said to have been founded by traders from Argos in the Peloponnese. Another legend offers a foolish etymology: the mythical hero Bellerophon, a great slayer of monsters, liked to travel on his winged horse, Pegasus. One day he fell off it and hurt his foot—whence the name Tarsus, from *tar sos,* the sole of the foot.

In fact, the city's true history can be traced back six thousand years. It stood at the mouth of the river Cydnus and was a junction of important sea and land trade routes. Where the river empties into the sea were swamps and lagoons, both at Tarsus and along the Cilician coastline. Mosquitoes flourished. August scorched, and it was then that an annual malaria epidemic started.

It was during this dangerous month that Alexander arrived at Tarsus, sweaty, dusty, and nearly overcome by the sweltering weather. Seeking coolness, he swiftly undressed in front of his troops, ran down to the river, and dived in for a swim. According to Arrian, the king suffered an "attack of cramp, violent fever and persistent inability to sleep." Barely conscious, he was carried to his tent.

What was the matter with him? It is too late for a doctor to examine him now, but the likeliest diagnosis is that he was bitten by a malaria-carrying mosquito. His recorded symptoms are consistent with a pernicious infection caused by the *Plasmodium falciparum* parasite, the most dangerous form of the disease. His first spasm or convulsion was followed by a violent fever and insomnia. After news arrived that Darius had left Babylon with his army and was bound for Cilicia, he suffered a bout of depression. He became unable to speak, had difficulty breathing, and lost sensation and then consciousness. This is very much how falciparum malaria develops, after which the sufferer either recovers or, without modern medication, more usually dies.

All but one of the available physicians feared he would not live and were extremely nervous about treating him, for they knew they would get the blame for a bad outcome. The only one to remain optimistic was Philip from Acarnania, a somewhat primitive region of mainland

Greece. He had been appointed as Alexander's personal doctor when a child and was totally devoted to him.

While the king was still able to communicate, Philip recommended a strong purgative and Alexander told him to administer it. But at the last minute a difficulty arose. For the second time in a few weeks, Parmenion received a report of secret treachery masterminded by Persia. The old general sent the king a note advising him to beware of the doctor, because Darius had allegedly bribed him to poison his employer.

Alexander put the note under his pillow. He passed it to Philip when the doctor gave him the medication in a cup and, in a gesture of complete confidence, drank it up. It appeared, though, that Parmenion's suspicions were justified, for the patient's condition took an immediate turn for the worse. Nothing abashed, Philip continued his treatment, applying poultices and stimulating the king's appetite with the smell of food. During periods of consciousness, he would talk to Alexander about his mother and sisters and the great victory that awaited him when he got better.

We do not know what Philip put into his potion and whether it did any good. Very likely not, but one way or another, Alexander, a young man in his prime, survived the infection and after two months' convalescence recovered. The illness came as a great shock both to the rank and file and to his commanders. There must have been confidential discussions at a senior level about what to do in the event of the king's death, although on his unlooked-for recovery amnesia quickly set in and no trace of them remains.

We have one clue to the dismay Alexander's near-death experience created among his intimates. He had an old schoolfellow called Harpalus, who was probably a nephew of one of King Philip's wives. Harpalus had some kind of disability that prevented him from soldiering. He stood by Alexander during the Pixodarus affair and was exiled for his pains alongside the crown prince's other friends. He accompanied the king to Asia. Because he was clever with numbers, he was appointed Alexander's chief financial officer.

Before the approaching battle, Harpalus absconded with money taken from the exchequer, probably in the belief that Cilicia would be a dangerous place in the event of the king's death. If cowardice played a part, he also seems to have been lured into criminality by a con man of his acquaintance, a certain Tauriscus. Knowing that the king had a long arm, Harpalus hid away in the small city-state of Megara in mainland Greece.

Harpalus was not alone in his anxiety about a post-Alexander future. Every soldier in the Macedonian army had received a sharp reminder of the vanity of human wishes. Officers and men must have wished that their invincible leader had an adult heir as competent as he had once been in his father's day.

The destiny of many thousands of men hung on a thread, the thread of a single life, which the Fates, merciless and immortal hags, spun on their wheel and were ready to snip off whenever they chose.

MEMNON'S UNTIMELY END ON Lesbos in the early spring of 333 was an event of the greatest importance. A skilled tactician and, even more usefully, a strategic thinker, the mercenary general exploited the Persian command of the seas, especially after Alexander's decision to disband his navy. If he could re-enslave the Ionians, attack or at least block off Macedonia, and provoke an uprising among the disgruntled city-states of mainland Greece, he would halt the Macedonian invasion in its tracks.

In Memnon's absence, the Great King lost confidence in the Aegean campaign. He resolved to pool his military forces and crush the Macedonians in one great land battle. The substantial force of Greek mercenaries from the fleet would be of most use to him in the army he was gradually mustering. So he recalled them.

Darius convened a council of his Friends, or inner cabinet, and asked for their advice. According to Diodorus, he laid out alternative courses of action:

> Either to send generals with an army down to the coast or for himself, the king, to march down with all his armed forces and fight the Macedonians in person. Some said that the king must join in battle personally, and they argued that the Persians would fight better in that event.

However, a Greek mercenary commander called Charidemus disagreed. He was a plain-speaking middle-aged professional soldier. Apparently he had known King Philip, but he was an Athenian citizen and had spent most of a distinguished career fighting the Macedonians. In his thirties he had served under Mentor and Memnon. Like other Hellenes, he was blunt and he patronized "barbarians." He was neither liked nor trusted at court.

Charidemus recommended that Darius should on no account stake his empire on a throw of the dice. Instead of leading his army against Alexander, he should send a competent general with a substantial force (the empire was rich in human capital) and hold himself and most of his military strength in reserve. One third of this force should be Greek mercenaries, better fighters by far than Persian levies. Charidemus unwisely hinted that if asked he would willingly assume responsibility for the success of his plan.

The Great King's courtiers, however, insinuated that Charidemus wanted the command for himself so that he could betray the empire to the Macedonians. Charidemus lost his temper and insinuated in turn that Persian soldiers were unmanly. Darius, upset, grabbed Charidemus's belt, a traditional gesture for ordering an execution, and handed him over to attendants, who led him off to his doom. As he left the room, he shouted that the king would change his mind, for he would soon witness the overthrow of his empire, repayment for his unjust punishment.

Darius did in fact recognize the superiority of the Hellenic hoplite and soon reproached himself for having made a serious mistake. Belatedly taking Charidemus's point, he looked about for a competent general. But he had liquidated the leading candidate and accepted that he would have to be his own commander-in-chief.

Some weeks later, Darius again sought advice. His army had gathered at Babylon and slowly made its way west, a journey of more than 570 miles. It was perhaps 100,000 men strong, including about ten thousand each of cavalry, of the Immortals (elite infantry), and of Greek mercenaries.

By October the Great King had reached the wide, flat plain east of the Amanus Mountains and encamped near a town called Sochoi. He was filled with optimism. Here was an ideal spot for a battle on his terms, for it gave his multitudinous host plenty of space to spread out and outflank the Macedonians. But a question nagged at him. Should he remain where he was and wait for Alexander to turn up? This would be difficult: a large army could not stay for long in any one place before it exhausted local food supplies. The Persians would soon have to move on in any event.

Or perhaps Darius should hunt down Alexander. That would mean pushing on through one or other of the narrow passes that led to the Cilician plain. The Persians had heard of Alexander's illness and suspected that he may have lost heart for a fight. Perhaps he would never come out into the open.

Darius reconvened his Friends, who were optimistic about his chances. It mattered little, they argued, where the battle was fought, for his powerful cavalry would trample Alexander's army underfoot and win the day. A renegade from the Macedonian court, Amyntas (yet another one), son of Antiochus, had joined the Persians and took an opposing view. He insisted that the Persians should not budge. He knew his Alexander and told Darius: "He will come and find you wherever you are. In fact, he is probably already on his way."

The Great King also questioned the leaders of the late Memnon's Hellenic hoplites as to the wisest course of action. They were presumably aware of Charidemus's grisly end and their reply was candid but careful. They counseled Darius to retreat to the plains of Mesopotamia, where food and animal fodder would be plentiful, and to resist any temptation to move into the mountains, where he would lose the advantage of numbers.

Darius was prepared to give the proposal serious consideration, but his Persian officials reiterated the ingrained suspicion of Greek military experts that had done for Charidemus. The Greeks were of dubious loyalty, they claimed, and could be bought and sold. In fact, while it is true that unemployed Hellenes of fighting age hired themselves out to every comer, there is little evidence that the Great King's foreign troops ever betrayed him. And, as Memnon's career illustrated, they knew more about the art of war than did upper-class Persians.

The counselors suggested that the army be ordered to surround the Hellenes and spear them all to death. Darius rejected the idea out of hand. He remarked: "If giving advice brings danger of death, I will soon run out of advisers." He thanked the Greeks for their concern for him, but explained that retreat would mean certain defeat.

In that case, the logic of logistics left him with no alternative—if he would not go back, he would be obliged to go forward. That would mean leaving the plain and marching into the mountains.

AS FOR ALEXANDER, NOW RECOVERED, he too consulted with his senior command about the approaching battle. He agreed (for once) with the opinion of his senior general Parmenion. Curtius writes:

> In [Parmenion's] view, it was imperative for the Macedonians to avoid flat ground and open spaces where it was possible for them to be surrounded or caught in a pincer-movement. What he was frightened of was that they would be beaten by their own exhaustion rather than the enemy's courage—fresh Persian troops would keep coming to the front if they could take a position which did not restrict their movements. Such soundly-reasoned strategy was readily accepted.

So Alexander delayed the encounter with the Great King for as long as he could. He guessed that, the harvest long over, shortage of supplies would lure the hungry Persians into the defiles. He waited for Darius to move. He was learning to be cautious.

To keep himself busy, he left his base at Tarsus and passed by the supposed tomb of the Assyrian king Sardanapalus, whose capacity for self-indulgence was legendary. Alexander was told that the epitaph included this wish: "You, stranger, should eat, drink and have sex, as all other concerns are not worth this" (signifying a handclap). Here was the—entirely fictional—image of the effete barbarian, whom all good Greeks would easily vanquish. It was grist to the mill, we may take it, for Callisthenes and the Macedonian publicity department.

The king reduced the pro-Persian port of Soli in western Cilicia and spent a week with some elite infantry subduing mountain tribes; these actions secured his rear, but equally to the point they used up time. Returning to Soli, he staged massive celebrations in the Hellenic manner, which were a sharp (surely intentional) contrast with the "oriental" decadence of barbarian monarchs.

Careful of his troops' morale, the king announced a public holiday and a festival of culture. Punctiliously devout as always, he sacrificed to the healing god, Asclepius, in thanks for his return to health. He personally led a parade of the entire army. The entertainment program included a torch race and competitions in athletics and the performing arts.

Spirits, now high, were further lifted by the good news that the garrison guarding Caria had soundly defeated Ada's irrepressible son-in-law, Orontobates, and recovered parts of Caria that had been lost to her.

Parmenion was sent forward with troops to garrison the mountain passes that led into the plain where the Great King's host was waiting for orders. He drove out Persian guards from the Amanus Mountains. Alexander rode over to confer with him and reunite the army, which then marched along the coast through one of the passes and reached the ancient settlement of Issus.

Here Alexander again conferred with his senior commanders, who all recommended an immediate advance against the Persians, presumably directly into the plain. We now encounter a puzzle. Rather than accept this unsatisfactory advice and abandon the safety (and the advantage) of the mountains, the king turned south and followed the narrow littoral between the Amanus Mountains and the sea in the direction of Syria. He passed through a coastal defile called the Pillar of Jonah (where the whale reputedly spat out Jonah) and proceeded toward the Phoenician seaport of Myriandrus.

What did he expect to achieve by this maneuver? It is hard to say. If we assume that the Persians were still at Sochoi, he may have hoped that they would attack him through one of the passes to the coast. Supply always worried him and access to the sea would guarantee it.

The true answer to the question may lie with what Darius did next: he finally decided to make a move. Under the protection of a small military escort, he diverted his baggage train and noncombatants to Damascus in Syria. He also sent there all his money and "most precious treasures." Following imperial protocol, his mother, Sisygambis; his wife, Stateira; his unmarried daughters; and his small son stayed with him.

Knowing that the Macedonians held the Pillar of Jonah, Darius now led his entire army on a flanking maneuver. Leaving the plain, he crossed through the mountain barrier by a northern pass called the Amanus Gates, expecting to catch Alexander in his rear. If he was lucky and some of the Macedonian army was still in Cilicia, he might even be able to cut it in two.

The odd thing is that the Gates had been left unguarded and the Persians met no opposition when they passed through. It is most unlikely that Parmenion would have omitted to place a garrison there. The facts as we know them suggest that this was a carefully laid trap, luring Darius to enter Cilicia and then to pursue the Macedonians down the coast. Alexander would then turn around and face the enemy on narrow ground of his choosing.

It may be that Alexander decided to evacuate some or all of the mountain garrisons as his army moved south. Now that he was ready for action, it would have been illogical for him to prevent the enemy from leaving the plain, when that was exactly what he wanted him to do.

THE PERSIANS REACHED ISSUS, where Alexander had left his sick and wounded, who were unable to keep up with his column. Darius was now more sure than ever that the Macedonian invader had lost his nerve and was evading an engagement. Optimism made him cruel: egged on by his courtiers, he had the Macedonians' hands cut off and cauterized with pitch.

According to the Roman historian Curtius, "he then gave orders for the men to be taken around so that they could get an impression of his troops and, when they had sufficiently inspected everything, he told them to report what they had seen to their king."

Lacking modern means of communication, ancient armies often did not know where exactly their enemy was in the run-up to a pitched battle. They blundered about in a fog of unknowing. Alexander was exceptional in his careful use of mounted scouts who gathered as much information as possible not only about an opponent's location, but also about the lie of the land, distances, and the availability of fodder, food, and water. The scouts were, one might say, his binoculars.

He appears to have been surprised when told that Darius was behind him. He did not immediately trust the report and wanted more data than his mutilated men were able to give. He sent some of his Companions in a thirty-oared ship with instructions to sail up the coast and see if what he had been told was true or not. Was the Great King there in person with his entire force? For all he knew, a second army group was planning a pincer attack from another direction. As evening fell, the Companions had their answer. From their safe vantage point on the water, they sighted a huge body of men. Campfires were lighting up everywhere in the darkening panorama. This was the Persian multitude at its full extent—and only eleven and a half miles from the Macedonian army.

Whether by luck or good judgment, Alexander had got his way. If he retraced his steps, he would meet Darius somewhere along the thin coastal strip he had just marched along, where the Persian army would be cribbed and confined. For all that, his nerves were on edge. In the darkness he climbed to the top of a ridge and by the light of torches sacrificed to the tutelary gods of the locality to win their favor.

The Macedonians were exhausted and out of sorts. In the past couple of days they had marched seventy miles and on the previous night been washed out of their tents by a torrential downpour. Now on the morrow they had to march back the way they came and face a vastly more numerous enemy.

Aware of the need to boost morale, Alexander gathered round him his generals and Companion cavalry squadron leaders and gave them a brief, intense, and outrageously optimistic talk. In summary, they had already beaten the Persians once, the gods were on their side, and Macedonians were better soldiers than Persians (Xenophon and the Ten Thousand had proved it years ago). The men gathered round him, shouted their approval, and urged him to lead them on then and there.

There was indeed no time to lose. Alexander arranged for the army to eat its evening meal and sent off a few horsemen and archers to reconnoiter the route. Then as dusk thickened the entire army marched back to the Pillar of Jonah, where they slept among the crags.

THE THIN RIBBON OF LAND expanded into a plain about one and a half miles wide, stretching from the shore to a line of foothills. It was bisected by a shallow river, the Pinarus, which ran obliquely to the sea. Here and there steep sides were covered with brambles. Except near the water itself, the ground was uneven and broken by gullies and small streambeds.

The Great King was encamped north of the Pinarus. He was shocked when he watched the Macedonians spread out into open country. He had expected to encounter a whipped enemy in full retreat, but here was Alexander ready to strike. He sent out his cavalry south of the river to screen and safeguard the deployment of his forces. The space at his disposal was uncomfortably restricted. He lined up his best fighters, the Greek mercenaries, in the center. These were flanked by lightly armed infantry, the Cardaces, who were covered by archers and protected by an improvised stockade along the riverbank (clearly they were not altogether to be relied on). Their role was defensive rather than aggressive. There was no room for the rest of the infantry, presumably Asian levies of one sort or another, which had to be stacked up at the back.

According to Curtius, the Great King "wanted the battle to be decided by a cavalry engagement, for he took it that the phalanx was the main strength of the Macedonian army." A conventional arrangement would have had cavalry on each wing with infantry in the middle, but Darius decided to mass almost all his horse on the right. These would deliver a massive blow that would rout the heavily outnumbered Macedonian cavalry opposite; they would then turn left to charge Alexander's phalanx on its flank. Meanwhile the Persian left wing reached the foothills, crossed the river, and occupied high ground beyond the expected limit of Alexander's line, thus posing a serious threat of encirclement.

The Macedonian army took some time to arrive. It had been marching in column of route, infantry first and afterward cavalry. As it debouched onto the plain, its front line broadened to fill the land available. The powerful but inflexible phalanx took the center and on its immediate right stood the hypaspists.

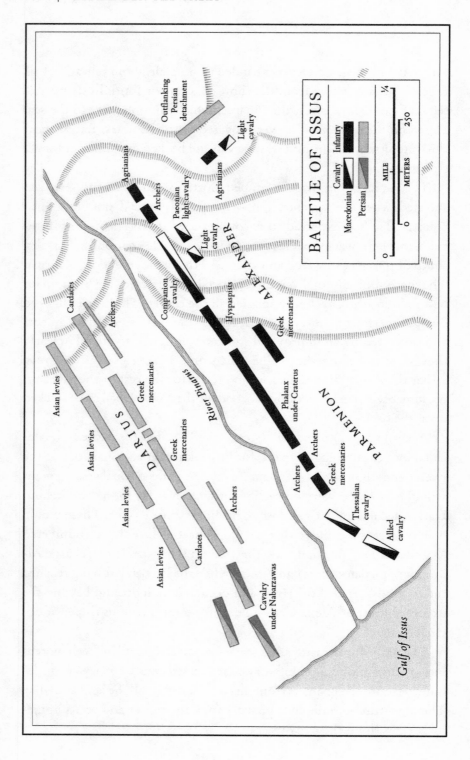

BATTLE OF ISSUS

Macedonian
Persian

Cavalry Infantry

Cavalry

MILE
METERS

Outflanking
Persian
detachment

Light
cavalry

Agrianians

Agrianians

Archers

Paeonian
light cavalry

Light
cavalry

Companion
cavalry

ALEXANDER

Hypaspists

Greek
mercenaries

Archers

Cardaces

Asian levies

Greek
mercenaries

Asian levies

DARIUS

Greek
mercenaries

River Pinarus

Phalanx
under Craterus

PARMENION

Asian levies

Greek
mercenaries

Archers

Greek
mercenaries

Archers

Asian levies

Cardaces

Archers

Thessalian
cavalry

Allied
cavalry

Cavalry
under Nabarzawas

Gulf of Issus

As the cavalry filtered out from its coastal track, Alexander sent the Greek and allied contingents to his left wing, which he placed under Parmenion's overall command with strict instructions not to allow the slightest gap between his forces and the sea. It would be a disaster if the Persians were allowed to outflank him.

On his right wing, Alexander placed the Companion cavalry and the elite Thessalian horse next to the hypaspists, whose function was to act as a flexible link between them and the phalanx. In addition, there were the scouts, or *prodromoi,* and the Paeonian light horse; also the irregulars—slingers, Cretan archers, and, most trusted of all, the javelin-throwing Agrianians. These acted as skirmishers in front of the main blocks of cavalry and infantry during the preliminary stage of the battle before taking their places in the line. Foot soldiers contributed by the Hellenic allies were held in reserve behind the phalanx, not trusted to fight strongly against fellow Greeks.

Alexander's plan of action was the mirror image of the Great King's. He intended to ride with the Companions against what he assumed would be Persian cavalry opposite, clear them from the field, and then attack the flank and rear of the Greek mercenaries. His ultimate target was the Great King himself, who by tradition stood richly robed in a high, gorgeously decorated, gem-encrusted chariot at the center of his line (namely, amid the Greek mercenaries). He was protected by the royal bodyguard of crack Persian soldiers. If he could be killed or was forced to flee, the battle—probably even the war—would be won.

Once the Persians had taken up their battle stations, their cavalry withdrew across the river to their position on the right and Alexander had a chance to observe their dispositions. He was pleased that the enemy had adopted a strong defensive posture, for it was attack that won a battle.

However, he made two urgent corrections. Alarmed by Darius's last-minute massing of cavalry beside the sea, he ordered the Thessalians to gallop unobserved behind his phalanx to reinforce Parmenion's cavalry on the left. He filled the gap this created by bringing up some of the Greek reserve and moving along two squadrons of Companions.

The massing of the Persian cavalry posed an obvious threat, but in compensation the Companions mainly faced light infantry, which, all other things being equal, they should find it easy enough to sweep from the field.

Alexander also took steps to eliminate the outflanking threat in the hills that curved round behind the Macedonian line. The Agrianians and a few archers drove off the Persians and then took their places at the end of the Macedonian line. Three hundred horse were delegated to keep an eye on the fugitives, and they caused no more trouble.

THE DAY WAS WEARING on and it may have been as late as half past four in the afternoon. But Alexander took his time.

He rode up and down the length of his front, encouraging his men to show what they were worth. They cheered back enthusiastically. The enemy stood watching and made no attempt to interfere. The king called out officers by name and title, as well as individuals noted for valor in earlier battles. He kept motioning with his hand to slow the pace of the advance. He wanted to ensure that the phalanx kept its dressing. Every now and again he halted the army to calm nerves.

As soon as the Macedonians came within missile range, Alexander changed gear. He led the Companions in a sudden charge across the river, probably at the apex of a wedge formation. After weeks of vigilant calculation—for he had learned from the Granicus—he was free to be a daredevil again. Stockades were quickly knocked down and the light-armed Cardaces took to their heels. The cavalry then turned and drove aggressively into the side and rear of the Great King's Greeks.

Up to this point, these competent and disciplined foot soldiers were doing very well, as were the Persian cavalry by the seashore. And Alexander was on the verge of a humiliating defeat, for the hypaspists and the phalanx could not keep up with the Companions. They lost their dressing and a gap opened into which the Greek mercenaries opposite moved forward. The fighting was bitter. In some places the Macedonians struggled to climb up sheer riverbanks as high as five feet, and were pushed back into the water. One hundred and twenty of them and a phalanx commander fell in the struggle to hold the line.

The Great King's heavy cavalry, its riders armed in metal plate, charged across the river and trampled down a Thessalian squadron. The fighting was on a narrow front, so the Persians were unable to make the most of their numbers. Also they were not so mobile as the Thessalians. Nevertheless, they maintained their onslaught and Parmenion worried that his wing would collapse.

On the far side of the field, having cleared away the Cardaces (and the few cavalry whom Darius had not transferred to his right wing), the Companions turned the scale. They plowed into the Greeks from their side and rear. It may be that the hypaspists and one or two phalanx battalions joined them. The Greeks wavered and Alexander's hard-pressed foot soldiers recovered their dressing and at last pushed forward across the Pinarus.

Just as the Macedonian king had been the Persians' number one target at the Granicus, so Darius, dead or alive, was now Alexander's. He must have remembered Xenophon's description of Cyrus the Younger at the Battle of Cunaxa as the pretender cut a path with his scimitar to his brother, Artaxerxes, but was struck down before reaching him.

Driving through or behind the crumbling Greek formation, Alexander meant to succeed where Cyrus had failed. He rode pell-mell in the direction of the Great King. Although some accounts portray Darius as timid and cowardly, this was a man who (as we have seen) had fought an enemy in single combat and won. Other reports correctly show that he and his guards, including his brother Oxyathres, fought fiercely. Many Persian noblemen, among them the satrap of Egypt, fell defending their master; Alexander, as ever placing himself in harm's way, received a sword-graze to his right thigh.

The Great King saw that the left half of his army was in full flight. It looked as if the battle was lost. If resistance to the Macedonian invader was to continue, it was essential that he be neither captured nor killed. So, reluctantly, he turned his chariot round and withdrew. The ground he traveled over was so rutted and bumpy that he switched to a horse for ease and speed, leaving behind his shield and bow. To avoid recognition, he also discarded his imperial robe and insignia (later Alexander took charge of the abandoned chariot and the other items). Darius did not halt until he had placed the Euphrates between him and his pursuers.

His absence was soon noticed. The Greek mercenaries had learned from the massacre at the Granicus that they would have a short future if cornered. They quit the field quickly and in relatively good order. Thousands of horsemen tried to escape as the Thessalians galloped after them, and many came to grief.

A rout developed and it was now that most of the casualties occurred. The Asian levies in the rear fared especially badly. Their only role in the struggle had been to be stampeded and slaughtered when it was over. Overall, the losses in men and horses were very great—many thousands, although we cannot estimate a likely number. As for the Macedonians, 150 horsemen and 300 foot soldiers lost their lives, and 4,500 men were wounded. This was rather a long casualty list for a victorious army and bore witness to the fierceness of the conflict. Alexander played down his own injury when he sent a dispatch to Antipater in Pella. "I myself happened," he writes, "to be wounded in the thigh by a dagger. But nothing untoward resulted from the blow either immediately or later." Once more, he had been lucky.

Alexander waited until he was sure that Parmenion and his cavalry were safe and that there was no more fighting to be done before he set off in pursuit of the Great King. The day was nearly over, but he and some Companions rode into the deepening dusk for more than twenty miles. Ptolemy, one of his close friends and supporters, was with him and recalls crossing a ravine piled high with corpses. But Darius had too long a lead and after nightfall the pursuers turned round and made for the camp.

ALEXANDER AND HIS RETINUE ARRIVED, tired and grimy, at about midnight. They found the Macedonians busy looting the enemy's camp. Although the Persian baggage train had been sent to Damascus for safety, there were rich pickings.

The capacious royal pavilion had been set aside for Alexander's personal use and its contents had been left untouched, for traditionally this was his spoil. It was lavishly appointed, with luxurious furniture and well-dressed servants. The king's first priority was to clean up. He unbuckled his armor, saying: "Let's wash off the sweat of battle in Darius's bath." "No, in Alexander's bath, now," one of his Companions corrected, toadily.

According to Plutarch, when Alexander entered the bathroom

he saw that the basins and jugs and tubs and caskets containing unguents were all made of gold and elaborately carved, and noticed that the room was marvelously fragrant with spices and unguents and then, passing from this into a spacious and lofty tent, he observed the magnificence of the dining-couches, the tables and the banquet which had been set out for him. He turned to his companions and remarked, "So this, it seems, is what it is to be a king."

When Alexander sat down to supper he heard sounds of women wailing. He was told that Darius's mother, Sisygambis, and the other women of the family had seen his chariot and its contents brought back from the field, and deduced that their owner was dead. He sent one of his staff to reassure them that the Great King was alive. He also told them that Alexander had decided that they should retain the style and title of queens and princesses.

The following morning, in spite of his own injury, Alexander visited and comforted the wounded. He then paraded the whole army and presided over the funeral rites and cremation of the fallen. He gave instructions that the Persians should be given the same simple ceremony (with so many casualties, this must have been a burdensome business). He allowed Sisygambis to bury whomever she wished in the more elaborate traditional Persian fashion, but, not wishing to irritate her captor, she restricted her choice to a few close relatives.

The king consecrated three altars on the banks of the river Pinarus to Zeus, his ancestor Heracles, and Athena, the goddess of war and wisdom. He allowed his army some days for rest and relaxation and then made for Syria, sending Parmenion ahead to Damascus where the king's baggage train was to be found.

Later in the day, Alexander and Hephaestion paid the royal ladies a courtesy call. They were both wearing plain Macedonian tunics. Because Hephaestion was the taller and more handsome of the two, Sisygambis took him to be the king and prostrated herself at his feet. Some captive eunuchs pointed out her mistake. She was covered in confusion, but gamely did obeisance again, this time correctly.

"Don't worry, Mother," Alexander replied. "You didn't mix us up. Actually, he is Alexander too."

It was a telling exchange. For one thing, it demonstrated the king's public closeness to Hephaestion, the one man who shared all his secrets. Even more remarkable was his use of the word "mother." Sisygambis was to be the latest middle-aged woman on whom he bestowed filial affection, even love. They became close and remained the best of friends until the end of their days.

As always with the king, behind sentiment lay practical calculation. The royal women were valuable pawns in any future negotiations with Darius. But they would be best held in reserve, for Alexander could not imagine a price high enough to be worth their return.

THE PROPHECY AT GORDIUM was proving to be accurate. The lordship of Asia lay within Alexander's grasp. But there was still much to do.

Both the kings at Issus had shared the same plan, but there proved to be differences between them in practice. The Macedonian troops (and especially the Companions) were of an altogether superior quality, thanks to rigorous training and attention to morale. Alexander's dash and sense of timing had no equivalent in the Persian high command. He was a soldier as well as a general and his personal bravery gave a material psychological boost to the cavalrymen under his direct command; his targeting of Darius led directly to his flight and the resulting Persian collapse.

The Macedonian king had found a winning battle formula, which he hoped to repeat—a defensive role on the left, maintenance of the bristling phalanx in the center, and a carefully timed aggressive cavalry charge from the right. His eagle eye for interpreting enemy movements and reacting instantaneously to them was as sharp as ever. He had learned to be cautious in his preparations and to manage his impetuosity.

One of Alexander's traits was a talent for delegation. This brought out the best in his officers, as their strong performance during the height of the fighting went to show, when noise, confusion, dust, and his own exertions isolated him from them and they themselves had to decide what to do.

Issus was a humiliation for Darius. He was a competent and courageous leader, but he was limited to being a symbol. He was compelled by tradition and his subjects' expectations to show himself on the battlefield in all his regal splendor. He did not have the agency his rival did. His role was to be seen; he was not supposed to take part. He had to be, not do.

The victory was total, but it was not a knockout blow. Indeed, one could say that it was a grave disappointment. The strategy of capturing the empire in a single great battle in which Darius was killed or captured had failed. Everything would need to be done again. The invader controlled Asia Minor, but otherwise the empire was intact.

The Great King gathered together a good number of loyal Greeks and other stragglers from the debacle, returned to his capital cities of Susa and Persepolis, and recovered his balance. A body of survivors tried hard to recapture the Anatolian plateau, although ultimately without success. The Macedonian renegade Amyntas with four other Greek defectors led eight thousand Greek mercenaries to Cyprus. On the principle that "in the present circumstances a man could hold whatever he seized as a rightful possession," he recruited more men and ships and sailed for Egypt, where he pretended to have been sent by Darius as the new satrap (to replace the one killed at Issus). For a man whom iron fate had condemned to repeated disappointment, nothing changed. He was cut to pieces in a skirmish outside Memphis.

Alexander faced two intractable questions. First, what should he do now? The simplest answer was to march his army eastward, somewhere catch the Great King, who would not have had time to assemble a new army, and win a final showdown—perhaps in Babylonia or in Persia.

There were objections. The Macedonians knew little, apart from what they had gleaned from Herodotus and Xenophon, about the territory through which they would be traveling, and for a commander passionate about logistics that was a grave weakness. The whereabouts of Darius were unknown and tracking down an elusive foe in remote mountains and deserts could trigger some sort of unpredictable guerrilla conflict.

Worse still, so long as there was a Persian fleet sailing around the Aegean Sea, Alexander faced the prospect of losing the western provinces of the empire while pursuing Darius in the east. To eliminate this danger he needed to persuade the great Phoenician city-states such as Sidon and Tyre, which provided most of the Persian navy's crews, to transfer their loyalty to him. They were already wobbling, but the king needed certainty.

So the answer to the first question was to leave the Great King to his own devices while Alexander himself completed the conquest of the Mediterranean seaboard as far as and including the satrapy of Egypt. Darius would need a year or so to raise a new, even larger army. This was just what Alexander wanted, for it would give him the chance to win another, and this time surely final, set-piece battle.

The second question was more fundamental. What was Alexander's war aim? Had the verdict of Issus changed it? It is difficult to imagine him declaring victory and marching home to Macedonia at the head of his men. He was already governing most of Asia Minor, appointing satraps and levying taxes, and he presumably meant to continue as he had started. And, as has already been argued, if he did leave, or even if he accepted the new status quo as sufficient, it would not be long before the Persians were back, seeking retaliation and demanding their old lands.

Unless he defeated Darius definitively, his territorial gains would be precariously held. So the war had to continue. But if he overthrew the Great King, who would govern the empire? There could be only one candidate: Alexander himself.

A fly was caught in the amber. His Macedonians were enjoying their wonderful escapade, but they expected to return to their native land in the not-too-distant future. After all, the king had promised in his pre-battle pep talk that victory would "put an end to their labors and crown their glory." They had not the slightest intention of spending the rest of their lives fighting their way mile by mile through the world's largest empire and becoming an army of occupation.

There was no need to resolve the contradiction yet, but intelligent observers could see that there was trouble in store. They kept their mouths shut, though, and Alexander did not repeat a promise made in the heat of the moment.

CHAPTER 8

IMMORTAL LONGINGS

Unfamiliar gusts of snow blew across the inland plateau on which the Syrian capital of Damascus stood. An unusually hard winter threatened. Faint dustings whitened the farmland and irrigation channels outside the walls.

Through this landscape a long trail of noble Persians and camp followers was abandoning the city. The governor had claimed it could not be defended against the triumphant Macedonians and ordered an evacuation. A crowd of porters, guarded by an armed escort, were carrying the treasures and cash that Darius had sent to Damascus for safekeeping. These included fabulously expensive robes, stiff with purple and gold embroidery. The temperature was so low that the porters put on these costumes in an attempt to warm themselves.

The governor was playing a double game, for he wanted to hand over the entire contents of the baggage train to Alexander, but not be seen to do so. He sent a message to Parmenion, who was on his way to take it over, that he was willing to bring the Great King's store of gold and silver out of the city into open country where it would be easy to confiscate without opposition.

When the Macedonian general at the head of his troops arrived on the scene and saw a crowd of refugees, the exotically dressed porters, and the armed escort, his suspicions were aroused. This looked like a trap. He ordered his Thessalian cavalry to charge.

The porters dropped their goods and took to their heels, while the guards, no braver, also threw down their weapons and made for familiar side roads. Seven thousand pack animals were now on the loose. The royal treasure was scattered across the snowy fields in vast quantities: more than 2,500 talents of coined money—an enormous sum—golden vessels, golden bridles, elaborately decorated tents, and wagons laden with uncounted wealth. Our sources speak of more than two tons' worth of gold goblets and cups inlaid with precious stones.

This was many Macedonians' introduction to the luxury of the barbarian way of life and, as Plutarch says neatly, "From now onwards, like dogs that have picked up a scent, they pressed on to track down the wealth of the Persians."

Everything was safely gathered up and a report sent to Alexander. This was accompanied by a beautifully made casket, which was regarded by the keepers of Darius's treasure as the finest item of all. Alexander asked his friends what he should keep in it as his most precious possession. Many different suggestions were aired, but in the end Alexander announced that he had decided to keep his copy of the *Iliad* there.

Alexander instructed Parmenion to return Darius's baggage train to Damascus and told him to guard it carefully. He also charged him with the military oversight of lowland Syria, the province in which Damascus was situated, and gave him authority to mint coins.

So far as human valuables were concerned, Parmenion took into custody the Great King's household. This included 277 caterers, seventeen bartenders, and, evidence of Darius at leisure, more than three hundred concubines. Of greater political value were a number of senior Persians, including women of the imperial family: three unmarried daughters of Darius's predecessor Artaxerxes Ochus; Ochus's widow; and the daughter of Darius's brave brother Oxyathres. Among other prisoners of war were the wife and daughter of Pharnabazus, Memnon's successor as commander-in-chief of Asia Minor's coastal area and of the navy. All these people would raise a great deal of money if ransomed. But Alexander was now, without exaggeration, rich beyond the dreams of avarice and may have kept his captives at court along with Sisygambis and Stateira. He never again suffered from financial difficulties.

Some envoys from Thebes (or the memory of it), Athens, and Sparta had the bad luck to be visiting the Great King at the time of the Issus catastrophe. Their city-states wanted to break up the League of Corinth, of which they were reluctant members, and were seeking an entente with the Great King. Ordinarily this would have been a serious offense in Alexander's eyes, but he was minded to be lenient. As he had laid waste their city, the Thebans' enmity was understandable, even praiseworthy. So he released them. The Athenian ambassador was the son of a famous military commander, Iphicrates, whom he admired, and he retained him as an honored guest; when the ambassador died later (of natural causes), Alexander arranged for his bones to be sent to his family in Athens.

AMONG THE PERSIAN WOMEN at Damascus was a great beauty. She was Barsine, one of the copious offspring of Artabazus, nephew of Artaxerxes III. As we have seen, Barsine spent time in Pella as an exile with her father when Alexander was a child. Her date of birth is unknown, but she was probably now in her early to midthirties.

She had led a life crowded with incident. Her mother came from the Greek island of Rhodes and was sister of the two wily military commanders in Darius's service, Mentor and Memnon. Consanguinity was no bar: Barsine married the first of her uncles, perhaps not long after reaching puberty. By him she had three children, all daughters. But by 336 or earlier Mentor was dead, and Barsine wedded Memnon, by whom she had a son. As reported, her new husband sent her to Darius as a pledge of his good faith when he signed up for service as the Great King's admiral and military commander in the Aegean and Asia. This was why she found herself in Damascus as a member of the royal court. By now she had been widowed for a second time and was without a male protector.

Alexander's sexuality seems to have been enlarging its scope, for he is reported to have fallen in love with Barsine. Apparently she was the first woman he had sex with. She was well equipped to please; being some ten years older, she could bring the expertise of a mature woman to bear on a callow (at least so far as straight sex was concerned) male.

As well as good looks, she had received a Greek education and was, Plutarch observes, "of a gentle disposition." It was helpful, too, that Achaemenid blood ran in her veins.

Parmenion had been pressing Alexander hard for years to do what was necessary with a socially distinguished woman and produce children. On this occasion he seems to have played the part of matchmaker. The lovers settled into a couple and Barsine gave birth to a son. They named him Heracles after the demigod and hero who was Alexander's ancestor. But however fond they were, they never married. (The whereabouts of Barsine's father, Artabazus, at this time is unknown, but unlike his daughter, if she had a choice in the matter, he remained loyal to Darius.)

Despite his new love interest, the old asexual Alexander had by no means disappeared. When he met his female captives, he said jokingly: "These Persian women are an irritation of the eyes." The remark picked up on a phrase in Herodotus; some ambassadors from the Great King once complained that royal Macedonian women "irritated their eyes," and then scandalously touched their breasts and tried to kiss them. In self-conscious contrast, Alexander made a show of his chastity, or so writes Plutarch, by paying the members of Darius's harem as little attention as if they were stone statues.

The king strongly objected to the sexual trafficking of slaves or prisoners. Philoxenus, the commander of his forces on the seacoast, who had satrapal powers, wrote to him to say that he had with him a slave merchant from Tarentum in Italy who was offering two exceptionally good-looking boys for sale. Would Alexander be interested in buying them? The king was furious. He asked his friends what evidence of depravity Philoxenus could ever have seen in him that he should waste his time on such a monstrous proposal.

A rich and influential courtier called Hagnon, who was one of Alexander's Companions, made a similarly ill-judged proposition. He sent the king a letter saying that he wanted to buy him a young slave boy whose beauty was the talk of Corinth. Hagnon received a sharp rebuke for his temerity. (These stories, we may note in passing, do confirm a general perception among his contemporaries that Alexander had sex with males.)

When the king heard that two Macedonian soldiers serving under

Parmenion had seduced the wives of some Greek mercenaries, he allegedly wrote to the general that if convicted they should be put down like wild animals.

It would seem that he repeatedly discussed sexual topics with Parmenion. He commented in the same letter: "So far as I myself am concerned, it will be found that not only have I never seen nor wished to see Darius's wife, but I have never even allowed her beauty to be discussed in my presence." If Alexander seems to be protesting too much, it is worth noting that no ancient commentator accused him of sleeping with the queen.

When he was a child, Alexander lived in Philip's boisterous court where sex with people of every gender was rough, ready, and routine. Pretty slaves will have been welcomed with enthusiasm. Our less than trustworthy sources assert no linkage, but it is not a wild surmise that Alexander's childhood experiences fed into adult distaste. He expected his own behavior and that of those around him to promote, if not virtue, then at least restraint.

DARIUS SENT A LETTER to the king of Macedonia. He wrote as "monarch to monarch," quite a concession for a ruler who admitted no equals, and asked for the release of his close relatives—his mother, wife, and children—in return for a large ransom. The fantastic sum of ten thousand talents was mentioned. He also proposed a treaty of friendship and, according to Diodorus, agreed to cede the territory and cities of Asia west of the Halys River. In other words, the war aim of annexing what is now Turkey and marching no farther east, as set out by that international intellectual Isocrates and probably endorsed privately by Philip, would be fully achieved.

Darius thought it a very good offer. So did Parmenion when the king brought the letter to his advisory council. He said, perhaps recalling military planning conversations with his previous master: "I would accept those terms if I were Alexander." "So would I, by Zeus, if I were Parmenion," came the crushing rejoinder.

In fact, the offer was suspect and the king was right to reject it. The treaty of friendship was not based on a true meeting of interests and was, rather, a long-term booby trap. The Macedonians would have had to defend an immensely long frontier; instability and war would have been permanent.

Alexander's reply opened with a rhetorical reminder that his campaign was a response to the two invasions of Greece more than a century before. He was not the aggressor, but was acting in self-defense (not the most convincing of claims). Darius had suborned Philip's assassins (almost certainly untrue, but plausible) and bribed Greek statesmen to rise against him (true, but in reaction to threats and invasion). Darius himself was a usurper (arguably so; a eunuch had placed him on the throne). Alexander went on:

> It is for you, then, to come to me as lord over all Asia. If you are afraid I will harm you when you come, send some of your people to bring you back my guarantees. And when you have come you can ask me for your mother and wife and children and anything else you wish, and you shall have them. Whatever you persuade me to give shall be yours. And in future address any communications to me as the king of Asia, and do not write as an equal, but tell me as the master of all your possessions what it is that you need. Failing this, I intend to treat you as a criminal. But if you wish to dispute the kingship, stand your ground and fight for it. Do not run away, as I shall come after you wherever you are.

When Darius received this forbidding missive, he abandoned hope of negotiation and began to recruit another army, this time from his eastern provinces. It was exactly the response Alexander had hoped to provoke.

THE MAN, DRESSED IN RAGS, worked as a gardener and water carrier in the suburbs of the Phoenician seaport of Sidon in Syria. Called Abdalonymus, he struggled to get by on a tiny income. Preoccupied with his labors, he had not noticed the political and military activities of the day.

The Battle of Issus passed him by, as did the arrival outside Sidon of the Macedonian army. Alexander accepted the surrender of the northern cities of Syria. The king of Sidon handed over his mini-state, although this did him no favors with the popular party, who believed that he was at heart pro-Persian. He was unceremoniously deposed and Alexander instructed Hephaestion to find a new king for Sidon.

Abdalonymus knew nothing of these high events.

Hephaestion was billeted with two wealthy young Sidonians and asked them for advice on suitable candidates. He was impressed by his hosts and inquired if they might be interested in the job. They declined, saying that Sidonians would only accept as king a member of the royal family. As a matter of fact, they claimed, they knew the very man for the job. He was distantly related to the ruling family and was an honest man.

Abdalonymus was drawing water from a well or doing some weeding when the two young men, in armor, came unannounced into the garden where he was working, carrying the royal robe and insignia. They hailed him as king. He was sure he must be dreaming and asked the visitors not to mock him. They eventually persuaded him of their good faith, got him washed, threw away his rags, and dressed him in purple and gold.

The city's upper class strongly objected to the appointment on the grounds of Abdalonymus's poverty and obscurity, so Alexander called him in for an interview. He asked him: "How well were you able to endure poverty?" to which Abdalonymus replied: "I only hope I will be able to put up with power as contentedly. I had nothing, and I lacked nothing." Alexander was impressed by the man's sangfroid and confirmed the nomination.

His reign seems to have been successful, if only in the sense that it lasted long enough for a son to follow him on the throne. But nothing is known of his activities during Alexander's lifetime, saving a gift of perfume made from henna, a specialty of Sidon, and some lilies that he sent to Alexander.

THE CAPITULATION OF SIDON was a necessary precursor of the main event, the siege of the great mercantile seaport of Tyre farther down the Phoenician coast (in today's Lebanon).

The city stood proud and unconquerable (its inhabitants were certain of this) half a mile from shore. It was built on a rocky island with a circumference of two and three quarter miles and was surrounded by a towering wall, 150 feet high on its landward side. Space within these fortifications was limited, and multistory houses were crowded together to provide homes for some forty thousand souls.

Tyre was the richest and most powerful of the many Phoenician settlements along the Syrian littoral. It had two fine harbors, the Sidonian in the north and the Egyptian in the south. Across the water on the mainland, Old Tyre was the city's original site although now a suburb of the island. Herodotus paid a visit in the mid-fifth century B.C. and was told Tyre had been founded more than two millennia previously.

The historian was much impressed by the temple of Melqart, the city's tutelary god, whom the Greeks equated with Heracles. He reported: "I visited the temple and found that the offerings which adorned it were numerous and valuable, not the least remarkable being two pillars, one of pure gold, the other of emerald which gleamed in the dark with a strange luminosity."

For centuries Tyre had made its living, and a very prosperous one, from trade, and its ships did business across the Mediterranean. As long ago as the seventh century B.C., the Jewish prophet Ezekiel had Jehovah pronounce:

> You say, Tyre, "I am perfect in beauty."
> Your domain was on the high seas;
> your builders brought your beauty to perfection.
> They made all your timbers of juniper from Senir;
> they took a cedar from Lebanon to make a mast for you.
> Of oaks from Bashan they made your oars;
> of cypress wood from the coasts of Cyprus
> they made your deck, adorned with ivory.
> Fine embroidered linen from Egypt was your sail
> and served as your banner;
> your awnings were of blue and purple
> from the coasts of Elishah.

Tyrians' income in kind included copper, lead, and other metals, ivory tusks and ebony, perfumes, oil, and precious stones. They were famous for the production of a purple or dark red dye, especially prized for the fastness of its color. The dye was extracted from sea snails of the family Muricidae. It was difficult to manufacture, in great demand and very expensive. Phoenicia, the semitic region of which Tyre was a leading member, was so named after the Greek word for dark red, *phoinos*.

A shadow fell across Tyre's uninterrupted prosperity. According to Ezekiel, Jehovah would not forgive the city for its hostility to his chosen people and predicted its destruction:

> Your end will be sudden and terrible,
> and you will cease to exist for all time.

But ages passed without catastrophe and the city's future remained as bright as ever.

The verdict of Issus and the surrender of Phoenician cities such as Sidon captured the attention of the Tyrians, but they did not expect serious trouble even when in January 332 the Macedonian army marched down from Sidon twenty miles away and encamped on the mainland opposite the island city.

At heart the Tyrian authorities, including the crown prince (in the absence of their king, Azemilcus, in service with the Persian fleet), were loyal to the Persian empire and, faced by the force majeure of a victorious Macedonian army, preferred alliance to capitulation. They did not want to let foreign troops into their city. Already on cordial terms with Alexander, they had supplied provisions to the Macedonian army, but they knew they had to tread carefully. They sent envoys across the channel and presented the king with a golden crown, offering to obey any orders he might give.

The king thanked them warmly, but seems to have sensed that something was being withheld. He asked the envoys to tell their government that he intended to "pay his dues to Heracles," or in plain terms sacrifice to Melqart, at his sanctuary on the island. In other words, he was going to enter the city. This was closer to surrender than entente.

When the embassy returned, the message had slightly changed. The Tyrians would obey any orders Alexander might give, except to allow either Persians or Macedonians to enter their city. In an attempt to sweeten the pill, they added that there was a temple of Melqart in Old Tyre, where he would be more than welcome to sacrifice.

Unlike Sidon, Tyre had opted for apparent neutrality. Alexander lost his temper and dismissed the embassy with the bleak promise: "I will either enter your city, or storm it." The envoys were shaken by Alexander's performance and once back home they advised their fellow citizens that it might be wise to let him in after all. However, the Tyrians were certain that, thanks to its fortifications, their island fastness was impregnable. Besides, the Persian navy ruled the waves. Their colony, the powerful north African merchant city of Carthage, promised practical aid. Alexander's threats were empty.

According to Diodorus, they cheerfully agreed to undergo a siege:

> Because they were doing Darius a good turn, they were confirming their loyalty to him. They thought they would get great rewards from the king for this favor, which involved drawing Alexander into a protracted and difficult siege. In that way they would give Darius a breathing space for his preparations.

But Alexander determined to destroy Tyre and nothing would hold him back. His first step was that of a typical Macedonian monarch; he took counsel of his army. He summoned his Companions and army leaders and explained his case for capturing Tyre. He was aware this would not be a popular decision, for sieges tended to be bloody affairs.

He said that it would be unsafe to proceed to Egypt, their next stop, with a hostile or at least ambivalent Tyre in the rear. The Persians still held Cyprus and with their fleet, mostly consisting of Phoenician galleys, they could very well win back the Mediterranean seaboard and stir up an already restless Greece, as Memnon had once planned. On the other hand, with Tyre taken most of Phoenicia would fall under Macedonian control. There was then every likelihood that their navies would defect and join Alexander's fleet. The Great King would lose Cyprus and his supremacy at sea would be at an end.

Alexander concluded:

When we have conquered Egypt, we shall have no further worries for Greece or our own country, and we can then make our move on Babylon with security ensured at home, our reputation enhanced, and the Persians cut off from the entire sea and all the land this side of the Euphrates.

To make assurance doubly sure, the king announced that in a dream Heracles had ushered him into Tyre. The ever reliable Aristander was on hand to offer the correct interpretation, namely that Tyre would fall (not too difficult a deduction). The gathering applauded and work began at once on the siege.

THE CHALLENGE FACING THE Macedonians appeared insurmountable and Alexander knew he would have to deploy every resource at his disposal. The engineer Diades, together with his fellow Thessalian Charias, headed his siege team. More artillery specialists were recruited from Phoenicia and beyond.

Their task was simply expressed. Using a battering ram and catapults, they had to break down a section of wall through which troops could then launch an assault. Tall wheeled towers would be pushed up against the wall. Once inside Tyre, the besiegers would face fierce opposition, but the defenders would almost certainly be disorganized and panic-stricken, and resistance would soon be over. Alternatively, if Alexander was not in a hurry, he could set up a blockade and starve the defenders to death. That could take months and was a less desirable option.

But how would it be possible to accomplish any of these things when the city in question was inaccessible, heavily fortified, and encircled by the sea? Furthermore, it had its own warships and could call on the Persian navy for assistance. The newly recommissioned Macedonian fleet was not yet battle ready, except for twenty Athenian triremes.

For the king, this was simply another Gordian knot through which to slice. Dash and determination would find a way. The siege was opened in January 332. The first hugely ambitious step was to build a mole or causeway, reportedly two hundred feet wide at its maximum, from shore to island. The army was put to work, aided by local people. In the beginning the going was easy, for the first part of the channel consisted mainly of shallow pools and mudflats. Nearer the island, though, the water deepened to three fathoms.

Old Tyre was demolished to provide the large quantities of stones and wood needed. Stakes were driven into the mud to hold the rubble in place, and planks were laid on top. Little by little the causeway lengthened. Then the Tyrians disrupted proceedings. Their ships sailed up to the mole and shot missiles at the unarmored workers. They jeered at these "famous fighters loaded down like donkeys." Construction came to a halt until two towers, covered in animal hides to resist burning arrows, were pushed to the end of the mole.

The Tyrians now began to take the siege seriously. To reduce the number of mouths to feed, the women, children, and men too old to fight were evacuated to Carthage and the Tyrians requested military reinforcement from their colony. They were daring and imaginative in their response to the inexorably lengthening causeway. They converted a broad-beamed horse transport into a fireship. They stuffed it full of dry branches, wood shavings, pitch, and sulfur. They rigged a double yardarm from which they suspended buckets of some flammable substance (probably naphtha), and then set them alight. Triremes pulled the boat toward the mole and at just the right moment the crews lit the yardarms. These burned through and the buckets fell onto the fuel-packed fireship. The triremes then released the fireship and flames shot high into the air just when it plowed into the towers. To prevent firefighters from approaching, the men in the triremes maintained a barrage of arrows at the towers, which soon blazed out of control.

This was a major setback for Alexander. He gave orders for the mole to be widened and for new towers to be built, but he realized that he would never take the city without command of the sea. Taking with him the hypaspists and the Agrianians, he marched to Sidon to pick up some warships there and bring them back. He then had a marvelous stroke of luck—or, rather, his policy of marching through Phoenicia collecting capitulations paid off almost immediately.

Phoenician contingents made up the better part of the Persian fleet. As their various cities surrendered to Alexander, these felt obliged to sail home and abandon the Great King's cause. Unexpectedly, eighty

Phoenician ships put in at Sidon and agreed to sail under the Macedonian flag. Then ten triremes arrived from Rhodes, three from Cilicia, ten from Lycia, and, as a small bonus, a penteconter (a fifty-oarsman galley) from Macedonia. Not long afterward, 120 ships came in from Cyprus, whose kings had collectively decided that it was time to join the winning side.

All of a sudden, Alexander controlled the eastern Mediterranean.

WHILE PREPARATIONS WENT AHEAD to sail his warships in battle array southward to Tyre, the king amused himself by leading a small force on a ten-day campaign against Arab tribes in the Lebanese mountains. His aim was probably to protect his supply lines. This was essential if he was to continue feeding his army in front of Tyre as days became weeks and months, and the city still stood. Water was abundant, but most provisions were either requisitioned locally or had to be ferried in by sea.

Here was an opportunity for Alexander to behave with the utmost irresponsibility. His onetime tutor Lysimachus insisted on accompanying him on the march, but he was old and fell behind the main body. Alexander and a few others loyally stayed with him. The sun was setting and it became bitterly cold. With nightfall, the king saw in the distance some scattered watch fires. According to Plutarch,

> trusting to his speed and agility, he dashed to the nearest campfire, dispatched with his dagger the two barbarians who were sitting by it and, snatching a firebrand, ran back to his own party. They quickly built up a huge fire which scared some of the enemy into flight, while those who dared to attack were quickly driven off and the Macedonians spent the rest of the night in safety.

Circumstances had allowed the king to act out something very like an episode in the *Iliad*. This was the occasion when the brave warrior Diomedes and the wily Odysseus crept by night into the Trojan encampment, slaughtered sleeping soldiers, and made their way back to safety. Diomedes, Homer recounts,

laid about him with his sword and killed them right and left.
Hideous groans came up from the dying men
and the earth ran red with blood.

This otherwise pointless incident in the Lebanese mountains was a
reminder that Alexander lived in the age of heroes as much as he did in
the present. It hardly occurred to him that he had been reckless. In the
flickering darkness, he was Diomedes reborn.

THE KING RETURNED TO SIDON, where his grand fleet was now prepared for action. With himself in command, it set out in battle formation on the short journey south to the island city. The Tyrians had
intended to offer battle, but knew nothing of the recent reinforcements and were astounded when they saw the number of warships approaching. They went about and retreated to their two harbors. To
prevent the Macedonians from finding anchorage in them, they blocked
the entrances, using warships lashed together sideways. The following
morning Alexander ordered the Phoenicians to set up a permanent
blockade of the Egyptian harbor, and the Cypriots to blockade the
Sidonian. This meant that at last the enemy navy was out of action.

During the king's absence a large number of siege engines had been
built. Some of them were mounted on ships and others pushed to the
end of the mole, which was creeping nearer and nearer to the high
walls of Tyre. Floating battering rams were a remarkable technical innovation. They probably rested on platforms supported by two vessels
and, provided that they were anchored firmly, could do a great deal of
damage.

For their part, the ever ingenious Tyrians came up with trick after
trick. Among the torments they devised were metal containers filled
with red-hot sand, which they poured onto agonized attackers below.
They built towers on the battlement facing the mole, which overshadowed Alexander's, and hastily put up an inner wall in case the main one
was breached. They also placed catapults on the battlement, which released showers of fire arrows at the floating rams. To blunt the force of
flying stones, they hung over the wall hides stitched together and
stuffed with dried seaweed. They dropped large rocks into the water at

the foot of the wall to deter ships from coming near. The Macedonians then had the awkward task of moving the rocks into deeper water with ropes and cranes.

The siege reached a hyperactive stalemate. Both sides could see that something radical had to be done to break it. But what? The defenders' answer was to send in some vessels, armored against missiles, to cut the anchor hawsers of the Macedonian ram ships. When these were driven off, they were replaced by divers with knives. The problem was solved only when the hawsers were replaced with chains. At last, despite the temporary inconvenience of a violent storm, it proved possible to get alongside the wall.

The Tyrians recognized the threat posed by the maritime blockade and attempted a desperate remedy. They noticed that the ships' crews went ashore every day for lunch and that Alexander usually took a nap at the same time. They decided that this would be the ideal moment for a surprise sortie. Sails were erected across the entrance to the Sidonian harbor to hide the preparations and then, at about noon one day, ten of the Tyrians' most powerful ships, with picked crews and their best armed marines, sailed out and fell on the temporarily empty Cypriot ships.

Luckily Alexander had forgone his siesta and was visiting the Phoenician fleet in the Egyptian harbor when he received news of the breakout. He immediately assembled a squadron of the quickest galleys to be crewed and rowed at full speed around the island. The Tyrians on the battlements saw what was afoot and shouted warnings to the men on their own ships. These were inaudible because of the din of the engagement, but eventually the men got the message and turned tail. A few of them reached their harbor in time, but most were caught and put out of action, sunk or captured. It was the Tyrian navy's last gasp; from now on, the Macedonian fleet could sail wherever it wanted without hindrance.

About this time, the mole reached the city wall, but despite the blood and toil that had gone into its making, it did not bring the end of the siege any closer. The Tyrians put all their energy into defending the fraction of the wall where it met the mole. Alexander belatedly realized this and, now that the enemy was excluded from the sea, sailed round the island looking for any weakness in the fortifications. He brought his battering-ram platforms to the battlement near the Sidonian harbor, but without success.

He then settled on a stretch of weak-looking wall immediately south of the Egyptian harbor. His battering rams soon shook it loose and partly broke it down. A drawbridge or ramp was laid across the breach and a tentative assault launched. This failed, but the king knew he had found a weak spot.

A couple of days later Alexander ordered a major attack by detachments of hypaspists, led by an officer called Admetus, and of infantry Companions. The breach had been widened and two ramps were laid down. Alexander joined the hypaspists and was in the middle of the mêlée (how could it have been otherwise?). Admetus was first to clamber through the ruined fortification, but a spear hit him and he died where he stood.

Meanwhile the fleet encircled the island, equipped with archers and missile-throwers. Squadrons attacked the two harbors and broke through into them. Arrian writes: "Under fire from all directions the Tyrians were confronted with danger wherever they turned."

Alexander and the infantry captured several towers and the curtain wall between them. They moved on along the battlements toward the royal palace, an area that offered an easy route to the city center. The main body of the defenders abandoned the wall and regrouped for a last stand at the Shrine of Agenor, a legendary king of Tyre who was credited with introducing the Phoenician alphabet. They saw that the city and its harbors were lost and sold their lives as dearly as they could. According to Arrian,

> the Macedonians stopped at nothing in their fury. They were enraged by the wearisome length of the siege, and by the behavior of the Tyrians when they had captured some of their men sailing in from Sidon. They had paraded them on the wall in full view of the camp, then cut their throats and thrown them into the sea.

The slaughter was terrible, although from compassion for their fellow Phoenicians, Sidonian sailors saved many defenders and hid them away in their ships. Some eight thousand Tyrians died, whereas over the whole siege Macedonian losses were about four hundred.

A number of dignitaries sought refuge in the temple of Melqart, including the Tyrian king, Azemilcus, and other government officials together with a delegation from Carthage, which in the event had done nothing at all to help its founder. They were all pardoned, but other survivors were not so lucky. Two thousand men of military age were crucified. A total of about thirty thousand Tyrians and other foreigners found in the city were sold into slavery.

At last Alexander was able to make the sacrifice to the god for which he had sought permission seven months earlier. As was his custom at the end of a campaign, the king held a celebration. He staged a parade of his entire army in honor of Melqart and also a naval review. Athletic competitions were held and a torch race in the temple precincts.

As in the case of Thebes, the complete destruction of a renowned city whose merchants were a familiar sight across the Mediterranean made an indelible impression on public opinion. The world learned that it was wisest to cooperate with the young Macedonian conqueror.

What Ezekiel foretold had now come to pass in all its terrible finality.

Nobody could be bothered to dismantle the mole; as the centuries passed, it silted up and slowly became a permanent isthmus. Tyre was repopulated and, whatever Hebrew prophets may say, thrives again today. But beneath the impedimenta of the modern city, its streets and buildings, lies the stone causeway, an unforgotten but unseen reminder of the wrath of Alexander.

A COUPLE OF MONTHS after the fall of Tyre, the king's life hung in the balance again. He was hit by a catapult bolt, which went straight through his shield and breastplate into his shoulder. This characteristic incident took place during the siege of Gaza, the last of the Phoenician cities before the wide desert that separated Egypt from Asia like a cordon sanitaire.

The royal physician, Philip, extracted the missile. Apparently, Alexander's cuirass had prevented those around him from seeing how deep the wound was, and when blood began to gush out, they became seriously alarmed.

Alexander himself did not even lose color. He had the bleeding stanched and the wound bandaged. According to Curtius,

> for a long time he remained on his feet before the standards, either concealing or mastering his pain, until the blood which had shortly before been suppressed by the application of a dressing began to flow more copiously and the wound, painless while still warm, swelled up as the blood cooled. He began to faint, his knees buckled, and the men next to him caught him and took him back to camp.

Gaza's commander, Batis, a corpulent black eunuch, was loyal to the Great King and, despite the grim news from Tyre, was determined to resist the triumphant Macedonians.

Gaza was a wealthy and well-fortified stronghold, an entrepôt for the spice trade, which occupied a high plateau, or tell, two miles inland. It had only a small garrison, but to the besieger, it presented two insuperable difficulties and one excellent opportunity. The tell was 250 feet high and siege engines could not reach the walls themselves. The ground was relatively sandy and soft and it was almost impossible to move wheeled traffic over it. But on the credit side, sappers would easily be able to tunnel under the town's defenses and take away the subsoil; the wall above would then fall in.

It was going to be the most testing of sieges, even harder perhaps than Tyre, but this only made Alexander the more determined. Hephaestion arrived with the fleet and transport vessels carrying the siege engines used at Tyre; he was also in charge of the commissariat and was responsible for procuring and supplying the large quantities of water and grain needed by the Macedonians outside Gaza (and later for the journey to Egypt).

The king ordered tunnels to be dug out of view into the tell and, as a diversion, arranged for some mobile towers to be moved toward a section of wall (presumably near a city gate where there was a road or ramp leading up to it).

The towers got stuck in the sand, and the Arabs inside Gaza sallied out to set them alight. The king led the hypaspists to the rescue; it was at this point that he received his wound. While he presided at a sacrifice earlier in the day, a carrion bird dropped a clod of earth, which fell on his head and broke up, or so the sources say. According to the seer Aristander, this omen meant that the city would fall, but also that the king risked serious harm. He was warned not to fight that day, and despite his annoyance he did stay in the rear for a while. But the temptation to lead the counterattack was too strong.

The wound did not heal easily, but Alexander continued to manage operations. He had the town surrounded with an earth mound or ramp. The siege engines were moved up the ramp and started battering the wall. A section of the wall crumbled, and the sappers' tunnels caused a more general collapse.

Ladders were laid over the rubble and three attacks were launched, without success. In the fourth assault the king surrounded Gaza with his heavy-armed infantry. The Macedonians pressed forward and opened every gate they found.

Alexander's shoulder was still very painful, for a scab had not yet formed on the wound. However, he insisted on joining the fighting. He was struck on the leg by a rock and had to support himself with his spear, but he stayed in the front line.

Gaza fell. The defenders, some ten thousand of them, fought to the bitter end. The city's women and children were sold into slavery. Batis struggled on bravely and was taken alive. Alexander, presumably unhinged by pain, restaged another incident in the *Iliad*. This was when the furious Achilles kills Hector, the great Trojan warrior; he ties the corpse to his chariot and drags it back to the Greek camp. Batis suffered a similar fate, with the significant difference that *he* was still alive. His ankles were slit and attached by thongs to a chariot, which drove around the ruined walls of Gaza until the eunuch was dead.

Many spices were found in Gaza's warehouses, including five hundred talents of frankincense and one hundred of myrrh. This was the occasion when the king dumped a huge consignment of spices on his old tutor Leonidas with a tart covering note that he no longer needed to be stingy with them.

———

OCTOBER WAS A BAD month to cross the 130 miles of desert from Gaza to Pelusium, a border fortress and the gateway to Egypt. The annual rains did not start until November and the water from wells, which were few and far between, was often too brackish to drink and anyway at this time of year were probably dry. Nevertheless, Alexander was too impatient to wait and he set off with his entire army for Egypt.

His "entire army" was not what it once was, for he was acquiring so much new territory, which everywhere required garrisons, that its numbers were falling. He sent off Amyntas, son of Andromenes and a trusted friend of Parmenion's son Philotas, with ten ships to Macedonia, with orders to enlist young men who were fit for military service.

Alexander and his men marched from Gaza to Pelusium along the seacoast, which was covered entirely with sand dunes. They had to keep to the wet shoreline, for otherwise the horses and wagons would have sunk into the sand. Food depots had been set up along the coast, and the fleet sailed alongside the army and ferried water to the thirsty troops. All went well and the Macedonians reached the border fortress without incident. In order to save on supplies, they had covered 137 miles in one week, or nearly twenty miles a day, a speedy rate.

Alexander was received with delight and open arms. Huge crowds were waiting at Pelusium to welcome him to the land of the pharaohs. In fact, everyone knew that he was set to become the next pharaoh.

The Egyptians had smarted for centuries under the Great King's yoke. Every so often they drove the Persians out, sometimes for years, but the insurrections were always suppressed. The eldest son of the last rebel pharaoh, Nakhthorheb (known to the Greeks as Nectanebo), fought on Darius's side at the Battle of Issus. His fate is unknown, but another Egyptian collaborator unpronounceably called Sematawytefnakht fled the battlefield. Shocked by the debacle, he abandoned the Persian cause and made his way home as quickly as he was able.

It may seem odd that Alexander was not regarded as just another foreign invader greedy for the country's wealth, but anyone who showed signs of destroying the Persian empire, as he did, was bound to be popular. Perhaps the Egyptians were persuaded by Alexander's self-promotion as a true liberator.

The king took ship to the great political and religious center of Memphis, at the base of the Nile Delta, where he met the governing elite, priests who were also administrators. The city's mud-brick walls were painted white, and to the approaching visitor it must have appeared as a blinding mirage, a shining city. Persian officials had not awaited the king's arrival and had made themselves scarce, except for the acting governor (the satrap himself had fallen at Issus). He stayed at his post and handed over all the gold he had, more than eight hundred talents, and, curiously, all the royal furniture. He was rewarded with a job in the new administration.

EGYPT HAD MANY GODS, but Ptah was among the greatest. He was the divine craftsman, the demiurge who preceded everything in the universe. In fact, it was he who brought the universe and its deities into being by the sheer exercise of thought. He took many forms; sometimes he was shown as a naked and deformed dwarf (the Greeks equated him with Hephaestus, the divine but lame blacksmith), but usually he appeared as a man with green skin, wearing a tight-fitting shroud.

At Memphis Ptah was embodied in a sacred bull, the Apis. The bull lived in state in a temple and was allotted a harem of cows. He was worshipped as an aspect of Ptah and when he died he was immortalized collectively as the Osiris Apis. A bull calf was chosen to succeed him, which had various precisely defined markings. His mother was impregnated by a flash of lightning from the heavens. She too lived a life of luxury. A lucky cow.

Alexander took care to sacrifice to the Apis, knowing better than to tamper with other people's beliefs. He may also have paid his respects at the funerary temple at Saqqara, where the dead, mummified bulls were laid to rest. The comparison with Artaxerxes Ochus, who on his invasion of Egypt a decade earlier had slaughtered the divine bull of the day, as had the Great King Cambyses in the sixth century B.C., was seen as doing him great credit.

While in Memphis, Alexander was officially recognized as pharaoh, the priest-king whose spiritual duties matched his political authority. However, he did not have time to stay in the country for the year-long round of ceremonies that the new ruler traditionally observed.

A pharaoh was recognized, in a symbolic sense, as son of Amun, chief deity in the Egyptian theogony. He had five official names or titles. Those of Alexander in hieroglyphic inscriptions reflected his military success against the Persians and announced his duty as guardian of Egypt. His throne name was Setep en Ra, mery Amun ("Chosen by Ra and beloved of Amun"). His title in his capacity as the incarnation of the falcon-headed god Horus, Egypt's tutelary deity, was "The Brave Ruler Who Has Attacked Foreign Lands." Other titles were "The Lion, Great of Might, Who Takes Possession of Mountains, Lands, and Deserts" and "The Bull Who Protects Egypt, The Ruler of the Sea and of What the Sun Encircles." His birth name was given as Aleksindres.

Splendid religious rituals marked the accession to power; once they were completed, Alexander decided it was time for Hellenic culture to receive its due share of attention. The new pharaoh staged games for his troops both in athletics and in the arts of drama, music, and dance. These celebrations must have been planned well in advance, for leading practitioners in the Greek world, the stars of the day, traveled to Egypt to take part.

Perhaps we have here an early hint of the principle that underlay Alexander's politics—namely, equal respect for different cultures. He disagreed with Aristotle, who advised him, according to Plutarch,

> to treat the Greeks as if he were their leader, and other peoples as if he were their master; to have regard for the Greeks as for friends and relatives, but to conduct himself toward other peoples as though they were plants or animals; for to do so [i.e., to do as Aristotle advised] would have been to cumber his leadership with numerous battles and banishments and festering seditions.

There was a practical consideration in the king's thinking; if he was to govern Asia he would need the services and the consent of the local inhabitants. There were not enough Macedonians to go round. However, he seems to have rejected from conviction the racism ingrained in most Greeks, and indeed his Macedonian subjects, and made sensitive appointments on grounds of merit rather than ethnicity.

This was one of the key assumptions that underlay his administrative arrangements for Egypt; the other two being "divide and rule" and noninterference in the lives of ordinary citizens. He appointed two Egyptians, presumably on advice from the priestly bureaucracy, to share the country between them according to an immemorial division, one for the governance of the Upper and the other of the Lower Kingdom.

Military matters were separated from the civilian government. Two Macedonian Companions were to be garrison commanders, and the leadership of a regiment of Greek mercenaries was shared between a Greek general and a Macedonian Companion. The eastern and western frontier districts were to be overseen by a couple of Greeks, one of whom was to be responsible for the finances of the entire province. This was the extremely able but extremely corrupt Cleomenes, from the port of Naucratis on the Nile Delta. We are not told, but he and the military commanders presumably reported directly to their Macedonian pharaoh.

For the individual Egyptian, nothing changed. District officials collected taxes as usual, but delivered the proceeds to Cleomenes rather than to a Persian satrap, and went on managing local affairs.

These dispositions were primarily designed to ensure that nobody had enough power to threaten his, Alexander's, control over this vastly wealthy province. At the outset they worked well enough, but, as we shall observe, in time the king's best-laid plans were subverted and he had to step in and retrieve the situation.

At about this time, good news arrived by ship about the naval situation in the Aegean. After Issus, Pharnabazus, whom Darius had appointed as admiral after Memnon's unexpected death, had failed to prevent the Greek islands of Tenedos, Chios, and Cos from breaking with Persia and had been captured. He managed to escape, but the days of the Great King's dominance of the seas were over for good.

Formal business being completed, Alexander sailed downriver, taking the western or Canopic tributary. He was accompanied by a small infantry detachment and the Royal Squadron of cavalry. At this time he was saddened by a personal tragedy. Parmenion had three sons, two of whom, Philotas and Nicanor, were senior commanders in the army. The youngest, Hector, was in his late teens and was particularly close to the king. Curtius writes that, during the voyage, he

> wanted to catch up with [Alexander], and boarded a small vessel along with a complement of men exceeding the boat's capacity. The boat sank, leaving all those aboard in the water. Hector fought against the current for a long time. Although his sodden clothes and tight-fitting shoes made swimming difficult, he still managed to reach the bank in a half-dead condition.

However, there was no one there to help him, for his companions had swum to the other bank, and he died. He was given a splendid funeral.

The army reached Naucratis, through which Egyptian grain, linen, and papyrus were exported and silver, timber, olive oil, and wine were imported. The fall of Tyre and Gaza had given the city a once-in-a-lifetime commercial opportunity. However, Alexander was not greatly impressed by the place and, as luck had it, when sailing around the huge and shallow saltwater lake Mareotis he stumbled on the perfect harbor.

This was a long limestone ridge or spur of land. To the south behind it was the lagoon, and on the Mediterranean side lay the island of Pharos. Ridge and island were separated by a stretch of deep water, where ships could moor in safety. The place had a temperate climate with mild winds, fresh water, limestone quarries, and easy access to the Nile. There was no unbearable heat, no malarial marshes.

Here Alexander chose to build a new city in his name: Alexandria. He was reassured in his decision by the endorsement of Homer. In the *Odyssey,* the bard has Menelaus, the cuckolded king of Sparta, whose wife Helen's elopement caused so much misery, sail home from Troy. He was blown off course to Egypt and found himself at "an island in the rolling seas off Egypt and men call it Pharos. . . . It has a harbor with good anchorage, where men can draw fresh water and launch their ships on an even keel into the deep sea." A good anchorage was just what Alexander had been looking for, but at the moment he had another more personal project in mind.

——

WHILE IN EGYPT, ALEXANDER suffered a mental crisis. We do not
know enough of his psychological interior to know exactly what it
was, but its external impact was visible.

As we have seen, he was a religious man and a punctilious observer
of sacrifices and ceremonies. He paid attention to oracles, and Aristander was always on hand to advise on the will of the gods. His spiritual life was egocentric; his chief concern was with his place in the
spiritual cosmos. As we have seen, he believed that the Argeads, Macedonia's royal family, could be traced back to Heracles, hero and demigod, a son of Zeus. Heracles was the only human being to have been
granted immortality. Perseus, too, slayer of the Gorgon Medusa whose
gaze turned onlookers to stone, was among Alexander's forebears. And
Olympias belonged to the Molossian ruling dynasty, which claimed
descent from Neoptolemus, son of Achilles.

Surely, he mused, his achievements were as awe-inspiring as those
of his glorious ancestors. They merited recognition on Olympus, and
reward. As pharaoh he was named the son of Amun, or in its Greek
spelling, Ammon. Chief of the gods, Amun was the local incarnation
of Zeus. Could Alexander conclude that he was literally the son of
Zeus? If so, what about Philip? Did he really have nothing to do with
his son's birth?

These questions were difficult to answer. We have seen that Alexander's relations with Philip had been stormy and with his mother very
close and loving. A late literary source reports that Philip publicly
doubted Alexander's paternity and that Olympias claimed that "she
had conceived Alexander, not by him, but by a serpent of extraordinary size." We do not need to believe these stories to sense domestic
unhappiness. They were probably later inventions, but if they did
originate in gossip from the early years of Philip and Olympias's marriage, they pointed to adultery. One can imagine the queen dropping
dark hints to her little boy. At least one might infer that he sensed dis-
cord, sided with his mother, and saw Philip as a hostile stranger.

It is uncertain whether or not Alexander, with or without Olympias, had plotted Philip's assassination. If he had, parricide was the most
terrible of crimes, on which the gods could be depended to visit their

wrath; Alexander would have thought of Oedipus, the legendary king of Thebes, who murdered his father (as well as marrying his mother) and ended up as a blind outcast.

Had Alexander by some chance learned of a conspiracy against Philip he had taken no part in, but failed to report? If so, he might have to shoulder a share of blame and seek purification, or perhaps the gods would not require that of him. It would be worth eliciting a divine ruling on the guiltiness of guilty knowledge.

Another worrying possibility was that his mother played a part in her husband's death without informing her son.

The king felt "an overwhelming desire" (*pothos,* again) to consult one of the most famous oracles of the ancient world, the temple of Zeus-Ammon. This would entail a risky journey from the Libyan coast across 160 miles of desert to the oasis of Siwah, where the oracle was situated. The place had a special significance for him because, according to legend, two of his ancestors, Heracles and Perseus, had paid it a visit.

He intended to raise the fundamental issues that were exercising his mind.

ALEXANDER AND HIS MILITARY escort left Lake Mareotis on a day in March 331. He went west along the coast, and near the little port of Paraetonium he turned south into the unknown. Camels were hired to carry supplies (the first time the Macedonians are reported to have used them). After two days progress was slowed by deep sand dunes. A severe windstorm blew up, common in Egypt at this time of year and caused by the differential heating of the Libyan desert and the rest of the Middle East during spring. The wind gusted to gale force, the temperature rose sharply, and the humidity fell. Worst of all, a sandstorm blasted its way across the desert and obliterated landmarks. After four days, the water ran out and the guides lost their way. If something did not turn up, the little expedition's survival was at stake.

The Fates were generous. A sudden downpour allayed the men's thirst, and two crows were seen flying ahead of the party. On the assumption, correct as it proved, that they were making for the oasis, Alexander followed their lead, and Siwah came thankfully into sight.

Even today, it is reported, the flight of two crows is regarded by residents of the oasis as a good omen.

Six miles long by four to five miles wide, Siwah lies below sea level. It has about 200 springs, including a hot water fountain the temperature of which varies. Date palms and olives abound. Rock salt deposits were farmed (they still are) and exported to Egypt. On a rise stood the temple of Zeus-Ammon.

Ammon was usually represented as a male figure with ram's horns, but at Siwah the cult image was a navel- or omphalos-shaped stone studded with emeralds and other precious stones. When the oracle was consulted, eighty priests carried it in a gilded boat with silver cups hanging from it. It seemed to move involuntarily where it willed. Women followed behind and chanted hymns. A priest interpreted the boat's movements in answer to questions put to the oracle.

After his arrival, Alexander walked up a path to the shrine and entered the first of two halls. He was welcomed by an elderly priest and seer, who said: "Rejoice, my son." Pharaohs were used to being called the Son of Amun and the priest must simply have been addressing him with formulaic politeness. He said as much, noting that "Ammon [that is, Zeus] is by nature the father of us all." However, the king took the greeting as a direct message from the god, which confirmed his suspicion that he was indeed the son of Zeus. He was then led through the second hall and into a small sanctuary.

The priest listened to the king's questions (or read them if they had been submitted in advance in writing). Presumably he left the sanctuary to watch the divine boat sway about for a while and returned with his interpretations. The matter of paternity now being settled, Alexander asked whether he was fated to rule the world. The flattering priest answered that the god agreed to his request.

The second question was a thunderbolt. "Have all my father's murderers been punished?" The priest corrected him: if Ammon was his father, he was a god and obviously could not be murdered or die. However, he confirmed that all Philip's murderers had paid for their crime.

It was a most surprising issue to raise: perhaps Alexander worried that there had been a wider conspiracy which remained to be uncovered. But surely this was old business, long since dealt with. It would cast a painful light, though, on his conscience if he *had* been implicated in some peripheral way in the murder or, indeed, if Olympias had been secretly involved.

What was said was said in private. Arrian is one of those who kept the king's confidence and offered no comment. He writes with unexpected brevity: "Once there [in Siwah], Alexander toured the site with keen interest, and put his questions to the god. Having heard all the answers he had hoped for, he set out back to Egypt." Other ancient sources publish the contents of the conversation. Are we to believe that these accounts were invented? Maybe. The oddity of the king's question about Philip, though, lends them credibility. The king could have spoken indiscreetly in later years, or the people at Siwah allowed themselves to gossip.

Whether or not the contents of Alexander's private conversation with the priest at Siwah were widely known, many senior Macedonians, whose careers were nourished and flourished in Philip's day, were upset by his son's apparent rejection of his earthly paternity when he accepted Ammon as his divine father. It is reported that Parmenion's son Philotas wrote to the king, advising him that it would be more dignified to keep quiet about the matter than to publicize it. One leading Macedonian lamented: "We have lost Alexander, we have lost our king!"

These first signs of discontent led nowhere at the time, for the thrill of successive victories reinforced loyalty and enthusiasm.

ALEXANDER STOOD ON THE long ridge and surveyed the scene. Having marched back without incident from Siwah the way he came, he found himself again at Lake Mareotis. He was surrounded by officials, among them the celebrated town planner Deinocrates and Alexander's Egyptian treasurer, Cleomenes of Naucratis, who was to be in overall charge of the development. On one side lay the lagoon and on the other, separated by a stretch of sea, the island of Pharos.

The king's mind was focused on the design of his new city. He wanted a Hellenic look with a grid pattern of streets. According to Arrian, he was seized with a passion for this project, and took personal charge of mapping his city on the ground—where its central square was to be built, how many temples there should be and to which gods (some Greek, but also the Egyptian Isis), where the surrounding wall should run. He made sacrifice in hope of sanction for these plans, and the omens proved favorable.

He also made provision for a large and splendid palace, from which it may be inferred that Alexandria was to be Egypt's administrative capital.

Alexander must have proposed a causeway connecting the ridge to the island of Pharos (it was not constructed till the following century). This would create two harbors, one for commercial shipping and the other for the fleet. When tracing the course of the circuit wall, Alexander followed Macedonian tradition by using ground pearl barley. When flocks of birds flew down to eat it up, Aristander and other seers prophesied (uncontroversially, for Egypt was the breadbasket of the Mediterranean) that the city would prosper "especially from produce of the earth."

The area within the walls was very large, for Alexander had in mind a megalopolis; indeed, for a century or two Alexandria became the largest city in the world, until Rome overshot it. People from neighboring towns and villages were drafted in, and incomers, mostly Greeks, were recruited from around the eastern Mediterranean world. A democratic constitution was planned, with an assembly, a council, and a board of elected officials, which would be responsible for local administration.

The king officially founded his new, as yet only imagined city on April 7, 331 B.C., and then immediately left what turned out to be his most lasting monument. He did not visit Egypt again and never saw his Alexandria complete. Much of the building work was done after his death, including its most famous edifice, the massive lighthouse of Pharos, one of the Seven Wonders of the World.

ABOUT A YEAR HAD passed since the fall of Tyre. Despite two bitterly fought sieges, Alexander's strategy had succeeded. He now controlled the entire coastline of Asia Minor and North Africa from the Hellespont to Libya. As expected, Persian seapower had collapsed. Following a short return visit to Memphis, the king rejoined his army, cheerful after wintering in the Nile Valley. It was now time to march eastward into the Persian homeland and do battle with the new host that Darius had been assembling since Issus.

But what Alexander appreciated as much as his thrilling victories by sea and land was his encounter with Zeus-Ammon. He could now legitimately claim to be a hero and a demigod on a level with the great warriors of old. In following the course of his life, a cumulative impression emerges that his hyperactivity had both an external and internal dimension. To his contemporaries and those who served him, he could hardly have seemed more real, more energetically, more dangerously, even unpleasantly present, whereas he himself appears to have seen the world as no more than a means of reenacting a dreamed past.

He dipped in and out of his own parallel universe, at will.

CHAPTER 9

AT THE HOUSE
OF THE CAMEL

———

ALEXANDER LED HIS ARMY DOWN THE LOW HILLS ONTO THE
wide plain of Gaugamela in Mesopotamia. He had his first view of the
enemy about three and a quarter miles away in the distance and was
shaken by what he saw. The Persians vastly outnumbered his own force
and would have no trouble at all outflanking him. There was no mountain or sea to protect his wings, just acres and acres of flat, empty land.

Worse, the Great King had obviously learned a lesson from Issus:
that his infantry could not be relied on to put up a good fight. So his
front line was nearly all cavalry, as at the Granicus, except for the center where Alexander could see Greek infantry mercenaries and the
royal bodyguard.

He realized that the spectacle was dampening his men's spirits, but
was at a loss for what to do next. So he called a conference of his Companions, generals, and squadron commanders. He asked whether in
their opinion he should attack there and then or, surprisingly on past
form, follow Parmenion's cautious but canny advice. This was to stay
where they were for the time being and make a thorough search of the
terrain. It looked as if Darius had cleared a large area of brush and
smoothed irregularities.

Alexander agreed to a delay and, guarded by a substantial escort,
spent much of the rest of the day riding about the ground the Persians
had cleared and noting its edges with care. He was less concerned with

the possibility that the Persians had laid traps for his troops as they advanced than with understanding the meaning and purpose of the enemy's battle order. On a humpbacked hill not far away, the village of Gaugamela (which translates as the Camel's House, and is today's Tell Gomel) looked down on the level expanse where the decisive encounter of the war was to take place.

On his return the king reconvened his officers and said that with their record of success they needed no encouragement from him, but he told them to fire up their men. They would be fighting to decide who would rule Asia Minor. It had been an open secret for some time that the king saw their mission no longer as revenge but as conquest. Now it was official.

As dusk fell on September 30, 331 B.C., Alexander ordered the army to eat its evening meal and then rest. Meanwhile a nervous Darius held a torchlight review and insisted that his men stay under arms in case of a night attack. Perhaps he had some spy among the Macedonians, for the possibility of just such a shock move was exactly what Parmenion and some of his older companions were now discussing.

According to Plutarch, they looked out across the plain and saw it

> agleam with the watch-fires of the barbarians, while from their camp there arose the confused and indistinguishable murmur of myriads of voices, like the distant roar of a vast ocean. They were filled with amazement at the sight and remarked to one another that it would be an overwhelmingly difficult task to defeat an enemy of such strength by engaging them by day.

They went to speak to Alexander about the idea and found him in front of his tent. He was in an anxious mood and was deep in discussion with Aristander, his bridge to the gods. The seer was dressed in white, with a sacred bough in his hand and his head veiled. He performed certain mysterious ceremonies and led the king in prayers for the assistance of Zeus, his "father," and Athena of Victory. Tellingly, the king offered a special sacrifice to the divine personification of Fear.

Once he had finished these rituals, Parmenion broached the topic of a night attack; the moon was early in its last quarter and he argued that in the lunar light they could catch the enemy unawares and disorganized. The king was not impressed. Darkness left too much to chance. In case anyone thought he might be losing his nerve, he was resolutely optimistic. He replied: "I will not steal my victory."

He then retired inside his tent, but seems to have gone on worrying about his tactics for the following day, balancing various options. When he had come at last to a fixed decision, his mind calmed, and in the small hours he went to bed. He fell into a deep untroubled sleep.

Dawn came and the king failed to wake up. His commanders were awaiting his orders with rising anxiety. No one dared to enter his tent to rouse him. Some even suspected that he was bottling it. Parmenion took it on himself to tell the men to take breakfast. The Persians were moving into battle formation, but still Alexander slept on.

It was bright day. Was the battle to be lost before it began?

TWO MONTHS EARLIER, in late July or August 331, the Macedonian army, returning from Egypt, had reached the ruins of Tyre. Here Alexander staged the grandest so far of his arts festivals. The program included sacrifices to the gods, solemn processions, contests of choral singing and, as in Athens from its heyday in the fifth century, the competitive staging of classic tragedies.

Drama was the most popular form of entertainment in the fourth century as well as being a religious obligation. In Greece, large open-air marble theaters were built to meet audience demand. However, Phoenicians were not enthusiasts of Greek tragedy, and perhaps the Macedonians' engineers erected a temporary wooden structure. The actors were all male, including those playing women's parts. The best of them were international stars who appeared in drama productions across the Hellenic world. Wearing masks, long ornate robes, and high-heeled boots, they were literally larger than life.

These performers were highly regarded. They knew personally the political leaders of the day and often acted as ambassadors between states. One who took on such a role was Thessalus, who was twice a winner at the prestigious festivals of Dionysus at Athens. He had been envoy for the teenaged Alexander during the Pixodarus affair and very nearly came to grief as a result. He and a fellow star and rival, Athenodorus, headed the bill at Tyre.

In Athens rich individuals, called *choregoi,* produced and funded the various drama productions and choral concerts. On this occasion the sponsors were the kings of Cyprus, who had just transferred their loyalty from Darius to Alexander during the recent siege.

Although he did not reveal his preference, Alexander hoped that his friend Thessalus would be the victor in the competition. But a majority of the judges chose Athenodorus. As he left the theater, the king remarked: "I endorse the jury's verdict, but I would have given part of my kingdom rather than see Thessalus defeated."

The winner had been due to perform in the Athenian festival of the Little Dionysia that winter, and was fined for breaking his contract by appearing at Tyre. He asked the king to intervene on his behalf with the Athenian authorities. Alexander refused, but privately paid the fine himself.

At first sight it seems more than a little odd, even frivolous, for a major military campaign to be suspended for a cultural celebration. But the king always kept a close eye on his public image. The festival was a powerful assertion of the Hellenic values for which he and his Macedonians were waging war with barbarians.

Everyone knew that a battle to win the Persian empire was imminent. What better time to advertise the superiority of Greek civilization?

THE LEAGUE OF CORINTH sent its warmest congratulations on Alexander's achievements "for the salvation and freedom of Hellas" and presented him with a golden crown. But as a matter of fact, affairs in Greece had been unsettled for some time. The fiercely independent and militaristic city-state of Sparta, and its homeland of Laconia, refused to participate in the league (as we have seen) and became a hotbed of discontent. Sparta had once been a major power, and dominated its resentful neighbors in the Peloponnese. After a crushing defeat at the hands of Thebes forty years before, it was now only of local importance. But the Spartans never forgot their claim to lead Hellas and refused to cooperate with Alexander's father. He once sent them a message: "If I conquer Laconia, I will turn you out." The Spartans, who had a reputation for brevity, responded with a single word: "If."

Their young king, Agis III, schemed to undo Macedonian control of the Hellenic world. But he was patient: Sparta had not fought at Chaeronea nor had it joined the failed rebellion that followed Alexander's accession. Then in late 333, while the Macedonian army was more than a thousand miles away and unable to interfere, Agis decided to stir the pot again. The Aegean basin had become a Persian lake, and Miletus and Halicarnassus had been recaptured. So, despite Alexander's success on land, Agis was optimistic about Darius's chances. He sent an envoy to Susa to open talks about a Greek uprising.

Not hearing back from Darius, Agis decided to see for himself what was going on. He sailed across the Aegean in a single trireme to meet Pharnabazus, admiral of the Persian fleet, and ask for the Great King's support.

Agis wanted the largest possible force of ships and troops to take back with him to the Peloponnese. But unluckily the Battle of Issus supervened and broke his hopes. Pharnabazus's priority was now to save his Aegean possessions. All the Persians could afford to give Agis was thirty talents and ten triremes. He sent them to his brother at Sparta and instructed him to secure Crete for the Persian cause. The island was a traditional Spartan sphere of interest and would be a useful base for the fleet. He himself stayed for a time in Asia helping the resistance to Alexander. Then in 332 or 331, Agis returned to Sparta and raised the standard of revolt.

The Macedonian king regarded him as no more than an irritant. Alexander was annoyed that the league was failing to do its job of keeping a lid on dissent, but he had no intention of returning to Greece to defeat the insurgents in person. That would be left to his deputy in Pella, Antipater. But he knew that he needed to win opinion to his side. While in Egypt he had welcomed numerous Greek delegations and made a point of giving them whatever they asked for. Most important of all, he knew that although Athens was weaker than it had once been, it was still worth having as a friend. The insurgency would be easily put down if only he could dissuade Athens from joining.

This is the likely background to a murky story concerning a handsome young long-term lodger in the house of Demosthenes (on terms unknown but perhaps sexual). The great orator was a fierce opponent of Macedonia and feared for his life. The lodger set up a back channel via Hephaestion to Alexander, who was happy to give Demosthenes "a certain degree of immunity" in return for his neutrality.

At Tyre during the arts festival the Athenian state galley turned up and a delegation once again asked the king to pardon those fellow citizens who had fought against him at the Battle of the Granicus and were still prisoners of war. He immediately agreed to the request.

At about this time, his former treasurer, the rascally Harpalus, arrived at the camp, begging pardon for having run away with a large sum of money before Issus. His con-man partner had disappeared to Italy and conveniently died. Unlike Alexander, Harpalus enjoyed sex, especially with expensive female prostitutes, and he may have been running short of cash. It says a lot for his charm that it was the king who made the first contact and persuaded him to return. He promised Harpalus that he would not be punished—in fact, on his arrival in Phoenicia the king gave him his old job back as treasurer.

It is a puzzling story. Alexander was not a man for pardoning betrayal. That said, they *were* old friends. Some speculate that in fact Harpalus was on a confidential mission, but it is hard to imagine what project would have required the secret involvement of such a senior figure. However, Harpalus could well have picked up useful information about the planned insurgency and passed it on to a grateful Alexander.

In any event, despite all the Hellenic fine words and smiles, Alexander suspected that friendliness might not be enough; he dispatched warships to intervene in Crete and keep a watch over the Peloponnese.

Alexander could be a diplomat when he chose. His combination of velvet glove and iron fist predictably failed to win over King Agis, but it did persuade the Athenians to steer clear of revolt.

IT WAS TIME TO find the Great King and fight him again. Around the first week of July, Alexander and his entire army left Tyre and marched up through Syria, probably along the seacoast (to facilitate supplies of food, fodder, and water). At the place where the great port of Seleucia would stand in later centuries, he turned right and made for Thapsacus, an ancient town on the western bank of the Euphrates.

As always with Alexander, logistical planning was meticulous. It seems that supplies were to be transported by boat south down the river toward Babylon, the assembly point for Darius's horde. The army was to have marched alongside the ships. Unfortunately, the newly appointed Macedonian satrap of Syria had failed to gather enough food and fodder and was sacked. By itself the narrow Euphrates Valley would not support the army, and in any case grain stores from the recent harvest were locked up and inaccessible in walled towns, so this route was now out of the question. Instead, Alexander decided to march east to the Tigris through the fertile fields of northern Mesopotamia, where there would be plenty to eat and the sun's summer heat would be less intense than farther south.

Hephaestion was sent in advance to build two pontoon bridges across the Euphrates. The farthest sections were left unfinished to deny them to the enemy. A prominent Persian, Mazaeus, commanded a sizable force of three thousand cavalry and the same number of infantry (of whom a third were Greek mercenaries). He was charged with preventing the Macedonians from crossing the Euphrates, and for a time he kept guard on the bank. But when he caught wind of Alexander's imminent arrival, Mazaeus quickly withdrew, perhaps feeling that the forces at his disposal were not strong enough to deter the Macedonians. It could also be that his heart was not in the fight.

The bridges were completed and the army spent an estimated five days tramping over them. The king paused for a few days to rest his men and prepare them for a forced march of 125 miles to the Tigris. He wanted to prevent any Persian force from reaching the river first. Luckily, Darius had probably expected Alexander to descend the Euphrates Valley, and by the time he had worked out that he was in fact making for the Tigris it was too late to stop him.

For an army to cross a river when an enemy was nearby could be very dangerous. It was also slow and difficult if the water was deep and fast-flowing. However, modern travelers record that the average depth of the Tigris in September is no more than one foot; there is no reason to suppose it was different in the past. Mazaeus reappeared, but did not attack the Macedonians directly; instead, he set about laying waste the land some distance east of the river. This scorched-earth policy (much like what Memnon had advocated before the Granicus) could have decided the war in the Persians' favor, but it was initiated far too late to cause Alexander any serious trouble. Once again he had gained advantage by speed and surprise.

Not long after the crossing, a regiment of Persian horse did put in an appearance. Alexander dispatched some scouts to charge it at full gallop. Their commander ran through his Persian counterpart with his spear, hurled him from his horse, and decapitated him while he struggled on the ground. He took the head back with him and, to loud applause, laid it at the king's feet.

IN FARAWAY BABYLON, which Darius and his army were in the process of leaving to fight with Alexander in northern Mesopotamia, temple astronomers were recording their daily observation of the heavens and weather conditions, as they had done for centuries. They believed that the gods had created the movements of the planets to give people on earth indications of the future.

In a collection of celestial omens known as Enûma Anu Enlil, the astronomers asserted causal links between movements in the sky and political, economic, and other important events, both after they happened and as prophecies of the future. They warned the authorities of impending troubles. Although they did not have telescopes, their observations were fairly accurate and they were able to anticipate eclipses.

The stargazers recorded a nearly total lunar eclipse that occurred at 9:20 P.M. on September 20 in the year 331:

> Sunset to moonrise: 8°. There was a lunar eclipse. Its totality was covered at the moment when Jupiter set and Saturn rose. During totality the west wind blew, clearing the east wind. During the eclipse, deaths and plague occurred.

According to the priest-astronomers, the predictive significance of this event was that an intruder will come with the princes of the west; for eight years he will exercise kingship; he will conquer the enemy army; there will be abundance and riches on his path; he will continually pursue his enemies; and his luck will not run out.

However, Alexander did not know of this helpful prognostication when he and his men saw the moon dim and grow blood-red in color. His soldiers were terrified. They were more than a thousand miles from home and were marching into the unknown. Religious awe was swiftly followed by panic.

Aristander and Egyptian seers who specialized in the movement of heavenly bodies knew perfectly well that the eclipse was the result of the sun, the earth, and the moon coming into perfect or nearly perfect alignment, with the earth's shadow falling on and covering the moon. But Alexander was certain that the common man would not accept such a rational explanation. This was the work of the gods. He called a full meeting of his generals and officers in his tent and asked the Egyptians to give their opinion. Using their imaginations, they ruled that the sun represented the Macedonians and the moon the Persians. An eclipse of the moon signified disaster for the latter. The grateful king sacrificed to the moon, the sun, and the earth (incidentally demonstrating that he understood the true explanation of the lunar eclipse). Aristander announced that the animals' entrails had been scrutinized and the omens were good. They indicated a victory for Alexander. The army calmed down and morale rose to its normal temperature.

The march resumed, but the Macedonians had no clear idea of where Darius was. Then, on September 24, Macedonian scouts encountered a body of Persian horse. They captured one or two of them and learned that the Great King's army was only eight miles away, at Gaugamela, on the far side of a low range of hills.

Alexander established a permanent camp with a ditch and a palisade on this higher ground. Defensiveness of this kind was unusual for him, as indeed it was for Greek commanders in general, and indicated his nervousness. He gave his men a further four days' rest, leaving the Persians to swelter in the plain.

——

AN INJUDICIOUS LETTER FROM the Great King was intercepted and brought to Alexander. It sought to suborn the Greek soldiers in the Macedonian army to murder or betray him. He wondered whether it would be a good idea to read the letter aloud at a general assembly. It would helpfully arouse anger on the eve of battle, and he was fairly confident of the loyalty of his League of Corinth forces. But Parmenion advised otherwise. Darius's scheming should not be allowed to reach the men's ears, for that would simply further publicize the Great King's criminal intentions. It would take only one soldier to kill Alexander. Alexander conceded the point, and the letter was set aside.

It was about this time that the death of Darius's wife, Stateira, was announced. It seems that the constant discomfort of traveling in an army baggage train had exhausted her, but she was probably only in her midthirties and in the ordinary way of things should have been able to manage. She may have been struck down by some fatal, and doubtless little understood, disease.

Perhaps her comparative youth provoked the unlikely story that she had been pregnant and miscarried. Certainly Darius was afraid that Alexander had slept with her. However, an attendant eunuch who had escaped from the Macedonian camp and brought the news of Stateira's death reassured the Great King that all the imperial women had been treated with respect during their captivity. Apparently, Alexander had only seen her once, in the immediate aftermath of Issus. He gave her a full funeral in the traditional Persian manner.

The two armies were nearing each other and Darius, moved by his opponent's kindness to his dead wife, launched a third peace initiative. He sent ten envoys to put new proposals to Alexander. These were even more generous than their predecessors. The Great King agreed to cede to Alexander all his lands west of the Euphrates, pay the sum of thirty thousand talents of gold as ransom for his mother and daughters, and give him the hand in marriage of one of the daughters. His son Ochus would stay with the Macedonians as a token of goodwill. The two rulers would become friends and allies. Presumably, although this was not spelled out, Darius's new son-in-law could expect to succeed him on the imperial throne. There was a precedent for this, when

Alexander's father, Philip, set aside his little brother Amyntas to take the throne himself.

But the experienced observer might well wonder how two suns could occupy the same sky. A reconciliation would be most unlikely to last long. Apart from anything else, it would require good faith—a tall order after the revelation of Darius's assassination plot. Moreover, with a decisive battle only a few days away, it was impractical to stand down all the military preparations at the last minute in favor of a sudden peace conference.

The Persian delegation left having achieved nothing, made its way across the plain Darius had chosen for his battlefield, and reported the failure of its mission.

WHAT WAS TO BE DONE? The young king went on sleeping and his immediate entourage did not dare enter his tent. It was high time that the army began to form up in order of battle, and nobody but he knew what that order was to be.

Eventually Parmenion went in, stood by the bedside, and called Alexander by name two or three times. Once the king was awake, the general asked how he could have slept so soundly when he faced the biggest battle of his life. Alexander replied: "Why not? Don't you see we have already won the battle? We won't have to wander any more around endless burnt-out plains, chasing an enemy who never stands and fights." This was an unfair slur on Darius, but bravado suited the moment.

The conundrum that had kept the king awake for much of the night was this. The Macedonians were massively outnumbered and could easily be outflanked. They faced a long, fearsome row of massed cavalry, some in shining armor of flexible laminated mail. In front of them at various points were the Great King's secret weapon—chariots with sharp scythes fastened to the yoke and to the axle housings.

We do not know exactly how large the Persian army was, but it greatly exceeded the Macedonian. Arrian's estimate rose as high as a million infantry and 400,000 horses. That was absurd hyperbole, but it is convincingly reported that as the two armies approached, Alexander's right wing found itself facing Darius's center. The largest number

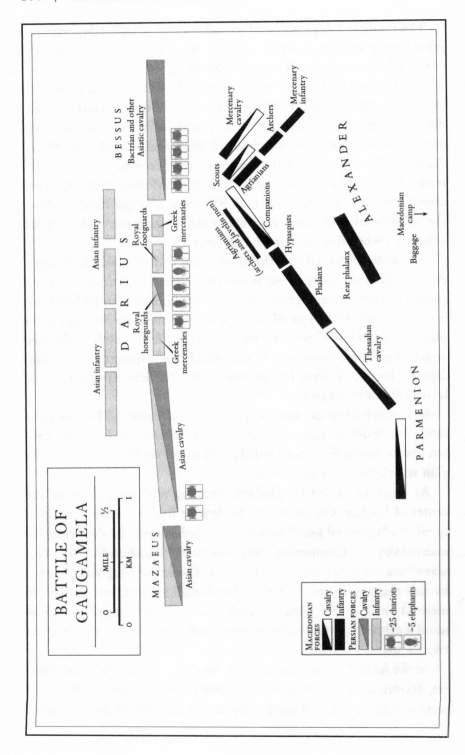

BATTLE OF
GAUGAMELA

BESSUS
Bactrian and other Asiatic cavalry

DARIUS

Asian infantry

Royal footguards

Greek mercenaries

Royal horseguards

Greek mercenaries

Asian infantry

Asian cavalry

MAZAEUS

Asian cavalry

Scouts

Mercenary cavalry

Agrianians

Archers

Mercenary infantry

Companions

Agrianians and javelin men
(archers and javelin men)

Hypaspists

ALEXANDER

Phalanx

Rear phalanx

Macedonian camp

Baggage

Thessalian cavalry

PARMENION

MACEDONIAN FORCES
Cavalry
Infantry

PERSIAN FORCES
Cavalry
Infantry

~25 chariots

~5 elephants

MILE
0   ½   1

KM
0   1

Menidas. Behind them, refused were lancers and Paeonian cavalry, and farther back still the other halves of the Agrianians and the archers. Close to the latter were some 6,700 highly experienced veteran Greek mercenary foot soldiers.

Both the flank guards were hidden from Persian view by lines of cavalry. These were designed to look temptingly weak and ready to be rolled up. In fact, they concealed foot soldiers detailed to cooperate with the riders and repel or maul the Persian attackers.

Because of the danger of complete encirclement, Alexander placed behind the phalanx a second line of infantry, mainly Greeks from League of Corinth member states. This rear guard was under instruction to turn about and engage with the enemy if it succeeded in outflanking the Macedonian wings.

THE KING, FULLY AWAKE NOW, sent round his orders, and the great military machine he had led across a continent to meet this day, the first of October, 331, slowly but surely geared itself for action.

He was already wearing his armor when he emerged from his tent—a belted tunic made in Sicily and over this a thickly quilted linen corselet that had been among the spoils captured at Issus. We see him wearing it in a mosaic depicting the battle that was found in Pompeii; a similar one, perhaps his very own, has been found in one of the royal tombs at Aegae in Macedonia. His steel helmet glowed like polished silver and was attached to a steel neckpiece studded with precious stones. His sword, tempered and lightweight, was a present from a Cypriot king; he had trained himself to use it as his principal weapon in hand-to-hand fighting. Finally, he wore an ornately decorated cloak.

Altogether Alexander was quite a sight on the battlefield. Instantly identifiable, he was not only a human flag or standard to be followed and protected at all costs, but also a key enemy target. Any self-respecting archer or javelin thrower or slinger on the Persian side would do his utmost to bring him down.

During the early maneuvers, Alexander used another mount to spare Bucephalas, who was past his prime. Only when he was ready to go into action was the elderly horse led up for him to ride. He delivered a long speech to the Thessalians and other Greeks and was greeted with a roar of approval. In response, the king shifted his lance into his left hand and, raising his right, prayed to the gods that if he really was the son of Zeus, they should protect and strengthen the Greeks. Aristander in a white robe and a golden wreath rode along the ranks pointing out an eagle flying overhead in the direction of the Persians, a wonderful augury. Once the king had cheered up his left wing, he crossed over to the right, greeting officers and anyone near to him. He then took up his position among the cavalry Companions. His presence was enough to raise morale.

At last, with the sun high in the sky the king gave the order to advance. The Macedonian army marched toward the enemy in oblique order, with the right wing leading. The point was to throw the enemy's line out of gear; if the cavalry on *its* right wing galloped forward to meet the distant Macedonian left they would risk attack from the side and would uncomfortably stretch the Persian center. To avoid envelopment, Alexander's left-flank guard and the Thessalians would be prepared to give ground.

The angle of the Macedonian approach was perhaps as steep as forty-five degrees. As a result, the specialist units at the tip of the left wing could not sensibly be echeloned back, but stood out parallel to the Persian line. They were a combination of Greek cavalry and Thracian forces.

Alexander was approaching the moment when commanders inevitably lose control of events. Dust thrown up by thousands of tramping feet, and the noise of shouting voices, neighing horses, and clashing armor and weapons meant that after a certain point Alexander would no longer be sure what was going on. Messages were taken to and fro by riders, but they were slow and not guaranteed to arrive at all. Even when a battle was lost and won, few participants would have been able to give a coherent account of what had taken place.

However, Alexander's officers had been fully briefed; they were used to their supreme commander delegating authority to them and would do what was required according to the circumstances and their instructions. He himself was at the place where the key decision was to be made: the timing of the crucial charge of the Companions that would determine the outcome of the battle.

As his army approached the enemy, he allowed it to drift to the right. If this continued, he would almost entirely cross over into unleveled ground. Darius could see the danger and ordered Bessus with the Scythians and Bactrians to advance and wheel around the Macedonian right flank. As soon as Alexander saw this, he reacted by ordering Menidas and his single rank of six hundred mercenary horse to charge them. To nobody's surprise, weight of numbers forced them back.

Alexander then sent two small cavalry units—the scouts and the Paeonians—backed by the veteran mercenaries, to attack the Scythians, who began to waver and give way. Arrian does not explain how this was achieved with so few horsemen, but we can deduce what happened from a passage in Xenophon, with which we may assume that Alexander was familiar. He points to the weakness of cavalry in the absence of infantry:

> If he has got some infantry, a cavalry commander should make use of it. A mounted man is much higher than a man on foot, and infantry can be hidden away not only among the cavalry but in the rear as well. . . . If the infantry, hidden away behind the cavalry, came out suddenly and went for the enemy, I think they would prove an important factor in making the victory more decisive. I have noticed that a surprise cheers men up if it is pleasant, but stuns them if it is alarming.

Alexander had fed into the fighting small groups one after another with brilliant economy and precise timing, while Bessus committed more and more of his massed horsemen. It is clear that the veteran mercenaries had delivered an unpleasant surprise to the Scythians and Bactrians and that the flank guard were in a thoroughly good mood. However, their good fortune could not last forever. Sooner or later the weight of the enemy would tell.

At this point Darius released a force of a hundred chariots against the Companion cavalry, who were as yet untouched by the enemy despite Persian hope that Bessus would roll up the entire Macedonian wing. The light skirmishers in front (Agrianians and the rest) grabbed the reins, pulled out the drivers, and slaughtered the horses. Trained in advance, the Companions simply let through their ranks those that got away.

They were captured by army grooms at the back and by royal shield-bearers. The Great King's surprise weapon had been a total failure.

The complete Persian army, jaded from having had to stay awake all night but splendid to look at, was now moving forward. However, Bessus's attempt at outflanking the Macedonians had drawn off so many horsemen that the line between him and Darius's entourage in the center thinned. This was the moment for which Alexander had been waiting. Arrian explains:

> The cavalry sent out to engage the Persians encircling the right wing had forced a break in the front line of the barbarian line of battle. He [Alexander] wheeled for the gap, formed a wedge of the Companion cavalry and the immediately adjacent infantry section [the hypaspists] and led them at full speed and in full cry straight for Darius.

In the space of a few minutes the whole situation turned upside down. Out of the noisy dust thundered the Macedonian heavy cavalry, shouting, "Alala alala" at the top of their voices. Heading the Royal Squadron at the apex of the wedge rode the scarlet and silver Macedonian monarch on his enormous horse Bucephalas. He and his horsemen were followed by the hypaspist infantry. The formation may well have outnumbered the Persian cavalry facing it, but in any event the Macedonians had superiority at point of contact.

Alexander and the Companions sliced through the enemy horse, turned left into the now unprotected flank of the Greek mercenaries, and fought hand-to-hand with the royal guards to reach the Great King. They pushed and shoved with their horses and stabbed with their lances at the Persians' faces. The infantry soon joined in and pressed their long pikes into the mêlée. The two kings were coming closer and closer together. Darius himself threw javelins to help ward off the onslaught. Alexander returned the compliment, but missed and killed the driver next to him.

WHAT WAS HAPPENING ELSEWHERE in the field? Here the news was bad.

Mazaeus on the right was mauling Parmenion and the Thessalians. He was faring well enough, he must have felt, to send three thousand horse round the edge of the Macedonian line and to capture the lightly guarded permanent camp ten or more miles away. He probably did so on the Great King's direct orders, for this was where prisoners of war, including Darius's mother and other family members, were held. To retrieve them would be a great prize. The detachment had no difficulty breaking in. Astonished attendants ran to Sisygambis's tent to bring her the good news that they had been rescued. She knew better than to commit herself, though, until she was sure of the day's winner. Curtius writes that she

> retained her former demeanor. Not a word left her lips and there was no change in her color or expression. She sat motionless—afraid, I think, of aggravating fortune by expressing joy prematurely. People looking at her could not decide which outcome she would prefer.

Then there was trouble in the center. The four phalanx battalions nearest to the hypaspists followed them when Alexander and the Companions advanced, and the two left battalions were distracted by Mazaeus's charge against the Thessalians. As a result, a gap opened in the middle of the phalanx, through which a body of Persian and Indian cavalry poured. They probably intended to take Parmenion from behind, but they became overexcited (as has often happened to horse riders throughout history) and charged unswervingly onward. They punched through the Macedonian infantry reserve and reached the temporary baggage deposit area not far from the back lines of the Macedonian army.

Arrian writes:

> The commanders of the infantry reserve behind the front phalanx soon realized what was going on, turned their division about face, as were their standing orders, and fell on the Persians' rear. Many Persians were killed where they were caught hugger-mugger among the baggage-animals, but some broke away and escaped.

The situation was becoming serious for the Great King, for he feared that he was not only being attacked in the flank, but would soon be taken in the rear and his escape foreclosed. High-born relatives were being slaughtered in front of him. For the second time he was forced to behave like a coward while not being one. Alexander and the Macedonians were getting nearer, and he would soon be taken or killed. If he was to fight another day, as he fully intended, there was no alternative to flight.

Unfortunately, it was difficult to turn his chariot round and drive it away, for it was snagged by dead bodies and wounded soldiers. The horses began to rear and plunge so that his charioteer was unable to control them. Hidden by clouds of dust, the Great King stepped down from his chariot and galloped away on a mare. Now he was there; now he was not.

At about the time Alexander launched his charge, Parmenion sent off a dispatch rider, a trusted Thessalian called Polydamas, from his position on the left. He was to inform the king that the enemy was engaging his forces heavily. It was a signal arranged in advance to help Alexander make the tricky decision when to launch his decisive charge. As things turned out, the messenger arrived when the king was already in the thick of conflict and could not be immediately reached. He delivered his dispatch in a probable lull after Darius's departure.

A later story suggested that Parmenion had issued an unnecessary cry for help, which fatally delayed the pursuit of Darius, and that his performance during the battle had been sluggish and unenthusiastic. In fact, it is clear that his task was explicitly defensive. As we have seen, he was under orders to hold the line long enough for Alexander to win the battle. His forces, especially the Thessalian horse, had acted with great gallantry and managed to stop the Persians from advancing.

The news of Darius's flight was spreading throughout his army. Bessus decided that the best course was to withdraw while in reasonably good order. Slowly and confusedly, the Persian line in general broke. The unimpressive infantry at the back had not done any fighting and wished to avoid it now: they ran as fast as their legs would take them.

Alexander was too good a general to leave a battle before he was quite sure of the outcome. He did not know whether Parmenion on the left had succeeded in holding off Mazaeus. He had to find out and intervene if necessary, for there was no point in having won on one side of the field if he had lost on the other. So, having disposed of the Great King in the center, he proceeded behind the enemy cavalry's positions on the Persian right to reach him.

To do so he was obliged to traverse terrified flows of fleeing Persian horsemen. According to Arrian,

> what ensued was the fiercest cavalry battle of the whole action. The barbarians rallied . . . and hurled themselves head on at Alexander's troops. They had no use now for the usual cavalry tactics—no throwing of javelins, no maneuvering of horses— but it was each man for himself, trying to force his own way through as the only means of survival. They were not fighting now for someone else's victory, but for their very own lives.

In this engagement, about sixty of Alexander's Companion cavalry were killed; Hephaestion himself suffered a spear wound in the arm, and two other commanders were injured.

Many Persians broke through, but Alexander did not chase them. He pressed on toward Parmenion. By the time he arrived, Mazaeus's cavalry had realized that all was lost and was disengaging as well as they could from the Thessalians, who had been putting up a stiff resistance. As soon as the king saw that all was well, he wheeled around and set off in pursuit of Darius. The day was won, but not yet over.

An ancient battle was like a weaponized rugby football scrum. It was relatively bloodless while the fighting was going on; only when there was a clear winner did blood flow copiously. So it was at Gaugamela as at the Granicus and Issus. The exulting Macedonians caught up with the fleeing enemy, cavalry overtaking and trampling on infantry, and went on killing for as long as there were men to kill. Many ransacked the luxuriously appointed and now desolate camp. Implausibly high estimates of casualties abound, but Persian deaths may well have been counted in tens of thousands. The best guess for Macedonian losses are one thousand foot and two hundred horse.

The pursuit of Darius went on until darkness fell. The king gave his men and horses an hour or two to rest and then resumed the hunt at midnight. He and his party (probably the Royal Squadron) galloped through the darkness. They covered seventy-five miles and with dawn arrived at the ancient city of Arbela (today's Erbil), but Darius had passed through it sometime before. For the second time the bird had flown, and Alexander returned crestfallen to his marauding army.

On the following morning he buried his dead and pondered his next step. He had been king for five years and was only twenty-five years old. He had already changed the world.

"ONCE THE BATTLE HAD had this result, the Persian empire was re-garded as having been totally dissolved," Plutarch observed of Gau-gamela. At Gordium, Alexander had been guilty of hyperbole in calling himself lord of Asia, when all he actually controlled was Asia Minor. But now the cap fitted. He had beaten the Achaemenid dynasty in a fair fight.

Darius had made good preparation and chosen his ground intelli-gently. Gaugamela was a wide plain with no convenient river or foot-hills with which an invader's undersize army could guard its flanks. He had assembled an even larger host than at Issus. He had given his inex-perienced infantry new weapons and some training. He had recruited mounted troops from the empire's horse-loving eastern provinces. He had learned from his previous encounter with the Macedonians and had given Alexander the shock of his life when he first laid eyes on the Persian battle formation—miles and miles of cavalry.

But during his dark night of the soul, the Macedonian king had devised the most brilliant of tactical schemes, which turned his nu-merical deficit to advantage. Unlike Darius, who made a virtue of pre-ponderance, he understood that victory would depend on movement and quickness of eye. By luring Bessus and his cavalry to overcommit themselves around the right-hand edge of his line, Alexander created the gap or thinning of the ranks opposite the Companions, into which he led his decisive charge. At Gaugamela he tempered his natural im-petuousness into disciplined energy.

But if Alexander had vanquished the Great King, had he over-thrown him? Were contemporaries right to recognize the end of an empire, or at least of a dynasty? No, Plutarch was mistaken. Despite

Alexander's best efforts, Gaugamela was the second time he had tried and failed to capture Darius dead or alive. He still could not claim the imperial throne without contradiction. If the Great King wished, as indeed was likely, he could continue the war from the far east of his dominions.

But for now there was nothing to do but rejoice. The empire and its great cities lay all before the jubilant conquerors.

CHAPTER 10

"PASSING BRAVE
TO BE A KING"

―――

W HAT WAS ALEXANDER TO DO NOW?

He had three choices, the first of which he rejected at once. He knew that many officers and rank-and-file soldiers wanted him to declare peace immediately and go home happy and glorious. To silence them, he stuffed gold into their mouths. Plutarch writes: "Alexander was proclaimed king of Asia, and after offering splendid sacrifices to the gods, he proceeded to reward his friends with riches, estates and governorships." His men knew how much trouble he took over their comforts, and he was very popular with them. He made it clear that he would soon give them the holiday of a lifetime. For the time being, this calmed any nascent dissent.

The Macedonian king was well aware that the war was not yet over. An alternative was to continue the hunt for Darius, who was plunging eastward past Media through a rough and unfertile landscape which a large army would find awkward to cross. His aim was to put as much distance as possible between him and his pursuers, buying time to raise a third army.

The Great King had with him Bessus's Bactrian cavalry, which had withdrawn from the battle relatively unscathed, a retinue of senior Persians, and a few of the Golden Apple guards. During his flight he was joined by some two thousand Greek mercenaries who had regrouped after the battle.

This was not a large force and, ideally, the Great King remained Alexander's chief strategic target. But we may safely assume that the Macedonians had little topographical knowledge of the eastern half of the empire, and Alexander made a point of not straying into territory which had not undergone a logistical analysis. In his military career so far, he had always sent scouts ahead of the main body of the army and tasked them to assess the nature of the terrain and negotiate supplies from the locals. No exception was to be allowed on this occasion.

There was a third and more attractive option, and this was the one Alexander chose. It was to march south down through Mesopotamia to the fabled city of Babylon with its Hanging Gardens and luxurious lifestyle. He intended to encamp his army outside the city walls for a month's relaxation inside them and then proceed to Susa and palatial Persepolis.

The enemy corpses on the battlefield were beginning to stink in the heat, and the Macedonians did not linger. Pausing only to pick up the treasure Darius had abandoned at Arbela, they marched south. The distance from Gaugamela to Babylon was nearly 290 miles and, when necessary halts are taken into account, the journey through the fertile lands of Mesopotamia lasted three weeks.

It would take a further three weeks to reach Susa, and the king was worried that the treasure stored there might be removed and taken east to Darius. So he sent a senior officer to ride at top speed to Susa to warn against this and to require the city's capitulation.

THE MACEDONIANS SAW THE high walls of Babylon appear in the distance. Alexander had formed them up in battle order, just in case of any trickery. Through a gate, a long procession was winding its way toward them. Priests and government officials led, and every sector of the community, bearing gifts, was represented. There in the throng was Mazaeus. After Gaugamela he had fled to the city, with which he had a personal association as his wife was Babylonian. Together with his grown-up children, he presented himself as a suppliant and formally surrendered the city to the Macedonian conqueror. The defection of a member of the Great King's inner circle was a coup for Alexander and had presumably been negotiated in advance. It was a blow to Darius's authority and would encourage others to follow suit.

The Persian in charge of the citadel and the Babylonian exchequer was highly competitive and refused to be outdone by Mazaeus. He carpeted the road with flowers and garlands. At intervals on either side, he set up silver altars and heaped them with frankincense and all kinds of perfume. Behind him as he walked came a moving zoo—lions and leopards conveyed in cages and, more usefully, cattle and horses. This was his present for Alexander—generous if inconvenient.

Zoroastrian wise men, or magi, chanted holy songs; after them walked Chaldean astronomer-priests, whose role (as we have seen) was to reveal and interpret heavenly movements and seasonal changes. Musicians followed; they usually sang the praises of Persian kings, but presumably rewrote their lyrics in favor of the Macedonian conqueror.

The cavalcade was rounded off by Babylon's cavalry; dressed in exotic uniforms they were chocolate soldiers rather than serious warriors.

The king rode into the city on a chariot, passing through the huge Ishtar Gate, with its glazed lapis-lazuli bricks, with its animals and rosettes, into a grand processional avenue that had been built by Nebuchadnezzar in the seventh century B.C. Alexander immediately took possession of the Southern Palace and the treasury. He may have had himself crowned king of Babylon.

FAR FROM ENCOUNTERING ANY HOSTILITY, the Macedonians were welcomed with open arms. Babylonians fondly remembered their glorious past. They had twice had their own empire, first of all briefly in the eighteenth century B.C. under the famous lawgiver Hammurabi; then, for a hundred years from the last quarter of the seventh century, they had ruled a wide-stretching territory from Egypt in the west to the Persian homeland, Persis, in the east. It was during this last period that the Hanging Gardens were built, and it has been estimated that for a time the city was the largest in the world, boasting a population of more than 200,000.

In 539 Babylon fell to the Persians and was governed thereafter by the Great King. At first sight, Alexander's arrival promised freedom from the foreign yoke. Sensitive to local feelings, he met the astronomer-priests and took their advice on appropriate sacrifices to the gods and in particular to Bel-Marduk, the city's guardian deity, whom Greeks saw as a barbarian version of Heracles.

In a bid for popularity he ordered the rebuilding of the great temple of Marduk, the Esagila. The Great King Xerxes is reported to have destroyed it, but it may simply have fallen into decay with the passage of time. Either way, Babylon's new ruler wanted it put to rights. The gesture may have been less appreciated when he made it clear that the local authority would have to pick up the bill.

We are not told if the Chaldeans briefed him on their astronomical records of the recent lunar eclipse and its political significance. It would seem likely that they did, for it was their duty to make their revelations available to the government of the day. In that case, Alexander will have learned at this early stage that his luck would continue for eight years, but no more. Iron must have entered the soul. In consolation, he must have gratefully recognized the parallel with Achilles, who preferred to die young but famous rather than long-lived and unknown. It is said that the court historian, Callisthenes, commissioned translations of the Astronomical Diaries and sent Aristotle a list of lunar eclipses in past centuries.

In the short term, there were issues to be addressed at once. What was to be done about the administration of the city and the province of Babylonia? Mazaeus had already taken control and Alexander named him as his permanent satrap (to guarantee security, Macedonians were given matching military responsibilities). They had probably been in confidential contact in the weeks following Gaugamela before coming to an understanding. But the appointment was unpopular in every quarter. For the patriotic Persian, Mazaeus was a deserter; for the Babylonian, who had thought he had been liberated, he was a symbol of Persian oppression; and for the true-blooded Macedonian he was living evidence that their king was going native.

But what else could Alexander have done? As the army marched farther and farther east it met fewer and fewer Greek-speakers. Even the king's cloud of traveling experts knew little of the peoples through whom they passed, nor were they personally familiar with local elites. The Babylonians spoke a version of Aramaic and only a tiny minority will have understood Macedonian or Greek. Their chief secondary language must have been Persian. It is highly unlikely that any Macedonian officer was fluent in either tongue, although interpreters were on the payroll.

From a practical point of view, a senior and trustworthy Persian nobleman was an obvious solution to the problem. Mazaeus turned out to be loyal and dependable; before he died in office a few years later, he was living evidence that further resistance was pointless, for the Macedonian king intended to retain Darius's officials in important posts provided they cooperated.

Alexander also appointed Mithrenes as satrap of Armenia. He was the Persian who had surrendered Sardis, the capital of Lydia, to him three years previously. The promotion was a mixed blessing, for Armenia had not yet been conquered and the new governor was obliged to fight for his job. We hear no more of him, so he was probably killed in the attempt. These two senior Persians were the first of many to be promoted to senior positions under the new regime.

While the business of government was being conducted at the palace, the army was encouraged to relax. Other-rankers were probably encamped outside the city, but spent their leisure in town having a good time. The local inhabitants feasted them lavishly.

The prudish Roman historian Curtius expressed his feelings about Babylonian degeneracy:

> The moral corruption there is unparalleled. . . . Parents and husbands permit their children and wives to have sex with strangers, provided this wickedness is paid for. . . . The Babylonians are especially addicted to wine and the excesses that go along with drunkenness. Women attend dinner parties. At first they are decently dressed, then they remove all their top-clothing and by degrees disgrace their respectability until (I apologize to my readers for spelling it out) they finally discard their most intimate garments. This revolting conduct is characteristic not only of prostitutes, but also of married women and young girls, who regard such disgusting fornication as "being friendly."

It may be that this garishly colored account reflects the ritual of divinely endorsed prostitution, which seems to have been an immemorial tradition in Babylon. Many centuries before, the lawgiver king

Hammurabi gave protection to the women involved. Premarital sex was practiced with strangers, although it was followed by strict conjugal chastity. Apparently, the act was associated with the divinity Mylitta (whom the Greeks identified with their goddess of love, Aphrodite). We are told that it had to be done at least once in a woman's life and was compulsory; earnings were handed over to the goddess. More probably, the custom may have been restricted to sexual priestesses.

Writing in the fifth century B.C., Herodotus evoked the scene:

> There is a great multitude of women coming and going; passages marked by line run every way through the crowd, by which the men pass and make their choice. Once a woman has taken her place there, she does not go away to her home before some stranger has tossed silver into her lap, and had intercourse with her outside the precinct; but while he throws the money, he must say, "I invite you in the name of Mylitta." . . . It does not matter what the fee is; the woman will never refuse, for that would be a sin, the money being by this act made sacred.

Whatever we make of these claims, Babylon was evidently a free-and-easy billet and, like all soldiers, the Macedonians enjoyed breaking a period of enforced celibacy.

AFTER A MONTH'S HOLIDAY, the Macedonians were on the move again. Their destination was Susa.

Alexander was approaching the empire's heartland. Until now he had crossed through subject populations who regarded him with goodwill, but now he faced opposition from inhabitants for whom he was the enemy. In effect, his army was a moving island in a hostile sea. He had always made sure to obtain advance information on roads, resources, terrain, and climate, but in future this would be much more difficult, albeit more essential than ever.

The march led through abundant country, and supply was easy enough for the time being, but after Susa Alexander tended to divide his troops into two or more groups. Each would take a different route and so would need to consume less food and water. Sometimes the main body would stay behind and Alexander would advance alone with a fast-moving special force. Only when he had subdued a hostile territory would he call forward the rest of the army.

During the march Alexander was joined by Amyntas, son of Andromenes, with substantial reinforcements from Macedonia. Amyntas had been dispatched after the siege of Gaza and now returned with 500 Macedonian cavalry and 6,000 infantry, 4,100 Thracian cavalry, and 4,000 infantry and just under 1,000 cavalry levied from friendly states in the Peloponnese. Alexander took the opportunity to review the performance of his senior officers, making promotions on merit rather than seniority. In the cavalry he abolished tribal groupings, and squadrons were led by men of his own choosing He also introduced improvements to the living conditions of the rank and file. All received generous bonuses from the money surrendered at Babylon.

Soldiers in the ancient world expected their wages to be supplemented by the rewards of victory—plunder plucked from the flames of enemy cities. But Alexander had no intention of letting his men loose on the empire's rich and civilized urban centers. To do so would simply create unnecessary political, economic, and social difficulties for the Great King, a post he expected soon to hold.

Diodorus comments: "He brought the whole force up to an outstanding devotion to its commander and obedience to his commands, and to a high degree of effectiveness, looking toward the battles to come." Up to a point. His men did adore him and he did look after them well, but underneath the cheeriness and pride in victory, early stirrings of opposition could be detected. Some asked themselves whether this war would ever end.

Amyntas brought with him fifty grown-up sons of Macedonian noblemen to act as an intimate bodyguard. These were the Royal Pages. They served the king at dinner, brought him his horses when he went into battle, and accompanied him on the hunt. They also took turns to be on guard outside his bedroom door. These young men were, in the politest sense, hostages for their fathers' good behavior, but they also marked a stage in the development of Alexander from an informal leader, a first among equals, to a ruler with a formal court where access to the king's person was ever more carefully controlled.

With Amyntas and his men came some potentially very bad news. Alexander had learned as long ago as the siege of Tyre that Greece was unsettled and Sparta was agitating for revolt. Now he was told that a general he had appointed as a governor in Thrace was involved in an insurgency. The threat this posed was very real, and Antipater had been compelled to lead a substantial force against him and to raise a fleet (which in due course won a convincing victory). Meanwhile Alexander had ordered reinforcements for his Persian campaign. Soldiers were beginning to be in short supply.

King Agis saw that these pressures on Macedonian military capacity gave him a unique opportunity. He left Asia Minor for Crete, where his brother was bringing the island under Spartan control. Here he signed up eight thousand Greek mercenaries who had taken refuge there and, probably in spring 331, sailed with them to the Peloponnese. Despite Sparta's unpopularity among its neighbors he negotiated an anti-Macedonian alliance with a number of them and was soon leading an army of twenty thousand infantry and two thousand cavalry. Agis inflicted a stunning defeat on a Macedonian force, which greatly enhanced his credibility among mainland Greeks.

Sparta's chances were improving. As an Athenian orator put it later: "Alexander had withdrawn to the uttermost regions of the North Star, almost beyond the borders of the inhabited world, and Antipater was slow in collecting an army. The whole outcome was uncertain."

IT WAS AT THIS POINT that Amyntas left for the east. He knew nothing of subsequent events and, unsurprisingly, his report alarmed Alexander. There was little he could do to help, but around this time he wrote to the Hellenic city-states announcing that all tyrannies had been abolished and that they lived under their own laws (this was more public relations than fact, for a number of tyrannies backed by Macedonia existed on the Greek mainland). As a reminder of the official purpose of the war, he commanded the citizens of Plataea to rebuild their tiny ruined town in Boeotia, as a symbol of the great victory nearby which saw the end of the Persian invasion in 479.

At his next stop, the empire's administrative capital, Susa, Alexander ordered a senior officer to take to Antipater the considerable sum of three thousand talents, to be used at will. At Susa he discovered a pair of statues looted from Athens by the Great King Xerxes in 480. They commemorated two youths, Harmodius and Aristogeiton, who assassinated the brother of the then tyrant of Athens—an event that paved the way to the creation of a democracy. Harmodius and Aristogeiton were heroes of the people and Alexander took care to send the statues back to Athens. This was the latest of a number of conciliatory gestures. They seem to have worked. When Agis attempted to win the city to his alliance, it continued with its cautious policy of nonalignment.

The Spartan made a bad mistake when he used force to gain allies in the Peloponnese. He laid siege to Megalopolis, the leading city of Arcadia in the north of the peninsula. People began to wonder whether his true objective was less to confront Alexander than to recover Sparta's old domination of southern Greece.

The siege came to nothing and wasted valuable time. Above all, it allowed Antipater to come to terms with the Thracians, recruit soldiers from states in the north, and march down to confront Agis. Soon Antipater commanded an army of about forty thousand men.

At a battle outside Megalopolis, Agis and his troops fought the Macedonians bravely, but he was badly wounded in the thigh and bled heavily. He was taken back to his camp, but the battle was lost. When he saw enemy soldiers approaching, Curtius writes that he "gave orders that he be put down." Not being obeyed, he covered himself with a shield and started brandishing his spear. Nobody would risk hand-to-hand combat with him, and he was killed at long range with javelins.

With this defeat the insurrection ended and Greek city-states made what peace they could with their Macedonian overlord. Alexander received the good news on the way from Susa to Persepolis. He ought to have been grateful, but he liked to make light even of a threat that could have brought his Persian campaign to a halt. He commented on Antipater's victory: "It would seem, my men, that while we were conquering Darius here, there has been a battle of mice over there in Arcadia." But when he first learned of Agis's campaign he had been rightly alarmed. What would the point have been of conquering Persia if he lost Macedonia?

Antipater was no fool. Sensitive to his master's amour propre, he handed over the peace negotiations to the council of the League of Corinth. They were equally cautious, merely giving the Spartans permission to put their case to Alexander in person.

The story is a sad one. Agis was as courageous as Alexander, but less lucky. His springboard was not a rich and thriving state like Macedonia, but a small provincial power past its peak. He did his best.

AN INSCRIPTION FROM 330 or the early 320s reveals that there was a famine in Greece. We know little about it, or indeed about civilian life in general during these years, but the disruptions to trade caused by Agis's revolt and more widely by Alexander's campaigning seem a likely cause. The stone tablet lists the states supplied with grain by the Hellenic city of Cyrene, on the coast of northern Africa west of Egypt. The city probably charged the usual price, in an attempt to discourage inflation.

Only two individuals are cited by name as recipients or purchasers—Olympias and her daughter Cleopatra. Although the details are unclear, they had a fraught relationship. The mother exercised influence, if not power, in Macedonia alongside Antipater. Meanwhile Cleopatra ruled as regent in Molossia when her husband (and uncle) went to southern Italy as a condottiere in the service of the powerful port of Tarentum. He was killed in battle. His body was mutilated and cut in half. What was left of him was cremated and the bones sent home to Molossia.

Presumably these royal women distributed the grain they purchased to the populations of their respective kingdoms. That they were singled out for mention in this fashion shows that they were well-known international political figures.

At some stage, Olympias fell out badly with Antipater. She seems never to have accepted that her son had placed him in charge of European affairs. After the end of the Agis rebellion Antipater was in a strong position to act as he wanted and there was no advantage in undermining him. Olympias disappeared to Epirus, where she took over the government. She and her daughter acted in concert for a while. However, there usually being no room for two queens in one beehive, Cleopatra decamped to Pella.

At some point, the young queen had sex with a good-looking man. Olympias found out about it, but for once reacted calmly, observing that her daughter ought to get *some* enjoyment from her royal rank.

ON THEIR WAY TO Susa, the Macedonians came across unrefined petroleum oozing from the soil, so copiously that it formed a small lake. The substance was highly inflammable and could be set alight, Plutarch observes, "by a flame's radiance without actually touching it." One evening as it was growing dark, some Persians arranged a demonstration. They sprinkled a small quantity of petroleum, or naphtha, along the street that led to the king's quarters and then set light to it at one end. In a fraction of a second the flames flashed to the other end, an effect that the ancient world had never before witnessed.

On another occasion, a servant boy called Stephanus was in attendance while the king took a bath and rubbed himself down with olive oil. Thinking that the flames moved so fast that they would not burn flesh, a courtier suggested that naphtha be tried out on Stephanus. Surprisingly, he agreed to the experiment and coated himself with the liquid. The fire took and Stephanus was enveloped in flames. Alexander was horrified, and if servants had not been able to put the fire out by pouring water over the boy, he would have died. As it was, he was badly burned.

Scientific experts of the day speculated (wrongly, it goes without saying) that naphtha flows from soil that is oily and combustible. It was no accident, they flatteringly inferred, that their king's own nature was equally fiery. No wonder he was conquering the combustible soil of Mesopotamia with such ease. Although the sources do not name him, this was just the kind of sycophantic idea that Callisthenes would have thought up.

THE FIRST TRACES OF human habitation at Susa have been dated to about 7000 B.C. Over that time a Neolithic village gradually grew into the leading city of the Elamite civilization, in the far west and southwest of today's Iran. Its fortunes fluctuated as conquerors came and went, and the city was razed three times.

One of these Ozymandiases was the Neo-Assyrian monarch Ashurbanipal. He sacked the city and boasted about it:

Susa, the great holy city, home of their gods, seat of their mysteries, I conquered. I entered its palaces, I opened their treasuries where silver and gold, goods and wealth were amassed. . . . I destroyed the ziggurat of Susa. I smashed its shining copper horns. I reduced the temples of Elam to nothing; their gods and goddesses I scattered to the winds.

Alexander may have been the latest in a long line, but, as he had demonstrated in Babylon, he was more interested in maintenance than destruction.

In early December he arrived outside Susa's walls. He was met by the son of Abulites, the Persian satrap for the region, and the Macedonian officer he had sent to the city after Gaugamela, and was presented with speedy dromedaries and a dozen elephants. The surrender took place as had been agreed and was peaceful. On entry, Alexander sacrificed in the traditional Macedonian manner, held a torch race for the men, and, as ever, staged an athletics competition. The contents of the treasury were handed over. These amounted to the staggering sum of more than forty thousand talents of gold and silver bullion that had accumulated untouched over many years, and nine thousand talents of minted gold in the form of gold darics.

Important appointments were made, confirming the king's policy of reconciliation with senior Persians. Abulites was confirmed in place. We hear of no protests, but throughout the army there will have been widespread puzzlement at best, and at worst silent resentment. As counterweights, the garrison command was given to a Companion and overall military authority to a Macedonian.

Alexander had been taken aback by Darius's luxurious lifestyle when on campaign. He was now shown round the "fabulous royal palace" and received a lesson about the trappings of majesty at home. He found a daily bill of fare for the Great King's lunch and dinner engraved on a brass column. Huge quantities of culinary ingredients were listed, including four hundred geese, three hundred turtles, three hundred goslings, thirty horses, and many kinds of herb (among them an aromatic plant called silphium, which, it was believed, conveniently doubled up as an aphrodisiac and a contraceptive, but is now regrettably extinct).

Evidently, the exchequer funded all the meals of a numerous court. The expense was colossal. Alexander knew how to be generous (always for a purpose, of course), but he disapproved of waste. Convinced that cowardice was the sure consequence of luxury and dissipation, he ordered the metal menu to be destroyed. In the royal bedroom a golden vine studded with clusters of jewels hung over the bed. An inventory conducted a decade or so later listed a large number of objets d'art together weighing fifteen thousand talents.

Alexander seated himself on the Great King's throne. It was too high for him and his feet did not touch the floor. One of the Macedonian pages saw this and pulled up a table beneath his dangling legs. It fitted and Alexander was pleased by the boy's presence of mind. Then he noticed that a eunuch on the palace staff was crying and asked him what the matter was. It was from that table, the man replied, that the Great King used to eat, and he was upset by the disrespectful use to which it was now being put. Alexander was embarrassed and, no doubt, did not want a reputation for impertinence to spread through the Persian court. He ordered the table to be removed.

Philotas, Parmenion's son, interrupted. "Don't do that, Sir. Take this as another omen, that the table on which Darius once dined is now your footstool." On second thought, the king agreed and kept the table where it was. This casual incident was to be understood as a divine sign of approval for the transmission of power.

Demaratus, the aged fixer from Corinth, believed in the revenge justification for the war. When he saw Alexander in Susa, he wept. Through his tears, he said that all the Greeks who had died before this hour had been deprived of a great joy, since they had not seen Alexander sitting on the throne of Darius.

A CLOUD BRIEFLY SPOILED the fine weather. The dowager queen, Sisygambis, and her granddaughters were still with the army and Alexander decided to park them permanently in Susa. He gave them tutors to teach them the Greek language. He was still on excellent terms with Sisygambis, but nearly ruined the relationship by committing a faux pas.

The king had been sent examples of national dress from Macedonia and a large amount of valuable purple fabric had been found in the palace. He ordered it all to be presented to the dowager queen, together with the women who had sewn the clothes. He added a message that if she liked the Macedonian garments, she would be able to have her granddaughters trained how to make them. Alexander still had much to learn about Persian cultural attitudes. Sisygambis took the gift as a grave insult, for high-status Persian females would have been humiliated if compelled to work with wool. Alexander was mortified when he learned of his mistake. Although "Sorry" was not in his usual vocabulary, he went to her in person to apologize. Greek women, like his sisters, he explained, were brought up to weave and spin and he had been led into error by his own customs. He begged her to excuse his ignorance of hers. Warmth returned between them. He went on calling her mother.

FOR A VICTORIOUS ARMY, the journey to Persepolis, the empire's ceremonial capital, was surprisingly hard going.

In the ancient world, wars were usually fought only between spring and autumn, but Alexander needed to reach Persepolis before anyone else took the opportunity to make off with the treasury. The Zagros Mountains stood in his path, and the passes were covered in snow. It is a mark of his urgency that he left Susa during the depths of winter in mid-January 330.

The distance from Susa is some 370 miles and the Macedonians marched through the land of the Uxii, a corridor that led to Persis, the Persians' "sparse and rugged" motherland. Some of these tribespeople lived in a fertile plain; they were governed by a Persian satrap and paid their taxes. The mountain Uxii were a different matter; they were not subjects of the Great King and fiercely maintained their independence. They made their living from taxing travelers—or, more exactly, from organized brigandage. The Persian authorities thought it would be too much trouble to subdue them and agreed to pay a toll.

After the king entered the Uxiis' territory, the dwellers on the plain immediately capitulated. However, those who lived in the mountains controlled a strategic pass leading eastward, and they insisted on levying their customary charge. Alexander told them to meet him at the pass, "where he would pay them what was owing." They assumed he meant to give them their money.

That was a mistake. The king advanced at top speed with only a portion of his army, up to fourteen thousand men in total, comprising nine thousand infantry, three thousand mercenary archers, one thousand javelin-throwing Agrianes, and one thousand Thracian horses. They fell on the Uxii villages, destroying and pillaging. Then Alexander marched to the pass, arriving before the tribesmen, shocked by the attack on their homesteads, had taken up position. He sent Craterus forward to occupy the heights to which he guessed the tribesmen would withdraw when hard pressed, and then he launched a full-scale assault. As he had predicted, they scattered in Craterus's direction and either were cut to pieces or fell to their deaths from cliff paths.

The Uxii were allowed to live in peace on payment of an annual tribute of one hundred horses, five hundred draft animals, and, cripplingly one assumes, thirty thousand sheep. An irritant which Great Kings had put up with for centuries had been removed in a few days.

The king then split the army between himself and Parmenion. The old general was given command of the Thessalian cavalry, the more heavily armed infantry, and the baggage train, and took the high road to Persepolis. They would inevitably proceed slowly. Meanwhile Alexander chose a more direct route with the remaining infantry, the Companion cavalry, the light cavalry used for skirmishing, the Agrianians, and the archers, and made a forced march to the Persian Gates, a narrow and easily defended gorge between high mountains. It was six miles long and at its narrowest six feet wide, cliff to cliff. The satrap of Persis, one Ariobarzanes, had guessed the impatient Macedonian's journey plan and occupied the pass with a substantial force of 25,000 men and some cavalry. Worse, he had had a wall built across it.

Alexander faced an awkward problem. He meant to defeat Ariobarzanes, but he would have to do so in a way that prevented the satrap from making a getaway. If the Persians withdrew in good order, they would most probably speed to Persepolis. Once there they would either defend the city or, much worse, take possession of the hoard of bullion reported to be stored there and run off with it. If they could deliver the gold and silver to Darius, who was skulking somewhere in the eastern wastes, the defeated monarch would be able to afford a new army.

Alexander started badly. With typical overconfidence, he launched a direct assault on the wall, but his men were bombarded from above by catapults, slingers, and archers. Large rocks were tumbled down onto their heads. The king had no choice but to sound the retreat, leaving his dead behind in the defile. It was a humiliating setback. To abandon the bodies was unthinkable, but a second assault would be pointless. What was to be done? How was Ariobarzanes to be defeated quickly and decisively before he withdrew to Persepolis?

The Macedonians built a fortified camp a few miles back and waited for a while. The king cross-examined some prisoners of war, who volunteered to show him a rough and narrow path that would take him round behind the Gates. Ever the risk-taker, he immediately accepted the offer. He placed Craterus in charge of the camp, leaving him a couple of phalanx brigades, some archers, and five hundred cavalry. He was to keep up the camp's usual appearance and increase the number of fires so that it would appear that nothing had changed.

At nightfall he led the rest of the army along the secret path. As they climbed, snowdrifts held them up and progress was slow. After eleven miles, the king divided his forces once again. For himself he selected a flying column consisting of the hypaspists, a phalanx brigade, the lightest-armed of the archers, the Agrianians, and two cavalry squadrons. He ordered the remaining troops, led by three senior generals, Philotas the cavalry commander, his friend Amyntas, son of Andromenes (now back in post after having brought the reinforcements from Macedonia), and Coenus, Parmenion's son-in-law, to march down into the plain on the far side of the Gates. They were then to build pontoon bridges over a river that would have to be crossed before reaching Persepolis.

The motive for this third detachment was presumably to ensure that there was a substantial force blocking the way to Persepolis, should the Macedonians fail to crush Ariobarzanes at the pass.

Alexander and his elite unit struck out along a rough and difficult track through dense forest. About midday they halted for a meal and some sleep. Darkness had fallen when they set off again. Just before dawn they came out onto a high point at the back of the Gates, overlooking an enemy outpost. They quickly annihilated it and also killed many in a second outpost. At the third, most of the guards escaped, but into the mountains rather than to the main camp. So, luckily, the alarm was not raised. Then Alexander led an attack on the enemy camp. At the perimeter ditch he had a trumpet sound as a prearranged signal to alert Craterus, who immediately launched a frontal assault.

Surprise was complete and the Persians, seeing that they were surrounded, panicked and fled. Many were killed. Ariobarzanes himself escaped into the hills with forty cavalrymen and five thousand foot. Just as the king had feared, he pushed on to Persepolis, but the authorities were realists and refused to let him in. He turned to face his Macedonian pursuers and fell fighting alongside his men.

It would have been an eccentric fate if the victor of Issus and Gaugamela had been defeated in a skirmish. Impetuosity had led the king into serious trouble, but if that quality was a fusion of speed and determination it had also rescued him.

Resistance being over, the royal treasurer surrendered the city to Alexander. The king had spared Babylon and Susa, but he had something different in mind for Persepolis. As Xerxes had sacked Athens all those years before, the Persians were now to suffer the same fate in a symmetry of punishment.

MOST GREAT CITIES GROW over the centuries from small beginnings. Persepolis was different, for it was invented by Darius the Great, the invader of Greece.

He envisaged the need for a splendid collection of palaces where festivals could be staged, grand receptions held, foreign ambassadors received, and religious ceremonies conducted. Here Great Kings could be buried in suitable splendor. Persepolis was to be the symbol and showcase of empire and was designed to evoke awe and respect. (But its remote location meant that it never grew into an urban community with its own character and social momentum.)

A huge platform, 450 by 300 meters in extent, was constructed, which abutted against a mountain. On it was built an audience hall approached by grand stairways; its roof was made from cedar, ebony, and teak and was supported by seventy-two columns twenty-five meters high. It could accommodate hundreds, perhaps thousands, of people. Nearby a treasury was used to store war booty and tax receipts. A large collection of cuneiform clay tablets has survived which shows that a bureaucracy of more than a thousand employees was responsible for the empire's financial management. Fine bas-reliefs, probably carved by Greek sculptors, depict all the different peoples of the Persian empire as they bring tribute to the Great King. These include, cheekily, the Ionian Greeks, whose rebellion set off the historical process, now reaching its climax with Alexander's doom-bringing arrival.

Darius's successors on the throne further developed the site, commissioning their own palaces and halls. His son Xerxes was an energetic builder and boasted in an inscription:

> I am Xerxes, the great king, the king of all countries and all languages, king of this great and wide world. . . . When I became king, I did much that was excellent. What had been built by my father, I protected, and I added other buildings. What I built, and what my father built, all that by the grace of Ahuramazda [the creator and sole god of Zoroastrianism, the official religion of the Achaemenids] we built.

Alexander sent advance guards to take possession of the city, after which he climbed up onto the high terrace. According to Plutarch, he came across a statue of Xerxes that had been toppled from its pedestal and was lying on the ground.

> He stopped and spoke to it as though it were alive. "Shall I pass by and leave you lying there because of your invasion of Greece, or shall I set you up again?" For a long while he gazed at the statue and reflected in silence. Then finally he walked on.

The treasury was found to contain the phenomenal sum of 120,000 talents in gold and silver coin and bullion. A further six thousand talents was removed from the vaults of Pasargadae, the empire's original capital some fifty miles from Persepolis where the tomb of Cyrus its first ruler was (and is still) to be found.

Once the entire army had come up, Alexander gave his men permission to loot the city for twenty-four hours, but not to touch the royal precinct, which was his share of the spoils. He authorized them to kill any adult males they met, and all prisoners were slaughtered on his orders, according to Plutarch, "because he thought that would help his cause." The Persians of Persis were bitterly hostile to their new master and no doubt would rise up against him if given the chance. Devastating their sacred city would, the king felt, show them that their days of grandeur were over and that resistance was futile. The rape of Thebes had aroused as much disgust as fear, but Alexander knew that terror would enforce submission.

Pillage was a military perk and the soldiers had not been allowed a good sack since the fall of Gaza. They seem to have gone berserk. The city was emptied of valuables and inhabitants. Those who had not escaped into the countryside were dead.

Once the bloodletting was done, the king held games in honor of his victories, as was his custom. He performed costly sacrifices to the gods and staged lavish entertainments.

What happened to the palaces is not so clear. According to one story, shortly before the army's departure from Persepolis in April, Alexander and his intimates were holding a party in one of the staterooms. Drink flowed. Some young men "giddy with wine" persuaded a reluctant Alexander to let them stage a *komos*. This was a ritual drunken procession, celebrating a wedding, athletic success, or, no doubt as now, victory in war. A chorus of men would sing rousing victory hymns (*epinikia*).

The constituents of a *komos* were quickly assembled—torches for all the guests and musicians (the female players who had been performing for the king's party). Unusually some other women were present as guests, along with their patrons or lovers. One of these was Thais, a hetaira (a female companion or courtesan) from Athens. She was to become the mistress, and later the wife, of Ptolemy.

The tipsy king led them all from room to room to the sound of singing and flutes and pipes. Thais organized the procession and was the first, after Alexander, to fling her blazing torch into one of the buildings. Everyone else followed suit. The wooden roofs caught fire and soon a large part of the complex was in flames.

The army was encamped outside the city. It was evening and when a brightening of the sky was noticed, soldiers ran to help put out the flames. Once they saw that in fact the king was directing the conflagration, they dropped the water they had brought and began throwing dry wood onto the blaze themselves.

THERE IS ANOTHER VERSION of what took place. This makes the arson an act of policy rather than an accident of alcohol. Immediately on arrival in the city, the king convened a meeting of his generals and set out his position. Curtius writes that he restated the obsolete war aim of retribution for the Persian invasion. He wanted to punish the Persians for wrecking Athens and its temples. No city was more hateful to the Greeks than Persepolis, he said. To appease the spirits of their forefathers they should wipe it out.

This not only gave his troops permission to pillage, as we have seen, but also announced his own decision to demolish Persepolis, just as he had Thebes. Parmenion urged him to change his mind. There could be little point in destroying what was now his own property. He added an argument close to the king's heart. The peoples of the empire would be less inclined to accept him as their ruler if they thought he had no plan to govern them, but, in Arrian's phrase, was simply there for "a tour of conquest."

The king had maneuvered himself into an impossible position by running two contradictory strategies at the same time—revenge and reconciliation. On the one hand he continued giving jobs to the Achaemenid elite and appointed a Persian as satrap of Persis. He very probably agreed with his wise old general. On the other hand, he had an acute sense of symbolism. In his eyes, east and west had fought one another tit for tat down the ages, and now a new Achilles had retaken Troy. He convinced himself that the Hellenic world would be dismayed if the leader of the League of Corinth failed to deliver a coup de théâtre that would bring the millennial drama to a conclusion. And such a gesture might remind any remaining Greek rebels of what had happened to Thebes; some were still sore and resentful after Antipater's victory at Megalopolis and would profit from a fiery assertion of who was master.

Even if the destruction was ill-advised in the medium to long term, we should note that Darius's personal authority was damaged by the surrender of the empire's four great cities without a fight and by the flames of Persepolis. It must have been about now that some high officials decided to switch sides to Alexander and that others began to consider secretly the deposition of the Great King.

The hypothesis that the fire was the outcome of policy is borne out by evidence on the ground. It is telling that many structures on the raised platform were left intact. The fire-raisers focused their attention on Darius's great audience hall, the palace of Xerxes, and the treasury. These were the two guilty men, and the buildings they created were compelled to pay postmortem for their crimes.

The ashes of the Acropolis were matched by the ashes of Persepolis, as modern archaeologists can confirm, for they have found scorch marks on columns and layers of charred detritus at both sites. The flames rhymed.

The two versions of the sack of Persepolis turn out not to be mutually exclusive. In its essentials Alexander's *komos* is best regarded as a historical event, but not so much an improvisation as a carefully staged performance.

And what was more natural than to dance around a bonfire?

ON THE MORNING AFTER the party, though, the king is reported to have had second thoughts. He came to regret what he had done. This is the last time we hear him talk of his crusade against barbarians. He was learning that if he was to be the Great King he had to behave like a great king. To ensure his power, military force was not enough. He would have to win the consent of those he ruled.

Burning down palaces was not the way.

CHAPTER 11

TREASON!

———

ALEXANDER DID NOT HAVE A MOMENT TO LOSE.

In two battles he had tried his hardest to kill or capture Darius, but each time the man had slipped through his fingers. It was obvious that the war was won, and should be over and done with. Instead, he was obliged to chase after the Great King wherever he was. The Macedonian army needed to move fast if it was to catch him. If too much time passed, Darius might be able to raise a third army from the eastern satrapies, which so far had made only a minor contribution in the field.

Why, then, did Alexander linger so long in Persepolis? He had arrived in January and did not leave until late May or June.

THE ANSWER TO THE PUZZLE lies in the terrain the Macedonians would have to cross before reaching their next destination. That was Ecbatana (today's Hamadan), capital of the northern province of Media and the empire's fourth great city, where the imperial family spent their summers. The route lay through a high pass in the Zagros range, snowbound and all but impassable in winter months.

Obtaining supplies in this desolate landscape, much of which was uninhabited in ancient times, was another challenge. In March 330, Alexander led a small exploratory force of a thousand cavalry and a few light infantry to face down a hostile tribe, the Mardi, and almost certainly to arrange food depots.

They had a terrible time of it. The rank-and-file soldiers clamored to go back to the comforts of Persepolis. Curtius, always well informed on geographical matters, writes that the king, leading from the front as usual,

> jumped from his horse and proceeded to make his way on foot through the snow and hard-packed ice. His friends were ashamed not to follow him and the feeling spread to his officers, and, finally, the men. The king was the first to clear a way for himself, using an axe to break the ice, and then the others followed his example.

Once they had defeated the Mardi, the Macedonians returned to base after a month's absence. The five-hundred-mile journey to Ecbatana lay across a rocky solitude of ice and snow, in many places three or four feet deep. Alexander accepted that he would be stuck at Persepolis until spring or the early summer. The only consolation was that Darius, reported to be at Ecbatana, would also be immobilized by winter.

DURING THE EMPTY MONTHS at Persepolis, Alexander had time to catch up on his correspondence. In the ancient western world, letters were scratched onto soft metal, such as lead, or onto wax-coated wooden boards. Papyrus was also available in quantity, presumably manufactured in Egypt and expensive. Trusted messengers would travel along the well-maintained highway that ran from the Persian capitals to the provinces of the west.

According to Plutarch, "It is astonishing that Alexander could find time to write so many letters to his friends." Everyone of any importance in Greece and the former Persian empire will have had reason to communicate with the world conqueror, and he was snowed under by official inquiries, to which he would be obliged to reply when decisions were required. A secretary, an intelligent young Greek called Eumenes, managed the king's correspondence. He had worked for Philip and had the rare virtue of being popular with Olympias.

The complicated issues Alexander had to adjudicate by long distance are well exemplified by the crisis at Eresos, a hill town by the sea on the island of Lesbos. It was a place of no importance, but its politics were savage. Alexander never went there, but found himself having to intervene by letter in its affairs more than once. During the 350s, three brothers seized power as joint tyrants (the word signified an authoritarian ruler but did not have pejorative connotations). At some point the brothers were expelled, and early in Alexander's reign two new tyrants emerged who were pro-Persian.

After Granicus, Alexander had these men removed from office and (presumably) a democracy installed, but during Memnon's brief but effective maritime campaign they were reinstated. Then the town was liberated again and the ci-devant tyrants were sent to Alexander, then in Egypt, for judgment. He sent them back, accompanied by a letter telling the people of Eresos to set up a court to decide themselves what should be done with them. This was arranged, the men were condemned to death and, it would appear, executed.

The family of the tyrant brothers now sent a delegation to ask the king to reinstate them. So Alexander wrote to Eresos about this. According to fragments of a marble inscription, the king ruled that

> the people should decide whether or not they should be allowed to return; the people hearing the edict set up a court for them, in accordance with the law and the edict of king Alexander, and when speeches had been made on both sides decided that the law against the tyrants should be valid and that they should be exiled from the city.

Plutarch reports an instructive comment of the Roman emperor Augustus, who expressed his surprise that Alexander did not regard it as a greater task to set in order the empire he had won than to win it. The criticism does not appear to be well-founded. Although our sources pay scant attention to matters of governance, inscriptions found at the site of ancient cities, such as those from Eresos, suggest that the king took an active interest in administration. Either he personally, or his staff, kept a close eye on the political activity and legislation of local communities.

What is more, the attention the king gave to the logistics of a military campaign and his careful management of his soldiers' welfare are evidence that he was a human-resources manager of the first order. We know too little of that aspect of his leadership skills to say much more.

ALEXANDER OFTEN CORRESPONDED WITH his mother, usually to fend off her many complaints. But she did also interest herself in his creature comforts: we are told that she urged her son to buy a slave of hers who was highly skilled at ritual cooking.

Like many of the king's inner circle, Olympias could not stand Hephaestion, rival as he was for her son's undivided love and attention. However, Hephaestion gave as good as he got. When she sent him threatening letters, he responded in high dudgeon: "Stop quarrelling with us and do not be angry or menacing. If you keep on, we won't pay much attention. You know that Alexander means more to us than anything." We can imagine the fury he aroused in Olympias by his use of the royal "we" with reference to himself. He surely meant to tease. He was certain of his place in his lover's heart and could risk goading his impossible "mother-in-law."

But the king did not allow him a completely free hand, for as a rule he kept Olympias's letters to himself. Otherwise, they regularly went through the post together. On one occasion, though, Hephaestion's eye fell on a missive from Olympias that had already been opened. Alexander let him read it, but took off his ring and pressed the seal to Hephaestion's lips, "so much as to tell him not to say a word."

Alexander liked to keep in touch with his friends and share the ups and downs of everyday life. He wrote to them fondly when they were away. They were all keen hunters, for whom any animal with legs was a fair target. He wrote to a Companion who had been bitten by a bear, complaining that everyone else had heard of the incident except for himself. "Now," he went on, "you must write to tell me how you are, and whether you were let down by any of your fellow-huntsmen, so that I can punish them." The sting in the tail was meant as a joke rather than a serious threat. The king had a heavy-handed sense of humor.

Another day he was out hunting a mongoose when Craterus accidentally wounded another general, Perdiccas, in the thigh. Alexander wrote to inform Hephaestion, who happened to be absent on a mission. Hephaestion was not well liked by his colleagues, but he and Perdiccas got on and the news must have worried him. The injured man survived.

Slavery was endemic in Mediterranean societies and domestic slaves were numberless. To be useful, they had to be allowed freedom of movement and, understandably, some took the opportunity to run away. The king somehow found time to help retrieve friends' slaves. He ordered a search to be made for one runaway and sent a letter of congratulation on the discovery and arrest of another. In the case of a third, who had sought sanctuary in a temple, the king advised caution. The man should be lured out and not taken by force from a sacred precinct. The son of Zeus always respected the gods.

THE GREAT KING, WHILING AWAY the winter in Ecbatana, had no intention of giving up the struggle.

He had with him a substantial force (if much reduced from the usual multitude) of thirty thousand infantry. They included a fiercely loyal regiment of mercenary Greeks under the command of Patron, a man from the home of the Delphic oracle, Phocis. Alexander saw them as traitors, for they had fought against his Hellenic crusade. They would never be allowed home, and if captured they faced a bleak fate. They had no choice but to be steadfast.

Bessus, the able and energetic satrap of Bactria, led a formidable troop of 3,300 horse. Four thousand slingers and archers completed the complement.

This was not a large enough army to defeat the Macedonians in a third trial of arms, and the Great King sent round to the eastern satrapies calling for soldiers. He was awaiting the requested reinforcements.

But spring had arrived and with it reports that his nemesis was closing in. There was no alternative but to hurry off to the increasingly remote provinces of Hyrcania, Parthia, Bactriana, and Sogdiana. Space would buy time, and time would buy soldiers. But time would lose him soldiers, too, for withdrawal from Ecbatana opened important allies, the Cadusii and the Scythians, to Macedonian attack

At one point Darius ordered his army to veer off the military road a little, telling the camp followers and the men guarding the baggage to go on ahead. He then called a meeting of his council. Among its members were his chief executive officer or chiliarch, Nabarzanes, and Artabazus, who was the father of Alexander's mistress Barsine but nevertheless a faithful servant of the Great King. Satraps from the east were also present.

The mood must have been gloomy, but everyone protested their loyalty. Below the surface, though, these high officials of empire were weighing their options. Darius's withdrawal after Gaugamela had depressed morale, and Alexander's obvious desire for continuity meant that jobs, position, life could be maintained under the new regime. Treason could be presented as being in the public interest.

Artabazus gave a rousing speech: "We shall follow our king into battle," he said, "dressed in our richest robes and equipped with our finest armor." But with no troops forthcoming from the east, the satraps saw little advantage in throwing away good men after bad. They sat on their hands.

Behind the scenes, Nabarzanes and Bessus made common cause. They decided to arrest the Great King. Curtius writes:

> They reasoned that if Alexander overtook them they could ingratiate themselves with the victor by handing over their king alive—he was sure to set great store by the capture of Darius—whereas, if they managed to get away from him, they would kill Darius, seize his kingdom themselves and restart hostilities.

These were ruthless and ambitious grandees, but they genuinely believed that Darius's cause was lost. They would be patriots if possible. Otherwise they would look out for themselves.

Nabarzanes laid the ground for their plan, turning to Darius and addressing him directly: "Temporarily transfer your authority and your command to another, who can carry the title of king only until the enemy quits Asia. When victorious, he can then return your kingdom to you."

His intention was to raise the notion of regime change without risking a charge of betrayal, but seldom has advice been less convincing. The Great King lost his temper. He drew his sword and threatened to cut down the speaker. Bessus and some Bactrians crowded around him. Ostensibly, they were upset; they begged the Great King to stay his hand. He did so, but if he had persisted they would have arrested and chained him.

The gathering began to break up. Nabarzanes slipped away and was soon joined by Bessus. They decided to move the men under their command away from the main body of the army. Meanwhile, Artabazus did his best to placate the Great King, telling him that he could not afford to estrange any of his supporters. Darius agreed, but, depressed and despairing, withdrew into his tent.

No one seemed to be in charge. Patron was worried by the turn of events. He told his Greeks to get their weapons from the baggage train, where they were stored during a long march, and await his orders. The Persian troops remained loyal, believing that "it was impious to desert a king." Artabazus assumed the role of commander-in-chief and worked hard to build their morale.

The conspirators decided it was time for action. They knew that the Greek mercenaries and the Persians were still loyal and dared not arrest Darius openly. When Artabazus told them that he had mollified the Great King, they put on a show of weeping and begging for forgiveness. A night passed; with dawn, they moved their men back into the camp and presented themselves at the door of the royal tent. They prostrated themselves in front of Darius.

Having accepted their apologies, the apparently unsuspecting Darius gave the order to march on and climbed onto his chariot in the usual way.

PATRON SUSPECTED THAT BESSUS and Nabarzanes meant the Great King harm. He walked as near as was permissible to Darius's carriage (Darius had left the uncomfortable chariot) and looked out for a chance to talk to him. But Bessus, fearing that the Greek was planning to betray his plot, would not step away from the Great King; he behaved more like a guard than a traveling companion.

Patron hesitated and sometimes fell back, not daring to speak. At last Darius noticed him and told an official to ask Patron whether he had anything to tell him. Patron replied that he did, but only in the absence of others. He was told to step forward without an interpreter. Alone in his entourage, Darius spoke some Greek, so the two men were able to converse in plain sight with nobody else able to understand what they were saying.

Patron asked him to pitch his tent in the Greek area of the camp, where he would be properly guarded. Darius asked why, and Patron told him that Bessus and Nabarzanes were plotting against him. The monarch replied that he was well aware of the mercenaries' loyalty but that it would be very difficult for him to leave his compatriots. He made a good point, for his Persian soldiers were doubtless considering their position and any sign that the Great King no longer had confidence in them could loosen theirs in him.

BESSUS WAS ON TENTERHOOKS; he knew no Greek but the setting aside of the interpreters made him certain that Patron was giving him away. He once more loudly protested his loyalty and warned that a mercenary like Patron would do anything for hire. Darius gave him a look that signified acceptance. In fact, he had accepted the truth of Patron's accusations: he later said as much to Artabazus. The old nobleman advised him to move across to the Greeks, but he again refused.

Night gathered and silence fell throughout the camp. Men in the bodyguard began to make themselves scarce. A few eunuchs stood around in the royal tent, not knowing what to do. Darius told them to leave and look after themselves. They began wailing and others joined in.

Misinterpreting the noise, soldiers reported to Bessus and Nabarzanes that Darius had committed suicide. They mounted their horses and, with a picked group of supporters, rushed to the royal tent, where they found that Darius was alive. They ordered him to be arrested and bound (in gold fetters, it was said).

The conspirators and their forces rejoined the highway and began marching east toward Bactriana, Bessus's province on the edge of India.

Darius was brought with them, still wearing his official robes. He was transported in an old wagon, which was covered in dirty animal skins so that its occupant should not be recognized. He must have told himself that his future would be bleak and short.

—

IN MAY OR EARLY June 330, Alexander was at last able to leave Persepolis. The snows had shrunk if not altogether vanished and the approaching harvest would help to provide supplies of food and fodder.

He was to march north to Ecbatana at the head of seventeen thousand men. He decided to take with him some of the money surrendered to him; with this, he would pay his army. The remainder of the money he ordered to be stored under guard at Ecbatana's citadel. To carry it all there, a vast number of mules, as well as three thousand camels, were recruited from Susa and Babylonia. Parmenion was placed in charge of the operation and ordered to hand over the treasure to the repentant and reinstated Harpalus. After that he launched a punitive expedition against the aforementioned Cadusii, a hostile tribe of mountaineers by the Caspian Sea.

Along the way, the king kept picking up contradictory rumors. Were the Macedonians to advance, he was told, Darius would abandon Ecbatana, fleeing eastward and ravaging the land as he went. Later it was said that the Great King meant to offer battle. Then, when Alexander was three days' march from the city, he was met by a renegade Achaemenid, who was an illegitimate son of the previous Great King, Artaxerxes Ochus. He reported that Darius had been expecting reinforcements, but when they failed to arrive had left Ecbatana four days previously, taking with him seven thousand talents from the exchequer.

Ecbatana was a remarkable sight, if we are to believe Herodotus, writing in the fifth century:

> Its walls are of great size and strength, rising in circles one within the other. The plan of the place is that each of the walls out-tops the battlements of the one beyond it. . . . There are seven circles, the royal palace and the treasuries standing within the last.

Apparently, the battlements were each painted in different colors—to start from the outside, white, followed by black, scarlet, blue, and orange. The inner two battlements were coated with silver and gold.

Alexander's priority was to catch Darius and once he had arrived at the city he spent as little time as possible admiring it before moving on. However, he chose this moment to introduce an important military reform. He demobilized all the League of Corinth troops, including the Thessalian cavalry. It was his final signal, after the burning of Persepolis, that the crusade was over. He treated the men with typical generosity: as well as all his back pay, each cavalryman received an enormous bonus of one talent; foot soldiers were awarded the smaller but still lavish sum of one thousand drachmas.

Many of these men had spent years in foreign service and will not have welcomed the prospect of a long march home to their small native city-states, where jobs were scarce. The king had something to offer them. They were invited to reenlist, and those who did so were given a handsome "golden hello" of three talents (eighteen thousand drachmas).

But from now onward they would exchange their Hellenic allegiance for loyalty to Alexander alone. He had in mind an army of professional soldiers, disciplined and well-trained according to his rule book. They would be ready and willing to go wherever he chose to lead them. They would fight alongside other recruits from the empire he had just vanquished, barbarians and Greeks marching together.

ALEXANDER WAS NOT INTERESTED in money, but now he had it in almost uncountable quantities. He was a masculine version of the nymph Danaë on whom Zeus—his father—had showered gold. His wealth allowed him to display munificence. This was a quality expected of a king which he will have learned from his famously open-handed father.

Plutarch discusses the topic in his biography: "Alexander was by nature exceptionally generous and became even more so as his wealth increased. His gifts were always bestowed with grace and courtesy, and it is this alone which truly makes a giver's generosity welcome."

However, he had no compunction in using prodigality as a weapon of control, and his gifts often had a bullying undertone. They were delivered to the recipient with the force of a blunt instrument. On one occasion the king saw a Macedonian soldier who was driving a mule laden with Persian gold. The animal was exhausted and the man took the load onto his own shoulders and tried to carry it. He was obviously in difficulty and Alexander called out to him: "Hold on, keep going, and you can take what you are carrying to your own tent."

When a Companion asked for help with dowries for his girls, Alexander presented him with the enormous sum of fifty talents. The Companion replied that ten would be more than enough, upon which the king remarked dryly: "Enough for you to accept, but not enough for me to give."

People close to the king registered their anxiety about what they saw as his excessive liberality. Olympias for one gave him a piece of her mind. She wrote: "I wish you would find other ways of rewarding those you love and respect: as it is, you are making them all the equals of kings and enabling them to make plenty of friends, but leaving yourself without any."

(Olympias knew nothing of today's dismal science of economics. If she had, she would also have been able to point out to her son that in time, the release of so much money into the classical marketplace was highly inflationary.)

Alexander himself noticed that some of those around him had developed a taste for vulgar and extravagant lifestyles. Hagnon survived his faux pas of offering the king a beautiful boy and remained an influential courtier; as a mark of conspicuous waste, he wore silver nails in his boots. Leonnatus was one of Alexander's closest friends from their schooldays and had been with him on the day of Philip's assassination. He was brave, hardworking, and true, but he was also very fond of Persian luxury. He enjoyed wrestling as a pastime and had special dust sent from Egypt to sprinkle on his body before a bout. His armor was ornately decorated and his horses' bridles gilded. Senior Macedonians cossetted themselves, hiring masseurs and personal servants.

The king noticed such things, but expressed no more than gentle disapproval. He asked: "How can a man look after his horse, or keep his spear and his helmet clean and bright, if he has lost the habit of using his hands to look after his own adorable body?" Plutarch, ever the moralist, believed that inordinate wealth sapped the fighting spirit of the Macedonians. He claimed that "[the king's] friends, because of the wealth and pomp with which they were surrounded, wished only to lead a life of luxury and idleness. They found his expeditions and campaigns an intolerable burden, and little by little went so far as to abuse and find fault with the king."

The evidence points in the opposite direction. Alexander's long run of victories, forced marches, and exposure to climatic extremes is proof enough that there was nothing degenerate about the Macedonian army. The king did not countenance poor performance when his men were on duty, and self-indulgence was unthinkable. When at leisure, though, they could let their hair down. As we have seen, Philip's court was notoriously filled with warriors who delighted in bling and excess. Alexander had no quarrel with that. Like father, like son.

AT ECBATANA THE MACEDONIAN army came back together again as an integrated whole. Word came that Darius was in full retreat and was heading for the satrapies of Parthia, Hyrcania, and, at the farthest edge of empire, the rich and powerful province of Bactriana. He was believed to be in danger of assassination, but at this point he still seemed to be in full command of his forces. His followers were losing heart, though, and many deserted, traveling back to their home regions. Quite a few voluntarily surrendered to Alexander, who as a result was kept well-informed about Darius's progress.

He set off in hot pursuit. He took with him only the Companion cavalry; the scouts or light cavalry and the mercenary horse; some of the phalanx; the archers; and the Agrianians—in sum, the fastest troops at his disposal. The rest of the army was to follow at its own pace.

The king set a course for Rhagae, a town with Zoroastrian associations (near today's Teheran). About 240 miles from Ecbatana, it stood on an ancient highway south of the Caspian Sea and the Elburz mountain range, brown and bone-dry below snowcapped peaks. It was only a day's march to the Caspian Gates, a mountain pass that opened the way to the eastern parts of the empire. Alexander wanted to get there before Darius.

The Macedonians proceeded at a punishing pace, with men falling behind and horses dying. They arrived at their destination after eleven days of forced marches only to find that Darius had already passed through the Gates. It was clear that he could not be easily overtaken. So Alexander gave his men five days' rest to recover from their exertions. He took the opportunity to appoint a Persian called Oxydates as satrap of Media; he had been imprisoned by Darius at Susa and condemned to death (for what offense we do not know), which, Arrian writes, "inclined Alexander to trust him."

The Macedonians resumed their march via the Caspian Gates and into cultivated territory. The next stage of their journey was to be across desert; the king sent Coenus, Parmenion's reliable son-in-law and one of his most trusted lieutenants, with a small party to forage for supplies. Soon afterward, one of Mazaeus's sons and a Babylonian nobleman, both escapees from the Great King's disconsolate army, presented themselves to Alexander and gave him the startling news of Darius's arrest by Nabarzanes and Bessus.

This galvanized Alexander. He had to reach and rescue the Great King before, as seemed very likely, his captors killed him. That way lay disaster, for some other Achaemenid would surely lay claim to the vacant throne and the struggle would resume. But with a living and breathing Darius in his possession, Alexander would be able to command events and find some way of persuading his prisoner to give up his crown in his own favor.

He pressed on without waiting for Coenus to return, taking with him only the Companions, the light cavalry, and some infantry chosen for their stamina and speed on the march. They had nothing with them apart from their weapons and two days' worth of food. The rest of the army was told to come after him at their ordinary speed.

The party traveled all through the night and till noon the following day. After a short rest, they resumed their journey and marched through the next night. At first light they arrived at the camp from which the renegade Achaemenid had set out to find Alexander. Darius's interpreter, ill and unable to keep up with the Persian force, was caught and was debriefed on the latest developments, the most important of which was that the Bactrian cavalry had acclaimed Bessus as supreme commander. He had declared himself Great King, giving himself the regnal name of Artaxerxes V and wearing the upright tiara of office. Artabazus and his troops, together with the Greek mercenaries, were furious. However, there was nothing they could do to reverse the coup, so they left. They turned off the main road and made for the hills. The Persians soon drifted back, for "they had no one else to follow."

Having heard all this, the king saw there was not a moment to be lost. He had to carry on: men and horses were exhausted, but he insisted. After another night and morning march, the Macedonians arrived at the place where Bessus and Darius had camped the day before. From the locals Alexander learned that the Persians were traveling by night. When he asked whether there was a shortcut to catch up with them, he was told that there was, but it was waterless.

That did not discourage Alexander. He selected five hundred of his toughest infantrymen and mounted them on the best of the surviving horses. He instructed Parmenion's son Nicanor, commander of the hypaspists, and the Agrianian chief to lead the rest of the attack force along the road taken by Bessus. He himself and his elite troop, assisted by a guide, rode from dusk for forty-five miles through the desert. It was an extraordinary feat. At dawn they came across the Persian rear. The soldiers were straggling and few of them had weapons. They offered no resistance and fled.

The scene was obscured by clouds of dust. Bessus did not see that his Bactrian cavalry heavily outnumbered the Macedonians and could have annihilated them. As ever with Alexander, audacity made luck.

THE CRISIS HAD ARRIVED. Darius had become a liability, chained as he was in his dilapidated wagon. He would soon be overtaken, and Bessus and some colleagues tried to persuade him to avoid capture by mounting a horse and galloping off with them. Darius refused. He would take his chances with Alexander.

With the commotion of the enemy's unexpected arrival audible, time was short. The conspirators' priority was to prevent their distinguished captive from falling into Macedonian hands. If they could not take him with them, they would have to leave him behind, dead.

This a couple of dissident satraps swiftly accomplished, hurling their spears at the king and running him through many times. Also, they tried to maim the wagon's draft animals, and they put to death the two slaves who were accompanying Darius (presumably the last of the eunuchs).

Then Nabarzanes and Bessus panicked. They were sure that Alexander would not thank them for killing Darius. In fact, he was more likely to punish them and, if he learned of the existence of the new Great King Artaxerxes, definitely with extreme prejudice. Most of their troops refused to fight. They decided to abandon the scene of the crime, riding off immediately to their different satrapies, Hyrcania and distant Bactriana.

Much of Darius's last army probably melted away. Patron and his Greek mercenaries surrendered unconditionally to Alexander. But the Bactrian cavalry remained fiercely loyal to their satrap Bessus and some of the infantry transferred their allegiance to him. At the empire's farthest frontier, they would make a last stand against the invader.

Meanwhile, maddened by their wounds, the draft animals pulled the wagon off the road and came to a halt some distance away. There was a spring nearby. Local people pointed it out to a Macedonian soldier who was tormented by thirst; he went over to drink the water and found Darius, not dead yet but at his last gasp. The king asked for a drink and when he had swallowed some cold water he is said to have sent a message of goodwill to Alexander. "Through you, I give him my hand." As he spoke, he took the soldier's hand and died holding it. He was about fifty years old.

Alexander soon came up and stood around respectfully for a short time, with a tear in his eye. He laid his cloak on the body, which he sent to Persepolis for a full-dress state funeral. As the self-proclaimed king of Asia, he knew he should stand for continuity and act as Darius's grieving heir. He vowed to punish the Great King's murderers.

A few miles away stood the city later known as Hecatompylos (Greek for City of One Hundred Gates). Built in the flat, dust-blown desert, it was fed and watered by the fertile strip that lies along the foot of the Elburz Mountains. Here Alexander made a fortified camp or base. His army was given a few days' well-earned rest.

DARIUS HAS BEEN PORTRAYED as weak and "effeminate." According to Arrian, he was "a consummate coward and incompetent." In fact, he was an effective ruler who possessed charm and attracted loyalty from those around him. His doom was to face a military commander of genius.

As Darius was only a distant member of the royal family, Arta-xerxes Ochus, well-known butcher of close male relatives, saw him as no threat to his throne. He was appointed satrap of Armenia and later promoted to a senior position in the postal service. He can never have counted on becoming the Great King.

His victorious duel with a tribal rebel was evidence of physical courage. Plucked from the imperial bureaucracy, he soon consolidated his rule and showed that he knew how to make and implement swift decisions, as when he removed the venomous kingmaker Bagoas from the stage.

With Philip's murder, he judged, quite reasonably, that the Mace-donian threat was just an irritant and could be dealt with by local forces. In any case, the inexperienced boy king might very well aban-don his father's invasion plan. Darius's only error was not to appoint a commander-in-chief, but he did not trust the best qualified candidate, Memnon.

The battle at the Granicus sounded the alarm; the Great King had no choice but to go to war in person. He was obviously a fine orga-nizer—he assembled a vast host with speed and efficiency—but he suf-fered from two material disadvantages: he had never had experience as a battlefield commander, and he was isolated from the world in a court of flatterers and fools, who underestimated the opposition.

Darius was adaptable enough to learn from failure. Seeing that the Macedonians at the Granicus had longer swords and light but tough cornel-wood spears, he re-equipped Persian soldiers with similar weap-ons. However, no experienced general would have fought at Issus along the narrow ribbon of land that constrained his greatest strength, cavalry. Darius learned that lesson, too, and made sure that his next battle would be fought on a broad plain. And this time his battle plan made the most of his cavalry. He nearly won.

For the second time he had to flee the field. The day was going well elsewhere, but that would mean little if he was struck down. It was the right, the brave decision.

Not only was Darius good at his job, but also the institutions over which he presided and the governing system were working satisfacto-rily in most parts of the empire (Egypt being a notable exception). The provinces were acquiescent and the Great King took care not to interfere in local affairs.

The Achaemenids did not fall through structural decay or misrule, but from straightforward military defeat. The victor had no plans for reform and saw himself as the heir to a going concern. He behaved as if he were an Achaemenid, and the slogan of continuity calmed the traditional ruling elite.

THE YOUNG MACEDONIAN MONARCH was changing. He began to wear exotic clothes that combined features of Persian as well as Greek costume. He dressed himself in a white robe with a sash around his waist, though not in the trousers and the typically Persian long-sleeved upper garment. He gave his Companions cloaks with purple borders and dressed the horses in Persian harness. He took to wearing the blue-and-white diadem, although not the upright tiara.

When sealing letters to European destinations he used his old Macedonian ring, but when writing to Asians he adopted Darius's royal signet (which he had presumably removed from the dead man's body).

Apparently, he maintained a Great King's costly perquisite of a harem containing 365 concubines, one for every night of the year. From what we know of his sexual interests it is most unlikely that he went to the trouble of recruiting hundreds of young women himself or that he brought them with him on campaign. We can assume that he inherited Darius's harem and simply took on the responsibility to pay for its upkeep.

Alexander continued to protect and promote distinguished Persians. He asked Hephaestion to parade outside the royal quarters the many prisoners of war who had accumulated over time, and to separate nobles from commoners. A granddaughter of Darius's predecessor, Artaxerxes Ochus, was identified; her possessions were returned to her and a search instituted for her husband, who was missing. The most important personage who came to light was Oxyathres, a younger brother of Darius, to whom Oxyathres had been devoted. At Issus, he had defended his Great King bravely from Alexander's decisive cavalry charge.

Oxyathres transferred his loyalty to Alexander, who took to him and enrolled him among his inner circle of friends. Evidently the Persian had been unimpressed by Bessus and, whatever his personal feelings, accepted that the Macedonian king was the new power in the land. He could see that Alexander wanted to govern the empire with the assistance of the Persian political elite. By joining his court, he publicized his endorsement.

The king was aware that his philo-Persian policy of retaining local administrators divided his generals. According to Plutarch,

> It was Hephaestion who approved of these plans and joined him in changing his habits, while Craterus clung to Macedonian customs. He therefore made use of the first in his dealings with the barbarians, and of the second with the Greeks and Macedonians. In general, he showed most affection for Hephaestion and most respect for Craterus, for he had formed the opinion and always said: "Hephaestion is a friend of Alexander, while Craterus is a friend of the king."

Unsurprisingly, the two men's mutual hostility grew and festered over time. On occasion they quarreled openly and Alexander was forced to mediate between them.

THE DEMOBILIZATION OF THE Greeks at Ecbatana some weeks earlier had upset the rank and file more than had immediately appeared. During the brief furlough at Hecatompylos, a sudden irrational rumor swept through the army that the king was satisfied with what he had achieved thus far and had decided on an immediate return to Macedonia. Curtius writes: "The soldiers scattered to their tents like madmen and prepared their baggage for the journey. One might have thought a signal had been given for the general packing-up of the camp. The bustle of men looking for their tent-mates or loading wagons came to the king's ears."

Alexander was rattled, for Bessus had yet to be defeated. Also, he had already privately decided on an exploratory expedition to India, thought to be at the final rim of land before the encircling ocean. He convened an emergency meeting of his senior officers. With tears in his eyes, he told them that his men were not cowards, but that they were threatening to bring his career to a premature end with this sudden pining for home. It was not possible to reverse the march of events. Having conquered Persia, they could hardly walk away now. Whatever their true feelings, each of the generals offered his support and volunteered for the most difficult tasks. They would calm their men down, they promised, provided that the king reassured them with kind words.

A general assembly was called and the king addressed it. He reminded his audience of the long list of victories they had won, but warned that those gains could be easily lost. Bessus and his friends would catch at any sign of weakness. He said, "The moment our backs are turned, they will be after us" and would fall upon the Macedonians "as if they were so many women." But one last push and the war would be over. The men cheered him to the echo, as he wrote in a dispatch to Antipater, and promised to follow him wherever he chose. The crisis was over. Two days later, in August 330, the army set off to the province of Hyrcania, where Persian refugees were hiding out.

But had there been a crisis at all? The episode leaves an impression of hysteria, of a lovers' quarrel, fierce to the outside gaze but playful for participants. Alexander's leadership style—risking his life at the drop of a hat; never ordering something to be done he would not, indeed did not, do himself; providing reliable supplies; arranging frequent rest breaks and quality entertainment; above all, winning—meant that his men had complete confidence in him. Their relationship had an undertone of infatuation.

Alexander had always paid great attention to his soldiers' morale, but from about this time he went a step further and began regularly providing lavish feasts overflowing with food and alcohol. They would be opportunities for bonding, for backslapping, for camaraderie. Also, as the military campaign stretched into the indefinite future, the king sought to deflect a natural homesickness and foster a desire to settle down. So, farsightedly, he encouraged his soldiers to marry and start families. Life in the camp was to become increasingly civilian and domestic.

Importantly, he backed this policy with a basic welfare system for soldiers' sons (nothing is known of provision, if any, for daughters). According to the Roman historian Justin, writing in the second century A.D.,

> maintenance was provided for the boys, and arms and horses were given them when they grew up; and rewards were assigned to the fathers in proportion to the number of their children. If the fathers of any of them were killed, the orphans notwithstanding received their father's pay; and their childhood was a sort of military service in various expeditions. Inured from their earliest years to toils and dangers, they formed an invincible army; they looked upon their camp as their country, and upon a battle as a prelude to victory.

In late August 330, a real crisis emerged which showed that Macedonian traditionalists were not to be bought off; it exposed the depth of disaffection in some quarters and, indeed, threatened the king's life.

DIMNUS WAS INFATUATED WITH a rent boy called Nicomachus, whom he had taken off the game and whose favors he now monopolized. A member of the Companion cavalry, Dimnus was a young man of no importance except for the fact that he was keeper of an enormous secret, which he was bursting to reveal to his boyfriend.

Almost beside himself, he took his beloved to a temple when nobody else was present. He asked him, in the name of their love and the pledges they had exchanged, to swear a solemn oath never to divulge what he was about to tell him. Nicomachus took the oath, not supposing that this would involve him in any illegality.

Dimnus then announced that he had joined a conspiracy to assassinate Alexander. The attempt was to be made in two days. He named eight plotters, apparently including a certain Demetrius, one of the king's seven personal bodyguards. The literary sources do not discuss their motives, but the timing suggests that Alexander's reconciliation policy and his refusal to end the war were powerful motives, and as we have seen, killing their kings was something of a Macedonian tradition.

Nicomachus was horrified by what he had heard. He made it clear that his oath did not justify treason nor free him from his duty to report a crime; self-interest will have reminded him that secret schemes of this sort often fail. Demented by passion and fear, Dimnus tried to persuade his lover to join the conspiracy and, failing that, at least to keep quiet about it. He drew his sword, pressing it to each of their throats, one after the other.

Eventually Nicomachus pretended that, out of affection, he would do what he was asked. He was a boy of a practical cast of mind and understood that he was in very real danger. Somehow he had to extricate himself, even if that meant betraying Dimnus.

He decided to confide in his brother Cebalinus, who was also endowed with common sense. They recognized that the sooner a message could be got to the king the safer they would be. Nicomachus should stay where he was. Other conspirators might realize that they were betrayed if he was seen near the royal tent. So Cebalinus went instead. He hung about at the entrance, waiting to ask someone entering to take in an urgent message.

This was a rare day when no visitors arrived. At last one of Alexander's leading commanders, Philotas, son of Parmenion, commander of the Companion cavalry, arrived on business with the king. Cebalinus, upset and anxious, stopped him and poured out his story. The general commended him and said he would report the matter to Alexander. He had a long conversation with the king, but in the event did not mention the conspiracy.

Cebalinus waited until Philotas came out toward evening and asked if he had done as he promised. He replied that Alexander had had no time to talk to him and then went on his way. Cebalinus refused to be put off and the next day he was back outside the royal tent. Philotas, on his way in again to see the king, said he was seeing to the matter, although in fact he did not inform Alexander.

The young man's suspicions were aroused. Rather than continuing to press Philotas, he gave his information to a young nobleman called Metron. He was one of the Royal Pages, who was responsible for the royal weapons and armor and had routine access to the king. He acted without delay, discreetly slipping Cebalinus into the armory and breaking in on the king, who happened to be taking a bath.

Events now speeded up. Alexander sent guards to arrest Dimnus and questioned Cebalinus. When he learned that it had taken two days for the boy to report the conspiracy, he doubted his loyalty and ordered his arrest. Cebalinus cried out that he had gone at once to Philotas, who had done nothing. He was obviously telling the truth and Alexander saw a huge political crisis bearing down on him. What was one of his senior generals and son of his deputy thinking of when he refused to pass on Cebalinus's warning? Had treason penetrated the heart of his regime?

He burst into tears.

DIMNUS SAW THE GUARDS approaching and guessed that the game was up. He stabbed himself with a sword he was wearing and collapsed. He was carried to the royal quarters for interrogation, but had lost the power of speech. He groaned, turned his face away from the king's gaze, and died.

Alexander invited Philotas to meet him and asked him, as though there must have been some misunderstanding, to clear up the issue of the two-day delay. The general was not at all taken aback. Yes, he admitted, Cebalinus had mentioned the plot to him; but (according to Curtius) he said he was afraid that reporting "a quarrel between a male prostitute and his lover would make him a laughingstock." Now, he admitted, he could see he had made a bad mistake, and he begged Alexander to forgive him.

To buy himself time, the king offered Philotas his right hand as a token of reconciliation. He commented that in his opinion this was a case of information not being taken seriously rather than being deliberately suppressed.

The trouble was that Philotas had form. He was brave, hardy, and almost as openhanded as Alexander. However, according to Plutarch, he

also displayed an arrogance, an ostentation of wealth and a degree of luxury in his personal habits and his way of living which could only cause offense in his position as a private subject. At this time, in particular, his efforts to imitate a lofty and majestic presence carried no conviction, appeared clumsy and uncouth, and succeeded only in provoking envy and mistrust.

Olympias, no slouch when it came to complaining, wrote to warn Alexander against him. And Philotas was heartily disliked by his colleagues. His father was worried enough by the poor impression he was making to remark: "Son, don't make so much of yourself."

Philotas had a mistress called Antigone. A beautiful young woman, she came from Pydna, a Greek port on the Thermaic Gulf. Sailing to Samothrace for the Mysteries, she was captured by the Persian fleet. After Issus she found herself in the Great King's baggage train at Damascus. There she fell into the hands of Parmenion, who passed her on to Philotas. She may or may not have been a slave, but appears to have been of low birth. She had little choice but to make her living as a high-class prostitute or hetaira.

By the time of the Egyptian campaign, Philotas and Antigone had become a settled couple. When he was drunk, he enjoyed engaging in indiscreet pillow talk. He complained of Alexander's claim to be the son of Zeus-Ammon. In his opinion, the king was a mere boy and his successes in the field were thanks to Philotas and to Philip. Antigone gossiped about these remarks, which eventually reached the ears of Craterus, Philotas's political enemy and rival. He brought her privately to Alexander, who told her to maintain the relationship with her patron and send in regular reports. He tended to discount carping among his subordinates and took no further action.

Alexander may never have been very close to Philotas, who appears to have taken Philip's part during the Pixodarus marriage fiasco. That was a long time ago, but Alexander saved up his resentments. However, he drew a line between inactive boastfulness and active disloyalty. He valued his cavalry commander highly for his military skills and had no wish needlessly to offend Parmenion. Best let sleeping, if tactless, dogs lie.

FACED WITH THE POTENTIALLY damning evidence of Nicomachus and Cebalinus, the king knew that, according to Macedonian custom, he would be expected to act consultatively and democratically. He called a meeting of his senior officers, except for Philotas, and arranged for Nicomachus to repeat his account. He then asked for advice.

Craterus twisted the knife: "The enemies we are about to pursue are still numerous enough. Protect yourself against the enemies within. Eliminate *them* and I have nothing to fear from foreigners."

The commanders could find no plausible explanation for Philotas's failure to warn the king. The pretense that Alexander had had no time to talk with him was a direct lie. If he had not believed Cebalinus, he should have rejected his charges and sent him away. Instead he had let the affair drag on, with the implication that the claims were credible.

The meeting agreed unanimously that there was enough evidence to justify interrogation under torture. We do not know enough about the Macedonian legal system to judge whether torture was regularly used when investigating serious crime, but in ancient Greece its use was usually restricted to slaves; by contrast, the honor of a citizen compelled him to speak the truth. However, because no one objected to the decision, it seems probable that the king in his judicial capacity was entitled to authorize torture.

Great care was taken with the arrest of Philotas. He was invited to dinner with the king and other guests and, to give an impression of normality, a route march was announced for the following day. Cavalry units were posted at all entrances to the camp with orders to block the roads. This was to make sure that no hint of what was about to happen reached the ears of Parmenion. He may have been innocent of any crime, but whether he was or not was immaterial. The old general would be furious at the news of his son's downfall. He was popular with the men and could be counted on to make trouble on Philotas's behalf.

In the middle of the night, when all lights were out, some of Alexander's most trusted officers—Hephaestion, Craterus, Coenus, and Erigyius, along with Perdiccas and Leonnatus from the bodyguard—gathered secretly in the royal tent. Small military detachments arrested all those who had been named, and a force of three hundred men surrounded Philotas's tent. The commander was in a deep slumber and was only half awake when he was arrested and shackled. A cloak was placed over his head so that he would not be recognized by any insomniac soldier.

The following morning Alexander ordered a general assembly in arms. About six thousand soldiers as well as assorted camp followers gathered outside the royal tent. Philotas was concealed from view by a column of soldiers, but Dimnus's corpse was placed on open display.

According to Macedonian law, the king acted as prosecutor in a capital trial, and Macedonian soldiers (or citizens if at home) were the jury. They stood on their rights and would not necessarily come to the desired decision. A sensitive case such as this needed careful handling.

Alexander marched out with his entourage to the assembly, looking gloomy and upset. He stood staring at the ground for a while, then pulled himself together and spoke. He announced the discovery of an extensive criminal conspiracy headed by (of all people, his listeners must have thought) his aged deputy Parmenion. He named Philotas and others as among the plotters and pointed to the dead Dimnus.

Nicomachus, Cebalinus, and Metron were then summoned and repeated their accounts. Although there was evidence of a conspiracy, it did not implicate Philotas and Parmenion as among its members. After an initial outburst, what the three young men said was received in silence.

Alexander resumed his address. He quoted from an intercepted letter sent by Parmenion to his two sons. The text read: "First of all take care of yourselves, and then of your people—that is how we shall accomplish our purpose." The king explained that anyone in the know would understand the passage, but it would be meaningless to other readers if they came across it.

Some people in the audience criticized the accused man, including Coenus (despite the family connection). He picked up a stone to throw at Philotas, but the king stayed his hand. At this point Alexander left the meeting, without explanation. So far, Philotas appears not to have been tortured, but he was in poor shape. Dazed and fainting, he wept. However, after wiping his eyes he spoke strongly in his defense.

He made two main points: first, neither he nor his father had been named by Dimnus and there was no evidence of their involvement in a plot. Secondly, his inaction after listening to Cebalinus was justifiable. He explained: "Unfortunately for me, I thought that what was coming to my ears was a tiff between lover and boyfriend. I doubted

Nicomachus' reliability because he did not bring the information in person but induced his brother to bring it." He would have looked a fool, he thought, if he had taken the matter any further.

Philotas was then led away. Perhaps he had displayed some of his old arrogant manner, for a veteran officer who had risen from the ranks infuriated the assembly with tales of Philotas's extravagance and boastfulness. The general mood hardened against him. However, the prosecution case was thin. It had not established the existence of a large conspiracy involving the two generals.

With uncanny timing, Alexander returned and promptly adjourned the session to the following day. He convened another meeting of his advisers, who agreed that Philotas should be executed by stoning, the traditional Macedonian form of capital punishment. However, first of all there had to be a conviction.

Clearly what was needed was a confession. Hephaestion, Craterus, and Coenus volunteered to question Philotas under torture. The king withdrew into the inner section of his quarters and waited on events (although some say he listened in behind a tapestry).

PHILOTAS WAS SHOWN THE instruments used to inflict pain. He immediately confessed to everything. "Why hurt me? I planned the crime and I wanted it to succeed." However, Craterus insisted that any admissions had to be given under torture. We are told that Philotas was subjected to "fire and beatings." Bloody and broken, he agreed to give a detailed confession, provided that the torture was halted and the instruments removed.

The story began with a certain Hegelochus, a relative of Attalus, whose niece and ward was King Philip's last wife. He was close to Parmenion and while the army was in Egypt complained bitterly about the visit to the Siwah oasis. Like many other Macedonians, he was furious that Alexander now claimed he was the son of Zeus Ammon, thus casting doubt over Philip's paternity. He asked the old general to join a plot to kill the king.

Parmenion had no objection to the project in principle, he said, but believed that the timing was wrong. According to Philotas, with Darius still alive, Parmenion thought the plan premature, since killing Alexander would benefit the enemy, not themselves, whereas with Darius removed the reward of killing the king that would fall to his assassins would be Asia and all of the East. The plan was approved and pledges given and accepted on it.

Philotas pleaded guilty to this grand conspiracy. Its implementation was now an urgent task, for Parmenion was old and likely to be retired soon from active service. However, he insisted that he had no knowledge at all of Dimnus's activities. His onetime comrades showed him the instruments again and he conceded on that point too.

Alexander now had a complete case to offer his Macedonian jurors, whom he reconvened on the following day. Philotas was carried to the assembly on a chair, for he was unable to walk. His confession was read out aloud. A mysterious incident followed, when he unexpectedly inculpated a high-ranking individual who was present and had not been previously named. Then Philotas and all the other conspirators were stoned to death. (Demetrius, the bodyguard, loudly protested his innocence and may have been spared for the time being, in which case he was done away with later when the fuss had died down.)

Far away in Ecbatana, Parmenion knew nothing of the catastrophe that had overtaken his one remaining son. The king realized that "it would be too dangerous to let him survive." He suborned Polydamas, a trusted and long-standing associate of the general, and dispatched him to the Median capital. Polydamas rode for eleven days on a racing camel through desert lands. Arriving secretly at night, he delivered instructions for the assassination. Parmenion's second-in-command, Cleander, orchestrated the murder on the following day. Delighted to greet the new arrival, the old man was unsuspectingly struck down in his walled Persian garden while reading a forged letter from his son.

It was an ungenerous reward for a lifetime's service to the Macedonian crown, but Parmenion knew that he played in a rough game. He would not have registered surprise at his fate, had he been given time to do so.

Alexander decided the moment was propitious to settle some unfinished business. Once the guilty men had been put to death, he brought forward before the assembly the hapless Alexander of Lyncestis, imprisoned since before Issus for treasonable correspondence with the Great King and possible involvement in Philip's assassination. He was suddenly brought forward in front of the assembly and required to defend himself. Three years of imprisonment in the baggage train had taken its toll. Curtius writes: "Although he had had all of three years to rehearse his defense, he was faltering and nervous, deploying few of the arguments which he had stored up in his mind, until finally his very thought processes, not just his memory, failed him." Without more ado, the Lyncestian was put to death.

After the body had been removed, Alexander had the four sons of Andromenes put on trial. The eldest, Amyntas, had the calamitous misfortune to have been a close friend of Philotas. Also, as a boy he had been educated alongside Amyntas, son of King Perdiccas, whom Alexander executed in 336 as a potential rival to the throne. However, the brothers had a proven record of loyalty and were liked by the troops. The youngest, Polemon, was in his teens. He was panicked by the Philotas affair and ran away from the camp.

The other siblings stayed to face prosecution. Amyntas convinced a truculent assembly of his innocence and the trio was acquitted. Amyntas promised to bring back Polemon and, when he had done so, the boy too was exonerated. The outcome showed that Macedonian justice could be fair-handed and generous. A suspicious mind, though, may wonder whether it was the king's intention to calm the feverish atmosphere and bring a melancholy sequence of trials and deaths to a happy conclusion.

THE ACCOUNT GIVEN ABOVE is a great lie, or at least dust thrown in the face. So say modern scholars who propose that, ever since inheriting the throne, Alexander had wanted to discredit Parmenion and his sons and rid himself of them. They were a constant reminder that his army was not truly his, but was the creation of his father. A helpful fate had disposed of Nicanor and Hector, and now at last after years of waiting the opportunity had arrived to put an end to this talented but independent-minded family. A scheme was hatched by a malevolent monarch and his cynical courtiers.

Is there any truth in this theory? And, more generally, how much of the narrative that has come down to us can be trusted?

To be clear, we are speaking of two conspiracies. The first was the amateurish group Dimnus joined. Curtius's account is the fullest: it is internally coherent and there is every reason to regard it as broadly historical. Apart from Demetrius the bodyguard, none of the named plotters were people of note; rather, they were probably discontented young men. We may speculate that their motives were in some way a reaction to Alexander's pro-Persian policy and his intention to continue the war.

The only point of interest was Philotas's opportunistic refusal to let its intended victim know what was planned, despite the fact that an attempt was said to be imminent. His explanation was weak. Even if he did not believe Cebalinus, the least he should have done was to investigate his claims. It is hard to resist the conclusion that his silence was malicious.

It is clear that Parmenion had no connection with Dimnus and his friends (pace his son's forced admission after two bouts of torture). If Philotas had been involved, it beggars belief that Cebalinus would have asked him to warn the king.

So far as the second, grander conspiracy is concerned, there is hardly a case to answer. At the beginning of his agony Philotas appealed to Craterus: "Just tell me what you want me to say." The detailed confession, in which a broken man asserted a long-standing plan to kill the king and tarred his father with premeditated treason, is most likely to have been devised by his tormentors. No doubt Alexander had already decided to eliminate Parmenion and needed some justification for his extrajudicial murder.

The only concrete piece of evidence that Parmenion conspired against Alexander is the dim tale Philotas told about Hegelochus, but that allegation could not be tested. Parmenion was absent and Hegelochus had conveniently died at Gaugamela.

Apart from this whisper, the slate is clean. Ancient histories cite the king as often rejecting Parmenion's advice. From this scholars deduce a propaganda campaign against him, which reflected the king's desire to remove him (and his sons). As we have seen, the charge is weakened by the fact that on a number of other occasions Alexander accepted his deputy's recommendations.

Parmenion had been Philip's man and married his daughter to Attalus, Alexander's great enemy. However, after the king's assassination, he quickly lined up behind Alexander and, as we have seen, put his son-in-law to death when asked to do so.

A great deal is known about Parmenion's activities during the Persian campaign as well as those of Philotas and Nicanor. They took leading roles in all Alexander's battles and made a major contribution to his victories. Why should the king seek to discard his best and most reliable commanders? And had he wanted to do so, Alexander's purge at the beginning of the reign showed that he was ruthless enough to have demoted or dismissed them at any stage. With his unbroken record of military victories, he could have ridden out a storm of protest. However, he kept Parmenion and his sons on in their posts. By the time of his death Parmenion was on the verge of retirement and two of his three sons were dead. Why bother to get rid of Philotas?

If there is a scintilla of truth in the charges, it may be attributed to the culture at the Macedonian court. Although an intelligent monarch could usually get his way, his noblemen insisted on treating him merely as a first among equals. They drank deep, led adventurous private lives, and spoke their minds. Philip was not literal-minded and had no objection to their candor, always providing they fought hard on the battlefield. Alexander had inherited that attitude. Only when talk turned into treason was he ready to intervene.

WE ARE NOW READY to sum up what we know or can reasonably guess of the facts.

Alexander was a hugely successful war leader, admired both by his officers and the rank and file. He had inherited his best generals from his father. He demanded a great deal from them, both under his direct command and as independent generals when he divided up his army into smaller units. And do their best they did. They fought well and served their master without stint.

As the distinguished Greek historian Polybius observed: "While we should perhaps give Alexander, as commander-in-chief, the credit for much, despite his extreme youth, we should assign no less to his co-operators and friends, who defeated the enemy in many marvelous battles, [and] exposed themselves often to extraordinary toil, danger, and hardship."

However, many were out of sympathy with his newfangled and un-Macedonian policies. They objected to his downgrading of King Philip, to his eccentric decision to claim Zeus Ammon as his father, to his promotion of Persians, to the growing luxury of his court, and to the continuance of the war. They did not keep their thoughts to themselves.

Mostly talk remained talk, but Dimnus and his friends were determined to act. Philotas felt much the same way as they did about the king and, when he was told what was afoot, he decided to keep his mouth shut. This can only have been because he was content for the plot to proceed undisturbed.

Once they understood the unpalatable truth, Alexander and his circle of intimates faced a difficulty. They were certain that Philotas had behaved treasonably and deserved execution. However, the fact that he had *done* nothing weakened the case against him. Furthermore, Alexander surmised that Parmenion would seek revenge in some way for his son's death, but that the army would accept a preemptive strike against him only if there were tangible evidence of his guilt.

Hence the need to fabricate a second conspiracy that smeared father and son. There was no evidence for what did not exist, so Philotas had to be tormented into a complete confession.

With the death of the conspirators, both genuine and alleged, the immediate crisis was over. Alexander had gotten away with it—just—at some cost to his reputation. He was not a prime mover in the scandal, but a responder. He had behaved promptly, rationally—and cruelly. If ever there was a case of *raison d'état,* this was it.

Alexander surely realized that the affair was not over. His policies were no more popular than before, and an undertow of fear now tugged at the loving relationship between him and his men. Of one thing he was certain: if loyalties were as slippery as now appeared, he could never again place the Companion cavalry under a single general who might turn them against him. He divided the command between Hephaestion and Cleitus, commander of the Royal Squadron. Hephaestion was dear to Alexander, but he possessed only a middling talent. He was no Philotas. The king usually advanced careers on merit; his lover's promotion suggests that he was running out of talent he could trust.

So far as Cleitus was concerned, his appointment was certainly deserved, but it also reflected a desire on the king's part to promote someone who reflected traditional Macedonian values and was popular with the army, as Parmenion had been. He was anxious about the men's mood. Letters sent home to family and friends were secretly read for disaffection and those who had criticized the king were reassigned to a special unit as a mark of disgrace (apparently their courage in the field turned out to be equal to any other's).

The Macedonian soldiery still loved their king; whatever they thought of Philotas, they were prepared to play their part in his destruction. But the atmosphere was becoming chilly. Alexander was increasingly remote, and the army was plunging to the edge of nowhere when all the men wanted was to go home.

When Antipater heard of the scandal, he commented: "If Parmenion plotted against Alexander, who is to be trusted? And if he did not, what is to be done?" And, he might have silently added, who would be next?

Boy Wonder

This portrait of Alexander in his mid-twenties conveys his youthful charisma. It was carved by the celebrated sculptor Leochares, who also cast the life-size bronzes of the Macedonian royal family that were displayed at Olympia, home of the Olympic games.

ACROPOLIS MUSEUM, ATHENS

Early Years

One of the caves of the shrine sacred to the nymphs at Mieza, now in ruins. Here Aristotle taught the teenaged Alexander and his friends. There used to be stone seats and shady walks where the class could talk and study free from interruption.

Hephaestion met Alexander when they were both schoolboys in their teens. They became best friends and (very probably) lovers. They were widely regarded as a couple and died within weeks of each other in their thirties. The head was sculpted in marble in the late fourth century B.C. within a few years of Hephaestion's death.

GETTY MUSEUM, LOS ANGELES

The city of Thebes erected the statue of a lion, signifying bravery, to mark the burial ground of the Sacred Band, its regiment of lovers, most of whom fell at the battle of Chaeronea. Here King Philip of Macedonia and his eighteen-year-old son Alexander decisively defeated a Greek army. On that day the great city-states of Athens and Thebes lost their freedom. Alexander led the cavalry charge that clinched the victory.

Death at Dawn

The theater at Aegae was built in the mid-fourth century B.C. and was still new when King Philip II of Macedonia was assassinated there in 336. Alexander, together with his terrifying mother, Olympias, may have been implicated in the crime. He certainly benefited from it, instantly seizing the throne and taking over his father's plan to invade the Persian empire.

After his assassination Philip was buried in one of the royal tombs at Aegae, which were discovered by archaeologists in 1977. His remains were placed in a golden casket. A gold crown or wreath was also found.

MUSEUM OF ROYAL TOMBS OF AEGAE, GREECE

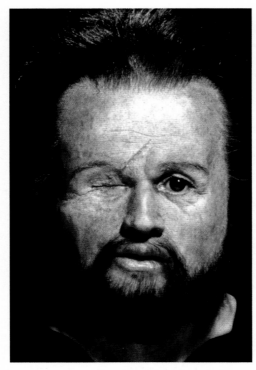

This facial reconstruction of Alexander's father, Philip, is based on remains found in the royal tombs, which have been identified as belonging to the king. He was blinded by an arrow at the siege of Methone in 355/54 B.C., one of many injuries incurred during a long military career. Philip laid the foundation of his son's later achievements.

MUSEUM OF ROYAL TOMBS OF AEGAE, GREECE

Evil Empire

The Great King of Persia was, supposedly, the all-powerful ruler of an empire that stretched from Egypt to India. In practice, he presided over a ramshackle collection of semi-independent territories. The transition from one Great King to his successor was often a bloodbath. To secure his place on the throne, Artaxerxes III Ochus, who reigned from 358 to 338 B.C., put to death all male members of the royal family on whom he could lay his hands.

Delegates bring tribute to the Persian court at Persepolis. In return, the Great King guaranteed peace and order. He did not interfere in his subjects' daily lives and allowed freedom of worship.

Alexander greatly admired Cyrus the Great, founder of the Persian empire, who died in 530 B.C. He visited the tomb, near the ancient Persian capital of Pasargadae, more than once and was enraged when it was robbed. Today the monument still stands, but empty of its owner.

Victory!

Alexander leads his Companion cavalry at the battle of Issus and charges straight at the Great King, whose eyes widen in alarm. He is wearing an elaborate linen cuirass, very similar to one found in the royal tombs at Aegae. The image is a mosaic made in the first century B.C. that copied a lost painting by Philoxenus of Eretria.

MUSEO ARCHEOLOGICO NAZIONALE, NAPLES

The battle of Issus, as imagined by the sculptor of a magnificent stone sarcophagus. This reconstruction is shown painted in bright colors, as was the custom in the classical world. The original, carved from high-quality Pentelic marble in the late fourth century B.C., and with traces of the original paint, was found in the royal necropolis of Sidon. It was probably made for king Abdalonymus of Sidon.

NATIONAL ARCHAEOLOGICAL MUSEUM, ISTANBUL

Winning the Peace

In this stone relief one of Alexander's Companions is hunting
down a stag. He is heroically nude in the Greek manner.
If Macedonians were not killing men in battle, they were killing
wild animals at their leisure. Alexander was a keen huntsman
and often risked his life in the chase.

NATIONAL ARCHAEOLOGICAL MUSEUM, ISTANBUL

Alexander as arsonist. He set fire to Persepolis, the ceremonial capital of the
Persian empire, in revenge for the destruction of Athens when the Persian
king Xerxes invaded Greece more than a century previously. For all his efforts,
the ruins still impress the visitor and Alexander soon realized he had made a
mistake. Without Persian cooperation he would have been unable to administer
his vast empire and for the rest of his reign he did his best to conciliate
his new subjects.

The marriage of Alexander and Rhoxane in 327 B.C. was celebrated in a painting by the fourth century B.C. Greek artist Aetion. The work itself is lost, but a detailed description survives, the inspiration for this fresco by Sodoma. VILLA FARNESINA, ROME

Coins were a unique means by which an ancient ruler "spoke" to his subjects. Here on the silver tetradrachm Alexander claims heaven's endorsement. He wears the lionskin of Heracles and on the reverse, Zeus, king of the Gods, sits enthroned.

Disaster in the Desert

The march through the Gedrosian desert (today's the Makran) lasted two months and was the greatest disaster in Alexander's career. Of more than 30,000 men only a quarter survived.

CHAPTER 12

WAR WITHOUT END

———

IN SPRING 330, ALEXANDER JOINED UP WITH THE ARMY UNITS HE had left behind during his pursuit of Darius. Also, on the sensible grounds that action lifts morale, Parmenion's troops were ordered to make their way to him. But instead of marching east to catch up with the usurper at the earliest opportunity, the king led his army of twenty thousand foot and three thousand horse north into Hyrcania (in its Persian form, the name translates as "Country of Wolves").

Alexander had good reason to turn toward Hyrcania. After Darius's murder, many of his courtiers had taken refuge there, together with the remainder of his loyal Greek mercenaries, and the king wanted to force their surrender. This would eliminate the danger of enemies in his rear before moving on.

The province lies between the southeastern end of the Caspian Sea and the rugged Elburz mountain range. Where it is not bare crag and cliff, it is tropically fertile, with a riot of vegetable color. Groves of tall trees abound in valleys. Vines and branches interweave, and sometimes pathways are hard to find or penetrate. The Macedonians were surprised to see the trees dripping with honey (the product of the Caspian honeylocust tree's sap, it is used today to make candy).

The army divided into two parts and the province was soon reduced. The king entered the Hyrcanian capital, Zadracarta—Yellow City, after the oranges, lemons, and other fruit that flourished in its outskirts. He found a group of Persian grandees waiting for him. Realizing they were cornered, they had come down from the hills to hand themselves in.

They had no cause to be nervous about their fates. They were quite a catch and, following his policy to conciliate the old ruling class, the king received them warmly. The largest fish to be hooked was Darius's chiliarch, Nabarzanes. With Bessus he had plotted the arrest and killing of Darius, and he took the sensible precaution of writing to Alexander in advance to ascertain his welcome. The king had no qualms about providing assurances of his personal safety.

The chiliarch presented Alexander with lavish gifts, one of which was to transform Alexander's personal happiness. This was an exceptionally beautiful eunuch "in the flower of his youth" (his emasculation probably entailed the removal of his testes). Called Bagoas, he was no relation, so far as we know, of his namesake, the poison-bearing kingmaker. He had been bedded by Darius.

Despite his past disapproval of those who used attractive slaves as sexual partners, Alexander fell head over heels in love with the boy. Little is said about Bagoas in the ancient histories, and what is said is disobliging. He makes few appearances in these pages, but the reader should bear in mind that he was present all the time, in the shadows, for the rest of the king's story.

Like most court eunuchs throughout the ages, Bagoas unjustly acquired a sinister reputation, but the rank and file regarded him with affectionate jocularity. We are not told what Hephaestion or (for that matter) Barsine made of him, but neither can have been pleased. He seems not to have sought a political role and to have retained Alexander's lifelong love. He survived the king, but his ultimate fate is unknown. It was probably nasty.

Two local satraps, Phrataphernes and Autophradates, surrendered and the king immediately reconfirmed them in office. An especially welcome arrival was the philoprogenitive Artabazus, accompanied by nine of his eleven sons. True to the last to the ancien régime, he now recognized that the Achaemenids' day was done and was transferring his loyalty to Alexander. This was not too hard a choice, for he had known Alexander since the distant years spent in exile at the court in Pella. As his new master's mistress Barsine would surely smooth her father's path into his favor. Artabazus joined the select circle of Alexander's most trusted advisers.

Messengers arrived from the sad remainder of Darius's Greek mercenaries, seeking an amnesty. Only fifteen hundred of them were left, but they were a force to be reckoned with. Alexander was unforgiving. Under no circumstances would he make any sort of terms with them. They had rejected the Greek consensus at Corinth and fought for the barbarians against their compatriots. They must surrender unconditionally, he insisted. A pause for thought ensued.

While in Hyrcania, the king launched a successful five-day expedition against a poor but fierce local tribe called the Mardians (not to be confused with the Mardi on pages 235–36), although his motive is obscure. They were "a culturally backward race," according to Curtius, who made a living from brigandage. The Great King had never managed to conquer them. They had done nothing at all to provoke Alexander, but they could field eight thousand capable warriors and were a potential threat. He probably saw the brief campaign as an adventure and a training exercise.

He may have had an additional motive. Apparently the Mardians were enthusiastic horsemen. Many Macedonian cavalry mounts having died of heat and exhaustion during the hunt for Darius, the king may have decided to round up replacements.

The Mardians retaliated in kind by kidnapping Alexander's much-loved Bucephalas. Although he was now elderly, he would not let anyone else ride him and remained the king's favorite animal. On hearing the news, Alexander exploded with rage. He sent an interpreter to deliver an ultimatum: either the Mardians gave back his horse, or he would annihilate the entire tribe, including their women and children. The tribesmen saw that he was serious and immediately returned Bucephalas, with gifts. Soon afterward they capitulated. Now that he had gotten exactly what he wanted, Alexander was all charm. He even paid the Mardians a ransom.

Alexander returned to his camp, where he found the Greek mercenaries waiting for him. Brought in with the assistance of (and doubtless good advice from) Artabazus, they had decided that further resistance was futile and placed themselves entirely at the king's disposal. In a generous frame of mind, he freed those who had joined up before the decision to go to war with Persia and incorporated the rest of them into his own army. The young men of Asia Minor were training in the Macedonian way of war, but were not yet ready for military service; perhaps Alexander was running out of experienced troops and was prepared to take in any that were available.

ALEXANDER SPENT TWO WEEKS in Zadracarta. During his stay, his sight began to fail, which probably explains the unusually long period of inaction. The cause was likely conjunctivitis or some other eye infection, a common affliction in the ancient world. For a time he was haunted by the fear of blindness, but in the event his eyes recovered.

As usual when resting his army, he offered sacrifices to the gods and staged an athletics competition. Then, in late August 330, spirits reignited, he set off with his entire army in search of Bessus, who was now recruiting horsemen in his satrapy of Bactria. So much booty had been won that the column could hardly move under the weight. The king ordered it all to be burned and, to dampen criticism, he put a torch to his own baggage first. The Macedonians gritted their teeth and marched eastward through Parthia to Areia, probably following the ancient Silk Road.

Some reinforcements caught up with the army, as did the satrap of Areia, Satibarzanes, who surrendered in person to Alexander. Like other senior Persians, he was given his old job back, but as soon as the Macedonians had gone on their way, he raised the standard of revolt. He massacred the few Macedonians left with him as a guard and proceeded to assemble an army.

A furious Alexander hardened his policy toward the regicides. There were to be no more accommodating deals for them. From now on, the king presented himself not only as Darius's successor but as his merciless avenger. He took a picked, fast-moving force (leaving Craterus with the rest of the army to besiege the provincial capital) and chased after the Areians. After two days and nights of forced marching he found them.

The astounded Satibarzanes slipped away with two thousand cavalry to neighboring Bactria, leaving the rest of his men to fend for themselves. Noncombatants and thirteen thousand troops took refuge on a large flat-topped mountain with steep cliffs and an extensive grassland plain at the summit. It was a natural citadel and Alexander was at a loss what to do. Luck came to his rescue. His soldiers cut down trees to make a ramp up a precipice. The wood accidentally caught fire and the blaze soon enveloped the entire mountain, roasting to death most of the defenders.

The king appointed another Persian as satrap and founded Alexandria Areion, the first of seventy or so garrison towns (either new or renamed). He was beginning to learn the novel art of guerrilla or asymmetric warfare. For the time being there was no place for the set-piece battle in which many thousands of men fought for a decisive result. Disaffection was spreading across the eastern half of the empire. Small groups of mounted fighters, swimming in the sea of the people, harassed the Macedonians, appearing and vanishing without warning. Alexander learned that territory won could easily be lost when his back was turned. It was essential to plant fortresses whose presence would deter a renewal of revolt.

There was a further obstacle to effective campaigning. Alexander and his generals had little or no knowledge of the geography and climate of the eastern half of the empire, much of which consisted of either mountains or deserts. The scientific experts accompanying the army were no better informed until they had conducted their researches. We have already observed that the Macedonians neither spoke nor even understood the languages of the peoples whose lands they were passing through—hence their dependence on not necessarily reliable Persians for data on routes and local power politics as well as for day-to-day interpreting.

Alexander did not feel ready to move directly against Bessus. Winter was approaching and it was essential to find an extensively cultivated region that could feed his army during a long stay. With this in mind, he turned south into the province of Arachosia. His destination was Lake Seistan, the land around which was populous and fertile, albeit plagued by midges, mosquitoes, horseflies, and venomous snakes, not to mention parching sandstorms.

Arachosia's satrap, a Persian regicide called Barsaentes, had declared for Bessus and needed to be dealt with. When the Macedonians approached, he fled to the safety of a neighboring Indian tribe. A few years later he was handed over to Alexander, who had him put to death.

On their way to the lake, the army passed through a place called Phrada. This was where the Philotas scandal played itself out and for a few days Bessus was forgotten. The king decided that Phrada should be renamed Alexandria Prophthasia, or Anticipation, in memory of the crisis. He was by no means ashamed of what had taken place and wanted the world to know that he would always be one move ahead of his enemies.

In January or February 329, the army began a two-month journey through the territory of the Ariaspi, also called the Benefactors because they had helped supply Cyrus the Great, founder of the Persian empire, when he and his soldiers were in extremis. Alexander was impressed by this long-ago good deed and rewarded the tribesmen with money and additional land.

Bad news arrived: Satibarzanes was back on the warpath, this time supplied with cavalry by Bessus. The king refused to halt now to deal with the uprising and dispatched a mobile force under Erigyius, an experienced commander well into middle age, to confront and destroy the former satrap. The army from Media (formerly under Parmenion's command) was on its way to join Alexander and would be able to help secure the south. Phrataphernes was asked to assist, but local troubles prevented him. Evidently the eastern provinces were in a fragile and unstable condition.

The two sides met and a fierce battle ensued. When Satibarzanes saw his fighters flag, he rode up to the front ranks, took off his helmet, and said that he would fight a duel with anyone the enemy put forward. Irritated by the man's bravado, Erigyius himself volunteered. Curtius writes:

> The barbarian threw his spear first. Moving his head slightly to the side, Erigyius avoided it. Then, spurring on his horse, he brought up his lance and ran it straight through the barbarian's gullet, so that it projected through the back of his neck. The

barbarian was flung from his mount, but still fought on. Erigyius drew the spear from the wound and drove it again into his face. Satibarzanes grabbed it with his hand, aiding his enemy's stroke to hasten his own death.

Resistance immediately ended and Areia was quiet again. The dead man's head was cut off and sent to Alexander. He was pleased with this display of old-fashioned, Homeric valor, recalling as it did the hand-to-hand combats on the windy plain of Troy.

A Macedonian was appointed as satrap of Arachosia, and for Areia a Cypriot replaced Satibarzanes. It looks as if the Persian policy was temporarily on hold.

IT WAS TIME AT last to confront Bessus. After founding another garrison town to watch over Arachosia, Alexander marched his Macedonians north 325 miles to the mountains of the Hindu Kush, beyond which lay Bactria, the pretender's base. They labored through harsh treeless highlands, inhabited only by an impoverished and backward tribe, the Parapamisadae. The ground was covered by a permanent frost and the sky was usually overcast. The army had a terrible time of it. According to Curtius, "The numbing cold of the snow, of which they had no experience, claimed many lives; for many others it brought frost-bite to the feet and for a very large number snow-blindness." The conditions were especially deadly for men suffering from exhaustion. Soldiers nearly lost consciousness from the cold. The only remedy was to force them at all costs to stay awake and keep going.

Toward the end of March, the shivering army reached an abundant and friendly valley where it rested for a few days. In front of them they saw their next daunting destination. This was the continuous chain of the Hindu Kush, which rises 16,872 feet above sea level. It was then mistakenly thought to be part of the Caucasus. It was here that Prometheus, one of the old gods, the Titans, who preceded the Olympians, was chained to a high rock. Each day an eagle swooped down and ate his liver, which regenerated overnight only to be eaten again the next day. This was Prometheus's punishment for stealing fire from the gods and giving it to human beings, who used combustion to nurture the technologies of war and peace. Local people pointed out his cave, the bird's nesting place, and the marks of his chains on the rock.

As usual Alexander sacrificed to the customary gods and founded another garrison town, Alexandria of the Caucasus. He could not spare any Macedonians, but settled seven thousand local people, who looked after food production; three thousand camp followers; and volunteers from among the mercenaries.

Then Alexander led his men across the lowest but longest pass through the mountains. This took sixteen or seventeen tedious days. The weather was atrocious. Many horses died, the grain ran out, and the men were reduced to eating herbs. The king ordered his soldiers to kill the baggage animals and eat them raw.

Emerging into Bactria, he found that the enemy had adopted a scorched-earth policy and supplies were still scarce. Arrian writes of a grueling march through thick snow, "but still they came on and on." The Macedonians had arrived in the province much sooner than Bessus expected and this unsteadied his nerves. At a drunken feast, one of his supporters, a Mede called Bagodaras, advised him to surrender to Alexander and seek mercy. Bessus lost his temper and had to be restrained from killing the man. Out of control, he rushed from the banquet. Bagodaras wisely took the opportunity to slip away. He handed himself in to Alexander, who took care to treat him kindly. His warm reception did not go unnoticed by other followers of the soi-disant Great King.

The plain fact was that Bessus had failed to unite the province he was supposed to govern behind a common plan of defense. He had only managed to recruit seven thousand cavalry and some Sogdian levies, insufficient to meet an army many times the size.

Bactria's northern frontier was the wide-flowing river Oxus, beyond which lay a land of extremes, alternating between the lush, irrigated green of river valleys and the dry ochre of deserts. This was the satrapy of Sogdiana, inhabited by nomads. Bessus, having lost confidence that he could hold his province, withdrew to Sogdiana. This was a sensible move, but it meant that his Bactrian troops deserted him.

Alexander did not relent in his advance; he soon captured Bactra, the provincial capital, and another town on first assault. Before following his adversary into Sogdiana he passed the administration of Bactria into the safe hands of Artabazus. He was then faced with the task of reaching the Oxus across a waterless desert. He took with him detachments of light troops, leaving the main army behind. It was now June and the heat was so unbearable that his troops were compelled to travel during the only slightly cooler night. The sand itself was scorching. Having just recovered from frostbite, soldiers now faced the prospect of heatstroke. Early one evening, Alexander arrived at the river, but many groups were straggling and fires were lit to guide them to the camp after nightfall. He stood in his armor to welcome them and took no refreshment until the entire column had arrived.

It was at this surprising point that the king demobilized and sent home older Macedonians who were unfit for military duty, as well as Thessalian cavalry volunteers. These men were presumably either sick or mutinous; whichever the correct explanation, they had had enough. It was in Alexander's interest that they leave in good humor, so he made sure to give them generous bonuses.

The next challenge was the river. It was three quarters of a mile wide and surprisingly deep. Bessus had burned all the riverboats after using them to reach Sogdiana. As previously, the king had the men collect their leather tent covers, stuff them with light rubbish, and sew them up. It took the army five days to cross the river on these improvised rafts.

SPITAMENES WAS ONE OF Bessus's leading supporters and a close friend. He was also a patriot who thoroughly disapproved of Alexander, but he and two Sogdian noblemen saw that the cause of Artaxerxes V was hopeless. They decided to surrender him to the enemy. That would both remove an incompetent leader and mollify the Macedonian king.

The conspirators tricked Bessus into granting them a private audience. Once they had him on his own, they overpowered him. They tied him up, took the diadem off his head, and removed his royal robes. Spitamenes informed Alexander that they would hand over Bessus if he sent a small contingent of troops to pick him up.

The king immediately dispatched Ptolemy, a Macedonian friend from his teens, with sixteen hundred cavalry and four thousand infantry (no small contingent, for he suspected a trap). The conspirators had second thoughts and were reluctant to play a direct part in the surrender. So they left Bessus on his own in a small village. The inhabitants, probably greatly relieved, handed over their involuntary captive and the royal insignia to Ptolemy at the first opportunity.

Ptolemy sent a messenger ahead to ask the king how Bessus should be brought into his presence. In his new role as avenger of Darius, Alexander ordered him to be placed on a roadside, which he and his army would be marching past. Bessus should be entirely stripped of his clothes, fettered, and tied to a post with a slave's wooden collar around his neck.

These instructions were followed to the letter. Alexander rode up in a chariot—an unusual vehicle for him, which he chose because it symbolized his role as Great King. He halted beside Bessus and asked him to justify Darius's murder. Bessus replied, lamely, that he had only claimed the crown to give it to Alexander. Under the supervision of Darius's brother, Oxyathres, now a Companion, the regicide was flogged. He was then taken to Bactra, where some months later Alexander put him on trial and charged him with treason against Darius. The city's population was invited to attend, not as jurors but as witnesses. The king was the sole judge. Bessus's nose and ears were sliced off, the terrible Persian penalty for traitors. He was then put to death in public. He may have had to endure the culminating cruelty of impalement up the anus.

Mutilation shocked Greeks and Macedonians. Arrian observed: "For my part, I cannot approve of this excessively severe punishment of Bessus, but regard the mutilation of extremities as a barbaric practice." If this criticism had been put to Alexander, he would have replied that he had no choice. Whatever his personal feelings, he was ruler of the Persian empire and felt obliged to follow traditional practice.

The ancient authors had little time for Bessus, and indeed he was neither effective nor lucky. He failed to take Alexander's measure. But for a Persian patriot, he may have acted less from personal ambition than in the national interest, as he saw it. He deposed and assassinated Darius in the hope that under his leadership the fortunes of war would turn in the Achaemenids' favor. The Bactrians took a more realistic view of their chances against the Macedonian conqueror and declined to enroll under his standard.

Bessus's moment came too late, for the Fates had already cut the empire's thread with their shears.

THE KING BELIEVED THAT only firm measures would pacify the eastern end of the empire. The cruel handling of Bessus was meant to set an example that would daunt anyone else who was planning an insurgency.

There were other demonstrations of Macedonian brutality at this time, of which the most extraordinary concerned a small town in Sogdiana. Its inhabitants were bilingual and turned out to be the descendants of the Branchidae, a noble clan members of which used to administer the oracle, sacred spring, and temple of Apollo at Didyma near Miletus. During the Persian invasions of Greece in the fifth century B.C., they were said to have sided with the Great King (either Darius I or Xerxes) when he destroyed the temple and made off with its contents, among them a cult statue of the god. The spring dried up and the oracle fell silent.

The Branchidae feared the wrath of their fellow citizens and persuaded the Persians to resettle them in some remote corner of the empire, where they hoped to live quietly and undetected.

After Alexander's arrival at the siege of Miletus, the water flowed again. Later the cult statue was recovered at Ecbatana and sent back to Didyma. The oracle was back in business. Now that the Branchidae had been found, what should be done with them? Alexander consulted Milesians in the army. They did not give a clear answer, so the king said he would decide the matter.

It is uncertain whether the allegations against the Branchidae were true or false, but it was possible that with the reopening of the oracle they might put in a claim to resume control. That may have been a factor in the king's mind: the ruling democracy would not stand for a return of the Branchidae. In any event, the Macedonian phalanx was ordered to surround the town, and at a given signal the city was sacked and every male inhabitant was killed. Curtius writes:

Neither community of language nor the olive-branches and entreaties of the suppliants could curb the savagery. Finally the Macedonians dug down to the foundations of the walls in order to demolish them and leave not a single trace of the city.

If ever there was a case of visiting the iniquity of the fathers on the children to the third and the fourth generation, this was it. Public opinion was shocked. Here was one more piece of evidence that Alexander had rejected reconciliation and was acquiring a reputation as a despot.

AFTER THE ARREST OF Bessus in the late summer of 329, Alexander set off across Sogdiana to the river Jaxartes (now the Syr Darya), the satrapy's northwestern boundary. On his way he visited the capital, Maracanda (today's Samarkand). His intention was to calm the people's angry mood and impose his control over the entire province. He brought his cavalry back to strength with local horses, having lost a good number during the crossing of the Hindu Kush and the comings and goings to and from the Oxus.

On the way, a party of Macedonians went on a foraging expedition and was set upon by a horde of Sogdians (perhaps as many as twenty thousand or thirty thousand, we are told). Many Macedonians were killed or taken prisoner, after which the attackers withdrew to a rocky crag. The king led several assaults, but was driven back by showers of arrows. He himself took an arrow through his leg which broke part of his fibula and was hard to dislodge. We hear nothing more of this wound, so presumably it healed quickly. Eventually the Macedonians captured the position, cutting down some of the enemy while others threw themselves off cliffs to their death.

Alexander was a fast learner and had mastered the principles of military action against irregular forces. He established a series of seven strongpoints to maintain his control of territory gained and prevent armed groups from moving about wherever and whenever they wished. These included existing townships, such as Cyropolis, founded by Cyrus the Great in 544 B.C., and completely new settlements, among which was Alexandria Eschate, or Furthermost, on the southern bank of the Jaxartes. With a circumference of five and a half miles, it was a substantial settlement. Its walls were built in three weeks. Once the work was complete the king made his usual sacrifices to the gods and staged athletic and equestrian competitions. This new Alexandria was to guard against incursions by nomads from beyond the Jaxartes; it was peopled with Greek mercenaries, some local inhabitants for cheap labor in the fields, and Macedonians who were no longer fit for service.

The king sought the help of Bessus's onetime supporter Spitamenes and his friends. He invited them to a conference at Bactra but, alarmed by his severity, they stayed away. Then, to his astonishment, they launched an insurrection across Sogdiana and Bactria. Hostile tribes overwhelmed the recently established strongpoints, and Spitamenes placed Maracanda's citadel and its Macedonian garrison under siege.

At first sight, this development fell from a blue sky. Up until then the Sogdians and Bactrians had been quiet. They had no particular objection to Alexander's replacement of Darius, nor had they supported Bessus; as for the Macedonian army, it was a temporary inconvenience and they believed it would soon go away. They did not feel threatened for themselves and their way of life. However, the establishment of Alexandria Eschate was a serious inroad into local liberty, signaling Alexander's intention to remain as a permanent presence. That could not be allowed, and so the provinces rose up in arms.

Alexander sent a modest relief force of sixty Companion cavalry, eight hundred mercenary cavalry, and fifteen hundred mercenary infantry to raise the siege of Maracanda. Then he divided his army in two groups. Craterus, who was filling the space left by Parmenion, laid siege to Cyropolis, while the king reduced the other forts at a rapidfire pace in two days. Their mud-brick walls were easy prey for his artillery. Alexander then rejoined Craterus and brought up siege engines to demolish the city wall. He noticed a dried riverbed beneath the wall. It left just enough room for men to crawl inside.

This was an opportunity too good to miss. An elite assault team was assembled, led (of course) by Alexander, who was not going to leave the thrill and the glory of an adventure to somebody else. The team squeezed into Cyropolis without difficulty. The defenders realized that all was lost, but some of them counterattacked the Macedonians.

Craterus was hit by an arrow and Alexander suffered a heavy blow to the head and neck. Everything went dark and he collapsed. As he lay senseless, the army thought he was dead and men wept openly for him. He regained consciousness, concussed, and with his voice almost inaudible. Typically, he insisted on returning to duty before his wound was healed. The city fell. Approximately eight thousand tribesmen lost their lives.

No wonder that the king was in an unforgiving mood. He put to death all adult males and sold into slavery the women and children of Cyropolis and the other garrison towns that had been recaptured. The conventions of war permitted besiegers who encountered resistance to act in this way, but this did not reduce the rising unpopularity of the Macedonians in Sogdiana.

ALEXANDER LIKED TO TAKE things in their proper order. Alexandria Eschate was attracting hostile attention from Scythian nomads who lived in the grassy steppes north of the Jaxartes. They were formidable horsemen and archers, whose technique was to gallop up to the enemy at speed, let loose a shower of arrows, and then turn tail. A large number had gathered and shouted insults over the water. The threat they posed needed to be dealt with before Alexander went to help dowse the flames in the south.

Somehow Alexander had to transport his army safely across the Jaxartes. The river was narrow near Alexandria Eschate, and the Macedonians would be vulnerable to the worst that archery could do while they crossed to the Scythian bank. Once they had reached it, they would have to face the mounted archers, who would surround them like a swarm of hornets.

The king was not deterred. Using the same method as at the Oxus, the Macedonians took only three days to prepare twelve thousand leather floats and rafts capable of carrying horses and catapults. The operation promised to be a risky one; when the king sacrificed for a successful crossing, his resident seer, Aristander, reported that the omens were unfavorable and prophesied danger to his own person.

Setting aside his piety for once, Alexander declined to cancel the attack. He said: "I would rather face the greatest possible peril than, as conqueror of virtually the whole of Asia, have the Scythians make a laughingstock of me."

An artillery barrage opened the action. The Scythians were amazed at the distance covered by the salvos and withdrew from range. This gave the Macedonians the opportunity they needed to negotiate the river, with the king out in front. The archers and slingers formed the first wave and joined the catapults to keep the enemy at bay.

Once the army had made it safely to the far bank, the Macedonians had to find a way of bringing the ever circling enemy horsemen to battle. The king had a plan. He ordered forward a weak cavalry contingent. The enemy horse took the bait and started riding around the Macedonian horsemen in their usual way. Not far behind, a screen of lightly armed foot soldiers, archers, and Agrianians advanced in a crescent formation. The Scythians went on galloping through the space between cavalry and infantry.

Then, in a surprise move, three regiments of Companion cavalry and mounted javelin men charged through the infantry screen and attacked the enemy horse from the wings. Many of the Scythians now found themselves surrounded on all sides and broke down into a disorderly, jostling crowd. About a thousand were killed. Although the Scythian army as a whole had not been defeated, it withdrew from the field, mightily impressed by this display of Macedonian power.

Alexander had hoped to lead a pursuit, but soon called it off. He had drunk some foul water and was incapacitated by a violent attack of diarrhea. Also his recent wound was still unhealed and painful. He was carried back to the camp in a critical state. Aristander notched up another accurate prediction.

The king's intention was never to annex the territory of the Scythian nomads. He simply wanted to demonstrate that it was unwise to provoke the Macedonians, who knew how to foil the nomads' hit-and-run tactics. His point was quickly taken, for Scythian envoys soon arrived, full of apologies. The recent incident had not been officially approved, they claimed, and the mistake would not be repeated. Alexander saw no advantage in rejecting this explanation and both sides agreed to forget a regrettable misunderstanding.

The campaign confirmed that, for all his other difficulties, the king was still at the top of his game. As before he had inspected the enemy with an open, inquisitive eye and confronted a novel problem with a novel solution. The military historian J.F.C. Fuller writes astutely that Alexander

> grasped the conditions which had hitherto rendered the Scythians invincible, and because he so shrewdly penetrated them, he compelled them to do the very thing they did not want to do— enter a circle of trained, disciplined, and better-armed soldiers. They set out to circle round the Macedonians, then suddenly their imagined circumference became the center of a hostile ring.

TERRIBLE DISPATCHES ARRIVED FROM Maracanda. The Macedonian relief force had been wiped out, almost to a man. It had been very poorly led by Pharnuches, a Lycian interpreter who was probably the father of the king's lovely Bagoas. Pharnuches had little experience of military command, but was expert in the languages of Bactria and Sogdiana. It would appear that the king appointed him anticipating negotiation with Spitamenes rather than fighting. Pharnuches knew he was out of his depth and tried to resign, but his subordinate officers, fearful of going against the king's wishes, all refused the command.

As the Macedonians approached the city, Spitamenes immediately abandoned his siege of the citadel and fled into the desert. The Macedonians wanted to expel the nomads permanently from the region and chased after them. Spitamenes added some six hundred Scythian cavalry to his force and halted on level ground, where he awaited his pursuers. He kept his horsemen circling in and out, firing their arrows into the infantry column. The Macedonian horse attempted countercharges, but the mounts were weakened from too much travel and too little fodder. The enemy was able to keep clear of them and came back hard when the Macedonians stood their ground or retreated.

Tormented by the arrows, Pharnuches formed his troops into a square and withdrew into a wood beside a river, where he hoped for some relief from the incessant cascade of missiles. The cavalry commander decided to fend for himself and tried to cross the river without orders or even consultation. He was followed by the panic-stricken infantry. The Scythians cannot have believed their luck. They shot at the enemy from the banks and went down into the water itself to take easier aim. The Macedonians took refuge on a small island in the river, but their situation was hopeless. The Scythians surrounded them and shot them down. A few were taken prisoner, but they too were put to death. No more than three hundred foot soldiers and forty cavalrymen survived.

This was the greatest disaster to have befallen Alexander in his entire career; indeed, it was the first recorded defeat of Macedonians since the year 353. It was more than a debacle, it was a massacre. As soon as he learned what had happened, the king rapidly concluded a deal with the Scythians and marched at top speed to Maracanda, where the victorious Spitamenes had returned and resumed the siege. Alexander covered 172 miles in three days, arriving at the city just before dawn on the fourth.

Once again, the ultra-mobile Spitamenes disappeared into the desert and lurked in small oases. If he was out of reach, the populace of Sogdiana was not. Alexander visited the scene of the catastrophe and buried the rotted corpses still lying on the ground. He determined on bloody reprisals. He systematically laid waste to the satrapy's most fertile land along the course of the gold-bearing river Polytimetus (a Greek word meaning Very Precious; Zarafshan today), overcame enemy strongholds, and butchered the inhabitants. Constant setbacks seemed to be brutalizing the king's nature.

There was nothing more he could do, so he spent the winter in Bactria's capital. Nearchus, a boyhood friend of Alexander, and Asander, probably Parmenion's brother and (remarkably) still loyal to the king, arrived with a substantial and welcome reinforcement of Greek mercenaries, and the satrapy of Syria presented newly trained native soldiers—in total, 19,400 infantry and 2,600 cavalry. To build up his forces he also recruited Bactrians and Sogdians locally.

A tribal chieftain from the lower Oxus paid a visit to the Macedonian court. In a friendly conversation, Alexander revealed his advance thinking. Once he had completed the conquest of the Persian empire, he intended a campaign in India. He went on to make his first recorded allusion to a plan for world dominion. According to Arrian, he replied to the chieftain's offer of military support that with India subdued he would then be in possession of the whole of Asia; with Asia in his control he would return to Greece and launch from there a full-scale naval and land campaign against the Black Sea regions through the Hellespont and the Propontis; and he asked Pharasmanes to save his present offers for redemption when that time came.

With the beginning of spring 328, the ice floes on the Oxus began to melt and Alexander crossed the river and returned to Sogdiana. Fruitless years were passing by and he resolved once and for all to put an end to the insurgency. What he had learned about asymmetric warfare he intended to practice. The king became a guerrilla.

As soon as he had entered Sogdiana, he broke down his army into five independent divisions, one of which he commanded; the remainder were placed under the general supervision of the (by now) indispensable Craterus, whose task was to guard Bactria. Alexander divided his own share of the army into five detachments. Keeping one for himself, he gave the command of the others to Hephaestion, Ptolemy, Perdiccas, and Coenus in association with Artabazus, who was doubtless included to assist with negotiations. Arrian writes that the divisions all

pursued their own line of invasion as and where opportunity presented itself, sometimes using force to annihilate groups concentrated in the strongholds, sometimes winning them over in voluntary surrender. Between them these divisions covered most of Sogdiana, and when his entire armament had reconvened at Maracanda Alexander sent out Hephaestion with a commission to repopulate the garrison towns already founded in Sogdiana.

This was a project of outright colonization that was achieved through ruthless military means. Gulliver-like, the satrapy was now pinned down by a network of strongholds and garrison towns and there was less and less free space in which Spitamenes and his fighters could hide or exploit as a base for his raids.

However, the rebel leader was still at large, bloody but unbowed. A frustrated Alexander spent the heat of the summer in the Sogdian capital. Here he accepted the resignation of Artabazus as satrap of Bactria on the grounds of age (he was in his early sixties). We know nothing of the rest of his eventful life. We may assume that his daughter, Barsine, was disappointed by the arrival of Bagoas and later by Alexander's marriage. However, members of his family remained high in favor. Two of his sons held commands in the army, and another daughter married the king's close associate Ptolemy. We may guess at a happy ending.

IN THE INTERVALS OF relaxation between campaigning, the king and his Companions loved nothing better than hunting. If they could not fight human beings, they would take on animals. In Greece the sport was largely utilitarian—for the pot and the table. Men with spears or bows and arrows hunted game such as hares and, more dangerously, wild boars.

In the Persian empire the Great King and his nobles built walled game parks or estates, inside which they pursued large game—deer, for example, and according to ancient sources the lion, king of beasts. Sometimes they were on horseback, sometimes on foot. Hounds and nets were used.

A finely carved marble sarcophagus dating from the end of the fourth century B.C. shows along one of its sides the king on a rearing horse as he spears a Persian at the Battle of Issus. On the opposite side he is seen hunting down a lion, as if the two encounters were of equal value.

Bravery at a hunt was a kingly virtue; Alexander was always out in front endangering his life. He strongly objected to other huntsmen getting in his way. Curtius describes a hunt on foot in Sogdiana when the king

issued orders for the animals to be beaten from their coverts throughout its length. Among these animals was a lion of unusual size which came charging forward to pounce on the king himself. Lysimachus [a somatophylax, or bodyguard] happened to be standing next to Alexander, and had started to aim his hunting spear at the beast when the king pushed him aside, told him to get out of the way, and added that he was as capable as Lysimachus of killing a lion single-handed.

This was an unkind reminder of a hunt some time before in Syria, when Lysimachus had killed a lion of extraordinary size on his own. However, his left shoulder had been lacerated right down to the bone and he had come within an inch of losing his life. Alexander backed up his taunt with action, for he went on to dispatch the animal with a single stroke—and without injury to himself.

Despite this victory, the army was displeased to see the king taking unnecessary risks away from the battlefield. A general Macedonian assembly decreed that in future he should not hunt on foot or unaccompanied by a select group of officers or Companions—a rare example of anyone telling Alexander what to do.

AFTER ITS LONG JOURNEY from the Mediterranean, a consignment of Greek fruit was delivered to the king at Maracanda. He was delighted by the fruit's beauty and freshness and decided to share it with the man he had just appointed to replace Artabazus in Bactria.

This was Cleitus, a grizzled warrior and a Macedonian of the old school. He spoke his mind as if doing so were a civic duty. Brave and loyal, he had thrived under Philip, and in the thick of the fray at the Granicus he had saved Alexander's life, lopping off the arm of a Persian nobleman who was on the point of striking Alexander with his sword. He liked to call the king by his given name rather than his title and he thoroughly disapproved of the policy to conciliate Persians. He was a conservative egalitarian, out of tune with the times, bitter as only a betrayed loyalist can be.

The new satrap of Bactria was ordered to prepare for a march on the following day. This, together with the opportune arrival of the fruit, was a good enough excuse for one of the king's early-starting banquets the previous afternoon.

Wine flowed and Alexander, a little tipsy, began to boast at length about his achievements, to the irritation of many guests. It was he, not King Philip, who had won the Battle of Chaeronea. Flatterers expressed their considered opinion that Philip had done nothing remarkable or great. Someone began to sing satirical verses about the Macedonian commanders who had been defeated by Spitamenes. Older members of the party took offense and booed. But Alexander and those sitting near him were obviously amused and asked the singer to carry on.

For true Macedonians, a party was not a party unless everyone got drunk as quickly as possible. The rules of polite behavior were suspended. This could be dangerous and few will have forgotten the disastrous banquet when Philip tried to kill Alexander in an alcohol-fueled rage.

Cleitus, who by now was not altogether sober, shouted that it was wrong for Macedonians to be insulted in front of barbarians and enemies, even if they had had some bad luck. Alexander retorted that by disguising cowardice as bad luck, Cleitus was pleading his own case. Cleitus jumped up and bellowed back sarcastically: "Yes, of course, it was my *cowardice* that saved your life at the Granicus." He went on to criticize the king for disowning his father Philip and claiming to be the son of Ammon.

"You scum," the king cried out. "Do you imagine you can go on saying things like this, stirring up trouble among the Macedonians—and not pay for it."

"But we *do* pay for it," replied Cleitus and blurted out his resentment against all the Persians at court. "We have to beg Persians for an audience with our own king."

Alexander's friends jumped up, while more responsible guests tried to calm both sides down. Now violently drunk, Cleitus refused to take back a single word and challenged the king to say in public whatever was on his mind, or else not invite to his table freeborn men who said whatever was on theirs. Otherwise Alexander ought to go and live among barbarians and slaves who were willing to throw themselves flat on the ground in front of his white tunic and belt, the insignia of a Persian monarch.

It looked as if the king would be able to manage his temper, but unhappily Cleitus had not finished. Some slurred praise of Parmenion and Attalus, both of them victims of the king, was the last straw.

At this point Alexander lost control of himself. He hurled one of the apples lying on his table at his tormentor and then looked round for his dagger. One of his personal guards had already taken the precaution of moving it out of harm's way. Companions crowded round and begged him to be quiet.

He leaped to his feet and screamed in Macedonian for the corps of guards, the signal for an extreme emergency, and ordered his trumpeter to sound the alarm. When the man courageously refused to obey he struck him with his fist. Afterward the trumpeter was warmly complimented for his conduct, for it was mainly due to him that the army was not thrown into an uproar.

Cleitus refused to shut up, but eventually his friends succeeded in pushing him out of the banqueting room and beyond the wall and ditch of the citadel where these events were unfolding. However, a little later he came back in by another door and quoted in a loud, insolent voice a line from Euripides: "There is a bad custom which now obtains in Hellas."

Euripides was the prolific Athenian author of more than ninety tragedies, of which nineteen have survived to the present day. He was very popular and many in the Greek world learned passages from his works by heart. Among the library of books Alexander took with him to Asia, Euripides held an honored place.

The sentence that Cleitus cited comes from the *Andromache,* a drama that addresses the demoralization and dehumanization of war. It does not seem at first sight to be especially offensive, but in truth it delivered a wounding blow. Cleitus did not quote the lines that followed, but the king and many others at the feast will have known them very well. The passage continued:

> When an army wins a victory over the enemy,
> No one gives credit to the men who sweat and fight;
> The general reaps the glory. Yet he, after all,
> Wields only one sword.

This was exactly Cleitus's argument: the army had dwindled into a one-man band.

Guests, embarrassed or alarmed or both, began to make their excuses and leave. Alexander grabbed a lance from one of the duty guards and tried but failed to wound Cleitus. Leonnatus wrenched the lance from his hand, while Ptolemy and Perdiccas held him by the waist. Alexander may have feared he was the victim of an assassination plot. In any case, he now broke free. He seized another spear, stood at the exit door leading to the vestibule, and watched those queuing to depart. Cleitus was last. The king challenged him and Cleitus answered: "Here I am, here is your Cleitus." As he spoke, Alexander plunged the spear into his side, saying (so we are told): "Now go and join Philip, Parmenion and Attalus!"

The vestibule was drenched in blood. Shocked and looking dazed, guards and Companions kept their distance from the king. He realized that he had done something terrible. His mood switched instantly to suicidal misery. He pulled the spear from the body and turned it on himself. Guards rushed at him and pulled away the weapon. They picked him up and carried him to his bed. He broke down in tears and wept noisily all night long, tearing at his cheeks with his nails as if he were a mourner at a funeral. He looked at his friends' grim faces and wondered whether they would ever speak to him again.

The inconsolable king had the corpse brought to his tent, but after a time his friends arranged for its removal. He grieved not only for the dead man, but also for Lanice, Cleitus's sister: she had been Alexander's nanny when he was an infant. She had already lost two of her three sons at the siege of Miletus and now, thanks to him, her brother was gone too. Alexander shut himself away for three days and refused to eat or drink. He also "neglected all other bodily needs." Gradually the people around him came to suspect that he really was set on dying and begged him to take nourishment. Eventually he agreed to do so, and the crisis eased.

Callisthenes, the expedition's chief philosopher, historian, and public relations officer, paid the king a visit, but to little effect, for he adopted a gentle bedside manner and failed to raise the subject of Cleitus's murder because he wanted to spare Alexander's feelings. Practical advice was required, not soft words. However, another philosopher friend did better. This was Anaxarchus, whose blunt manner hid a flattering heart. He criticized the king for "lying on the floor weeping like a slave, terrified of the law and of what men will say of him. And yet all the time it should be he who represents the law and sets up the criterion of justice." In other words, by virtue of his kingship, Alexander was unable to break the law. He was clear of guilt. This was a convenient and comforting doctrine indeed, which Alexander did not forget. It would have its uses in later times.

To add belt to braces, the Macedonian general assembly, distraught at the prospect of losing its leader in a remote and friendless part of the world, discussed the killing and formally declared that Cleitus's death was justified.

WHAT ARE WE TO MAKE of this unedifying episode? First of all, beneath the Hellenic high-cultural veneer, Alexander showed himself to be a typical Macedonian monarch in that he ran an alcoholic court. Its members played and drank hard. According to a contemporary historian, Ephippus the Olynthian, who joined the Asian expedition, they "had no notion of moderation in drinking, but started off at once with enormous drafts before eating, so as to be drunk before the first course was off the table, and to be unable to enjoy the rest of the banquet."

Alexander was a citizen-king, who by convention was obliged to tolerate the appearance of equality with the plain-speaking noblemen who served under him. He was expected to endure gracefully the odd hot-tempered remark when they were in their cups. It was a pity he had not done so on this occasion. The consequence of the death of Cleitus, following on as it did from the Philotas "conspiracy," was that respect among his subordinates began to be replaced by fear.

More significantly, it underscored the fierce opposition among some of the king's commanders not only to his slow transformation into an honorary Persian, but also to his increasingly autocratic manner. According to Arrian, he became quicker to anger; the obsequiousness in which he was now enveloped cost him the "old, easy relationship" with his Macedonians.

The disastrous evening at Maracanda brought out into the open three broadly defined groups: friends of the king (in particular, Asians of various national or ethnic types, and Greek mercenaries); Macedonians; and experienced soldiers of no fixed political views.

These divisions were replicated in his inner circle. Hephaestion supported the king's strategic approach to running the empire, while Craterus, by far the ablest of his commanders, was a Macedonian conservative.

As for ordinary soldiers, there is little firm information. We have seen that the king paid close attention to their interests. He gave them their regular holidays and entertainments, encouraged marriage and family life, kept casualties to a minimum, and set a personal example of endurance and valor. They followed willingly where he led, although the time might come when they lost patience. So long as the connection between him and his men remained secure, he could safely ignore his disputatious officers.

The king drew an important conclusion from the Cleitus episode. It did not persuade him to return to the old Macedonian ways, as one might have expected. Rather, by temporarily abdicating in a hysterical sulk as he had done on more than one occasion, he saw he could bully, even blackmail, those around him into accepting whatever he did, even committing murder. Despite the long history of assassinations in the Macedonian royal family, he did not listen to his critics. Although he still behaved, more or less, as a first among equals during drinking sessions, he continued to transform himself for the world at large into a Great King, an imperial despot.

MOST ANCIENT HISTORIANS CLAIM that from around this time Alexander began to drink more heavily than in the past. Had he practiced moderation, he would have "stopped short of killing his friends at dinner." So opines Curtius, a strict moralist, who asserts that the king's fine qualities were ruined by alcohol.

> Alexander had some great natural gifts: a noble disposition . . . ; resolution in the face of danger; speed in undertaking and completing projects; integrity in dealing with those who surrendered and mercy toward prisoners; restraint even in those pleasures which are generally acceptable and widely indulged. But all these were marred by his inexcusable fondness for drink.

Plutarch takes a different view. He acknowledges that the king could sometimes behave like an offensive and arrogant drunk, but claims that as a rule he was a moderate drinker.

> The impression that he was a heavy drinker arose because when he had nothing else to do, he liked to linger over each cup, but in fact he was usually talking rather than drinking: he enjoyed holding long conversations, but only when he had plenty of leisure. Whenever there was urgent business to attend to, neither wine, nor sleep, nor sport, nor sex, nor spectacle could ever distract his attention.

It is impossible to come to a firm judgment on so personal a matter as Alexander's alcohol consumption and the pressures or stresses that may or may not underpinned it. Even at the time observers had different views on the subject, but we can be sure that Alexander was not an alcoholic. For most of the time he was too busy and faced too many demands to sit around quaffing unmixed wine (a Macedonian custom in an age when wine was weakened with water). Mostly he was on campaign and needed, often round the clock, all the physical energy and mental acuity he could summon.

During intervals of rest and relaxation, Alexander may very well have often drunk in moderation as Plutarch says. However, evidence such as the Cleitus affair shows that on vacation he could be a binge-drinker. He was still in his twenties and, like many young adults throughout the ages, on a day off he liked to drink to get drunk.

AFTER TWO FRUSTRATING YEARS of hard fighting in cruel terrain, it was time to put an end to Spitamenes. The irrepressible rebel, with the assistance of the Massagetae, a Scythian nomadic tribe, overran a Bactrian outpost, killed its defenders, and moved on Bactra. The tiny garrison bravely counterattacked, with some success. However, it was caught in an ambush on the way home and suffered very heavy casualties. Craterus and his contingent were nearby; they arrived quickly on the scene and drove off the enemy. The network of fortresses was proving its worth.

The five sections of the army made a planned rendezvous at Maracanda. Alexander took over Cleitus's command of the Companion cavalry, and most of the army moved into winter quarters at the Sogdian settlement of Nautaca. Coenus was left in command of a substantial force at Maracanda with instructions to keep watch over the region and do his best to destroy the insurgents.

With his freedom of maneuver almost completely restricted, Spitamenes, who had recruited a large troop of Scythian horse, decided to launch an attack on Coenus. A fierce battle ensued, resulting in a decisive Macedonian victory. Spitamenes was deserted by most of his nomadic allies. Some Bactrians and Sogdians stayed with him, but lost heart when they heard that Alexander was on the move in their direction. So they beheaded Spitamenes.

According to Curtius, the story had a domestic twist. It was Spitamenes' wife who did the deed while he was in a deep sleep. Still wearing blood-drenched clothes, the widow brought the head to the Macedonian camp. So ended the most formidable and determined of all Alexander's opponents.

The insurgency was drawing to its close. With the arrival of spring 327, the king set off to mop up continuing resistance in the mountains. After surviving a fearful electrical storm, he came across the enemy in jaunty occupation of a natural fortress.

"YOU'LL NEED SOLDIERS WITH WINGS if you want to take this place!" shouted the defender peering down at the Macedonians from the lofty outcrop.

Alexander was inclined to agree. He had carefully scrutinized the Sogdian Rock, as it was called, and it seemed impregnable. The cliffs on every side were sheer, and a solitary path led up to the top. The Rock was a refuge for a large number of rebellious Sogdians who wanted to keep out of Alexander's way. Although winter was over, a heavy fall of snow impeded the approaches. The Sogdians had laid in copious provisions. They could melt the snow if water ran out.

However, the sneering response to his request for a parley irritated the king. He changed his mind. He would find a way. He announced a prize of twelve talents for the first man to scale the Sogdian Rock, an

almost incredible sum for a private soldier, with lesser but still generous prizes for runners-up. Three hundred volunteers were recruited,
all of them men who had experience of rock climbing. They gathered
a supply of small metal tent pegs to serve as pitons, and stout linen
ropes so that they could fasten themselves together. To avoid discovery, the ascent took place at night. It was an almost suicidal mission
and was the only special operation during Alexander's career which he
did not lead in person. Arrian picks up the story:

> Fixing their pegs where they could, sometimes into solid
> ground wherever it showed through, sometimes into the snow
> where it seemed least likely to crumble, they hauled themselves
> up the rock by various routes. About thirty of them fell to their
> death in the climb, and their bodies, lost in the snow where they
> happened to fall, could not be found for burial. The rest com-
> pleted the ascent toward dawn [and] established possession of
> the summit of the Rock.

The ascent was a remarkable achievement. It is interesting to observe
that climbing techniques and equipment have not changed in their essentials over the centuries.

A peak loomed above a large cave where the Sogdians had their
headquarters. Once on the summit, the climbers waved pieces of white
cloth to alert the king to their presence. He had a herald shout to the
Sogdians that they should surrender without further ado, for Alexander had found the men with wings.

The defenders turned round and looked up. They saw with amazement the young men on the crag above. A trumpet sounded in the
Macedonian camp, loud shouting was heard, and an assault seemed imminent. The Sogdians panicked and surrendered on condition that
their lives be spared. In fact, their situation was not hopeless at all; the
mountaineers were heavily outnumbered and Alexander had found no
way up the Rock for his army.

The operation displayed to advantage one of the king's special qualities as a military commander: he understood that psychological insight into the mind of the enemy could be as important to victory as
conventional military strength.

AS THE FIGHTING IN Sogdia and Bactria drew to a close, Alexander could announce a victory, but it contained the seeds of defeat. He had come to see that his angry hard-line policy of pacification by force had failed. At the first opportunity the nomadic tribes would rise again. Before leaving the region for India, he gave Amyntas, its new satrap (after Artabazus), a substantial garrison force of ten thousand infantry and thirty-five hundred cavalry. That was necessary but not sufficient. Macedonian rule would never be accepted unless brutality was replaced with the respect and reconciliation that he had successfully applied to his new Persian subjects.

The wife and daughters of a local baron called Oxyartes were among the refugees on the Sogdian Rock. One of his daughters was an attractive sixteen-year-old—of marriageable age by contemporary standards—called Rhoxane. She caught Alexander's eye and, although Arrian insists that he did not tamper with her, it is telling that the king compared the two of them to Achilles and Briseis in the *Iliad*. Briseis was a beautiful captive who was given to the warrior as a slave for his sexual use.

Oxyartes was alarmed to learn that members of his family were in Macedonian hands, but once he heard of the king's interest in Rhoxane he arranged to meet him and was well received. To further the affair, he staged, writes Curtius primly, "a banquet of typically barbaric extravagance" at which his daughter made a starring appearance. Alexander told Rhoxane's father that he was willing to formalize their relationship. He ordered a loaf of bread to be served, in accordance with Macedonian tradition, which he cut in two with a sword for himself and Oxyartes to taste. The marriage agreement was a decision taken by men; Rhoxane had nothing to do with it.

The army was displeased. Why did the king not take a Macedonian wife, as his predecessors had done? soldiers asked. This was an unfair question—Olympias, after all, was a foreigner, from Epirus. What the complainants really disliked was a *barbarian* wife from a conquered people. Probably in an attempt to calm these racist objections, the king insisted that this was a love match.

It was, of course, a political union. The eastern end of the Persian empire had long been quasi-autonomous, only half tamed. Painful experience over the last couple of years had taught Alexander that he could not alter this state of affairs, at least in the short run. His choice of Rhoxane was an implicit apology: it was a signal that he would no longer be a destructive foreign devil, but a respectful monarch who would leave the ruling elites in place and not interfere in the details of daily life.

Oxyartes helped the king deal with another, even larger mountain fortress. This was the Rock of Chorienes, some four thousand feet high and about seven miles in circumference. The Macedonians built a wooden bridge across a deep ravine on top of which an earth ramp was laid, thus enabling an assault on the stronghold. This risky plan was not put to the final test, for Oxyartes, now a traveling companion of the king, persuaded the Rock's commander to surrender on honorable terms.

He did more than surrender. The Macedonians were in a poor way. During the siege they suffered badly from a heavy snowfall, and there had been a shortage of food (one of the few occasions when Alexander's usually efficient logistics faltered). The commander offered to provision the army for two months and made an immediate distribution to each mess of grain, wine, and salted meat from his supplies on the Rock.

Craterus was sent to mop up two remaining rebel leaders and at last the great rebellion was over.

NOW, FINALLY, ALEXANDER COULD shake the dust of Bactria and Sogdiana from his feet. He readied himself for the expedition to India he had long dreamed of. The army he led would be very different from the expeditionary force of Macedonians and Greeks that had crossed the Hellespont a little more than five years previously. Now growing numbers of Asians were being recruited—among them, Lycians and Syrians and recently recruited cavalry from Bactria and Sogdiana.

He was still short of men. The pool of human capital in Macedonia was now more or less dry. As Alexander conquered wider and wider swaths of territory, the empire had to be guarded. Troops, often Greek mercenaries, were made over to satrapal armies and garrisons. Then there was "natural wastage": men grew old and retired, were killed in battle, or suffered disabling wounds.

Sometime in 327, satraps from the recently conquered territories and the numerous garrison towns brought thirty thousand local boys to Alexander. They were all about the same age and on the verge of puberty. They were to be taught Greek writing and the use of Macedonian weapons and tactics. A large number of instructors were employed for the purpose. After three years, the students would be conscripted as full-time soldiers.

They were called the Epigoni: the Successors. They were to be personally loyal to Alexander. The direct link to Macedonia would be broken. Their title was a clear hint that the king intended to create a brand-new army, designed no longer to conquer but to protect the empire.

CHAPTER 13

A PASSAGE TO INDIA

———

I T WAS ALL A GREAT MISUNDERSTANDING, THE QUARREL ABOUT *proskynesis*.

The word literally means "kissing toward" and designates an act of homage from a social inferior to his superior. However, there were two different ways in which the term could be applied—the Persian and the Greek. According to Herodotus,

> When the Persians meet one another in the street, you can see whether those who meet are of equal status. For instead of a verbal greeting, they kiss each other on the mouth; but if one of them is inferior to the other, they kiss one another on the cheeks, and if one is of much less noble rank than the other, he falls down before him in profound reverence.

The Great King expected full prostration from his subjects unless they were relatives or close friends, in which case a slight bow and the blowing of a kiss would suffice. The point of the ritual was secular, not religious. There was no question of the monarch being regarded as divine.

For Greeks, though, *proskynesis* was far more than an elaborate method of asserting class distinction. It was an act of worship that was due to the gods alone. It was generally performed standing up with hands raised to the sky, more rarely kneeling on the ground. For a free human being to prostrate himself to another was a humiliation. For a mortal to accept *proskynesis* was hubris.

As matters stood Persians regularly did obeisance and Macedonians regularly laughed when they saw it. Alexander wanted to unify court practices and so ensure that Macedonians and Persians felt that they were on equal terms in his presence. He persuaded his inner circle to accept *proskynesis* as a universally applied greeting, for Macedonians and Persians alike, when meeting the king.

An experiment was arranged. At a banquet *proskynesis* would be introduced without fuss or announcement, after which it would become a routine part of court etiquette. Presumably this was not to be the full prostration, but a bow. Or so it was hoped. Alexander drank from a gold loving cup and passed it to one of his friends, who stood up to face the household shrine, did obeisance to the king, received a kiss, and resumed his place on his dining couch.

The Greek court philosopher and historian Callisthenes deeply disapproved not only of the practice but of the entire Persianizing policy. Like his mentor, Aristotle, he believed that the Great King's subjects were in effect slaves whereas Hellenes, including Macedonians, were free men. When the cup came round, he drank from it, but, without doing obeisance, stepped up for a kiss. Alexander happened to be chatting with Hephaestion at the time and did not notice that the *proskynesis* had not been performed. However, one of the Companions told the king, who then refused to kiss him. Callisthenes replied: "Very well, I shall go back, the poorer by one kiss."

The incident attracted attention. The philosopher was well liked by the younger soldiers and the king decided, much to his annoyance, that he would have to let the matter drop.

The objection to obeisance was in part based on a fundamental error. The Great King did not see himself as a god and prostration before him was politeness rather than adoration. The Greeks wrongly applied their cult definition of the term to the Persian social context.

However, in another sense they may have had a point. In the background of the debate lay a growing suspicion that Alexander was beginning to think he was a god. The experience at Siwah had had a profound effect on him. Perhaps he was literally, not just symbolically, the son of Zeus, although this would not remove his mortality. Alexander's relationship to the god was why he was distancing himself from Philip.

The Greeks did not draw a line between the human and the divine. Great men were able to cross it and become *isotheoi,* equals of the gods or demigods. Heracles, whom Alexander was proud to count among his ancestors, became a demigod and was given the very rare accolade of immortality. The great Theban poet Pindar sets out the relation between the human and the divine in an ode celebrating the winner of the boys' wrestling at the Nemean Games:

> Single is the race, single
> of men and gods;
> from a single mother we both draw breath.
> But a difference of power in everything
> keeps us apart;
> for the one is as Nothing, but the brazen sky
> stays a fixed habitation forever.
> Yet we can in greatness of mind
> or of body be like the Immortals.

Alexander's achievements were colossal in the eyes of his contemporaries and it would not be unreasonable for him to claim that they were at least the equals of Heracles' labors. There were historical precedents for the establishment of cults of godlike human beings. The famous Spartan commander Lysander, who won the decisive sea battle at Aegospotami in the long war between Sparta and Athens, was awarded cult honors by Hellenic cities. He was probably the first living Greek to have altars erected in his name and sacrifices offered to him; the island of Samos changed the name of its national festival, which became the Lysandreia. Alexander's father Philip seems also to have received honors bordering on those accorded to the divine.

Ancient authors suggest that Alexander came to believe himself to be a god like Dionysus or Apollo. It is more likely, though, that he had no personal belief in his divinity, but saw political advantage in the establishment of a ruler cult devoted to him. Curtius has him say in a speech that the father of the gods held out to me the title of son; accepting it has not been disadvantageous to the operations in which we are engaged. I only wish the Indians would also believe me a god! For reputation determines military success, and often even a false belief has accomplished as much as the truth.

The words may be fictional, but the cynicism is supported by a recorded remark quoting the *Iliad,* which the king made when wounded by an arrow and in great pain: "What you see flowing, my friends, is blood, not '*ichor,* which flows in the veins of the holy gods.' " He hardly ever mentioned his godhead when in Greek or Macedonian company, but used it regularly to impress "barbarians."

Plutarch sourly commented that it was clear that the king was "not at all vain or deluded, but rather used belief in his divinity to enslave others."

In sum, Alexander may well have regarded himself as special, *isotheos,* and as having gods among his ancestors. His aching scars, however, reminded him that he was mortal.

THE ROYAL PAGES LIVED busy lives. They were the sons of Macedonian aristocrats and their presence at court was in part a guarantee of their fathers' good behavior, but they also played an essential role in the general administration of Alexander's daily routine.

Their duties were menial. They spent the night on watch outside the door of the royal bedchamber. They escorted in sexual partners by a private entrance out of sight of the official armed bodyguards. In the daytime they brought the king's horses to him and helped him mount one of them. It was widely seen as a special honor that they were allowed to sit and eat with Alexander. They accompanied him in battle and at the hunt. They were also expected to show an interest in cultural matters.

Access to the king was strictly controlled and the pages had a front-row view of everything that went on. In effect, they were apprentices in government, in the arts of war and peace, and could expect promotion in due course to important jobs in the regular army.

One day in 327 an incident took place when the pages were out hunting with Alexander that set off a tragic chain of events. One of their number was Hermolaus, a student of philosophy and an admirer of Callisthenes. He foolishly speared a boar that the king had marked down for himself. This act of lèse-majesté received condign punishment: the boy was flogged in front of his fellows.

Smarting from the humiliation, Hermolaus complained to another page called Sostratus, who was passionately in love with him. After they had exchanged oaths of loyalty, Sostratus persuaded Hermolaus to join him in a plot to assassinate the king at night in his bed. They enlisted seven other pages to join them.

It was a feasible scheme, but there were obstacles. The conspirators were on duty on different nights. The plan was to alter the work rota so that on a given night they would all be on duty together and able to murder the king without opposition. However, two official bodyguards also slept in the room and would have to be killed too. It took a month before the rota could be fixed. That left plenty of time for a security leak.

The conspirators were in luck, for none of them wavered and morale was high. On the evening when the assassination was to be carried out, the king was holding a dinner party and the pages stood outside the door into the dining room, intending to lead him to bed when the meal was over. But the company drank more deeply than usual and played party games. Time ran on; the pages feared that Alexander and his guests would continue drinking until morning, when they were due to hand over to a new shift.

In fact, the party broke up shortly before dawn and it looked as if there would be just enough time for the attempt. At this moment a mentally deranged woman appeared on the scene. She was a regular visitant and seemed to have been religiously inspired. She claimed to foretell the future and the king, impressed by some of her predictions, allowed her to wander about at will.

She was unusually agitated and as the king took his leave she threw herself in his way, telling him to return to the party. "The gods always give good advice," he remarked laughingly, and obeyed.

Alexander did not make up his mind to go to bed until about seven or eight in the morning. By then the hapless conspirators had lost their chance, but could not bring themselves to go away after being relieved.

When the king finally emerged from the dining room they were still hanging around. He told them to go and rest since they had been on their feet all night. Ironically, he praised them for their commitment and arranged for them to receive a gratuity.

The assassination was rescheduled. While the boys waited for the next opportunity, one of them, a certain Epimenes, had a change of heart. Perhaps he was touched by the king's kindness or, more probably, the events of the night persuaded him that the gods opposed the plot. Whatever the motive, he confided in his brother Eurylochus.

The specter of Philotas's fate was still hanging before everyone's eyes; Eurylochus knew better than to delay. He grabbed his brother and brought him at once to the royal quarters. There he found two Companions, Ptolemy and Leonnatus, who immediately opened the bedroom door, took in a lamp, and with some difficulty woke the king from a deep drunken sleep.

Once Alexander had regained consciousness, the two brothers gave a full account of the conspiracy. Alexander lost no time in pardoning Eurylochus and giving him fifty talents and the estate of a prominent Persian who had fallen from favor. The generosity of this reward seems excessive. It must be a measure of the king's shock to discover that those who spent most of their time in his company wanted him dead.

The guilty pages were quickly rounded up. The king asked what he had done to merit this treatment. Hermolaus was unabashed. "You ask as if you didn't know," he answered. "We plotted to kill you because you have started to behave not as a king with his free-born subjects, but as a slave owner."

Hermolaus was repudiated by his father. He and the other boys were tortured by their fellows and stoned to death, according to Macedonian practice.

THERE ARE NO DOUBTS about the Royal Pages affair. It was a serious plot and came within an inch of success. What is less than certain, though, is the motive that powered it. It confirmed the old adage that no man is a hero to his valet, but even if Alexander was a difficult employer there was more to the business than domestic backbiting: there was also a political dimension. The pages agreed with the king's Mace-

donian critics. As ever, the trouble lay with the king's policy of reconciliation with the enemy. Curtius has Alexander speak against
Hermolaus, who claims that

> I am foisting Persian habits on the Macedonians. That is true,
> for I see in many races things we should not be ashamed of copy-
> ing. The only way this great empire can be satisfactorily gov-
> erned is by our transmitting some things to the natives and
> learning others from them ourselves.

The king detected a figure standing in the shadows—namely Callisthenes, now fallen from grace. Unfortunately, it was difficult to link
him directly to the plot. It seems clear that the boys did not implicate
him in their confession. This is confirmed by Plutarch, who writes that

> not one of Hermolaus' accomplices, even in extremis, denounced
> Callisthenes. Indeed, Alexander himself, in the letters which he
> wrote at once to Craterus, Attalus and Alcetas, says that the
> youths had confessed under torture that the conspiracy was en-
> tirely their own idea and that nobody else knew about it.

However, it appears that Callisthenes cultivated young upper-class soldiers and shared with them his criticisms of the regime. He and Hermolaus were on friendly terms.

Callisthenes was his own worst enemy. He was tactless and saw no
danger in antagonizing Alexander. Once he was invited to deliver a
speech in which he eulogized the Macedonians. This he did to great
applause, upon which the king said: "Show us the power of your eloquence by criticizing the Macedonians." His vanity flattered, Callisthenes accepted the challenge. He did this so well that he infuriated all
his Macedonian listeners, Alexander included. Aristotle, who was his
uncle and had been his teacher, said that he possessed great eloquence,
but lacked common sense.

Rumors and accusations about Callisthenes were rife. Like Socrates,
he was believed to be a corrupter of the young. Although there was no
conclusive evidence of his disloyalty to Alexander, there was enough
to persuade the king. Furthermore, he suspected a Greek connection;

sophisticated opinion among city-states such as Athens laughed at Alexander's alleged aspirations to divinity and opposed his policy of reconciliation with barbarians.

Alexander was sure that Aristotle was behind much of this talk and was pouring poison into his nephew's ears. In a letter to Antipater at Pella, he reported:

> The youths were stoned to death by the Macedonians, but as for the sophist [i.e. Callisthenes], I shall punish him myself, and I shall not forget those who sent him to me, or the others who give shelter in their cities to those who plot against my life.

This sounds as if the philosopher, being Greek, was not brought before the Macedonian assembly, but was dealt with on the king's authority. Various versions of his fate have survived. He was tortured, he was crucified, he died of obesity or of an infestation of lice. The likeliest explanation is that he was arrested and died some time later in captivity.

We cannot easily tell how widespread was the discontent that the affair of the Royal Pages exposed, but it was probably limited to Macedonian noblemen, amplified and distorted by their teenaged offspring. That said, it does not appear to have weakened their resolve in battle or in using their initiative when operating independently from the main army. Alexander was extremely popular with the Macedonian rank and file and, so far as we can see, with private soldiers of whatever ethnic origin. His attention to their working conditions, avoidance of casualties, and insistence on leading from the front, whatever the danger, bound them to him. The new "barbarian" troops were presumably unaffected by what one might call the Macedonian infection, as were the Greek mercenaries.

INDIA WAS A SMALL triangular peninsula with high mountains to the north. It was longer than its width and a suite of great rivers, including the Indus, ran south through it. Not far beyond was the end of land, the farthest reach of the world. Here flowed the vast waters of the river Ocean, which surrounded the island of Europe, Africa, and Asia.

This was what Alexander and his contemporaries believed. They knew very little of the subcontinent and the void was filled in with fantasy. Giant ants dug in the desert sands for gold. Indians copulated in the open, like cattle, and their semen was black. Cannibals killed their old people before they fell ill and began wasting away, so that their meat was not spoiled.

After arriving in India, Alexander drafted a proud letter to his mother in which he boasted that he had discovered the source of the Nile. He supposed that the Indus was a higher reach of the Nile, which ran through a long desert before reaching Egypt. As evidence, he mentioned that he had seen some crocodiles in the Indus. He was soon reliably informed that the Indus was a river in its own right, which flowed into the Ocean rather than the Mediterranean. By good luck he had not yet sent off his letter; he silently removed the passage about the Nile.

Clearing up the geography of India was one of the tasks that the king hoped the experts he had brought along with him to Asia would undertake. He wanted to know where everything was and how long it would take to get there.

Gods visited India. During his visit the semi-divine Heracles spent much of his time impregnating local women. Only one of his offspring was a daughter, born late in his life. Unable to find a suitable husband for her, he had sex with the girl himself when she was only seven, so that his line would continue. Some said that Dionysus spent his childhood in the Punjab. He conquered India, founded cities, and taught the inhabitants the art of farming—and also of perfumery. It was from here that he started his celebrated procession through Asia to Greece where he introduced his worship and the blessings of viticulture.

According to Herodotus, India was the most populous nation in the known world and was reputed to be rich in gold, often sieved from the rivers. It paid in annual tribute to the Great King 360 talents in gold dust. Curtius notes that

the extravagance of [the Indians'] royalty . . . transcends the vices of all other peoples. When the king deigns to be seen in public, his servants carry silver censers along and fill with incense the entire route along which he has decided to be carried.

He lounges in a golden litter fringed with pearls, and he is dressed in linen clothes embroidered with gold and purple. The litter is attended by men-at-arms and by his bodyguard among whom, perched on branches, are birds which have been trained to sing in order to divert the king's thoughts from serious matters. The palace has gilded pillars with a vine in gold relief running the whole length of each of them and silver representations of birds (the sight of which affords them greatest pleasure) at various points.

Darius I had taken the boundary of his empire to be the Indus, but it is unclear how far his writ ran in practice. The Great King sent a maritime expedition down the river, which made its way as far as the Red Sea. By Alexander's day imperial control cannot have extended much farther than the Kabul Valley.

Although he seems not to have spelled out his thinking, the invasion of India was intended to achieve two objectives—one sentimental and the other practical. He had an overpowering desire, a *pothos,* to reach the river Ocean. With that achievement he would surpass Heracles and Dionysus. More basically, he longed to see the world's edge because it was there.

A more immediately pressing task was to restore the empire's authority in these remote marches. It is clear from the king's actions that he intended the Indus to be its permanent frontier. Defending it would not be a problem in the south, for it ran alongside the great Thar Desert. To the north, though, various independent native kingdoms flourished. Alexander aimed to crush them militarily, but not to annex them. They were to function as obedient buffers between the empire and whatever land waited to be discovered beneath the rising sun. As the Macedonians approached India, they learned that there was much more of that land than they had originally expected.

BY THE EARLY SUMMER OF 327, Alexander was ready for the new campaign. India promised mystery and glamour. He had heard the stories of the immense wealth of its rulers, and of their warriors gleaming in gold and ivory. Unwilling to be outdone, at least in appearances, he silver-plated his soldiers' shields and decorated their body armor with gold or silver. This may or may not have impressed the enemy, but it surely cheered up his men.

The army had ballooned; we are told that after the latest substantial reinforcements, which had joined him at Bactra, and the recruitment of many native fighters, it was 120,000 strong. This seems a rather high estimate and probably includes noncombatants in the baggage train. These were numerous, for the army was a mobile state, or at least city. Soldiers themselves probably numbered not more than sixty thousand. The king foresaw the need for more soldiers and gave orders for the recruitment of thirty thousand men from the provinces.

Northwestern India opened out before the conquerors. It was a patchwork of jostling riverine kingdoms, whose rulers were well aware of the imminent Macedonian threat. They could live with it and indeed work it to their advantage. They guessed that it was a violent form of state visit and would soon pass. A local dynast, Sisikottos (or Shashigupta) informed Alexander that Taxiles, the king of Taxila, whose realm lay between the Indus and Hydaspes (today's Jhelum) Rivers, would be seeking Alexander's friendship and his help against Porus, king of the Pauravas east of the Hydaspes.

A meeting was arranged; when Taxiles turned up he was in full battle array, with gaily decorated war elephants, and for a moment Alexander feared he was coming under attack. This was a dangerous misunderstanding, but was quickly cleared up and the two men got on very well. Taxiles, who was shortly to die and was succeeded by his equally accommodating son, insisted he was not spoiling for a fight. He said: "If I possess more than you, I am ready to be generous toward you, and if I have less, I shall not refuse any benefits you may offer." The kings began presenting each other with more and more valuable gifts. Alexander, competitive to the last drop of blood, ended by giving Taxiles a thousand talents in coin, much to the annoyance of his circle. One of his marshals, Meleager, drank too much at dinner and remarked sarcastically to him: "At least in India you have found a man worth a thousand talents!"

At last the Macedonians were ready to set off. They recrossed the Hindu Kush and called in at the new garrison town of Alexandria-in-the-Caucasus, where Alexander summarily dismissed the incompetent governor. Then they marched down into the Indus Valley. Applying the lessons learned in Bactriana and Sogdiana, the king again divided his army into smaller sections as called for by the occasion. His tactic was to assault and capture an enemy fortress-town, inducing others in the neighborhood to surrender without a fight. He founded a new settlement to watch for insurgencies. At one siege an arrow pierced his breastplate and wounded him slightly in his shoulder.

Alexander's first destination was the broad-flowing Indus. Fed by the snows and glaciers of the Himalayan, the Karakoram, and the Hindu Kush ranges of Tibet, it is the longest river in Asia. The king sent Hephaestion with a substantial force to prepare for a crossing by building a bridge across the river. The remainder of the army was put to laying a road and constructing a flotilla of boats and thirty-oared galleys, which were to sail down the river to the bridge and help convey personnel and impedimenta over the water.

THE KING RESUMED HIS POLICY of exemplary brutality. He had trouble with the Assacani, a tribe in the Lower Swat Valley. Their army, not being large enough to meet the invader, dispersed to various strongholds, one of which, Massaga, Alexander invested. The formidable Macedonian siege machines were brought into operation.

Someone on the wall shot an arrow at Alexander and wounded him in the leg. He reacted with typical, careless fortitude. Curtius writes that he

> pulled out the barb, had his horse brought up and, without even bandaging the wound, rode around fulfilling his schedule no less energetically. But as his injured leg hung down and, after the blood dried, the wound stiffened, aggravating the pain, Alexander is reported to have said that, though he was reputed to be the son of Zeus, he could still feel the damage done by a wound.

He should have lain on his bed, but (as at Gaza) he refused to stay still and wait for a scab to form. Instead, he insisted on inspecting some engineering work.

The Assacenian king was killed by a stray catapult bolt and his mother, Cleophis, took charge. After a few days the defenders saw that their cause was hopeless. The terms of a surrender were negotiated and the queen dowager with her ladies-in-waiting presented herself to Alexander. She sought pardon and confirmation of her standing as ruler. The king gave her what she wanted. Apparently, she was good-looking and joined the lengthening list of women of a certain age who caught the king's eye. A baby was born in due course, whom the queen named Alexander.

The Assaceni had hired seven thousand or so Indian mercenaries, who offered strong resistance, but came to an agreement with Alexander that their lives would be spared if they enrolled as regular members of his army. They came out of Massaga with their weapons and encamped with their families on a hill opposite the Macedonians. In fact, they planned to slip away under cover of darkness, for they had no wish to fight against other Indians.

The king got wind of this, ringed the hill with his forces, and slaughtered all the mercenaries. We can only suppose that the women and children were put up for sale. The incident shocked the civilized world and was another reminder of the destruction of Thebes. In extenuation, Alexander may have calculated that it was unwise to leave such a large body of hostile soldiers free to wreak havoc in his rear. The massacre was probably a case of cruel necessity rather than of gratuitous cruelty.

CRADLED IN A BEND of the Indus, a vertiginous massif rises to a height of five thousand feet above the river. It was called Aornos—Greek for "Birdless" because birds did not fly so high (it has been identified as today's Pir-Sar, in Pakistan). The rock is crowned by a narrow plateau about one and a half miles long, containing good arable land and copious springs; it can be reached only by one difficult route. At the northern end, a much higher conical hill rises above the plateau and is separated by a deep ravine from another lofty crag, now called Uni-Sar.

Many tribesmen had congregated on the plateau to escape the attentions of the Macedonian army. A local legend had it that a god, probably Krishna, had once besieged Aornos, but had given up because of

an earthquake. Once Alexander was informed that Krishna was an incarnation of Heracles, he developed a *pothos* to succeed where his great
ancestor had failed. He was determined to capture the rock, whatever
the cost.

But how to do it? Alexander marched to Aornos with a part of the
army. A direct assault was out of the question. Advised by some locals,
he sent Ptolemy with a lightly armed and agile advance guard to scale
the neighboring Uni-Sar out of sight of the enemy. They scrambled up
a rough and steep track, until they reached a spur facing Aornos. Here
they could be seen and would have to defend themselves, so they made
a camp with a surrounding stockade and ditch.

A prearranged beacon alerted the king that the advance guard had
established itself and he led his troops up Uni-Sar in Ptolemy's footsteps. However, tribesmen crossed over from the plateau and blocked
his way. Alexander was forced to pull back. The tribesmen then about-
turned and assaulted Ptolemy. They tried to pull down the stockade,
but at sunset they gave up and withdrew.

During the night Alexander sent a trusted Indian deserter to carry
a letter to Ptolemy, ordering him to go on the offensive the following
day as soon as he saw the main force resume its advance. This would
mean that the enemy would be sandwiched between two attacking
forces. The tactic succeeded. The Macedonians drove off the enemy
and reached a high top opposite the plateau.

However, a deep ravine separated the two rocks, Uni-Sar and Pir-
Sar or Aornos. Alexander was undeterred; he ordered his men to construct a bridge or causeway, probably a wooden cribwork construction
covered with earth. It must have looked like an early American railroad
trestle bridge, in a modern scholar's happy simile. After a few days the
causeway began to stretch across the void. Slingers and artillery engines were at last able to fire at the defenders (a light catapult could hurl
a metal bolt about 450 yards). A band of enterprising Macedonians
scaled a small hill on the far edge of the ravine and level with the plateau. The causeway was not far off and would soon reach the hill.

The tribesmen were stunned by the Macedonians' engineering skills
and their giddying combination of determination and panache. They
announced that they were ready to agree to terms of surrender; their
intent was to waste the day in negotiation and then scatter to their

homes during the night. The king was informed of this (we are not told how) and craftily removed troops guarding the exit route. After the tribesmen (literally) walked into his trap and began to leave the rock, he led seven hundred soldiers up the part of the plateau which they had vacated. At a signal, they attacked the retreating tribesmen and killed many of them.

According to Arrian's laconic comment, "Alexander was now master of the rock which had defeated Heracles." The king was modest enough, or perhaps sensible enough, not to boast about this. Nevertheless, Aornos was the most remarkable of his sieges and confounded the Indians. His reputation as a military leader was now such that many thought twice before opposing him.

THE ARMY WAS ACTING very oddly indeed.

Soldiers were roaming around lush mountain slopes in a drunken stupor and cavorting in clearings and shady thickets. Ivy (Dionysus's signature plant) or something very like it was growing everywhere and the men made wreaths from it which they put round their heads.

Some lay stoned on beds of leaves. Others sang songs to Dionysus and behaved as if they were Bacchants, drugged worshippers of the divine patron of wine and ecstasy. Although they are not mentioned in the sources, women from the baggage train must also have played a part in these ecstatic orgies (they certainly did on similar occasions elsewhere).

It was as if the revelers were living out the god's own behavior, as a hymn in his honor describes:

> He spent all his time wandering through woody coombes, thickly wreathed with ivy and laurel. And the nymphs followed in his train with him for their leader; and the boundless forest was filled with their screams.

The explanation of these bizarre scenes can be traced back to an embassy to Alexander from the citizens of Nysa, a town near the Indus at the foot of a mountain rich in flora and fauna. The delegates asked him not to attack their city because it had been founded by Dionysus and was reputed to be his birthplace. The king, whose mother was, as we know, a follower of the god and had taken part in his rites, was mightily impressed and agreed that the Nysaeans should retain their independence.

Arrian and Curtius had little time for the Dionysus connection. They thought the envoys had exaggerated a local legend to please Alexander. Perhaps they had even made up the story for the occasion. One way or another, though, the king allowed himself to be taken in, because, as Arrian suggests, he wanted Nysa to have been founded by Dionysus: if that was true, it would mean that he himself had already traveled as far as Dionysus and would yet go beyond him. Alexander calculated that the Macedonians would not be so reluctant to follow him on grueling campaigns in still more distant places if the ambition to surpass Dionysus's achievements spurred them on.

He announced a ten-day holiday and led his entire army up the mountain overlooking the town. There he sacrificed to Dionysus and held a lavish banquet. It must have been quite a party, for even senior Macedonians in his inner circle "became possessed by Dionysus, raised the cult cry of *euoi,* and fell into a Bacchic frenzy."

If only the Indians had known that the invincible invaders were stuck in the middle of a forest and helplessly out of their minds, the expedition could have come to a premature end. At last, though, the king and his men pulled themselves together and came down from the mountain.

They marched onward to the Indus, where they found serviceable timber which was felled for shipbuilding. The resulting flotilla sailed down the river to the bridge Hephaestion had been ordered to construct (probably planking over tethered boats). Here the king sacrificed to all his usual gods (Dionysus and Heracles surely among them) and staged athletic and equestrian competitions beside the river. The omens were favorable and the Macedonians made their way across without incident. More sacrifices followed, in thanks this time rather than prayer.

THE SKIES WERE GRAY and lowered above the river Hydaspes, one of the five great tributaries of the Indus which pour south from the Himalayas. The air was thick with humidity. Anything made of metal—swords and armor—rusted without constant attention. Rain was falling, heavy, constant, everlasting rain. The date was July 326; the monsoon—unfamiliar to the Macedonians, and a nasty surprise—had started and would last till September.

Alexander intended to march eastward, which meant crossing the Hydaspes, so he arranged for his flotilla on the Indus to be dismantled, transported overland to the river, and reassembled. He suspected that the Indian king Porus would cause trouble. As mentioned earlier, Porus ruled Pauravas, a territory between the Hydaspes and the Acesines (today's Chenab). Unaware that the Macedonian never took no for an answer, Porus alone of his fellow rajahs had refused Alexander's invitation to a meeting. He had made up his mind to fight the invader and was awaiting reinforcement from Abisares, who ruled an area of hill country (Kashmir) near the Hydaspes.

The river was in full spate—swollen and muddy with a fast current—but Alexander hoped that he would be able to make use of a ford (near today's railway station at Haranpur). When he arrived there, he found the entire Indian army lining the far, or eastern, bank. It was an alarming spectacle. And so, for that matter, was Porus himself. Curtius writes that he "rode an elephant which towered above the other beasts. His armor, with its gold and silver inlay, lent distinction to an unusually large physique. His physical strength was matched by his courage."

The sources vary, but a rational guess posits thirty thousand infantry and a modest four thousand horse, together with three hundred chariots. Porus also had about 130 elephants, trained for warfare. Alexander was skeptical of their value, for they could do as much damage to friends as to foes; however, they would frighten his horses, on whom he would be depending once again for victory.

What was to be done? The king opted for deception. He split his army into smaller units, which he and his commanders led here and there in the countryside, laying waste to enemy territory and apparently searching for easier places to ford the river. Supplies of grain were brought in to give the impression that the Macedonians were digging in for a long stay, until the monsoon was over and the water level had dropped. As Arrian observes,

With his boats plying up and down, leather rafts being stuffed with straw, the whole bank visibly crowded with troops, cavalry here, infantry there, Alexander kept Porus unsettled and prevented him from selecting a single vantage-point in which to concentrate his defensive capability.

Then night after night the king had most of his cavalry ride up and down the bank shouting and making all sorts of noise that suggested an army getting ready to cross over. Porus reacted by following the commotion with his elephants and other troops. Eventually, he realized that these were false alarms and no longer paid them any mind.

Once he was sure the Indian king had been lulled into inattention, Alexander put into effect an ingenious stratagem. There was no time to lose, for he learned Porus's ally Abisares was on his way to join him with a substantial force and would arrive within a couple of days.

The Macedonian scouts had discovered a pathless and uninhabited wooded island seventeen miles upstream (near today's Jalalpur). It concealed a tree-covered inlet on the near bank. This was where the king intended to attempt a crossing. The plan was to divide the army in two. Through the night Alexander would lead some five thousand horse and at least six thousand foot soldiers to the island. These were modest numbers, but he must have calculated that they were enough for the task in hand, and at any rate they were the maximum he could transport within a single night.

The king would take a roundabout route to avoid discovery. His men would bring with them the leather raft casings, which had been restuffed. The reassembled Macedonian boats would be waiting out of sight behind the island.

The larger part of the army, under Craterus, was to remain where it was at the Haranpur ford. The men would behave as if they were about to launch an attack. The king's pavilion would remain in place, and a double would wear the royal cloak and stand in for Alexander. Also, the Greek mercenaries were dispersed along the riverside. They too would cross the Hydaspes once it became clear that the forthcoming battle was on the point of being won.

The departure of the assault force would be masked by empty tents and blazing fires. The king gave Craterus strict instructions to stay

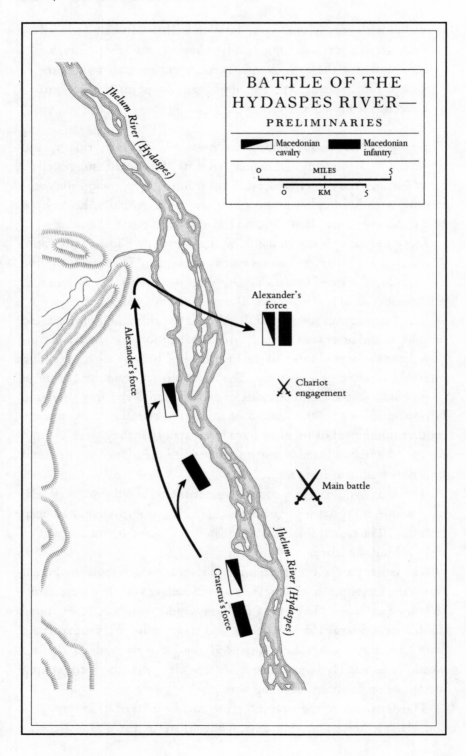

Jhelum River (Hydaspes)

BATTLE OF THE
HYDASPES RIVER—
PRELIMINARIES

Macedonian
cavalry

Macedonian
infantry

O   MILES   5

O   KM   5

Alexander's
force

Alexander's force

Chariot
engagement

Main battle

Craterus's force

Jhelum River (Hydaspes)

where he was unless Porus marched off to confront Alexander or was in retreat. In what appear to be his written orders, he continued:

> But if Porus takes part of his army against me and leaves part behind in the camp with elephants as well, you must still not make a move. If, though, he takes all his elephants with him against me, with some of the rest of his army left in the camp, then cross as fast as you can. It is only the elephants which make it impossible to land the horses—any other part of Porus's army will pose no problem.

One night Alexander put his plan into operation. He set out secretly and arrived at the island some hours later, where he found everything present and correct. Shortly before first light the cavalry were on their rafts and the infantry in their boats. The crossing was under way.

As often happens with a careful plan, fate interposed an obstacle. A tremendous storm broke. Water flooded down from the sky, restricting vision and drenching the men. The general misery was at least alleviated by the knowledge that the claps of thunder and the drumming rain would camouflage the sounds of thousands of troops on the move.

Worse was to come. The boats and rafts made for the bank and all the men and horses disembarked, only to discover that they were in fact on the shore of another smaller island. This was a serious setback. It would soon be broad daylight and the advantage of surprise would be lost. There was no time to reembark, so the king and his men struggled across the island and waded through a fast-flowing channel. This was hard going, for the water came over the chests of the foot soldiers and only the horses' heads were above the surface.

By now, the Macedonians had been observed by Porus's scouts; it was essential that the entire assault force reach land as soon as possible and be ready to oppose the inevitable Indian attack. The whole process must have taken several hours. The king placed his cavalry in the front behind a screen of mounted archers. (From his guerrilla years in Bactriana and Sogdiana, he had learned the value of mounted archers skilled at dashing in, shooting arrows, and dashing out with impunity.) The infantry formed up behind the cavalry as they emerged sodden from the river.

Porus now faced a painful dilemma. He saw that the Macedonians had divided into two. One part must have been a feint, a ruse, and the other the main force. Which was which? Or, to put the question another way, where was Alexander—at the Jalalpur island or at the Haranpur ford? He spent time pondering the problem, for he knew that his fate and the issue of the forthcoming battle hung on his choice. Meanwhile he quickly sent one of his sons with two thousand cavalry and 120 chariots to see if he could drive the invaders back into the river.

At first sight Alexander thought this force was the advance guard of Porus's entire army, but when he learned their true strength he decided to wipe them out. He immediately charged at the head of his cavalry. Once the enemy recognized Alexander, they pulled back in alarm. The chariots turned out to be useless, for their wheels sank into the monsoon-muddy ground. Porus's son was killed, as were four hundred of his horsemen.

At last, Porus did the right thing, but he did it too late. His cavalry had been mauled. The Macedonians had extricated themselves from the Hydaspes and were preparing for battle. Alexander had been seen leading the charge in person against his son. The Indian king realized that the real threat came from the assault force and moved the bulk of his army against it. He left a small contingent and a few elephants to frighten Craterus's cavalry away from the bank.

BOTH SIDES PREPARED THEMSELVES for a set-piece battle. Porus moved forward until he found a piece of well-drained ground where elephants and cavalry could maneuver safely. In his center he formed a line of between eighty-five and two hundred elephants at intervals of one hundred feet, and behind them he placed his infantry, which stretched well beyond the Macedonian phalanx. Diodorus remarks: "His whole array looked very much like a city, for the elephants resembled towers, and the soldiers between them curtain walls." His cavalry, now numbering after the recent skirmish only 3,600 riders in total, was divided between the wings, screened by 180 chariots and special infantry units.

Alexander took care to keep his forces out of sight for the time being while discreetly observing Porus's dispositions. The Macedonian troops eventually caught up with the cavalry and were allowed to rest and recover a little from the exertions of the night.

Meanwhile the king devised his tactics. Once more he brought deception into play. He arranged his army in a conventional lineup, with his phalanx and hypaspists in the center, flanked on both sides by Companion cavalry. He led two squadrons on the right and Coenus commanded two on the left. But Alexander introduced a twist. His squadrons and the center moved forward toward the enemy and came into view. However, Coenus at the far end of the field was instructed to hold back and stay out of sight behind trees or in dead ground.

The king sent mounted archers against the Indian cavalry and the chariots on Porus's left wing. In Arrian's words, their task was "to create havoc among the troops stationed there with their dense volleys of arrows and quick charges in and out." The enemy horse was soon in disarray and the chariots were more or less annihilated. Alexander then led a charge against them.

He was playing a mind game with the Indian king. He guessed that Porus would suppose that the Macedonians were fielding only two cavalry squadrons. He would know nothing of Coenus and his horsemen and would assume that the cavalry on his right wing had nobody to fight and nothing to do. He would be tempted to order it across the battlefield behind his lines and reinforce his cavalry on the left, which was now under fierce attack.

In this way, Porus would substantially outnumber Alexander's squadrons and would be able to prevent his left from breaking. With any luck, he might even drive off the Macedonians and win the battle. Coenus had been instructed in advance to keep an eye on the Indian right, and if the cavalry there left its station to follow on behind it.

Porus acted just as Alexander's psychological insight had predicted he would. With Coenus's arrival, the combined Indian horse unexpectedly found itself assailed in the rear as well as the front. They began to break up and fell back onto the elephants nearby.

The mahouts drove their animals against the Macedonian cavalry. The phalanx took this as a signal to encircle the elephants. They speared them, hacked off their feet, and chopped at their trunks. Some of the crazed beasts charged into the Macedonian infantry lines, which prompted the Indian cavalry to launch an unsuccessful counterattack.

The fighting now became general. The Macedonians soon gained the upper hand, with Alexander and his Companions charging again and again into the trapped enemy horse. The elephants went berserk. Arrian takes up the gory narrative:

> Crowded now into a narrow space, the elephants caused as much damage to their own side as to the enemy, turning round and round, barging, and trampling. The Indian cavalry, tightly corralled among the elephants, suffered massive carnage. Most of the mahouts had been shot down: wounded, exhausted, and with no one to control them, the elephants could no longer play their specific role in the battle but, maddened by pain, they began attacking friends and enemies alike, crushing, trampling, and killing indiscriminately.

The phalanx recovered its élan and pressed its bristling sarissas against the wavering line of enemy foot-soldiers. The Macedonian horse began to set a cordon around them and were perhaps joined by the Greek mercenaries who had been waiting at the riverside. The tiring and lengthy business of butchery began. Craterus moved his troops across the ford and joined in the mopping up.

By the end of the day it is said that twenty thousand Indian infantry and three thousand cavalry lay dead on the rain-soaked earth. The chariots were all wrecked. The Macedonians lost about eighty foot soldiers at most, ten mounted archers, and 220 cavalry.

One particular casualty of the battle or its aftermath struck Alexander to the heart. About this time, his horse Bucephalas died. He was thirty years old and probably succumbed not to a wound but to heat exhaustion. Alexander, who loved him as a comrade-in-arms, was grief-stricken. Of the two garrison towns he founded on the battle site and at the base camp, the first was named Nicaea, "City of Victory," and the other Bucephala in honor of a much-missed friend.

A gigantic figure towering over the field on his enormous elephant, Porus surveyed the ruin of his army and his hopes. He ran through

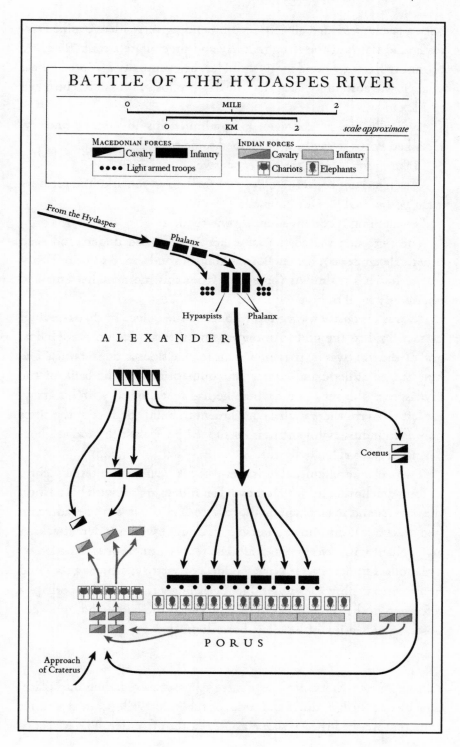

with a javelin a valued ally for recommending surrender. Unlike Darius he did not quit the struggle early and precipitate a rout. Bleeding profusely from a wound in his shoulder, he eventually accepted defeat when it was absolutely clear that the day was lost. He asked to be taken to Alexander.

Typically, the Macedonian king admired his adversary's bravery. He asked Porus to say how he wished to be treated.

"Like a king," came the perfect answer.

"As far as I am concerned, Porus, I shall do as you ask. Tell me now what you would like for yourself."

"Everything is contained in my one request."

The two men shared the same heroic code and understood each other. Alexander confirmed Porus's kingship and added some territory to the Indian's realm. As for Porus, from this moment he remained unfailingly loyal to his conqueror.

As was his custom, the victor honored the fallen. In thanksgiving, he sacrificed to the gods. Among them on this occasion was Helios, god of the sun (was he praying for more blue skies and less rain?). The king staged athletic and equestrian competitions on the bank of the Hydaspes at the very point where he had first crossed with his army. He left Craterus there with a detachment to build and fortify the cities he was founding, while he himself moved on against the Indians bordering the area ruled by Porus.

Two celebratory medallions were struck. One was a tetradrachm, or four-drachma coin, which showed an Indian archer with his bow on the obverse and an elephant on the reverse. The other was a decadrachm (ten drachmas); this shows a horseman, doubtless Alexander, attacking an elephant with two riders, doubtless representing Porus attended by a mahout. On the reverse Nike, goddess of victory, crowns a standing figure, presumably Alexander. He is clasping a thunderbolt, perhaps a reference to the thunderstorm that preceded the battle and, one supposes, an indication of his Zeus-born divinity.

THE PIECES OF ALEXANDER's strategic jigsaw were falling into place. One by one the kingdoms and states of the Indus Valley joined a buffer zone that marked the Persian empire's eastern frontier. The Macedonian conqueror was to be their overlord, but otherwise he would leave them to govern themselves.

Porus, now a close and trusted ally, was instructed to bring his best surviving troops and some elephants. The army was divided again into separate contingents, which roamed the Indus Valley requesting surrenders from the various states in the region. Most did as they were told, but some resisted. Taxiles was reconciled, a little reluctantly, with Porus. Abisares, who had been expected to join the Indian king at the Hydaspes but had failed to show up, sent an embassy, headed by his brother, to make peace. He was appointed satrap of his own kingdom. A force was dispatched to quash a revolt among the Assacenians.

Another king called Porus (the first one's cousin) offered his submission. However, he was alarmed by Alexander's favoritism toward his namesake, a long-standing enemy of his, and fled eastward with as many of his fighting men as he could persuade to join him. Hephaestion was sent off to annex his kingdom and pass it on to the first Porus; after he had done this, he founded a couple of fortified settlements.

A people called the Cathaeans rose up in arms and made a stand at the strongly fortified city of Sangala. They encircled a hill just outside the gates with three lines of wagons. Alexander captured these improvised defenses and the enemy retreated behind Sangala's brick wall. After an attempted breakout, the Macedonians built a double stockade which ringed the city except for a shallow lake. The king guessed correctly that the defenders would attempt another breakout across the water; his Macedonians, reinforced by Porus, slaughtered them as they emerged.

Siege engines were moved up, ladders were installed around the circuit, and Sangala was taken by storm. Seventeen thousand Indians were reportedly killed and seventy thousand captured. The city was razed.

The chivalry which Alexander had shown to his royal adversary had given way once more to ferocity and inhumanity. Indian public opinion was disgusted by the destruction of Sangala. Polyaenus, a strategy expert during the reign of the Roman emperor Marcus Aurelius, observes: "This act greatly damaged his reputation in the eyes of the Indians, who considered him a bloodthirsty savage."

Alexander's campaigning had been crowned with military success, but the morale of the troops was plummeting. The Battle of the Hydaspes had taken place in May, but in the following weeks the spring thunderstorms that announced the monsoon gave way to continuous heavy rain. As the Macedonians crossed one tributary of the Indus after another, the waters rose higher and flowed faster. The cities of Nicaea and Bucephala were washed away and had to be rebuilt.

Nothing is more injurious to a sense of well-being than being permanently wet. Alexander's men may have adored him, but there were limits to what they would put up with.

INDIA WAS TURNING OUT to be a much larger place than had originally been anticipated. Alexander and the Greek scientific experts he had recruited had assumed that it was no larger than today's Punjab and that a short march would bring them to the edge of the Ocean. Now that they were actually in the subcontinent, reports could not be ignored which showed that land, states, and populations stretched indefinitely eastward.

A local king spoke of a desert that would take twelve days to cross. The traveler would then arrive at a vast river, the Ganges. The ruler there had at his disposal two hundred thousand infantry, two thousand chariots, and four thousand elephants equipped for war. Alexander was impressed and consulted Porus, who happily confirmed the accuracy of the report (despite the fact that no such desert existed and the Indian army numbers were hyperinflated). Other accounts spoke of fertile lands with many elephants.

We are now confronted by an enigma. By now the Macedonians were approaching the last of the Indus tributaries, the Hyphasis (today's Beas). It was six fathoms deep and with a violent current, and would be difficult to cross. The king could not care less about obstacles; he had a *pothos* to journey to the ends of the earth, and that was that. According to Arrian, he "advanced with his army to the river . . . intent on subduing the Indians yet further to the east. In his mind there could be no end to the war as long as there was any enemy left."

The army disagreed. It had had a surfeit of water and refused to follow him. So far as they were concerned, the war was over.

Alexander had detected incipient discontent: after the victory over Porus, he had distributed large bonuses both to his generals and to other ranks. Soldiers' wives were granted monthly rations, and their children received an allowance calculated according to their fathers' military record. He gave generous rewards for bravery. None of this improved the mood. Men gathered in small groups and muttered. Some simply complained; others swore they would not take another step, even with Alexander as their leader. But no one spoke out openly.

The king saw that he had to intervene. He summoned his senior officers and gave them a pep talk. He had shared the work, the danger, and, notably, the recompense, with every member of the army, he said, and deserved their continuing loyalty. He told them: "All this land is yours, and you are its satraps."

The men said nothing and hung their heads. "I must have hurt you in some way without knowing it," added Alexander bitterly. "You don't even want to look at me. I seem to be completely alone—nobody answers me, nobody even says no to me."

A long silence followed. This was a political crisis of the first order. The future of the entire expedition depended on the trust that flowed back and forth between the king and his men, and that appeared to have drained away. At last one of the generals, the able and trusted Coenus, took his career in his hands and spoke for the army. He chose his words carefully and respectfully, but he did not mince them. The men wanted to see their homeland again and their loved ones. He referred pointedly to the poor condition of their equipment, their clothes, their armor, and their weapons. Arrian has him say, to loud applause:

> You should not now lead forward a reluctant army. You won't find them as ready as they once were to meet danger, when they have lost their will for battle. But, if you agree, go home with them to Macedonia, see your mother, settle what needs to be settled in Greece, bring back all these great victories to adorn your father's house. Then, if you so choose, begin again from scratch—and launch another campaign.

Alexander was unaccustomed to rebuffs, and he took this one very badly. Much of his fury was directed at Coenus. He abruptly suspended the meeting and recalled it in a foul temper on the following day. He announced that he himself was going on and anyone who wished to join him was welcome to do so. Everybody else was free to go home. They could tell their friends that they had abandoned their king surrounded by enemies.

With these words he jumped down from the dais and withdrew like Achilles to brood in his tent. For three days he refused to allow anyone in, even his closest associates and Companions. Learning from his behavior after the murder of Cleitus, he hoped this might compel the army to change its mind. In fact, it remained obstinate. The men were sorry that Alexander was upset, but they were not going to change their minds.

The only question now was how the king would give way without loss of face. As was his practice on important occasions, he conducted a sacrifice before crossing the Hyphasis. He found that the omens were inauspicious. Is it too much to suppose that a quiet word was dropped into Aristander's ear? In any event, Alexander called off the offensive, but made it clear that he was yielding to the gods, not to his men. The soldiers responded to the announcement with an earsplitting roar of joy.

To translate his renunciation into something that looked like a victory, the king arranged for twelve massive altars as high as his highest siege towers to be erected. He sacrificed on them to the gods in thanksgiving for his unbroken line of victories. As usual he staged athletic and equestrian competitions. This pause gave time for the army to recuperate after its exertions and ready themselves for the long return.

Within a few days of these events, Coenus took ill of some unspecified disease and died. Modern scholars have suspected foul play, but nobody did at the time. Alexander was saddened and the general was given a fine funeral.

THIS IS A CURIOUS TALE.

For all his *pothos,* Alexander was a practical man and did not give way to a random yen before assessing the risks and the benefits. Throughout his campaigning in Thrace and Asia, he had sought to secure his borders and resisted the temptation to annex new territory. If we judge the king by his deeds rather than by the rhetoric of war without end, his aims in the Indus Valley were rational and attainable. As we have seen, these were to protect the ramshackle, largely ungoverned eastern end of the Persian empire by establishing a reliable set of allied states that would stand between it and whatever and whoever lay beyond.

So the fact is that he never had any intention of marching to Ocean. He had displayed his standards along his empire's final frontier and now the Indian adventure was over.

In that case, what lay behind the quarrel with his men? His passion for travel and discovery, for global dominion, was a feature of his public image. Perhaps when planning his departure from India, he needed someone else to blame for not fighting his way across the subcontinent to the world's end. Otherwise he could be accused of losing his nerve. The obvious candidate was his army; he knew that if he broadcast his intention to carry on campaigning permanently, he would set off something approaching a mutiny. So that was what he did.

More mundanely, it can be argued that, while he had no serious plan to vanquish all India, he did fancy a brief foray, rather as when he crossed the Danube, to frighten the local people. It would also enable his experts to pursue their scientific inquiries and gain a more accurate notion of the geography of India. In the imagination of his men—and of ancient historians—this was inflated into a more all-embracing project.

We will never know the truth of the matter, but once the Indus Valley had been secured, Alexander's next step was predictable. The only imperial frontier he had not yet visited lay to the south—down the Indus, along the coastline of the Arabian Sea, and up the Persian Gulf.

THEN, WITH THE CONCLUSION of his circuit of empire, rest and relaxation awaited him in Babylon, city of wonders.

CHAPTER 14

SHOW ME THE WAY
TO GO HOME

———

A CITY WAS DANCING ON THE WAVES.

Timber had been floated down from the mountain forests and transformed over the summer into a fleet of open boats and thirty-oared triaconters, of war galleys and troop ferries or horse ferries. They were joined by a myriad of Indian river craft, making a grand total of nearly two thousand vessels. Men in the army with sailing experience were recruited as crew. They assembled on the Hydaspes at the new garrison towns of Nicaea and Bucephala, where an artificial harbor had been created. Their destination was the southern sea into which the Indus poured its iced waters from the Himalayas.

It was the autumn of 326; the monsoons had done their worst and the sun had reappeared. The multitude of sails and oars and rigging made for a brilliant spectacle. But this was no armada prepared for war. Its task was simply to transport Alexander's men and animals. The seers presided over the customary sacrifices for a lucky voyage, but, to make assurance doubly sure, insisted that they include in their devotions the Hydaspes.

It was about now that Alexander's wife, Rhoxane, gave birth to a son, but he was either stillborn or died within the first few days of life. The king buried him and offered sacrifices. A few months had passed between marriage and pregnancy, but the king had at least demonstrated his capacity, if not his enthusiasm. A little later he gave his father-in-law, Oxyartes, the satrapy of Parapanisadae, from which we may deduce that the marriage was at least a public relations success.

Just before dawn on a day in early November, the king stood in the prow of his own ship and poured libations from a golden bowl to the river god, to Heracles, and to his "spiritual" father Zeus Ammon; also to Poseidon, to Amphitrite, and to the Nereids. A trumpet sounded and the fleet put out.

The loyal but unimaginative Nearchus was appointed admiral. He had previously served as satrap of Lycia and Pamphilia. He was somewhat overshadowed by Alexander's helmsman, a Greek from Aegina called Onesicritus, who had constant access to the king while he was aboard, and used his influence to undermine Nearchus. Arrian notes drily: "One of the falsities in Onesicritus's history of Alexander is that he gives himself the title of 'admiral,' when in fact he was simply a helmsman."

Arrian evokes the scene of the departure:

> The noise of the simultaneous rowing by so many ships was like nothing else. The coxswains shouted the "in . . . out" command for every stroke and the oarsmen raised a cheer each time they struck the churning water in unison. The river banks, often higher than the ships, funnelled and amplified the noise, which ricocheted from bank to bank. Here and there wooded hollows on either side acted as echo-chambers, beating the sound back from their empty spaces. The horses visible on the transports caused amazement to the barbarians watching the spectacle, as horses had never been seen on ships before in India.

All went well to start with. The king was in no great hurry and after a few days' sail everyone camped on the banks for a brief rest before continuing downstream. But at the confluence of the Hydaspes and another great river, the Acesines, the gods forgot the generous burnt offerings and hit out at the Macedonians. As well as making a tremendous din, the meeting of the waters created powerful eddies. Broad-beamed boats were spun violently around and Alexander took his clothes off in case he had to swim for his life. However, no harm was done, Arrian observes, "except to the nerves of those on board."

War galleys, being long, thin, and low, came off much worse.

> They did not ride so high over the seething rapids, and those with two ranks of oars could not keep the bottom one clear of the water. When the whirlpools swung them broadside on, their oars collided with each other, and many ships were damaged. Two ran against each other and sank. Many of those sailing in them perished.

This was an entirely unexpected setback, but Alexander made the best of things. He moored the fleet on the right-hand bank where there was shelter from the current and damage could be repaired.

THE ARMY WAS IN good condition again. Substantial reinforcements had arrived during the journey back from the Hyphasis—nearly six thousand cavalry from Greece and Thrace; seven thousand Greek mercenary infantry raised by his treasurer in Asia, Harpalus; and 23,000 infantry raised from Greek allies in Europe, Asia, and northern Africa. It was now so tempting for men from all over the Mediterranean to follow Alexander's star, and make a fortune, that there was no need to recruit obstinate and contrary Macedonians. From Babylon came much needed medical supplies and 25,000 suits of armor inlaid with silver and gold. The equipment problem had been solved.

The fleet carried the hypaspist infantry, the royal cavalry squadron from the Companions, the invaluable archers and Agrianians, and (probably, although they are not mentioned) the baggage train and siege equipment. The remainder—in fact, the majority of the army—was divided in two. Craterus was to lead some of the cavalry and infantry along the river's right bank. Hephaestion was to advance down the other with the largest and strongest part of the army, including some two hundred elephants that various rajahs had presented to Alexander. The two generals were on bad terms and the fact the Hydaspes was never less than two and a quarter miles wide will have come as a relief to both of them.

On one occasion around this time, they actually drew swords and came to blows. Friends appeared and began to join in the disturbance. Alexander rode up and gave Hephaestion, who was evidently more in the wrong, a furious dressing-down. He told him he was mad or stupid if he didn't realize that without his, the king's, favor he was nothing. Later in private he sharply rebuked Craterus.

Finally, he imposed a public reconciliation. He said: "By Zeus Ammon and all the other gods, these are the two men I love most in the world. But if ever I hear of them quarrelling again, I will kill them both—or at the very least the one who started the quarrel." The king's outburst shocked them into obedience and neither man ever again did or said anything, even as a joke, to offend the other.

ALEXANDER'S BODY WAS A palimpsest of scars. He exulted in hand-to-hand combat and regarded wounds as a professional hazard. It was now that he received the last and most dangerous of them and it is very remarkable that he recovered from it.

His army faced one more hard-fought campaign before finding the sea, despite grumbling from the rank and file. The Hydaspes joined the Acesines, which then ran through the territory of the Oxydracae and the Malli; these were hostile tribes who would have to be overcome if the Indus Valley were to be completely pacified and the imperial frontier secured along the length of the great river. News came in that they were planning to obstruct the Macedonians' passage with a horde of one hundred thousand warriors.

In response the king divided his army into separate detachments and placed them at various points around the southern borderlands of the tribal territories. To the west and east of these territories were waterless deserts. Alexander decided to attack the Malli from the north and drive them into the arms of the forces that were waiting to receive them. He, of course, led an agile assault force, consisting of hypaspists, a phalanx battalion, some light infantry, half the Companion cavalry, and the highly valued mounted archers.

To ensure the maximum surprise he led his men through an arid wasteland. After some miles they paused at a small spring for a rest and then traveled for the remainder of the day and through the night. Altogether they covered forty-five miles before emerging from the desert at dawn, to the astonishment of the tribesmen, many of whom were out in the fields and unarmed. He killed most of them without any resistance being offered. Settlements in his path, probably little more than villages with mud walls, received the same treatment. Ruthlessness and intolerance had returned. The king had lost patience.

Faced with this blitzkrieg, the Mallians abandoned their capital, and most of their armed forces holed up in a well-fortified stronghold. The king laid the place under siege. The Macedonians broke through the outer perimeter and attacked the citadel. They set up scaling ladders, but morale had been shaken by the fierceness of the defense and some of the assault team nervously hung back. The king seized a ladder, huddled under his shield, and scampered up the wall by himself. Peucestas, an old school friend who was carrying the sacred shield from Troy, came up after him. Two other Macedonians, Leonnatus and a corporal, followed Alexander and climbed up beside him.

At the top was a parapet, against which the king propped his shield. He cleared his section of the wall, shoving some of the defenders off it and dispatching others with his sword. Arrows rained down on him from nearby towers on the wall.

His men could see how exposed he was and frantically jostled one another on the same ladder, which broke under their weight. Alexander realized he could not safely stay where he was for much longer. To take the Indians by surprise and goad his Macedonians to redouble their efforts to rescue him, he decided on an absurdly rash act. Almost suicidally, he jumped off the wall, not back into the arms of the besiegers, but into the citadel itself.

He had good balance, as well as luck, and landed on his feet near an old tree, which gave some protection from attack. After he killed two Indians at close quarters, his opponents stood back and hurled spears and arrows at him.

He took many missiles on his shield, but his helmet was broken and his legs began to buckle. He was hit by an arrow, which passed right through his breastplate and into his chest, above a nipple. He staggered back and fell to his knees. Arrian writes that

the blood escaping from the wound was bubbling with the air from his lung. As long as his blood ran warm, and although he was in a bad way, Alexander continued to defend himself: but when inevitably his breathing caused a massive hemorrhage he became dizzy and faint, and fell forward over his shield. Peucestas stood astride him as he lay there, protecting him with the sacred shield from Troy, and Leonnatus took his stand on the other side: these two were now the targets, while Alexander was slipping into unconsciousness from loss of blood.

Finally, Macedonians arrived on the scene in force and captured the citadel. Fury was fed by guilt and they slaughtered every Mallian in sight—women, children, and old men.

Meanwhile the king was stretchered away on his shield. There was no surgeon on hand and urgent action was needed. It was essential to remove the arrow from the king's chest. The head being barbed, this could only be safely done if the entry wound was enlarged. The shaft had to be sawn off first since the flights would not pass through the hole in the cuirass. One of Alexander's leading generals, Perdiccas, cut round the wound and then carefully drew the barb out. When he did so, blood spurted and pain and shock induced nature's anesthetic. Alexander passed out.

He was cared for where he was and when he was well enough to travel was brought to the river and boarded ship. There were fears that the indispensable leader would not survive, leaving his men in the middle of nowhere and thousands of miles from home. When Alexander heard that rumors of his death were spreading, he had two ships lashed together and a tent erected in the center of them. This allowed him to be seen in public and prove to both friend and foe that he was alive. Even so he was obliged to wave his arm before his survival was fully believed. He then proceeded downstream, keeping some distance from the rest of the fleet so that the stroke of the oars would not disrupt his sleep (which his very fragile condition still required).

The wound took more than seven days to close, but Alexander recovered with remarkable speed. The foam strongly suggests that his lung was pierced. The antiseptics of the day were weak and it is remarkable that within a few weeks the king was up and about.

We cannot doubt that his health was seriously and permanently affected. Very probably he had a splintered rib; a lung had been torn and both walls of the pleura perforated; and the intercostal muscles were lacerated. These damaged layers are all part of the breathing system and usually mobile. The process of healing, though, would knit them into stiff, ragged scar tissue. In future, with every breath he drew, Alexander would feel his wound, and every arm movement would hurt.

Senior officers in his intimate circle criticized him for taking needless risks. That was something an ordinary soldier might do, but not a commander. Alexander was irritated by these comments. Arrian offers his own convincing assessment of the king's attitude to risk:

> I would guess that Alexander's annoyance was because he recognized the truth of the accusation and his own responsibility in incurring it. Yet the fact is that in battle he was a berserker, as addicted to glory as men are to any other overpowering passion, and he lacked the discipline to keep himself out of danger.

IT WAS JULY 325 and the monsoon rains had started again, blown in from the southwest. While convalescing, the king had had more ships built and he was now impatient to get going again. He intended to deal decisively with any resistance as he moved down into the Lower Indus Valley. To the east of the river lay the wide-ranging Thar Desert, most of which was covered by huge shifting sand dunes. It reached down to the sea and was impassable.

To the west, though, Indian communities still resisted the invader, but their defeat was little more than a sanguinary formality. The Macedonians applied the tactic of the bloodbath. An insurgent prince was crucified together with the holy men or Brahmins who had egged him on. Soon southern Indians were either dead or terrified.

The fleet arrived at Pattala in the Indus Delta. This was the river's main port, but at the moment it was empty. The population had fled in terror and were only enticed back with difficulty. Hephaestion was ordered to transform the city into a military base with ship sheds and dockyards. Later, a second harbor was created farther south in the delta. While construction work was under way, Alexander explored the principal outlets leading to the Ocean. Out at sea, he sacrificed bulls to Poseidon and poured libations from a gold cup. The animals' bodies were thrown into the water in thanksgiving, as were the cup and some gold bowls for mixing wine.

The king and his fellow Macedonians were astonished by tides, which are hardly apparent in the Mediterranean. Shocked when the ebbing water marooned their ships on mudbanks, they were mightily relieved when it returned and refloated them.

They encountered a more serious problem, as Arrian explains:

> When they came to the point where the river spreads out wide, extending here to twenty-two miles at its broadest, the wind was blowing in strong from the open sea and the rowers could hardly lift their oars in the heaving water. Guided by their pilots, they ran for shelter again into a side-channel.

In due course, this southwest wind was to threaten the very survival of Alexander and his army.

THE NEXT STAGE OF Alexander's journey would take him 450 miles along the barren coast of Gedrosia (today called the Makran) that led from western India to the Persian Gulf. The monsoon passed it by, rain clouds only hitting mountaintops in the interior. The land was mostly desert—red, mountainous, and as dry as an ossuary. A nineteenth-century traveler reports

> chiefly a barren repetition of sun-cracked crags and ridges with parched and withered valleys intersecting them, where a trickle of salt water leaves a white and leprous streak among the faded tamarisk or the yellow stalks of last season's grass. . . . Here and there jagged peaks appear as if half overwhelmed by an advancing sea of sand. They are treeless and barren, and water is but rarely found at the edges of their foot-hills.

According to legend, Heracles, who appears to have visited everywhere, and the fabled Semiramis, queen of Assyria, had both tried and failed to cross Gedrosia. The king, always competitive, would be delighted to outcompete them. However, he was not suffering from a bout of overheated *pothos,* but rather had sound practical reasons for traveling through this unforgiving landscape. His prime motive was to inspect and if necessary strengthen the boundary of his possessions, but he also knew that traveling by sea was quicker than by land and far less arduous. The Makran could be developed as a trade route between rich and populous India and his empire's heart, Mesopotamia. Alexander planned to establish a string of colonies along this coast and on offshore islands, which he believed would become as wealthy as the city-ports of Phoenicia. It would also be much easier than before to keep in touch with his Indian provinces and protectorates.

Alexander recognized that guiding his men through the desert would be one of his greatest challenges and he took great pains over his preparations. The Indian soldiers who had swelled his ranks were dispersed. In June, he gave Craterus command of the bulk of the army, including more than half of the phalanx, some of the archers, all soldiers from whatever unit who were unfit for service and to be sent home, and the elephants acquired during the campaign in the subcontinent. They were to march westward through the eastern satrapies and rejoin Alexander in Carmania, the province next to Persis and Persepolis.

This left the king free to undertake his Gedrosian adventure. He still commanded a sizable force—the Macedonian troops not going with Craterus, the Greek mercenaries and cavalry from the eastern satrapies. In addition, the cumbersome baggage train, under Hephaestion's command, included all sorts of noncombatants from prostitutes to children, from traders to servants.

The most seaworthy ships in the fleet were to join in an amphibious operation. They were under orders to proceed at the same pace as the army along the littoral. The fleet would carry provisions for the troops on land, who in turn would dig wells and supply the sailors with water. They would also take water from the intermittent mountain streams that ran down to the sea and that were full at this time of year. Four months' supply of grain was gathered and stowed in about four hundred cargo vessels. Military detachments marched west partly to reconnoiter and dig wells and partly to punish two hostile tribes, the Oreitae, who were routed, and the Arabitae, who opted for discretion and fled. The king founded another of his garrison towns, where he left Leonnatus to ensure calm after his departure.

In late August, the king began his homeward trek. He chose the height of the monsoon for his departure because he calculated that dried-up riverbeds in Gedrosia would be briefly in spate and would help water his troops. Estimates of his numbers reach as high as 120,000 or more, if the baggage train is included, and as low as a more plausible thirty thousand. The wind was still blowing from the southwest and prevented Nearchus and his ships from leaving harbor. Alexander assumed that when it changed direction they would catch up with him.

This was a grave error, for gales were permanent during the rainy season; they were to last until October. The Macedonians' usually excellent intelligence service had let them down, probably because local people were so offended by the brutality of the campaign that they refused to give the invaders accurate information.

The ships did not come.

ALEXANDER WAS EVENTUALLY FORCED to accept that they would *never* come. He had no idea what had happened to them. Perhaps an Indian army had overwhelmed them, or perhaps they had been sunk in a storm. None of this mattered, for he had his own crisis to confront.

What was he to do now to save his army? He had three options. He could stay where he was, but the territory had been devastated and at the best of times would not have grown enough produce to feed his army. Alternatively, he could retrace his steps and go back to Patala, nearly three hundred miles away. But armies trash the land through which they pass, and his Macedonians would be unlikely to survive the march across a wasteland of their own making.

There was one final possibility—to keep calm and carry on. This was the one he chose, although he knew that he would have to use all his skill and imagination if he was to save his men. He sent out fast-riding messengers to the neighboring satrapies, ordering them to load racing camels and other pack animals with food and other necessities and deliver them urgently to the army at an agreed rendezvous.

A scouting party rode down to the sea to assess the situation on the coast. On being told it was desert, with a few fishermen "living in stifling huts put together out of shells and roofed with the backbones of whales," the king turned inland to the Jhau tract, a territory where modest quantities of food were to be found. Some was requisitioned and sealed with the king's seal; it was destined for the fleet, in case it had turned up, but famished soldiers broke it open and consumed the contents. Not wanting trouble, Alexander pardoned them.

From Jhau, 150 miles of sheer desert lay before the Macedonians. The scorching heat, the scalding sand, the lack of water, and the poor and minimal diet took their toll of lives. Men struggled through dunes. Arrian writes:

> One factor was the depth of the sand and the temperature to which it was baked, but in most cases the animals finally died of thirst. They had to negotiate high dunes of deep loose sand, into which they sank as if they were treading in mud or—a better analogy—a fresh drift of snow.

The army marched at night, probably following a well-trodden caravan route. It only stopped when a source of water had been reached. If they had to carry on into the day, they suffered terribly from heat and thirst. Horses and mules in the baggage train were illicitly slaughtered and eaten; in these dire circumstances all the king could do was to turn a blind eye. Wagons were sabotaged because it was difficult to keep them moving through the deep sand.

According to Arrian,

> All along the route men were left behind—the sick, those suffering from exhaustion, heatstroke, or crippling thirst—and there was no one to carry them or stay to look after them. The march was pressed on at all possible speed, and the concern for the general good necessarily involved the neglect of individual needs. With most of the marching at night, many simply fell asleep on the road. When they woke, those who still had the strength followed the tracks of the army in an attempt to catch up, but only a few survived: most were lost in the sand, like sailors lost overboard at sea.

Every now and again rainwater from the mountains flowed in torrents down the riverbeds without warning. On one such occasion, many women and children were drowned and the royal tent with all its contents was swept away. Whenever the men happened upon an abundant supply of water after hours of heat and thirst, their insatiable drinking often had fatal results. The king used to make camp a mile or two away from a spring or stream to prevent a stampede.

Alexander had not lost his knack for propaganda. He was as tired and thirsty as everybody else, but he insisted on leading his men on foot and from the front. He refused any special treatment. Once a party of soldiers found a dribble of water, filled a helmet, and hurried back to give it to Alexander. The king thanked them for their trouble and, with everyone watching him, poured the water into the ground.

We may pause to wonder why he did not simply pass the water to someone whose need was greater than his. However, the gesture was very well received, even if Arrian inclines to hyperbole when he reports: "The effect on the morale of the entire army was as if every man had been refreshed by a gulp of the water Alexander had poured away."

The local guides confessed that they were lost: a sandstorm had blown away route markers and they could not distinguish one featureless dune from another. Alexander suspected that they were traveling in the wrong direction. He guessed that they needed a turn to the left and rode off with a few cavalrymen to test his hunch. It was correct. He and five others found the sea and, better still, copious fresh water that was there for the digging.

The agony had lasted sixty days, but was at last reaching its conclusion. The bedraggled and emaciated survivors entered a land of plenty where there was an abundance of grain, dates, and sheep.

THE GEDROSIAN EXPEDITION OF 325 had been a disaster without mitigation. Plutarch estimates that a quarter of the army's fighting force died. "Diseases, wretched food, parching heat, and, worst of all, hunger destroyed them." The proportion of casualties among those in the baggage train must have been even larger.

Alexander was shattered and ashamed. There would have to be a reckoning. What had gone wrong with his best-laid plans? Who was to blame for the debacle? Where was the fleet? Did the fleet even exist anymore? Why had the satraps sent no supplies? The guilty would be punished, of that there could be no doubt.

Whatever the answers to these questions, he knew that first of all he had to apologize to his men for what had happened on his watch. He did so implicitly. For seven days he loosened the bonds of discipline. In an echo of the Dionysiac revels in the Punjab, his men marched in a drunken pageant. Their route was strewn with flowers, and wine was freely available. Wagons were rigged with tents so that soldiers could ride in them and take the weight off their sore feet. New uniforms and armor were distributed.

The king himself had been under very severe strain and needed to unwind.

Alexander himself feasted continually, day and night, reclining with his companions on a dais built upon a high and conspicuous rectangular platform, the whole structure being slowly drawn along by eight horses. Innumerable wagons followed the royal table, some of them covered with purple or embroidered canopies, others shaded by the boughs of trees, which were constantly kept fresh and green; these vehicles carried the rest of Alexander's officers, all of them crowned with flowers and drinking wine.

Before the year's end the fate of the fleet became clear. Nearchus had set sail in late September but was forced into a harborage, where he waited for more than thirty days until the monsoon came to an end together with its implacable southwest wind. At the outset he had had to deal with disciplinary problems by dumping unruly sailors in Leonnatus's lap in the territory of the Oreitae. Leonnatus did not complain and gave him some replacement sailors and ten days' worth of supplies.

However, Nearchus's journey along the Makran coast was marked by malnutrition and low morale. Provisions were scarce, although date palms were found in places. A local guide was recruited and the fleet eventually put in at a river on the shore of Carmania. Nearchus dragged the ships up onto the sand and built a double stockade and a ditch to protect them. He struck out inland with a small group to look for Alexander.

Meanwhile the king, with despair in his heart that the fleet was lost, received a report that it was safe and Nearchus was near at hand. He sent out search parties. When the admiral and his companions were found they were hardly recognizable, according to Arrian, "such was the great change in their appearance. They were long-haired, squalid, caked in brine, flesh shrivelled, pale from lack of sleep and every kind of hardship." Alexander burst into tears at the sight. The admiral debriefed him: "Sir, your ships are safe and your men too. We have come here to bring you the news of their safety." The king wept again. "They are here pulled up on shore . . . and being repaired."

There was good news, too, from Leonnatus. After putting down a rebellion of the Oreitae, he found his way to the king by land.

However, it was beginning to be clear that the great Indian victories were slipping like quicksilver through the conqueror's hands. He had crushed many tribes and their rulers, but it was a safe bet that the Macedonians would have their hands full elsewhere and would not soon return. Once the hurricane had passed, the defeated raised their heads and life resumed its normal course. The satrap Alexander had appointed to govern the Indus Valley was assassinated. Unrest grew in the Punjab under a young leader called Sandrocottus. He is better known today as Chandragupta, founder of the Mauryan empire, which at its height ruled over much of northern India. In future years, he was ably assisted by a king called Parvataka, who has been identified with King Porus, Alexander's ultra-loyal paladin.

AT PURA, THE GEDROSIAN CAPITAL, an arts festival was staged with dance and music contests. Bagoas, the lovely eunuch, won a prize. After his performance he crossed the performance space, still in his costume and wearing his winner's crown, and sat down next to Alexander. At the sight the soldiers applauded and shouted good-humoredly: "Give him a kiss!" For a time Alexander resisted the invitation, but at last gave way. He put his arms around Bagoas and kissed him.

This is a slight anecdote, but it demonstrates that the army's morale had already recovered from the Makran experience. Also, although eunuchs were often unpopular because of their reputedly cruel and devious nature, Alexander's favorite seems to have been well enough liked among the rank and file.

A famous work of art appears to confirm that the young man was still the apple of the king's romantic eye. We learn from the comic writer Lucian, who lived in the second century A.D., of a painting by the distinguished artist Echion—*Wedding of Alexander and Rhoxane*. It was exhibited at the Olympic Games of 324 and was surely a royal commission. It not only celebrates the happy couple's union, but also reminds the viewer of Alexander's other loves.

According to Lucian's eyewitness account, the scene was a very beautiful bedroom. Rhoxane, eyes modestly lowered, faces Alexander.

> There are smiling Cupids: one is standing behind her removing the veil from her head and showing Rhoxane to her husband; another like a true servant is taking the sandal off her foot, already preparing her for bed; a third Cupid has caught hold of Alexander's cloak and is pulling him with all his strength toward Rhoxane.
>
> The king himself is holding out a garland to the bride and their best man and helper, Hephaestion, is there with a blazing torch in his hand. He is leaning on a very handsome young man—I think he is Hymenaeus (his name is not inscribed).

Lucian's guess as to the identity of the youth is unconvincing. As the god of marriage, he ought to have been shown more obviously presiding over the ceremony. Also, it would have been Hymenaeus who traditionally held a torch to illumine the proceedings, not Hephaestion.

The figure is more likely to have been Bagoas, appropriately enough standing beside Alexander's other male lover. With its honoring of masculine affection, the picture made clear that there were limits to Rhoxane's command of her husband's heart.

If Bagoas was still riding high at court, he was rather less popular with the Persian nobility, as soon became apparent. After the collective orgy of food and drink, the king left Carmania and entered the province of Persis. As he had done on previous visits to the area, he made a point of paying his respects at the tomb of Cyrus the Great, first of the Achaemenid Great Kings and someone whom he much admired.

The tomb was (and still is) a small stone building standing on a high, stepped platform with a pitched roof. Inside there was a gold sarcophagus containing Cyrus's body, a couch, and a wardrobe of elaborate costumes. An inscription read:

> MORTAL, I AM CYRUS SON OF CAMBYSES.
> I FOUNDED THE PERSIAN EMPIRE AND
> WAS KING OF ASIA.
> SO DO NOT GRUDGE ME MY MONUMENT.

Alexander was deeply moved by these words, for they reminded him of the uncertainty of human affairs and the inconstancy of fortune.

On this visit he found that robbers had vandalized the tomb and thrown out the remains. He was furious. He ordered what was left of Cyrus to be put back and the contents restored or replaced. He had the tomb's priest-guards interrogated under torture, but without result.

However, it emerged that a descendant of Cyrus himself was responsible for the theft of the grave goods and the desecration. This was Orxines, who had taken over the satrapy of Persis without permission, on his predecessor's death in office. After Alexander's return to Persia, he knew he would have to work hard to persuade him to endorse the usurpation. He arrived at court laden with generous presents for the king's friends.

According to Curtius, he paid his respects to all and sundry, but refused to acknowledge Bagoas. When advised that this was unwise, he replied: "It is not the Persian custom to regard as men those who allowed themselves to be sexually used as women." Orxines was investigated and shown to have acted corruptly in office. He had plundered temples and royal tombs, including that of Cyrus, and illegally put to death numerous Persian citizens. On Alexander's orders, he was impaled.

Bagoas gave evidence against Orxines. The Persian was clearly guilty and, although the eunuch must have been hurt by the offensive put-down, there is no reason to suppose that he lied. His behavior in reporting what he knew to Alexander was perfectly understandable, but unlikely to please other senior Persians, who regarded him as a typically ruthless palace fixer.

ORXINES WAS NOT THE only guilty man. During Alexander's lengthy stay in India, for Greeks and Macedonians the very end of topographical knowledge, many newly appointed satraps misbehaved. They enriched themselves at the expense of their subjects and they executed objectors. Even the honest men were open to charges of incompetence.

It was widely supposed that the king, having completely disappeared from view, was unlikely to return. Defeat or disease would most probably carry him off. After the Mallian episode a rumor of his death circulated, which was not so far from the truth. However, once news spread that he was back, complaints flooded in from all over the empire. It appeared that fourteen of his twenty-seven satraps were guilty of corrupt practices and had even been openly rebellious.

Wherever he looked Alexander could only see turmoil, inefficiency, and half-hidden hostility toward him. Even at home, Olympias and the king's sister, Cleopatra, were plotting against the regent, Antipater. But first things first. The satraps who had failed to send Alexander provisions during his extremity in the desert had to face his wrath. He condemned to death in absentia Apollophanes, the Macedonian satrap of Gedrosia, unaware that he had already been killed during the Oreitiae uprising.

Two senior Persians, father and son, who were satraps respectively of Susiana and Paraetecane, were arraigned before the king. The father had brought the Macedonian army three thousand talents in place of supplies. Alexander had the money thrown to some horses. When they did not touch it, he asked: "What good are your provisions to us then?" The satrap was imprisoned and executed later, presumably after a summary trial. The king was so angry that he took a pike and ran the son through with his own hands.

The satrap of neighboring Carmania was suspected of plotting a revolt. The king concealed his feelings and spoke to him affably. But, as soon as he had studied the evidence carefully and decided on his guilt, he had him arrested. He was put to death during the recent revels.

The four generals in command of the garrison in Media faced many serious accusations. They were led by the Greek mercenary Cleander, brother of the recently dead Coenus, who had sided with the soldiers at the mutinous military assembly in India. These were the men who had put Parmenion to death on Alexander's orders and the king owed them a sizable debt, but, Arrian writes,

> this could not compensate for all the crimes they had committed. After plundering everything in the secular sphere, they had not even refrained from what was sacred: virgins and women of the highest breeding had been sexually assaulted and were bemoaning the physical abuse they had suffered.

Alexander commented that the prosecution had overlooked one charge—namely, the assumption of those on trial that he would not survive the journey to India. The defendants were found guilty and put to death. Six hundred common soldiers were executed for having been active accessories to their commanders' crimes. Throughout his career the king had given short shrift to men who sexually abused women. For a soldier to say that he was only obeying orders was no defense.

These punishments were intended as a warning that "oppression of the ruled by the rulers is not tolerated." This assertion of justice enjoyed widespread approval and helped reconcile the native population to the new regime. We may also assume (although there is no evidence for this) that the king was quietly pleased to have seen the end of men who knew too much about the gravest crisis of his reign. To do Alexander a great service was always risky, for it tended to arouse anxiety and irritation in him rather than gratitude.

Some governors who commanded Greek mercenaries were alarmed by the king's severity and threatened unrest. Alexander's suspicious mind may have feared a general revolt. He wrote to all his satraps, ordering them, as soon as they had read his letter, to disband their mercenaries instantly. They obeyed, but presumably (we are not told) maintained their security by raising troops from among the locals.

This was a very poor decision. Darius had employed numerous Greek mercenaries. After the Battle of Issus, many of them had reluctantly signed up as soldiers in Alexander's army. Not entirely trustworthy in the front line of battle, they were often deposited as garrisons and as guards battalions who were tasked with protecting satraps in their provincial capitals.

Now large numbers of unemployed Greek soldiers roamed the empire and brigandage was rife. Something drastic had to be done to restore the rule of law. As usual, Alexander acted decisively and rapidly. His solution was to send the mercenaries home to their native cities. At the Olympic games for 324 he had a decree read out by a herald:

> King Alexander to the exiles from the Greek cities. We have not been the cause of your exile, but, save for those of you who are under a curse [i.e. guilty of murder and other serious crimes], we shall be the cause of your return to your own native cities. We have written to Antipater about this to the end that if any cities are not willing to restore you, he may constrain them.

The decree referred to *all* Greek exiles, not only mercenaries but also men who had fallen foul of their domestic authorities for political reasons. Greek public life was bitter and quarrelsome. Losers were seldom allowed to form a loyal opposition but were expelled or put to death.

The decree killed two problems with one stone. The troublesome mercenaries would be cleared from the empire and no longer cause him and respectable citizens trouble. But also Alexander was aware that, despite the defeat of the Spartan king Agis and his allies at Megalopolis in 331, opposition to his rule was rising. The injection of political enemies into the anti-Macedonian city-states of Hellas would preoccupy their governments and discourage foreign adventures.

This was a thoughtless and malevolent policy, which in the long run was bound to backfire. A general restlessness would convert itself sooner or later into a new insurgency. It is as well not to poke a stick into a nest of hornets.

THE KING'S PERSONALITY WAS changing for the worse. He was acting more and more despotically, or so say the literary sources. Arrian writes that by this time he had become more inclined to accept as wholly reliable any accusation made to him against officials, and ready to inflict severe punishment on those found guilty of even minor offenses, in the belief that the character of a petty offender was equally capable of more serious crimes.

Curtius, who had no patience with Bagoas, put the matter more strongly, observing that "his degeneration from his former self was so complete that, though earlier possessed of unassailable self-control, he followed a male whore's judgment to give some men kingdoms and deprive others of their lives." Some modern scholars have taken the hint and conjured up a reign of terror. The disciplining of the satraps has been presented as a paranoid clearout comparable to the totalitarian show trials of the modern age.

A fair reading, though, of the surviving accounts suggests that Bagoas was innocent and that the purge was in the main a reaction to real cases of misgovernment, corruption, and political unrest. The satraps' failure to respond to his urgent requests for food when he and his army were in desperate straits strongly suggests malice aforethought, or at best criminal incompetence. The crackdown was ruthless but rational. The guilty men seem to have faced some sort of trial. We are told that Alexander had public support for the severe measures taken.

The signs of instability the king found on his return from India threatened to undermine his achievements and justified a firm and rapid response.

That said, it hardly comes as a surprise that a ruler with an unblemished record of military and political success over many years began to govern autocratically. One certainly senses a coarsening and a growing impatience with opposition. The king's lifestyle had become more and more formal, elaborate, and, in a word, Persian. When Macedonian traditionalists spoke of degeneration it may be this ceremonial grandeur to which they were objecting as much as to a psychological or moral decline.

An account of Alexander's receptions by the historian Phylarchus may have exaggerated the numbers of officials and soldiers involved, but it gives a flavor of the occasion. The king had a tent large enough to contain a hundred couches, and supported by fifty golden pillars; no doubt it had once been used by Darius. Embroidered golden canopies provided shade. Persian royal bodyguards lined the interior, dressed in purple and apple green. Also on parade were one thousand bowmen, some in fiery red uniforms and others in purple; many wore blue cloaks. And in pride of place stood five hundred Macedonian elite infantry.

In the middle of the tent was placed a golden chair, on which Alexander used to sit and conduct business, the bodyguards standing all around. Around the tent on the outside, was a troop of elephants regularly equipped, together with one thousand Macedonians in Macedonian uniform; and then ten thousand Persians, five hundred of whom wore purple fabric provided by Alexander. And though he had such a numerous entourage of friends and servants, not a single one dared to approach the king of his own accord; so great was his charisma and the awe with which they regarded him.

THAT MYSTERIOUS FINANCIER AND boyhood friend, Harpalus, put in an unexpected reappearance at this point. He had run away before Issus, been forgiven, and was now based in Babylon where he was responsible for the empire's finances. Alexander used his services to purchase high-quality goods. When wintering in Bactriana and Sogdiana, he asked for a shipment of books; Harpalus knew his taste and sent him copies of plays by Aeschylus, Sophocles, and Euripides, some choral hymns, and a history of Sicily. Later, as we have seen, he supplied the king, when campaigning in India, with 25,000 suits of armor finely wrought with gold and silver.

As soon as Alexander had disappeared to the ends of the earth and his back was turned, Harpalus embarked on a fantastically expensive lifestyle. He sexually abused many local women. With exchequer funds he bought a celebrated courtesan from Athens to live with him. She was the slave of a female flute player who in turn was owned by the madam of a brothel. The contemporary historian Theopompus called her "trebly a slave and trebly a prostitute." Harpalus pampered her with luxury gifts and when she died built a temple in her honor in

Babylon and an impressive and costly tomb outside Athens. He then acquired a replacement bedfellow, whom he installed as a queen in Tarsus. He also had a brass statue of her erected in Syria.

The return of the king, victorious and vengeful, was terrible news. The conviction of Cleander and his fellow officers was even worse. Harpalus had spent time in Ecbatana and knew them well. They had committed crimes similar to his own, and perhaps he had collaborated with them. He feared for his own head and took the fateful decision to flee to Greece for a second time. He did not travel alone. He brought with him six thousand mercenaries and five thousand talents from the Babylonian exchequer, which made him a power to be reckoned with among the hard-pressed city-states.

The treasurer's fondness for the ladies was a running joke at court and Alexander allowed the production of a farce that mocked his friend's obsession with sex. But when messengers told the king of Harpalus's desertion, he had them arrested for spreading false information.

The fugitive knew that the only way he could escape punishment was to foment a general uprising led by Greece's greatest naval power, Athens. However, the city was embarrassed when he arrived on its shores and asked for asylum. Not wishing to get into trouble with Alexander, it turned him away.

So Harpalus deposited most of his force at Taenarum, Sparta's port in southern Greece, which had become a center for unemployed and disgruntled mercenaries. He returned to Athens as a suppliant, with seven hundred talents. According to Plutarch,

> Harpalus was exceptionally shrewd at assessing the character of a man who had a passion for gold. He recognized it from the expression which crossed his face and the gleam that lit up his eyes. In this case he was not deceived, for Demosthenes could not resist the bait.

Harpalus was allowed in after Demosthenes, who fell for a beautiful and fabulously expensive gold cup, went over to his side. Demosthenes was not alone, for other leading politicians also accepted hefty bribes. This soon became the talk of the town and later the guilty men were indicted for corruption and sent into exile. In the meantime, Harpalus was locked up and his money confiscated. Antipater and Olympias demanded his extradition, but, ever a slippery customer, he soon escaped to Taenarum, picked up his fleet, and sailed it to Crete.

Here the story of Harpalus came to an abrupt end. In 323 his deputy assassinated him, and took charge of his money and his mercenaries.

WHEN IN INDIA, ALEXANDER had encountered Brahmins, a priestly aristocratic class, and been impressed by them. They wore very few clothes and led ascetic and contemplative lives. Their opposition to the Macedonians was fierce, spiritual, and absolute, and they pressed the local rajahs to resist the invader. The king's only riposte was to hang any of them who fell into his hands.

In fact, he admired them for the purity of their motives. They were free spirits and had no desire for anything in Alexander's power to give. Their estrangement from the day-to-day compromises of life, their indifference to captains and kings, recalled Diogenes, the philosopher in a barrel, for whom Alexander had a wary respect.

The king of Taxila introduced him to a Brahmin called Calanus, who refused to speak to him unless he first took off his clothes and listened naked. We are not told in so many words whether the king did strip, but in light of their later friendship we must assume that he did.

Calanus joined the Macedonians and traveled with them, much to the disapproval of his fellow Brahmins, who believed he had exchanged a divine for a human master. His motive was unclear, but he never hesitated to criticize the king when the mood took him. Probably before the Gedrosia tragedy, the sage told him a parable. He threw on the ground a dry and shrunken leather hide. When he put his foot down here or there on its outer edge, the leather would rise up elsewhere, but when he trod on the center the entire hide lay flat. Calanus's point was that Alexander should focus his authority on the heartland of his domains instead of wandering around the periphery.

At Pasargadae in Persis, Calanus, who was seventy-three years old, had suffered from a disease of the intestine for some time. He did not want to carry on as an invalid and decided that it was time to end his

life. He asked for a funeral pyre to be built for him on which he intended to immolate himself. According to Plutarch, death by fire was
acceptable in "Indian" (Hindu) religion. Alexander did his best to dissuade Calanus, but the Brahmin made it clear that he would find some
other way of killing himself if his request was denied. So the king gave
way and had Ptolemy build a pyre according to Calanus's instructions.

Apparently, the army laid on a military cortege. Incense was placed
on the pyre along with gold and silver cups and embroidered clothes.
The Brahmin was too ill to walk and a horse was made ready for him,
but he was incapable of riding it and was carried in a litter instead. He
managed to clamber onto the pyre and gave the horse, the cups, and
the costumes to members of his circle.

He addressed those present, urging them to make this a day of joy
and revelry. He concluded mysteriously: "Drink deep with the king,
whom I shall soon see in Babylon."

Then he solemnly lay down and covered his head. Trumpets
sounded when the pyre was lit. He stayed absolutely still as the fire
enveloped and consumed him.

The king decided to take Calanus's advice and give him a festive
send-off: he invited friends and officers to a banquet, at which he proposed a drinking contest. Whoever downed the most neat wine would
receive a crown worth a talent. The consequences were calamitous.
The winner downed the equivalent of thirteen liters—and three days
later died from the aftereffects. It is said that many other competitors
also succumbed.

> He believed that he came as a heaven-sent governor to all, and
> as a mediator for the whole world. Those whom he could not
> persuade to unite with him, he conquered by force of arms. He
> brought together into one body all men everywhere, uniting
> and mixing in one great loving-cup, as it were, men's lives, their
> characters, their marriages, their very habits of life. . . . Cloth-
> ing and food, marriage and manner of life they should regard as
> common to all, being blended into one by ties of blood and chil-
> dren.

This assessment by Plutarch offers the unexpected portrait of Alexander as an idealist, as the fully armed secretary-general of an international peace agency. The truth is plainer. What we have here is a fine example of the work of Alexander's propagandists.

The passage is an echo refracted from a mass wedding ceremony which the king staged on his return to Susa in the spring of 324. The Achaemenid princesses had been waiting for him there since the Battle of Issus. He had told them to learn Greek and promised that he would find suitable husbands for them. Now he was minded to honor his word.

But whom should the princesses marry? Persian aristocrats were ruled out, because their offspring might very well become pretenders to the Achaemenid throne and stimulate insurgency. The obvious answer was to find the women Macedonian spouses.

As part of his Persification policy, Alexander extended the principle of the mixed marriage to leading members of the court. He and ninety-one other Macedonians took Persian wives. A polygamist for reasons of realpolitik, as his father had been, the king married the eldest daughter of Darius and the youngest daughter of Artaxexes III. In this way he attached himself to the Achaemenid dynasty and created a veneer of continuity. Hephaestion was allocated another of Darius's daughters, for Alexander, rather touchingly, wanted his lover's children to be first cousins of his own.

The celebrations took place in the vast royal tent with its splendid appurtenances, specially modified for the occasion. The floor was covered with carpets of purple, scarlet, and woven gold thread. Sumptuous cloths were hung between the many golden columns, creating private spaces, inside which each bridegroom had his own couch.

A trumpet sounded to announce the official part of the ceremony. In front of 9,000 guests, chairs were set out in line for the grooms. The king took his place among them, for he had decided, in a characteristically populist touch, to take part in the mass ritual. After toasts, the brides came in and sat down beside their husbands-to-be, who took them by the hand and kissed them. After these formalities the couples withdrew to the privacy of their couches. Generous presents were given and the king paid for all the dowries.

The partying went on for five days. Both Greeks and Persians gave performances as did some Indian tribesmen. Conjurors did "wonderful" tricks; harpists played with and without voices. Flute players accompanied songs. Actors performed speeches from the tragedies, among them the famous Thessalus, now approaching the twilight of his career (he was a long-standing friend of the king and, as readers will recall, had acted for him during the Pixodarus affair).

One might suppose that a good time was had by all, but this was not the case. The Macedonians strongly objected, in private, to being forced into unwelcome unions with unknown barbarian women. This was yet another of the king's attempts to persuade his fellow countrymen that the empire could be governed only with Persian cooperation. However hard he tried, he failed to win the argument. The fun was skin deep. (We may well wonder, although we are not told, whether the brides were any happier with their fate than their grooms.)

Alexander was well aware of his critics and sought to deflect their discontents by enriching them. He awarded golden crowns for conspicuous service in the face of the enemy (with Peucestas first in line, for saving the king at the Mallian town).

More expensively, he promised to pay off all his soldiers' debts and invited them to register their names. Only a few complied, for there was a widespread suspicion that this was a survey to reveal who was living beyond his means or had extravagant tastes. The king denied the charge, but gave way. He had tables set up in the camp piled with gold coins and instructed his officials to pay against sight of promissory notes without taking down any names.

This gesture is said to have cost him the enormous sum of twenty thousand talents. Although the cancellation of debts was a popular gesture, it was a sign of weakness rather than strength. Morale among the troops was edgy and volatile and remained so.

Alexander's immediate priority was to build confidence among the peoples he had defeated, preferably without losing that of his men. In the long run he expected that the sons of the mass marriages would grow up to be a new mixed-race ruling elite.

If there was to be a "unity of nations," it was little more than a technique for governing his empire.

———

THE ARMY WAS CONTINUING to change its composition, with the Macedonian component increasingly diluted with Persians. Satraps from across the empire had brought with them the thirty thousand cadets the king had ordered in 327. Now, three years later, the Successors were old enough for military service and were to form a new and separate unit. They had been issued with Macedonian uniforms and armor and been trained in Macedonian techniques of warfare. Alexander was delighted by the progress they had made.

The Companion cavalry was strengthened in part with the recruitment of "barbarians," and senior Persians were introduced into the high-prestige Royal Squadron. In the following year twenty thousand seasoned Persian troops were to join Alexander's army, to be incorporated into the Companion infantry.

Arrian reports that the Macedonians "deeply resented all this and thought that Alexander was now going completely native in outlook and showing no regard for the Macedonian way of life or the very Macedonians themselves." Their suspicions soon received justification.

In May or June 324, Alexander and his troops left Susa, ultimately for the cooler summer capital of Ecbatana. (He had caught the wandering habit of the Achaemenids.) But first the king fulfilled a *pothos* to see the Persian Gulf: leaving Hephaestion in charge of the infantry, he joined the fleet and sailed along the coast and up the Tigris. He removed some artificial cataracts, which the Achaemenids had installed in the river as a defense against naval attack, and founded a new Alexandria at the Tigris estuary.

The summer heat was intense, shortening tempers. Alexander disembarked at Opis, a town alongside the river, where Hephaestion was encamped with the army. Here the king called an assembly of his Macedonian troops and announced the demobilization and repatriation of all those who were unfit for service through age or disability. He offered them generous bonuses and severance pay, promising that they would be the envy of their friends and relatives at home and inspire many of their countrymen to sign up for a life of adventure.

Alexander expected a warm reception. After all, his soldiers had long been agitating for an end to the ceaseless campaigning. In fact, his audience was outraged. It was obvious, they felt, that they counted for nothing and were quite useless as a fighting force. Fit young men shouted that he should dismiss them as well. Sneering at his claim to be the son of Zeus Ammon, they suggested that he just take his father on his next campaign.

What lay behind this behavior? It is hard to say, but it suggests the contradictory emotions of a lover at the end of an affair. The veterans had had enough of military service, but could not bear rejection by their charismatic leader. Perhaps an unstated grievance was the growing number of Persians in what had been a Macedonian army.

Alexander was completely taken by surprise and lost his temper. He jumped down from the speaker's platform, followed by his entourage, and ordered the arrest of the thirteen main troublemakers, pointing them out to the guards. He sent them off for instant execution. They were shackled and thrown into the Tigris (a traditional Persian punishment). Arrian notes: "He had become by that time quicker to take offense and the oriental obsequiousness to which he had become accustomed had greatly changed his old easy manner to his own countrymen."

The king mounted the platform again, and we are told he gave a long speech in which he itemized the many benefits King Philip and he had conferred on their soldiers. He concluded with wounded ferocity:

> And now it was in my mind to demobilize any of you no longer fit for service. They could return home to be envied and admired. But since you all wish to go, then go! Every single one of you!

He jumped down from the platform once more and disappeared into the royal quarters. Thunderstruck, the men stood rooted to the spot. They had no idea what to do or where to go.

The king sulked for three days, letting no one in to see him and taking no care of himself. It was not the first time he had applied the emotional blackmail of absence and breakdown to enforce his will and once again the trick worked.

Alexander called in Persian aristocrats in camp and began to appoint them to military commands. He gave them the title of kinsmen and the exclusive right to greet him with a kiss of friendship. Macedonian names were given to Persian military formations. When the troops learned of these developments, they could no longer contain themselves. They rushed to the royal quarters dressed only in their tunics, laid down their weapons, and started shouting and pleading to be let in. They promised to hand over those who had started the barracking. They said they would not leave until Alexander had taken pity on them.

This was what the king had been waiting for. He hurried out to meet the demonstrators. He saw how upset they were and his eyes filled with (surely crocodilian) tears. Before he could say a word, Callines, a squadron commander in the Companion cavalry, said that what really hurt the men was the king's decision to call Persians his kinsmen and let them kiss him.

Improvising with typical presence of mind, Alexander replied: "So far as I am concerned you are all my kinsmen and that is what I will call you from now on." To prove the pudding, Callines walked up and kissed him, and anyone else who so desired kissed him too. Then they all retrieved their weapons and happily dispersed to their tents, cheering and singing the *paean,* the song of victory. To cite a modern scholar, they still loved their "hero, friend, soldiers' father [and] their threatening, angry, terrorizing, melancholy king."

To mark the return of peace and to promote reconciliation, Alexander invited nine thousand guests to a lavish feast. After performing the usual sacrifices, he presided over the meal. He was surrounded by places reserved for Macedonians, then for Persians, and finally an outer tier for men of other nationalities.

Greek seers and Persian magi jointly led an ecumenical ceremony of libation, the pouring out of wine as an offering. Alexander prayed for harmony and fellowship between Macedonians and Persians as they ruled the empire together.

However, on the matter at issue, the king did not yield an inch. He now organized the discharges of some ten thousand veteran infantry and fifteen hundred cavalry. This time there were no protests. As promised, the redundancy terms were extremely generous. Salaries were extended beyond the time served to cover the homeward journey. Each man received a bonus of one talent.

Families were to be left in Asia to avoid trouble from relatives and wives at home, but the treasury would pay for sons to receive a good Macedonian education. They would grow up to be soldiers in the royal army and only then would they be allowed to visit the home country.

The king knew how to gild a lily: he instructed Antipater that at all cultural and athletic performances the veterans should occupy the best seats at the front and wear garlands on their heads. This was not only a highly visible compliment but also a constant reminder of Alexander's victories.

ANTIPATER, WHO HAD BEEN the king's regent in Macedonia almost from the beginning of his reign, was becoming something of a problem. This was a surprise, for he had organized a smooth transition from the assassinated Philip to the young crown prince and was utterly loyal to his new master. He had managed the quarrelsome nest of city-states in mainland Greece with tact and firmness and put down King Agis's rebellion.

He had been almost annoyingly competent; Alexander had even been a little put out by his victory at Megalopolis. The only real problem with Antipater was, in fact, Olympias, the king's mother. Put simply, she refused to accept the regent's authority and wrote endless letters to her son criticizing him. Antipater had little choice but to respond in kind. He objected to her headstrong personality, her violent temper, and her insistence on having a finger in every pie. Alexander had to admit that his mother "was charging a high rent for the nine months he lodged in her womb." On one occasion, in an implicit allusion to her, he warned his regent to keep guards about his person, for there were many plots.

But although he knew very well how demanding Olympias was, she was still his mother and he loved her. Once, Antipater wrote a long letter finding fault with her. Having read it, Alexander burst out: "Antipater doesn't understand that one tear shed by my mother will wipe out 10,000 letters like this one."

Olympias's case against the regent was that he had grown too powerful. Word reached the king's ear that he had regal aspirations. When some people praised the frugality of Antipater, who, they said, lived a plain and simple life, he responded: "On the outside Antipater is plain white, but inside he is completely purple." But ambition is an implausible charge against a man who was seventy-six years old and approaching the end of his active career. Arrian gives him a clean bill of health: "We hear of nothing Alexander said or did which could have invited the conclusion that his affectionate regard for Antipater had in any way diminished."

Nevertheless, the king decided it was time to intervene. Seeing that his best general, Craterus, was suffering from poor health, he instructed him to lead the demobilized veterans back to Macedonia, where he was to take over as regent. Antipater was instructed to gather Macedonian reinforcements and march them to Babylon.

The king's plans for Antipater's future are unknown. He could have been retired or, more probably, given a new, undemanding command. The regent advised the king that Greece was too unsettled for him to leave his post at present and the stock of Macedonia's young fighters was running dry. He dispatched his son Cassander in his place. As for Craterus, he was held up in Cilicia partly by illness and partly by local conditions there, for the satrap had been killed in battle.

DID ALEXANDER REALLY WORK toward the "unity of mankind"?

Regarding the relationship between Hellenes and "barbarians," the king was a pragmatist. So far as we can tell, he was not inspired by high-sounding ideals, apart from those hymned by Homer, but reacted to practical needs. Plutarch's admiring judgment masks the fact that the king's inclusive and antiracist strategies, as we would call them today, were an expression of realpolitik. In his eyes, the two "races" were not equal, or we would have heard of Macedonian females being offered as wives to Persian men, and the Macedonians would not have been given pride of place at the banquet of reconciliation. Persians may have dominated in the army, but positions of power at court remained in the hands of the victors.

Equality of esteem was no more than a pious hope in the minds of the king's traveling philosophers–cum–public relations officers.

LAST THINGS

IT WAS TIME FOR A PROPER HOLIDAY. THE LAST FEW MONTHS HAD been painful physically (the Gedrosian desert) and psychologically (the Opis mutiny) and a period of recovery and revelry was in order.

The king and his army marched north across the Zagros Mountains and arrived in Ecbatana some time during the late summer or autumn of 324. He staged a massive arts and athletics festival, with many plays and spectacles. Three thousand performers were imported from Greece, presumably most of the theatrical and musical professionals of the day.

There were also constant drinking parties. It is time to consult the Royal Journal, a day-by-day narrative of the king's actions. Aelian cites an extract which describes Alexander's carousing and probably dates to this stay in Ecbatana.

On the fifth day of the month of Dius [October/November] he drank to excess at Eumenes' [Eumenes was the king's chief secretary or *grammateus*], on the sixth day he slept off the alcohol, and was sufficiently refreshed to get out of bed and give orders to his commanders for the next day's exercises, saying that they should set out very early. On the seventh he feasted with Perdiccas, and again drank heavily. On the eighth he slept. On the fifteenth day of the same month he drank again, and slept through the next day. On the twenty-fourth he dined at Bagoas's place about ten stades from the palace. The following day he slept.

Although he is not mentioned, we can assume that Hephaestion attended such binges.

One day he caught a fever and was placed on a strict dietary regime. Glaucias, his doctor, kept an eye on him to make sure he followed it to the letter. On the seventh day of his illness, the stadium was packed for boys' sports. Alexander was there, and so was Glaucias, who had left his patient unsupervised. This was unwise, for Hephaestion enjoyed filling himself with food and drink whenever opportunity offered. He was feeling better and, in the doctor's absence, he sat down to breakfast. He devoured a boiled fowl and washed it down with half a gallon of chilled wine. He immediately fell ill again.

The king received a message that Hephaestion's condition was grave and deteriorating and he hurried to his side, but by the time he reached him the young man was dead.

The exact nature of Hephaestion's illness was unknown at the time and is irretrievable now, but the literary sources strongly imply that it had to do with excessive drinking. Nobody at the time raised the possibility of unnatural causes. The modern doctor would observe that Hephaestion's symptoms were consistent with a serious bowel infection (for example, typhoid). This produces a protracted bout of fever and often leads to stomach ulcerations. During recovery the sufferer should avoid doing anything that might perforate the damaged bowels—for example, eating a heavy meal. A perforation could quickly cause collapse, internal bleeding, shock, and death. For recovery to begin after seven days seems unusually early, but the fever could well have set in sometime before a busy and preoccupied patient reported it.

None of this was known to ancient medicine. Blame was thrown on the physician, either for prescribing the wrong medication or for allowing his patient access to alcohol.

Alexander's grief was total, inconsolable, and uncontrollable. Arrian remarks: "I believe he would rather have been the first to go than live to suffer that pain, like Achilles, who would surely have preferred

to die before Patroclus." In imitation of the Greek warrior, Alexander sheared off his hair above his dead lover. As at other moments of crisis he withdrew into himself. He spent a night and a day lying on Hephaestion's body, weeping, until his Companions dragged him off. He took no food and did not attend to any of his bodily needs. Plutarch writes:

> As a token of mourning, he commanded that the manes and tails of all horses should be shorn [this was a Persian and a Thessalian practice], demolished the battlements of all the neighboring cities, crucified the luckless physician and forbade the playing of flutes or any other kind of music for a long time.

A local temple of Asclepios, the god of healing, was destroyed as his punishment for not having saved Hephaestion.

The corpse was embalmed and Perdiccas, his successor as chiliarch, was ordered to accompany it to Babylon. Here a vast funeral pyre was to be constructed at the cost of ten thousand or more talents. Diodorus claims:

> Alexander collected artisans and an army of workmen and tore down Babylon's wall to a distance of ten furlongs. He collected the baked tiles and levelled off the place which was to receive the pyre, and then built it in the shape of a cube, each side being a furlong in length. He divided up the area into thirty compartments and[,] laying out the roofs upon the trunks of palm trees[,] wrought the whole structure into a square shape.

The elaborate design was to take the form of a ziggurat with gigantic sculptural displays on each floor—golden ships' prows; statues of soldiers; torches; eagles with outstretched wings and serpents at their feet; a wild-animal hunt; golden centaurs at war; lions and bulls; and Macedonian and Persian weapons and armor. At the top of the monument would stand statues of Sirens, hollowed out to allow singers inside to chant laments.

Mourning was decreed throughout the empire. Persians were ordered to quench temple fires until the funeral, a custom previously reserved for the death of a Great King. Hephaestion had not been universally popular, and astute courtiers with whom he had quarreled fell over themselves to display their sorrow. Many Companions dedicated themselves and their arms to his memory. Everyone of note commissioned images of him in gold and ivory. It became fashionable to swear an oath with the phrase "by Hephaestion." Eumenes was one of those who could not stand him, and he knew that the king knew it. He was careful to propose honors that would be most likely to enhance the dead man's memory, and he made a very generous contribution to the costs of the pyre.

Alexander was disempowered by his grief for some time. He left Ecbatana and set out unhurriedly south toward Babylon. As a distraction, he launched a winter campaign against the Cossaei, a warlike tribe that inhabited the highlands between Susa and Media; they made a living from brigandage but had been tolerated by the Achaemenids. He massacred the entire male population from teenagers upward. According to Plutarch, this was termed "a sacrifice to the spirit of Hephaestion," for it echoed the incident in the *Iliad* when a vengeful Achilles slaughtered twelve young Trojans and cremated them alongside Patroclus on his pyre.

The king's grief may have been excessive, but it was sincere. The ancient world was in no doubt that Alexander was "ruled by Hephaestion's thighs." We do not know their respective ages or even which of them was the older (Curtius observes in passing that the couple were coeval). However, as we have already discussed, it is plausible that in their teens, or at least in Alexander's teens, they followed aristocratic Greek practice and were pederastic lovers.

Alexander regarded Hephaestion as his alter ego. However, for many years he was careful not to promote him beyond his abilities and devoted time and energy to calming down colleagues whom he had annoyed. Hephaestion was a competent officer, but no more. He was never appointed to crucial positions, but was capable of handling complex administrative tasks. He matured and after the departure of Craterus for Arachosia and Drangiana in 325, he rose to the position of chiliarch and the king's deputy.

His finest quality was his adamantine devotion to his lover and friend.

———

ALEXANDER WANTED TO DO something unique for Hephaestion. An emissary was dispatched to the priests of Ammon at Siwah, where the king had learned of his "true" paternity. He asked whether divine honors could be paid to Hephaestion. The oracle said no, but prudently permitted the institution of a hero cult.

The king was delighted by this response, when it arrived after some months, and (cheekily slipping in the word "god") immediately arranged for Hephaestion to be worshipped as Associate God and Savior. He wrote to Cleomenes, governor of the Arabian portion of Egypt and treasurer for the entire country, and ordered the construction of hero shrines to Hephaestion in the Nile Delta city of Alexandria and on the island of Pharos. No expense was to be spared.

As we have seen, Cleomenes was much complained of by the Egyptian public, probably because he was corrupt. Alexander always took care to be well informed and now applied a metaphorical thumbscrew to guarantee the official's good behavior. He added to his letter: "If I find the temples in Egypt and these shrines to Hephaestion in good order, I shall ignore your previous offenses and guarantee that any future offense, of whatever nature, will not meet with any disagreeable consequence at my hands." Cleomenes understood the king's meaning and we may be sure that he moved fast to obey his terrifying master.

The question of Hephaestion's semidivine status turned, or returned, Alexander's attention to the possibility of his own divinity. Since his visit to the oracle at Siwah, this was a topic that attracted his full attention. He saw himself as the son of Zeus Ammon, but the claim was self-contradictory, for he did not seriously disavow Philip. As pharaoh of Egypt, however, he was an incarnation in some sense of Horus and acted as an intermediary between the gods and mortals.

How literally did the king, or anyone else at court for that matter, take all this? A hostile witness describes his behavior at banquets.

Alexander used to wear even the sacred vestments at his banquets; and sometimes he would wear the purple robe, and slit sandals, and horns of Ammon, as if he had been the god; and sometimes he would imitate Artemis, whose dress he often wore while driving in his chariot; having on also a Persian robe, but displaying above his shoulders the bow and javelin of the goddess.

Apparently he also used to appear as Hermes, messenger of the gods, and Heracles with a lion's skin and a club. If there is any truth in this account, it gives the impression of a costume party rather than a serious bid for godhood.

The witness continues:

Alexander also had the ground sprinkled with expensive perfume and sweet-smelling wine, and myrrh and other fragrant substances were burned in his honor, and everyone present remained respectfully silent out of terror, because he was impossible and bloodthirsty, and appeared to be un-balanced.

Yet again a traditionalist Hellene has placed the worst possible interpretation on Alexander's sensible but unpopular policy of adopting the rituals of a Persian Great King. The growing formality at court does not prove that the king had lost his mind and been transformed into a mad tyrant.

However, the coins he issued, or that were issued posthumously, show the king with divine attributes. Decadrachms struck at the mint in Babylon have him crowned by Nike, the personification of victory, and brandishing a thunderbolt as if he were the father of the gods, Zeus. As we have seen, Apelles, the most celebrated artist of the day, showed the king with the divine thunderbolt in his painting for the temple of Artemis at Ephesus, and received a handsome payment for the commission. In the famous tetradrachms of Lysimachus, Alexander is wearing the horns of Ammon, which also feature in portraits of him (for example, in the "Alexander Sarcophagus," a late-fourth-century-B.C. stone sarcophagus adorned with bas-relief carvings).

Coins express the propaganda of the day and are not necessarily evidence of intent; they neither request nor require their owners to worship a new deity. But it does appear that, with the passage of time, Alexander became increasingly serious when he claimed his divinity. En route from Ecbatana to Babylon for Hephaestion's funeral, he was met on the way by embassies from Greece. Arrian reports (with a smile, one senses) that "the delegates wore ceremonial wreaths and offered Alexander golden crowns, to all appearances as if these were official pilgrimages to honor a god." Word percolated through the Greek city-states that Alexander expected to be recognized, and indeed worshipped, as a god. Our information is fragmentary, but the king may have sent out an official letter of request. An Athenian orator hints, bitterly, at coercion:

> The practices which even now we have to countenance are proof enough: sacrifices being made to men; images, altars, and temples carefully perfected in their honor, while those of the gods are neglected, and we ourselves are forced to honor as heroes the servants of these people.

The orator wisely spoke in general terms, but everyone knew that the only men receiving such cultic devotions were Alexander and the late Hephaestion.

The Hellenes were in no position to resist the pressure. In Athens it was proposed in the *ecclesia* to erect a statue of "Alexander the Invincible God." Demades, the realist who had always got on well with Philip and his son, moved a decree conferring divine honors. The great opponent of the Macedonians, Demosthenes, conceded sarcastically that "Alexander might be the son of Zeus and Poseidon too if he wished." A witty Spartan summed up the general attitude. "Alexander wants to be a god? Very well, let's call him a god!"

As for the rest of Greece, there is little additional information, but we may assume similar honors were proposed and similar cynical remarks made.

WHAT DID HIS DIVINITY mean to Alexander? Much of the data is missing, but we know enough to sketch the outline of an answer. He seems to have filled his mind with mutually exclusive concepts. On the one hand, he was sincerely religious, believed in the Olympian deities, and was certain that he was descended from Heracles. For him the war at Troy was a historical event. Achilles and Patroclus had once walked on earth. He was a punctilious celebrant of religious rites, slaughtered hecatombs of sacrificial beasts, and regularly consulted the soothsayers who accompanied him on campaign.

On the other hand, he was a subtle and ruthless manager of men. So, for example, the context strongly implies that his personal seer, Aristander, produced bad omens to order when the king needed an excuse to retreat from India. Alexander made it clear that if he was a god, he was neither invulnerable nor immortal like Zeus and Apollo. He could bleed and die like any of his soldiers.

Alexander's success was truly astonishing, and even hostile contemporaries were profoundly, albeit unwillingly, impressed. His godhead was a memorable symbol which would express and promote his overwhelming power. When he let it be known, whether formally or informally, that the Greek city-states should establish his cult, this was less for religious than for political reasons. It would allow him to impose obedience more effectively than in his role as elected leader of the League of Corinth.

In this as in so many other matters, Alexander was following in his father's footsteps. The Philippeum at Olympia and the carrying of his statue alongside those of the Olympians in the theater at Aegae show that Philip was already flirting with the idea that his kingship had a divine dimension.

Maybe Alexander did not altogether know what his being a god might mean. Did dressing up as Zeus or Artemis or his ancestor Heracles, if correctly reported, hint at a certain playfulness, a lack of complete commitment to the project of deification?

HEPHAESTION WAS DEAD, but Alexander was still very much alive. He was in his early thirties and he intended to fill the years ahead with new and ambitious plans of conquest.

That was exactly what the Mediterranean world feared. On his way to Babylon, he was met by a multitude of embassies, eager to discover his intentions and to offer nervous congratulations. There were so many of them he had to arrange a schedule specifying the order in which he would see them. (He gave the highest priority to those who wanted to raise religious issues.)

The envoys came from every direction—from Ethiopia, from European Scythia, from the lands of the Celts and Iberians. The Libyans presented him with a crown as king of Asia. Envoys arrived from the Bruttians, Lucanians, and Etruscans, all Italian peoples. Delegates from the North African state of Carthage, the greatest maritime power of the age, put in an appearance; they were right to be apprehensive, for they had supported their mother city of Tyre during the siege and some of their citizens had been captured when the city fell. As ever, Alexander never forgot or forgave a disservice.

Intriguingly, some classical historians mention emissaries from the then little known city of Rome, which at the time was a middling Italian state embroiled with the fierce mountaineering Samnites. Most of these historians, writing after Rome had acquired an empire even larger than Alexander's, added all kinds of rhetorical and anachronistic flourishes. However, the king's contemporary Cleitarchus mentioned the visit without comment, so it is very probably historical.

Arrian notes that the arrival of these embassies marked the moment "when Alexander himself and those around him fully realized that he was indeed master of every land and every sea."

Of course, he was an explorer as well as a general. He seems to have envisaged a circumnavigation of Africa. He also sent a Greek officer with a party of shipwrights to the Caspian Sea. They were to build a flotilla and sail on a voyage of discovery. Their task was to establish whether the Caspian was linked to the Black Sea and whether one or both were inlets of the great river Ocean, which surrounded all land on earth.

The king's next important project, an invasion of Arabia, was imminent. Preparations for it had been made well in advance. His purpose was not conquest for its own sake, but rather the establishment of a secure trade route from India to Egypt. For this he would need to vanquish the Arabians, not to expropriate the entire peninsula but only to guarantee control of the coastline and offshore islands. He would govern existing ports and found new ones. Eventually there would be a chain of trading posts from the Indus Delta to the Red Sea.

Scouts were sent out to assess conditions and measure distances before launching the campaign. Three ships left on separate voyages of exploration, one of which sailed a good way up the Red Sea before returning to base. Nearchus also organized a reconnaissance of the immediate coastal areas. It transpired that Arabia was prosperous and was well endowed with many kinds of spice. The coastline was very long, with fine natural harbors and suitable locations for new cities.

A huge array of warships was gathering at Babylon. Nearchus's fleet was complemented by a flotilla from Phoenicia—two quinqueremes, three quadriremes, twelve triremes, and some thirty triaconters. They were transported in sections from the Mediterranean to Thapsacus on the Euphrates and reassembled. They then sailed down the river to join the armada. Meanwhile, a harbor and dockyards were constructed at Babylon large enough to house at anchorage one thousand warships.

IF THE ANXIOUS EMBASSIES had known what was in Alexander's mind, they would have found their fears amply justified. Alexander set out his strategy on paper; it had two related parts—conquest of the western Mediterranean and exploration.

A war with Carthage was envisaged, for the king had indeed not forgiven the city for the moral encouragement it gave Tyre. With this in mind he intended to build a thousand warships, all of them larger than triremes. They were to be made in the dockyards of Phoenicia, Syria, Cilicia, and Cyprus.

The defeat of Carthage would be only one element in a more ambitious plan to bring the entire coastline of northern Africa and Sicily inside his empire. As with the Persian Gulf and Arabia, economic development and international trade were the chief priorities. A great highway was to be constructed from Egypt to the Pillars of Hercules (Gibraltar), which would be punctuated at suitable intervals with ports and shipyards. It is said that Alexander also had plans for Iberia (the Spanish peninsula), although his geographical knowledge of it must have been sketchy at best.

The king also intended to erect six colossal, and colossally expensive, temples—on the sacred island of Delos, the birthplace of the god Apollo; at the world-famous oracle at Delphi; at the oracle at Dodona, second only to Delphi; dedicated to Zeus at Dium in Macedonia; to Artemis Tauropolos (Huntress of Bulls) at Amphipolis, a city in Thrace under Macedonian rule; and finally to Athena at Cyrnos in Macedonia, who was also to be honored with a shrine at Troy.

As a reminder that whatever his relation to Zeus Ammon, he was still deeply indebted to his natural father, Philip, Alexander would build him a tomb that would rival the Great Pyramid at Giza.

Most interestingly, the king intended to build on his policy of ethnic integration. Diodorus writes that he would "establish cities and to transplant populations from Asia to Europe and in the opposite direction from Europe to Asia, in order to bring the largest continents to common unity and to friendly kinship by means of intermarriages and family ties."

In the spring of 323, Alexander crossed the Tigris and approached Babylon, which he appears to have chosen as his permanent administrative base. He was met by some Chaldean seers, doubtless the astronomers in the city who (as we have seen) recorded movements in the heavens and from these measurements provided the governing authority with interpretations and predictions.

They advised the king to halt his march, for entry into the city would be "dangerous for him." At the time of the Battle of Gaugamela the astronomers had already offered a prophecy that Alexander would "exercise kingship for eight years." Because Callisthenes had been given access to these records, it is possible that Alexander saw them. If he had, he will have known that the eight years allotted to him were nearly up.

However, he politely turned away the seers with a quotation from Euripides: "The best of prophets is the one whose guess comes good." This admirable summation of the rationalist's opinion of clairvoyance suggests that Alexander had not sat at Aristotle's feet for nothing.

The seers persevered. "At least, your majesty, avoid the west and enter from the east." The king politely complied, only to find that the eastern side of Babylon was impassable by the army because of marshes and pools of standing water.

He suspected that the Chaldeans' motives were self-serving. For during his first visit to Babylon after Gaugamela, the king had promised to rebuild the Esagila, a vast ziggurat dedicated to Babylon's divine patron, Marduk. In the intervening years, nothing had been done.

Now was the time for action, and orders were given to clear the site of a great pile of rubble and bricks. The temple priests and administrators received an annual income from an endowment to defray the cost of running the temple and conducting sacrifices, and since its demolition they had had nothing on which to spend this revenue—except themselves. If Alexander could be dissuaded from settling in the city, there was a good chance the rebuilding scheme could be postponed again and their emoluments would remain untouched.

At about this time one of the king's Companions, Apollodorus, a Macedonian from Amphipolis, became anxious about his future. He was the commanding officer of the Babylon garrison and had watched with rising alarm the recent cull of the satraps. Was he next on the list for investigation and punishment? He wrote to his brother, Peithagoras, a seer who also lived in Babylon and practiced divination on the internal organs of sacrificial victims. He asked him to predict if he was in any danger. Peithagoras replied asking who was posing the threat and Apollodorus wrote back naming Hephaestion and Alexander.

So Peithagoras conducted a sacrifice to assess any threat from Hephaestion. The animal's liver did not have a lobe, so he assured his brother that there was nothing to fear from that direction. Hephaestion would soon be out of his way. As his letter arrived the day before the chiliarch's death, the ritual of divination had hardly been necessary to forecast a fatal outcome of his illness. Then the seer sacrificed concerning Alexander, and the results were the same. He sent the bad news to his brother.

There is little more dangerous than to write an autocrat's horoscope or to speculate on the date of his death. It may be seen as verging on an assassination plot and is often a capital offense. But Apollodorus trusted his king and immediately passed on to him the contents of his brother's letter.

Alexander thanked Apollodorus and once back in Babylon interviewed Peithagoras. What did the absence of a lobe signify? he asked. "Something very serious," came the reply. So far from being angry, the king was grateful to be told the unvarnished truth.

There is little reason to doubt the historicity of these tales, while keeping faith with Euripides. They are circumstantial and have the ring of truth: the prophecies may be menacing but they are also astutely vague. A professional seer would know that it was likely enough that "something very serious" would take place at some point in the not-too-distant future. Most people believed that there was a supernatural world and that the gods permitted glimpses of the future. A prophecy that did not come to pass could be reasoned away or simply forgotten.

These particular lucky guesses have been remembered because of their aftermath, and it is not necessary to suppose that they were planted later, when what they "foresaw" had actually taken place.

ALEXANDER IGNORED THE PROPHETS of doom and entered Babylon from the west, where he was briefed on the state of readiness of both the fleet and the army for the Arabian expedition.

While work proceeded, the king kept himself busy by sailing down the Euphrates, where he improved the river's drainage system. During seasons of flood, a canal diverted excess water to marshes and lakes. When the level was low, sluices were closed to shut off the canal. Because the soil was a soft, muddy clay this was a very difficult task. Three and a half miles downstream, the king noticed that the soil was hard and stony. He had a cutting dug there, which joined the canal and made it much easier to block the outlet and prevent leakages.

Having entered and then left Babylon without incident, Alexander believed he had evaded whatever grisly fate the Chaldeans had had in mind for him. Nevertheless, now that he was back from his river trip, he decided, obediently, to try again to return to the city from its eastern side. He sailed through a swamp, where lay centuries-old tombs of Assyrian kings. Some of the fleet got lost in narrow channels and the king sent them a guide to bring them back to the main waterway.

He was steering his own trireme and, we can suppose, thoroughly enjoying himself. He wore a felt sun hat with the royal diadem, a cloth headband, attached to it. A sudden gust of wind blew it off. The hat itself fell in the water, but the diadem was carried away on the breeze and caught on some reeds near one of the ancient tombs.

For a symbol of royalty to be associated with a grave was a bad enough omen, but worse was to come. A helpful Phoenician sailor swam out to recover the diadem. Wanting to keep it dry, he put it on his head and brought it back to his ship. This was lèse-majesté at its worst; the seers ruled that the head that had worn the diadem could not be permitted to stay on its shoulders. So the king gave him one talent for his prompt action and then had the hapless man decapitated. Another source says that he was merely given a good flogging.

Not long afterward the king was personally supervising some troop allocations when another alarming incident took place. He felt thirsty and walked away from the dais where he was sitting to get a drink. Some "insignificant man" saw that the throne was unoccupied, walked through a guard of eunuchs, and sat down on it. This was sacrilege and the eunuchs were prevented by Persian custom from removing him. All they did was beat their breasts and faces as though some terrible disaster had struck. When Alexander was told, he had the man tortured on the rack, but all he would say was that the idea had come into his mind and he had acted on it. It was clear that he was acting alone. The seers again advised the death penalty, which was carried out.

As we have seen, Alexander was rationally devout and took omens with a pinch of salt. But this catalogue of portents began to unnerve him. According to Plutarch,

> Alexander had become overwrought and terrified in his own mind, and now abandoned himself to superstition. He interpreted every strange or unusual occurrence, no matter how trivial, as a prodigy or a portent, with the result that the palace was filled with soothsayers, sacrificers, purifiers and prognosticators.

However, there was plenty of good news to lift the gloom. Army reinforcements arrived in large numbers. Brave Peucestas, who had been seriously wounded when fighting to save the king's life at the Mallian town and was appointed satrap of Persis, arrived with an army of twenty thousand troops drawn from the local population, which were incorporated into the Companion infantry or phalanx, and a substantial number of warlike mountaineers. Mercenary forces also came from Caria and Lydia under their satraps' command, and some cavalry recruits arrived from Macedonia.

Embassies from Greece presented themselves at court and were well received. During his invasion in 490, the Great King Xerxes looted the cities he captured, making off with many works of art. Alexander entrusted all these statues, images, and votive offerings into the envoys' care, to be returned to their original owners.

In May, Alexander's messenger to Siwah arrived after his long journey and announced the priests' decision to allow Hephaestion a hero cult. Alexander put aside his mourning and celebrated with sacrifices and drinking parties. Happy days were here again.

THEN TIME CAME TO A STOP. A slight indisposition led to a rising fever. The king took to his bed. For a fortnight of blinding Mesopotamian days and baking nights, he wavered between life and death. An endless line of soldiers walked past his prostrate form and took their leave. The end came on June 11.

The destroyer of the Achaemenids had himself been destroyed. Good riddance, thought many Hellenes. The Athenian politician Demades summed up the general mood. "Alexander dead? Out of the question. The stink of his corpse would have filled the whole world by now." In surprising contrast, when the dowager queen, Sisygambis, Darius's mother, heard the news, she went into mourning and refused food (and, we must assume, water). She died five days later.

A strange story soon began to spread: Alexander had not succumbed to natural causes as had appeared to be the case, but had been poisoned. The royal helmsman, Onesicritus, was the first to make this claim, but he was afraid of reprisals and declined to name the perpetrators. Nothing seems to have come of this at the time; if Plutarch is right, the rumor mill only began to grind five years later. A detailed narrative then emerged.

Two men were behind the assassination. The first was Antipater. His recall as regent of Macedonia and replacement by Craterus made him fear that he might be imprisoned for opposing Olympias, or might even be put to death if he obeyed the king and made his way to Babylon. At least, that was a rumor doing the rounds. The trouble was that Alexander had form. Antipater had not forgotten the murders of Parmenion and Cleitus in the king's drunken rages, nor the execution, even if justified, of his son-in-law for treasonous communication with the enemy. He profoundly disapproved of the multicultural policy at court.

The second plotter was the greatest philosopher of the age, Aristotle, who had tutored Alexander in his teens, but now was an embittered opponent. The regent was a close friend and agreed to be the philosopher's executor. Aristotle had not forgiven the king for the fall of Callisthenes; nor had Alexander forgiven Aristotle for recommending Callisthenes as his historian and public relations adviser in the first place. He suspected that Aristotle had been involved in some way in the conspiracy of the Royal Pages.

The two men agreed that it was time to terminate with extreme prejudice the world conqueror. Antipater's sons, Cassander and Iolaus, were to do the deed.

The regent's excuse for refusing to join the king that the Greek city-states were restive was false. His true reason was to save his career, and possibly his life.

Cassander, the son whom he sent in his place, was probably about thirty years old and a less than impressive specimen. He had suffered from poor health as a boy. Even when he was grown-up, his father forced him to sit on an upright chair at dinner as if he were still a child, instead of reclining on a couch as adults did. This was because he had failed to pass a Macedonian rite of passage by killing a wild boar without a hunting net.

He brought an important item in his baggage—namely, poison supplied by Aristotle, which

consisted of ice-cold water drawn from a certain cliff near Nonacris [near the river Styx, which leads down into the underworld], where it was gathered up like a thin dew and stored in an ass's hoof. No other vessel could hold the liquid, which was said to be so cold and pungent that it would eat through any other substance.

Cassander handed the poison to his younger brother, Iolaus, who was a Royal Page and official wine-pourer for the king. Iolaus had a grudge against Alexander, who had hit him over the head with a stick for some mistake. He was the lover of Medius, with whom he plotted Alexander's death and whose drinking party was to be the scene of the crime. The conspiracy included others in Alexander's immediate entourage, and many of those at the party, including Leonnatus and the admiral Nearchus, recent recipient of a golden crown for his services, knew what was about to happen. The senior generals Eumenes, Perdiccas, Ptolemy, and a few other guests were kept in the dark.

Iolaus slipped the poison into the wine; as the king downed a beaker, he screamed. He was in agony and his skin was painful to the touch. He decided to make himself vomit and asked Iolaus for a feather. The Royal Page found one, but before bringing it to Alexander he dipped it in the remaining poison. The king doubled up with pain.

He realized that he was dying and decided to make a mysterious end—to vanish from the earth and, it might be supposed, ascend into heaven. He crawled to a door that opened onto the Euphrates, intending to drown himself in its waters. But his wife Rhoxane found him and he returned to his bed.

The king's health gradually improved, but when he asked for a drink of water Iolaus brought him a poisoned cup. After draining it, he cried out again with pain. Death quickly supervened.

Meanwhile Cassander rode off to the mountains of Cilicia, where he would not be noticed and could wait undisturbed upon events. Some days later, after hearing from Iolaus in Babylon, he sent a coded message to his father in Macedon that "the business is concluded."

HOW MUCH OF THIS account is true? Was Alexander poisoned? Was there a conspiracy to put an end to him? Or can we trust the account with which this book opened? The reader who has followed his career in these pages is in a strong position to judge the general likelihood of an assassination plot.

The history of the king's campaigns shows how good he was to his men. He gave them frequent holidays, held athletic competitions, and staged arts festivals. He honored conspicuous bravery in the field with generous gifts. He paid much attention to supplies and his army seldom starved. Intensive deployment of scouts meant that the enemy delivered few surprises. Casualties were kept to a minimum.

Also, Alexander led from the front. He would never ask his soldiers to risk their lives without him risking his. His many scars were not simply evidence of an absurd valor, they were a means of forging loyalty.

The "mutinies' in India and at Opis were, in effect, lovers' quarrels. Once they were over, the affection and fundamental loyalty of the rank and file resumed.

Alexander's senior officers also had little to complain about. They served a brilliant commander and had the satisfaction of taking part in victorious campaigns. They also acquired riches beyond the dreams of avarice. Best of all, the king's habit of dividing his army into independent detachments meant that, within a clear strategic framework, commanders were often operationally independent. Job satisfaction must have been high.

Of course, there were complaints, as a rule privately expressed. Philotas and Cleitus were old-fashioned Macedonians who objected that their employer took too much of the credit for *their* victories. This was mostly barroom banter, although it could and did get out of hand and end in drunken disaster, as in the case of Cleitus.

In many ways, Alexander was a typical Macedonian king. Like Philip, he headed a boozy, rowdy court where noblemen spoke their minds freely to a monarch who was first among equals. Opposition grew among conservative Macedonians as Alexander took on the ceremonial formality and splendor of a Great King. However, an even-minded observer would understand that a Persianizing policy was inevitable. There were not enough experienced Macedonians capable of managing the vast Persian empire. In any event, few of them spoke the relevant languages. Without the cooperation of the old Persian elites the conquest would fail.

There were two serious conspiracies to assassinate Alexander, but they were amateur affairs organized by very young men. We know little about them, but they seem to have been powered by a combination of public and private motives.

Some modern scholars have detected bias in the ancient histories against Parmenion and his sons, Nicanor and Philotas. They speculate that Alexander wanted to replace his father's men with his own and schemed patiently for many long years to find a way of destroying them. According to this theory, the Philotas crisis in 330 was a put-up job. It was not a plot against Alexander, but by him. The evidence for this is thin. Great weight is placed on the times the king regularly rejected Parmenion's advice. True enough, but on other occasions his opinions were accepted and acted on—for example, the decision to delay the Battle of Gaugamela.

The fact is that for years the king placed the old general and his sons in crucial positions of command and that they rewarded him with sterling service. Had he wanted to eliminate them, he could surely have found a way whenever he wished.

In sum, the claim that a number of the king's generals were party not simply to a drinking session but to his murder is altogether out of character. They had enjoyable and lucrative jobs. Why should they put them at risk? Nearchus, to cite just one of them, was an old friend of Alexander and used to discuss maritime matters with him at length. He was in charge of the armada that was due in a few days to invade Arabia. He had no cause to kill.

AS FOR THE NARRATIVE of the assassination itself, it is infused with unlikelihood. Let us begin with Antipater. We know that he was shocked by Parmenion's death, but he was an old hand at Macedonian politics and understood its violent realities; indeed, he had taken part in them. He had spent the last ten years as a more or less independent agent and will not have welcomed his recall, but the excuses he gives for sending his son to Babylon in his place were plausible and very probably true. Alexander had no real grounds for complaint against his regent and was chiefly concerned to distance him from Olympias. Arrian observes:

> It could well be that Antipater's recall was not intended as a demotion, but as a means of preventing the quarrel between those two turning nasty on both sides, beyond any reconciliation that even Alexander could effect.

Neither man had anything much to fear from the other.

As for Aristotle, he and the king did indeed fall out over the destruction of Callisthenes, and it is true that this doctor's son knew something about poisons. Diogenes Laertius, the biographer, reports that he committed suicide in the year after Alexander's death by drinking aconite. This lethal plant is known by many names—among them, wolfsbane and queen of poisons. It can kill in two to six hours and in a large dose almost instantaneously.

If Antipater had intended to murder the king, he might well have asked Aristotle for advice, although at this time he was running his philosophical school at the Lyceum in Athens and, on such a highly confidential matter, may not have been immediately available for consultation to the regent in Macedonia.

Of one thing we can be sure. Had the philosopher offered information on handy toxins, he would not have proposed a draft from the river Styx. There is no known liquid that remains ice cold and can be safely kept only in the hoof of a dead donkey.

Plutarch writes: "Nobody had any suspicion at the time that Alexander had been poisoned." We remember Onesicritus's halfhearted attempt to sound the alarm, but it took five years before the possibility of foul play was taken seriously. In all probability it was a political move against Antipater, mounted by whom else but Olympias, still raging against him. Whether she believed the charge of murder or made the story up herself, we cannot tell. But she acted with her usual fury. Iolaus the onetime cupbearer, whom the Athenians honored for his role in the assassination, had died in the meantime, of what cause we do not know, but the vengeful dowager overturned his tomb and put his brother Nicanor (not to be confused with Parmenion's son of the same name) to the sword.

ALEXANDER'S DECLINE AND DEATH lasted thirteen days, according to the lost document known as the Royal Journal (or *Ephemerides*), from which our two chief sources, Arrian and Plutarch, quote. Presumably the journal reported the king's daily doings throughout his Asian campaign. It must have been the "memory" of the court and, one supposes, was necessary to ensure the smooth running of the king's business. Its main author was the royal secretary Eumenes.

Our sources trust the Royal Journal and we have little choice but to follow suit. If it were an invention, contemporaries would have been sure to cry foul. Arrian and Plutarch quote selectively from a lost original and use their own words. There are some inconsistencies, perhaps due to carelessness or to errors of transmission in some intermediary text. Broadly speaking, though, we can accept the sequence of events as given.

The main point we take from the journal is the extraordinary length of time the king took to die. The ancients were familiar with poisons, but not those with a slow effect over days or weeks.

A large or fatal dose of strychnine administered in unmixed wine has been suggested, but its bitter taste would be detectable. Symptoms of ingestion include muscular convulsions within a quarter hour or half an hour, soon followed by unconsciousness and death. If repeated small doses are given over time, the victim develops a slightly raised but not feverish temperature, muscular rigidity, and excessive sensitivity to light and sound. None of these is consistent with Alexander's symptoms—a raging but intermittent fever, loss of speech, and a sharp pain after drinking.

Two further relevant factors must be taken into account. Alexander's was the most public of dyings. The king was very seldom on his own. Every minute of the day, he was surrounded by Companions, officials, guards, and strapping young pages. He could have been stabbed or cut down with pluck and luck, but the assassin would have lived only a few seconds longer than his victim. More likely he would have been intercepted before reaching his target; and it would be next to impossible to administer poison regularly without being caught. Who would accept such a suicidal commission?

Also, Alexander had witnessed enough conspiracies in his lifetime to be wary of any unusual food or drink. If he had noticed something suspicious, he would have been the first to protest. He did not do so.

Plutarch wrote two thousand years ago that "most authorities consider that this tale of poisoning is pure invention." We do not need to disagree with their judgment.

THERE IS NOTHING TOTALLY certain in classical studies. Too much time has passed and too much evidence been lost. No investigation was held at the time, no postmortem. But we can say, on the balance of probability if not without a reasonable doubt, that the king was not poisoned.

So what did kill him?

Before identifying the direct cause, we must recognize that Alexander's formidable constitution had been weakened by the many wounds he had sustained during years of fighting. The arrow that pierced his lung at the town of the Malli in India had very nearly killed him two years previously and it left a permanent legacy of pain. It was immediately followed by the impact of the Gedrosian disaster on his health. Since then, he had not been seriously campaigning. As usual when he had time on his hands, he spent much of it downing heroic quantities of wine.

As long ago as the nineteenth century, it was noticed that Alexander's symptoms before his death were very like those of malaria caused by *Plasmodium falciparum,* regarded today as the deadliest parasite in humans. Typical symptoms of *Plasmodium* malaria are a fever with lucid intervals, speechlessness, and a sharp back pain when the malaria infects the spinal cord. The king seems to have contracted the disease twice. As reported, the first time was at Tarsus shortly before the Battle of Issus, and he was lucky to recover.

On this second occasion, we know that the king took boating trips among the swamps outside Babylon. The mosquitoes that communicate the parasitic infection to human beings are especially common in June or July. It looks very much as if the king died of an insect bite.

Alexander was a little short of his thirty-third birthday when he died. It seems appropriate, for he was not a man to settle down. He did not seek a long life. Hence his almost suicidal bravery in the field.

Like his hero, Achilles, he was doomed to die young.

CHAPTER 16

FUNERAL GAMES

————

Nobody had the first idea what to do now.

The power vacuum created by the king's unexpected death was testimony to the innocence of his marshals. After Philip's assassination, Antipater had superintended the transition to Alexander with exemplary efficiency, and if he *had* instigated a poison plot he would have made arrangements for a smooth succession.

Demades compared the Macedonian army without its leader to the blinded Cyclops, blundering about in agony. A confused and emotional conference in the royal tent led quickly to violence. Perdiccas, as holder of the signet ring that Alexander in extremis had passed to him, took charge. His proposal was to wait and see if the heavily pregnant Rhoxane gave birth to a boy. If she did, he would be king and, it went without saying, Perdiccas would be his protector until he came of age sixteen years or so into the future.

A commander of the phalanx called Meleager unexpectedly proclaimed Alexander's half-brother, Arrhidaeus, as king. Arrhidaeus suffered from an incurable mental illness of some kind and had been brought along on the Asian campaign (presumably to prevent him from becoming a magnet for disaffection). The startled Perdiccas and the cavalry rode out into the countryside while Meleager and the infantry stayed in Babylon. The standoff was soon settled when Meleager was tricked and killed.

In the event, the dowager queen gave birth a few months later to a boy, Alexander, and a compromise dual monarchy was agreed. With one king a baby (albeit "our expected hope" as the rhetoric had it) and the other an incompetent, whoever happened to be their guardian exercised their authority—Perdiccas and, a couple of years later, Antipater.

The Babylon conference agreed on the distribution of satrapies to leading generals, and the Macedonian assembly canceled all Alexander's ambitious future plans. None of the commanders had the *pothos* for more conquests. They would need their armies to fight each other.

Six days of angry argument elapsed before anyone thought of Alexander's body and its disposal. Curtius writes of its surprisingly good condition:

> Nowhere are more searing temperatures to be found than in Mesopotamia, where they are such as to cause the deaths of many animals caught on open ground—so intense is the heat of the sun and the atmosphere, which bakes everything like a fire. . . . When Alexander's friends eventually found time to attend to his corpse, the men who had entered the tent saw that no decay had set into it and that there was not even the slightest discoloration. The vital look that comes from the breath of life had not yet vanished from his face.

If we are to believe this eerie tale, it must be that the king had not died when originally thought to have done so, but had sunk into a deep deathlike coma. We can only hope he expired before the embalmers were allowed in to gut him.

The mummified Alexander, wearing a golden breastplate and covered with a purple-and-gold robe, was placed in a coffin of hammered gold filled with sweet-smelling spices. Although the king may have wished to be buried at Siwah, where he had learned of his divine paternity, it was decided to transport the body to Macedonia and lay it in the royal tombs at Aegae.

It was carried on a large and elaborately decorated carriage drawn by sixty-four mules. The roof was made of gold, with golden statues of Victory at the corners, and was supported by golden cornices. On the sides were four paintings of Alexander on a chariot, elephants armed for war, cavalry in battle formation, and warships ready for battle. A purple banner featuring a gold-woven olive wreath fluttered above the carriage. Large bells hung from tassels and alerted people to the carriage's approach. Huge crowds came to watch it pass on its long journey to Macedonia.

At the allocation of satrapies, Ptolemy had been given (or perhaps asked for) Egypt. This was a good choice, for the country was easily defensible. Rather than compete with all the other marshals for the entire empire, he had the more modest aim of establishing Egypt as an independent realm, with himself and his descendants as the ruling dynasty. He added to it Cyprus, Palestine, and parts of the Asia Minor coast.

The new mercantile settlement of Alexandria was already prospering, and the canny Macedonian chose it for his capital. In the south he would be pharaoh, but here in the Nile Delta he would rule as a civilized Hellene. The city needed a "unique selling point," some feature that would mark it out from all the other Alexandrias and place it on the same level as Athens or Babylon.

That selling point was to be Alexander himself. Ptolemy led an army into Asia, intercepted the lumbering hearse, and hijacked its precious cargo. It rested for a time in Memphis before it was moved to its permanent home in a specially built mausoleum in the center of Alexandria.

In the first century B.C., the gold coffin was melted down and replaced by a glass one. The ultimate fate of Alexander's tomb is unknown. It disappeared long ago and may have been destroyed in war or by earthquake.

In the early twentieth century, the young E. M. Forster spent time in Alexandria; he tells a story that all students of Alexander will dearly wish to be true. In 1850—so Forster was told—a dragoman from the city's Russian consulate said that he was looking through unexplored cellars beneath the mosque of the Prophet Daniel in the city center when he saw through a hole in a wooden door "a human body in a sort of glass cage with a diadem on its head and half bowed on a sort of elevation or throne. A quantity of books or papyrus were scattered around."

——

ALEXANDER PROPHESIED TRULY WHEN he predicted funeral games after his death. The generals formed shifting coalitions and conducted an intermittent but brutal civil war. In 317 Olympias, as ever ferocious, put to death King Arrhidaeus and his wife, Philip's granddaughter. She was captured by Cassander and was arraigned before the Macedonian assembly, which condemned her to death. The soldiers detailed to carry out the sentence were so overawed in her presence that they withdrew without touching her. Relatives of her victims did the deed themselves. She did not flinch.

The other king, Alexander IV, fell afoul of Cassander as well; in 310, when he was thirteen, he and his mother were put to death. At the end of her affair with Alexander, Barsine and Heracles, her son by Alexander, withdrew to the city of Pergamum in Aeolis, where they lived quietly. Heracles' claim to the Macedonian throne was generally discounted on the grounds that he was a child and illegitimate.

However, the boy seemed to have some promise and in 309/308, when he was about seventeen, Heracles was taken to Greece. The plan was to install him as king of Macedonia. Cassander, who followed Antipater—dead presumably of old age—as the kingdom's current ruler, did not take kindly to the idea. He suborned Heracles' patron to poison him one night at dinner.

ALEXANDER HAS ENJOYED A remarkable—and fantastic—afterlife.

In A.D. 221, someone claiming to be Alexander and looking very like him appeared beside the river Danube with a troupe of four hundred revelers dressed as followers of Dionysus. They wandered down to Thrace, took ship at Byzantium and crossed the Bosporus to Chalcedon. Here they conducted some sacred rites, buried a wooden horse—and disappeared. The oddest part of the story is that the public authorities through whose territories they passed gave them food and drink and provided them with lodgings as if the Macedonian king still commanded obedience—almost exactly five hundred years after his death.

All kinds of fanciful legends have attached themselves to the king's name, and with the passage of centuries his adventures transformed him into an early version of Sinbad the Sailor or Baron Munchausen. These tall tales bear no relation to reality, of course, but some of them give the flavor of the king's personality—inquisitive, disenchanted, decisive, open, and yearning for the apparently impossible.

We learn that on his travels he encountered: people who were thirty-six feet tall, with forearms and hands like saws; fleas as big as frogs; beautiful women warriors, the Amazons. He once fed a naked woman to an ogre. He visited a spring of immortality (when his chef dipped a dried fish into the water, it came to life and jumped out of his hands). He placed red-hot life-size bronze statues in the front line of battle.

The king constructed a prototypical bathysphere—a large glass jar with a plug inside an iron cage—and descended in it to the bottom of the sea. He only just escaped with his life when a giant fish took the cage in its mouth and threw it onto a beach. He told himself: "Alexander, you must give up attempting the impossible."

When in India he cross-examined some Brahmins and received telling answers to his questions.

"Which is the wickedest of creatures?"

"Man," the naked philosophers answered.

"Why?"

"Learn from yourself the answer to that. You are a wild beast."

This mythical monarch retains his power to enrage or engage. He is embedded in the cultures of lands as far apart as Spain and Malaysia. Hebrew tradition makes him a prophet; for Christian Greeks, he is an obedient servant of God; among some Persians, he is a malicious demon who destroyed Zoroastrian altars, but in their national epics he is a legitimate king, being the son not of Philip, but of Darius.

As recently as the twentieth century, on stormy nights in the Aegean anxious women used to shout from the seashore to their fishermen husbands:

"Where is Alexander the Great?"

They would reply, in ritual exchange:

"Alexander the Great lives and reigns."

———

IN THE MIDDLE AGES, the king was one of the Nine Worthies, and a pattern of knightly chivalry. His doings were a regular theme of Renaissance art. Handel devoted two operas to him. He has been the subject of feature films and, even, the hero of a rock opera. A heavy metal band, Iron Maiden, has composed a song about him. He has been the hero of historical novels (notably by Mary Renault).

HOW ARE WE TO assess the historical Alexander?

He lived the most extraordinary life, winning battle after battle, undefeated and perhaps invincible. He overthrew a great empire and was perhaps the most talented field commander of all time.

Even the ancients were in two minds. For many he was a hero of the first water. He was much admired by the imperialists of ancient Rome. Pompey the Great imitated his hairstyle and the way he held his head to one side. However, in others his glorification of war aroused distaste and even disgust; they saw his career as a long killing spree. Many thousands of deaths can be laid at his door. It could be argued that Homer was his evil genius. The *Iliad,* masterpiece though it be, gave cover for his bellicosity and for the long bloodbath of his career. Although he often behaved chivalrously by the standards of his time, even his contemporaries condemned his cruelty, and today he would undoubtedly qualify as a war criminal.

St. Augustine of Hippo tells of an entertaining exchange between the king and a pirate he had captured.

> When he asked the man what he meant by taking over the seas, the man answered boldly and proudly: "What do *you* mean by taking over the whole earth? Because I only have a petty ship, I am called a robber, while you who command a great fleet are called emperor."

Critics rightly point out the crucial role of his father. To Philip is due the credit for reviving Macedonia from its sleepy past, creating the most efficient army of the age, and establishing himself as the dominant power of the Greek world. His son sometimes undervalued his achievements, but without them the overthrow of the Persian empire is inconceivable.

At first sight, the king's premature death seems to have undone many of his achievements. His generals abandoned the Arabian expedition and his other plans. The empire split into separate, warring states. But, as ever, it is unwise to underestimate Alexander. He and Philip had transformed the world of the eastern Mediterranean. The old Persian order was gone for good and the once powerful Greek city-states became provincial backwaters. Eventually the fractured monarchy settled down into three stable entities—Macedon including Greece, Asia (that is, the Middle East), and Egypt under the Ptolemies. In the long run, Alexander's multicultural policy transformed the lands that stretched from the Mediterranean Sea to the Indus River. He was probably only motivated by practical concerns, but the proliferation of Greek-style "cities" and the promotion into government of local talent helped to fuse the cultures of Greece and "barbarian" Persia.

This process touched only the ruling elites, and its impact was weaker in the eastern provinces. Plutarch patronizes and exaggerates, but the essential point he makes has merit:

> Alexander . . . taught the Gedrosians the tragedies of Euripides and Sophocles. . . . Thanks to Alexander, Bactria and the Caucasus peoples worship the gods of Greece. . . . He planted Greek institutions all across Asia, and thus overcame its wild and savage way of living. . . . His enemies could not have been civilized if they had not been beaten.

The fact is that the king set the scene for the Hellenistic civilization that dominated the next few centuries. His nascent concept of a divine monarchy was enthusiastically developed by the successor kings in Asia and the eastern Mediterranean and lasted till the arrival of the Romans. The Egyptian Alexandria was a success and became the acknowledged center of Greek learning and arts. A form of Attic or Athenian Greek became the universal language or *koinē* (from *koinos*, the Greek for "common" or "shared"). This linguistic culture, which Alexander brought into being (without altogether understanding what he had done), survived the arrival of the Romans and in its final manifestation flourished in the empire of Byzantium until the fifteenth century A.D.

Alexander was essentially a soldier, but he was also a serious explorer. If we compare maps of the ancient world, we gain a clear idea of the new geographical knowledge for which he was responsible. In the world picture proposed by Hecataeus of Miletus two centuries before Alexander's time, the river Ocean wraps round a world disc with nothing much beyond Persia; a century after his death, Eratosthenes allocates nearly half the world to India, identifies the Persian Gulf, and distinguishes the Asian subcontinent from Africa. Alexander had made the world bigger.

Many people have regarded Alexander's invasion of India as a waste of lives and treasure. He won battles wherever he went, but could not always hold on to his conquests. That said, he understood the imperatives of international trade and opened up the subcontinent to Western commercial interests. This was no mean accomplishment.

WHAT WOULD ALEXANDER HAVE done if he had lived?

His plans for the conquest of Arabia and northern Africa suggest that he meant to go on and on, seeking out new enemies and overwhelming them. There is no particular reason to suppose he would have failed, although the simple technology and communications of his day must surely have placed a limit on what he could accomplish.

He was an eminently practical man, but his dominant motive was *pothos,* a longing for the unattainable. Had he survived into old age, he would have resembled Tennyson's superannuated Ulysses, still ready for adventure alongside his grizzled mariners, whose purpose held

> To sail beyond the sunset, and the baths
> Of all the western stars, until I die.

Could the aged Alexander even have made it to America?

GLOSSARY

---

agema: elite infantry or cavalry guards.

Agrianians: tribesmen from Paeonia, lightly armed javelin throwers. Much used by Alexander.

archon: chief magistrate (civilian), commander (military).

bematist: measurer of distances traveled.

chiliarch: Greek for "commander of a thousand"; the Persian king's chief executive officer or grand vizier.

choregos: producer of and investor in dramatic or musical performances.

Companion: see *hetairos*.

daric: a gold coin which, along with a similar silver coin, the *siglos,* represented the bimetallic monetary standard of the Persian empire.

drachma: silver coin worth 6 obols. Roughly the value of a skilled worker's daily pay.

erastes: older lover in a pederastic relationship.

eromenos: younger "beloved" in a pederastic relationship.

hegemon: military leader. Commander-in-chief of a league (e.g. League of Corinth).

Hellas: the Greek word for Greece.

hetairos: companion or friend. One of a select group who advised Alexander and acted as administrators. Member of the Companion cavalry and Companion infantry.

hipparch: cavalry commander.

hypaspists: literally, shield bearers, infantry more agile than the phalanx. They linked the *pezhetairoi,* or Foot Companions, to the Companion Horse. There were 3,000 of them, rising to 4,000 in 331. They were later named the Argyraspids or Silver Shields.

ilarches: cavalry squadron commander.

ile: cavalry squadron.

ile basilike: royal squadron. Commanded by Cleitus.

Mede: inhabitant of Media; used by the Greeks as a synonym for Persian.

nauarchos: admiral.

pais basilikos: literally, royal boy. One of the Royal Pages, who looked after Alexander's domestic requirements.

peltasts: lightly armed troops.

pezhetairoi: Foot Companions. The phalanx. It included six 1,500-strong *taxeis* or battalions, totaling 9,000 men. They were territorial levies.

Philippeum: a statue group in Olympia of the family of Philip II of Macedonia.

prodromoi: mounted scouts.

proxenos: a man from one state who represents to it the interests of a foreign state.

sarissa: the Macedonian pike.

satrap: governor of a Persian province.

somatophylax: one of seven close bodyguards. The term was also used of the Royal Pages and the hypaspists.

strategos: general or (civilian) senior elected politician.

syntrophos: coeval of a king's son, who is brought up with him.

talent: bar of silver worth 6,000 drachmas.

taxis: an infantry unit or battalion.

tetradrachm: silver coin worth four drachmas.

triaconter: thirty-oared ship.

trierarchos: commander of a trireme or the man who financed the fitting out of a ship.

trireme: warship with three banks of oars.

xenoi: foreigners, mercenary troops.

xenos: foreigner, a foreign friend.

TIME LINE

*S*ome dates are speculative or debated.

B.C.	
382	Philip II born in Macedonia.
c. 373	Olympias born in Molossia.
357	Philip and Olympias marry.
356	Their son Alexander is born at Pella.
July 20 or 26	Philip captures Potidaea.
c. 355	Their daughter Cleopatra is born.
354	Demosthenes attacks project for a crusade against Persia.
	Philip captures Methone; loses an eye.
352	Artabazus (with daughter Barsine) and Memnon seek refuge in Pella.
351	Macedonian fleet harasses Athenian shipping.
340s	Olympias's brother Alexander becomes king of Molossia with Philip's help.
343/42	Aristotle is appointed Alexander's tutor.

338	Battle of Chaeronea; Alexander leads Macedonian cavalry.
	Building of Philippeum at Olympia.
337	League of Corinth formed, appoints Philip as leader of an anti-Persian crusade.
	Philip marries Cleopatra, ward of Attalus.
	Alexander and Olympias escape from Macedonia.
	Alexander recalled to Pella.
	Pixodarus affair (possibly early 336).
336 spring	Parmenion and Attalus take an advance expeditionary force to Asia Minor.
June:	Accession of Darius III of Persia.
	Cleopatra, Philip's wife, gives birth to a daughter, Europa.
	Alexander of Molossia marries Cleopatra, Olympias's daughter.
	Philip assassinated.
	Alexander succeeds Philip as king of Macedonia.
Late summer:	League of Corinth appoints Alexander as leader of the anti-Persian crusade.
335 early spring	Alexander campaigns in Thrace and Illyria.
	Memnon campaigns in Asia Minor.
	Olympias puts to death Cleopatra, Philip's wife, and her daughter.
	Alexander orders the death of Attalus.
	Revolt and destruction of Thebes.
334 spring	Alexander's army crosses to Asia Minor.
	Battle of the Granicus River.
	Siege of Miletus.
Autumn:	Siege of Halicarnassus.
334/33 winter	Conquest of Asia Minor.
333 early spring	Naval offensive by Memnon.
	Memnon dies.
	Persian army musters at Babylon.

	Alexander at Gordium.
	Alexander marches to the Cilician Gates.
	Persian army moves westward from Babylon.
September:	Alexander in Tarsus, falls ill.
Autumn:	Battle of Issus.
	Darius makes peace offer, refused.
332 winter (?)	Submission of Byblos and Sidon.
	Siege of Tyre.
June (?):	Darius makes second peace offer, refused.
July 29:	Fall of Tyre.
	Disintegration of the Persian fleet.
Autumn:	Siege and fall of Gaza.
	Alexander welcomed as pharaoh in Memphis.
331 early spring	Alexander visits oracle at Siwah.
April 7–8 (?):	Foundation of Alexandria.
	Alexander returns to Tyre.
Summer:	Alexander reaches Thapsacus on the Euphrates.
	Darius leaves Babylon.
September 18:	Alexander crosses the Tigris.
September 20:	Eclipse of the moon.
	Darius's final peace offer.
September 30 or October 1:	Battle of Gaugamela.
mid-October:	Alexander enters Babylon.
	Revolt of Agis defeated at Megalopolis.
December:	Alexander captures Susa unopposed.
330 (?) January:	Alexander enters Persepolis.
May:	Alexander sacks Persepolis.
Early June:	Alexander sets out for Ecbatana.
	Darius leaves Ecbatana for Bactria.
	Greek allies dismissed.
	Alexander campaigns in Tapuria, Hyrcania, Parthyaea, and Areia.

July:	Darius murdered near Hecatompylos.
	Bessus in Bactria, appoints himself Great King.
Late August:	Alexander at Lake Seistan.
October:	"Conspiracy" of Philotas.
	Alexander marches through Arachosia to Parapanisadae.
329 spring	Alexander crosses the Hindu Kush into Bactria; Bessus retreats across the Oxus.
June:	Alexander crosses the Oxus, dismisses veterans and Thessalian volunteers, reorganizes his cavalry.
	Bessus handed over to Alexander.
	Revolt, led by Spitamenes, of Bactria and Sogdia; annihilation of a Macedonian force.
329/28	Alexander winters in Bactra.
328	Campaign against Spitamenes.
Autumn:	Murder of Cleitus.
328/27	Defeat and death of Spitamenes.
Late winter:	Siege and capture of the Sogdian Rock and the Rock of Chorienes.
327 spring	Macedonian army reunites at Bactria.
	Alexander marries Rhoxane.
	30,000 Persian "Successors" recruited.
	Pages' conspiracy, fall of Callisthenes.
Early summer:	Alexander recrosses the Hindu Kush; invasion of India.
	Hephaestion builds bridge and fleet on the river Indus.
327/26	Dionysus episode at Nysa.
	Capture of the Aornus rock.
326 spring	Macedonian army reunites at the Indus.
	Battle of the Hydaspes; death of Bucephalas.
	"Mutiny" at the Hyphasis.
	Reinforcements arrive from Greece.
November:	Macedonian fleet sets off downriver.

326/25	Campaign against the Malli; Alexander badly wounded.
325	Revolt in Bactria.
	Harbor and dockyard built at Patala in the Indus Delta.
	Craterus sets off for Carmania.
Late August:	Alexander marches through the Gedrosian desert.
October:	Nearchus sets sail for the Persian Gulf from the Indus.
	Harpalus, Alexander's treasurer, flees to Greece.
December:	Alexander meets Craterus in Carmania.
	Purge of the satraps begins.
324	Nearchus joins Alexander in Carmania; fleet is sent on to Susa.
	Tomb of Cyrus the Great King robbed.
	Alexander returns to Persepolis.
February– March:	Alexander in Susa; mass marriages at Susa.
Spring:	30,000 Persian Successors arrive.
Summer:	Recall of the exiles, announced at the Olympic Games.
	Mutiny at Opis.
	Craterus appointed to replace Antipater as regent; restores order in Cilicia and leads veterans toward Macedonia.
	Alexander moves from Susa to Ecbatana.
	Hephaestion dies.
323	Harpalus assassinated in Crete.
Spring:	Campaign against the Cossaeans.
	Alexander returns to Babylon.
	Arrival at court of Antipater's son, Cassander.
	Final preparations for Arabian campaign.
May 29–30:	Alexander falls ill.
June 10–11:	Alexander dies.

ACKNOWLEDGMENTS

———

I AM GREATLY INDEBTED TO RODDY ASHWORTH FOR HIS ADVICE AND assistance with research.

My literary agent, Christopher Sinclair-Stevenson, and his American colleague Tom Wallace have offered invaluable support; as has my editor, Molly Turpin. As in the past, the long-suffering Professor Robert Cape of Austin College, Texas, has read a draft and given me many valuable comments and suggestions. Any errors are mine alone.

BACKGROUND
AND SOURCES

My LINE OF BUSINESS IS NARRATIVE HISTORY. I AM INTERESTED in people and in the bustling life of the past. I set myself two cardinal rules: I am blind to the future, and I describe the lives of my characters as though I did not know what was going to happen next.

Second, I avoid so far as possible the acrid debates among Alexander experts. Despite his fame, many of the memoirs of those who knew him and took part in his astounding career have been lost. The sources we have are less than adequate and were composed hundreds of years after the fact. Modern classicists have clever minds and have cleared up many conundrums, but sometimes they go too far and stretch speculation beyond the limits of the data. Their speculations recall the attributions made by the professional connoisseurs of Old Master paintings.

Thus, there is scarcely any evidence for the modern claim that Alexander plotted over many years the destruction of a family of loyal Macedonian generals. I shave with Occam's razor. Of competing solutions to tricky questions, it is often simplest to accept what the ancient historians tell us if it is not obviously wrong.

I usually leave scholarly discussions to brief comments in the endnotes. Anyone who seeks further and better particulars will find the bibliography a starting point.

The inadequacy of the ancient historians brings with it another difficulty. We do not know enough to reconstruct Alexander's psychol-

ogy in detail. A picture does emerge, but in soft focus. We are told
what he did, and from those actions it is possible to make an educated
guess about the emotions that powered him. That is all.

The spelling and pronunciation of Greek proper nouns is problem-
atic. The Romans transliterated them into Latin, and it was these versions which the English-speaking world inherited and which are still in
common use today. So Achilleus became Achilles, and Alexandros answered to Alexander.

I have abandoned a search for rules other than the comfort of the
reader and have chosen names on a case-by-case basis. I accept Persian
names in their Greco-Latinate form—Darius, for example, rather than
Dareios (Greek) or Dārayava(h)uš (Old Persian). Some lesser-known
names I leave in Greek. A few, such as Athens or Tyre, have been angli-
cized. The Latinate Hephaestio just looks wrong. The Greek form is
Hephaistion, but I opt for a commonly adopted hybrid version, Hephaestion.

The pronunciation of most names is obvious, but the letter "e" at
the end is spoken as "ee."

In an effort to be easily understood, I sometimes use contemporary
appellations for places and territories—so, for example, the Punjab,
the Hindu Kush, and the Middle East instead of Greek place-names
that no one has heard of or for which no convenient Greek term exists.

THE STUDY OF ANCIENT HISTORY is rather like the reporting of current affairs. In each case, there is too little evidence to be sure of exactly what has happened. Either too much source material has been lost
or too little has yet been revealed. To fill the gaps we have to use our
judgment. The basic rules of politics—the making and breaking of
deals, the uses and abuses of power—do not appear to have changed
greatly since the days of Alexander and in this biography are applied in
much the same way as when we analyze the tergiversations at the
White House or the inscrutabilities of the Forbidden City. I will be
happy if my interpretations of a distant past are as plausible as the best
of today's political commentaries.

Most ancient historians, certainly the ones who have survived the
literary cull of time, write incompetently about battles. Almost invari-

ably they were not present and they make up for ignorance with invention, usually quantities of flyblown rhetoric. Sometimes they cite the reports of participants, but these can be unreliable witnesses too. A battlefield was a noisy and confusing place.

However, there is usually enough evidence to propose a broad outline of what happened. We can see that Alexander's extraordinary skill was to judge the enemy's intentions simply by looking at how he arranged his troops, scrutinizing the slightest of signs, and making last-minute dispositions (often a clever trap) while he could still communicate with his subordinates.

New technology has transformed warfare, but has not touched the imperatives of military strategy. Modern scholars have convincingly reconstructed Alexander's victories, but their accounts sometimes fail to make the battle real. I want the reader to understand what was in Alexander's mind, so far as we can tell, and how the day went.

Two giants bestride modern scholarship. They did their best to tell the truth about Alexander, but it is salutary to see how their accounts reflect the concerns of their own age as much as they do of his. In the first half of the twentieth century, Sir William Tarn was an admirer. His Alexander was the model of an English gentleman who played by the rules, believed in the "unity of mankind," and, if he had been alive at the time, would have helped found the League of Nations.

After the Second World War, the Austrian-born Ernst Badian had little trouble dismantling the Tarn version. But Badian, too, was a man of his time. For him Alexander was a prototype of the totalitarian dictator, a classical Hitler or Stalin. It is a powerful analysis, but leaves a disagreeable impression of animus.

ALEXANDER THE GREAT'S CAREER was so world-changing that some forty of his contemporaries or near contemporaries wrote books about his life and times, whether they knew him personally or not.

The king himself employed a secretariat and a Royal Journal was kept of his activities day by day. It was an essential feature of the royal administration. Other official records threw light on events—for example, the astronomical readings of the night sky (unearthed by modern archaeologists) which priests in Babylon translated into predictions of the future—on occasion with startling accuracy. Specialist members of the army that the king led into Asia must have written down useful information—for example, bematists' measurements of distance and engineers' designs of siege engines. Some of this material was published later.

Of necessity the king was a copious correspondent, and collections of his letters were published after his death. Unfortunately, many were spurious and it can be difficult to tell which is which when they are quoted in surviving sources.

Alexander took with him a relative of Aristotle called Callisthenes. His task was to record and interpret events as they took place, always making sure that they reflected the king's wishes and showed off his achievements to their best advantage. He may have had access to the Royal Journal. In truth, he was less a historian than a public relations officer. In 327, Callisthenes fell from favor after the conspiracy of the Royal Pages and was either executed or died of natural causes as a prisoner. His history was probably carried down to 331 or even 329. The first in its field, it was published not many years later and, although filled with information, was generally felt to be too hagiographical.

Cleitarchus, a Greek from Alexandria in Egypt, wrote the most popular account of the king's life, but although he was Alexander's contemporary they never met. Cleitarchus appears to have looked down on Macedonians and disliked Alexander. He was less interested in facts than in sensation. Quintilian, a rhetorician of the first century A.D. and a good judge, found him "brilliantly ingenious but notoriously untrustworthy" and sided with Callisthenes. He was a tutor of Ptolemy and sometimes exaggerated his role in events. His history was a substantial text in twelve books and was published by the end of the fourth century.

Two authors knew Alexander well. Marsyas was raised in Pella and was a *syntrophos,* or fellow-student, of Alexander. He wrote the *Makedonica,* which primarily dealt with Philip's reign and did not extend beyond the campaign in Asia Minor. The other writer who knew Alexander was Aristobulus, a Greek engineer, who accompanied Alexander from the beginning of the Asian campaign and remained with him until his death. He started writing his historical memoir only at the age of eighty-four and was more than ninety when he died. He enjoyed the king's confidence and was an apologist both for him and for Ptolemy.

Others who served under Alexander recorded episodes in which they played a special part—the admiral Nearchus described the voyage from the Indus to the Persian Gulf, and Alexander's helmsman One-sicritus wrote of the philosophy of the Brahmins and the utopian rule of an Indian rajah, Musicanus. Chares, royal chamberlain and usher, reported on etiquette and ceremonial at Alexander's court as well as events such as the murder of Cleitus.

Ptolemy, one of the king's leading associates and later pharaoh of Egypt, was the author of a substantial history of Alexander. He has been accused of writing up his role, but denied Cleitarchus's report, or (rather) invention, that he saved the king's life in India.

OF ALL THIS MASS of material nothing has survived except for the Babylonian tablets and numerous fragments, mostly overwritten papyrus palimpsests dug up from long-forgotten Egyptian rubbish dumps. To this should be added a miscellany of innumerable quotations from the fourth and fifth centuries B.C. in the *Deipnosophists* (Learned Banqueters) of Athenaeus.

Time has reduced the literary wealth freely available in ancient times to a few more or less complete texts, first published hundreds of years after Alexander's death. They are of variable value.

The earliest of these works is Book 17 of the *Historical Library,* a "universal history" written by Diodorus of Sicily in the first century B.C. Diodorus's custom was to base each book's text on a single, preferred source, in this case the unreliable Cleitarchus.

Not long afterward a Gallo-Roman historian called Gnaeus Pompeius Trogus wrote *Philippic Histories and the Origin of the Whole World and the Places of the Earth* in forty-four books. Its central theme was the Macedonian empire, but it was also a general history of all those parts of the world that came under Macedonian rule. Books 11 and 12 are devoted to Alexander. Trogus's work survives in an epitome or abbreviation written by Marcus Junianus Justinus Frontinus (Justin) in the second century A.D. It contains useful material, but like all summaries should be used with caution.

Quintus Curtius Rufus wrote the only full-scale study of Alexander in Latin. His dates are uncertain, but he may have flourished in the reign of the Roman emperor Claudius. The first two books of his ten-book *Histories of Alexander the Great* are missing and there are large lacunae elsewhere. Cleitarchus and Ptolemy were among his sources. Curtius is tendentious and moralizing; his style is heavily rhetorical and he composed many elaborate speeches for his protagonists. He was surprisingly well-informed about the geography of the Middle East (see Engels, *passim*).

The only author to write about Alexander who can be read with undiluted pleasure is the Greek biographer and essayist Plutarch, who flourished in the first and second centuries A.D. He is best known for his *Parallel Lives,* short biographies pairing and comparing distinguished Greeks and Romans. The longest was devoted to Alexander (who was coupled with Julius Caesar) and contains much interesting information. Other lives, such as those of Demosthenes and Phocion, also offer rewarding insights into Alexander and other leading personalities of the age, as do Plutarch's essays *On the Virtue and Fortune of Alexander I and II* and *Sayings of Kings and Commanders*. However, although he understood the principles of historical inquiry, Plutarch was not a historian and did not claim to be one. His interest lay in the personalities of his subjects and the ethical conclusions that could be drawn from their behavior. On occasion, he repeated stories because they were telling rather than because they were likely to be true.

The Metz Epitome (so called because the only manuscript was found in Metz) is a summary written in late antiquity of various fragments dealing with the campaigns of Alexander the Great from Hyrcania to southern India. It is indebted to Cleitarchus. The manuscript includes the so-called *Liber de Morte Alexandri Magni Testamentumque,* a curious account of the king's death and will.

Long passages in the above texts share a common source, probably Cleitarchus, and are sometimes corralled, not especially helpfully, as a group under the heading of the "Alexander Vulgate." They are set against an apologetic tradition which features the *Anabasis of Alexander* and the *Indica,* by Lucius Flavius Arrianus Xenophon, and the anonymous *Itinerary of Alexander.*

Lucius Flavius Arrianus, Arrian for short, was a Greek who enjoyed a distinguished political career culminating in a consulship under the Roman emperor Hadrian. His *Anabasis* describes Alexander's career from his accession to his death. Arrian modeled his style partly on that of his namesake, the Athenian soldier and author Xenophon, and also on the great historians Herodotus and Thucydides. His main sources were Ptolemy and Aristobulus. He is the best authority on Alexander's campaigns, but, while he could be critical of the king, his main purpose was to justify him.

In addition to the *Anabasis,* Arrian also wrote the *Indica,* the chief theme of which is the voyage of Nearchus's fleet from the river Indus to the Persian Gulf but which also discusses the history, geography, and culture of the Indian subcontinent.

The anonymous *Itinerary* was written about A.D. 340 and was dedicated to the emperor Constantius II. It tells the story of Alexander's journey of conquest and is influenced by Arrian.

OTHER CLASSICAL AUTHORITIES TOUCH on Alexander, among them the Greek historian Polybius during the second century B.C.; also the Greek geographer Strabo and the Roman historian Livy, both of whom wrote in the first century B.C. Three military authors cast light on tactics and siege warfare: Aelian, Polyaenus, and Vitruvius.

Perhaps the oddest text, or, rather, assemblage of texts and versions, is the *Alexander Romance.* Popular in medieval times and much translated, it mixes legends and sensationalist fantasies with accurate data.

Archaeologists have unearthed inscriptions in Greek cities which mainly record legislation passed by people's assemblies and displayed in public places. They reflect the impact of Alexander's doings, but seldom the doings themselves. Most remarkably, royal Macedonian tombs have been unearthed, most of them untouched by robbers.

A VOICE IS MISSING, that of the Persians.

In our literary sources, the fall of the Achaemenids is viewed entirely from the Greek and Macedonian point of view. The Great King made announcements, sent messages, and carved his successes into mountain cliffs; there was architecture and sculpture, but no histories, no dramas or poems, no letters have survived—indeed, we do not know whether they were ever written. What did the Persians think of the Greeks? What was their political worldview? What did their subject peoples think of them? How did the court and the Great King himself react to events?

There is not even a memory.

All we have is what the cold Hellenic stare saw.

ANCIENT SOURCES, ABBREVIATIONS

Many of the ancient authors cited below appear in the Loeb Classical series where Greek and Latin originals are accompanied by versions in English. Good translations for many of them can also be found in Penguin Classics.

Ael NA	Aelian, *De Natura Animalium*
Ael Tact	Aelian, *Tactica*
Ael VH	Aelian, *Varia Historia*
Aesch Ctes	Aeschines, *Against Ctesiphon*
Aesch Emb	Aeschines, *On the False Embassy*
Aesch Tim	Aeschines, *Against Timarchus*
Aeschyl Ag	Aeschylus, *Agamemnon*
Aes	Aesop, *Fables* (trans. Olivia and Robert Temple, Penguin Classics, London, 1998)
Alex Chron http://www.livius .org/cg-cm/chronicles/bchp -alexander/alexander_02.html	Alexander Chronicle (BM 36304)
Anti GA	Antipater of Sidon, see *Greek Anthology*
Ar Cael	Aristotle, *On the Heavens* (*De Caelo*)
Ar Anim	Aristotle, *Inquiries into Animals*
Ar Nic Eth	Aristotle, *Nicomachean Ethics*
Ar Meta	Aristotle, *Metaphysics*
Ar Met	Aristotle, *Meteorologica*
Ar Pol	Aristotle, *Politics*
Ar Rhet	Aristotle, *Rhetoric*

Arrian	Arrian, *Anabasis*
Arr Ind	Arrian, *Indica*
Arr Succ	Arrian, *Successors to Alexander*
Ascl	Asclepiodotus, *Tactics*
Athen	Athenaeus, *Deipnosophistae* (Learned Banqueters)
Aug	Augustine, *City of God*
Aul Gell	Aulus Gellius, *Noctes Atticae*
Cic Arch	Cicero, *Pro Archia*
Cic Att	Cicero, *Letters to Atticus* (trans. D. R. Shackleton-Bailey, Duckworth, London, 1971)
Cic Nat	Cicero, *De Natura Deorum*
Cic Rosc	Cicero, *Pro Roscio Amerino*
Cic Tusc Disp	Cicero, *Tusculan Disputations*
Clem	Clement of Alexandria, *Stromateis*
Nep Eum	Cornelius Nepos, *Lives of the Eminent Commanders, Eumenes*
Curt	Curtius Rufus, Quintus, *Historiae Alexandri Magni Macedonis* (The History of Alexander)
Dem	Demosthenes, *Speeches*
Dem Crown	Demosthenes, *On the Crown*
Did	Didymus, *On Philippics of Demosthenes*
Dio Chrys	Dio Chrystostom, *Discourses*
Diod Sic	Diodorus Siculus, *Library of History*
Diog Lae	Diogenes Laertius, *Lives of Eminent Philosophers*
Diog	Diogenes of Sinope, *Letters* (attrib.)
Dion Hal	Dionysius of Halicarnassus, *To Ammaeus*
Eur Androm	Euripides, *Andromache*
Eur Andr	Euripides, *Andromeda*
Eur Bacc	Euripides, *Bacchae*
Eur Med	Euripides, *Medea*
Ezek	Ezekiel (Bible, New International Version)

Alex Rom	*The Greek Alexander Romance* (trans. Richard Stoneman, Penguin, Harmondsworth 1991)
Gk Anth	*Greek Anthology*
GHI	*Greek Historical Inscriptions 359–323* B.C. (trans. P. J. Rhodes, London Association of Classical Teachers, 1971)
142 FS	Hegesias of Magnesia FGrH
Herod	Herodotus, *Histories*
Hes WD	Hesiod, *Works and Days*
Il	Homer, *Iliad*
Hom Hymns	Homeric Hymns
Hyp Dem	Hypereides, *Against Demosthenes*
Hyp Fun	Hypereides, *Funeral Oration*
Isoc Alex	Isocrates, *Letters to Alexander*
Isoc Phil	Isocrates, *Oration to Philip*
Isoc Plat	Isocrates, *Plataicus*
IG	*Inscriptions Graecae*
Itin	*Itinerary of Alexander (Itinerarium Alexandri)*
Jos Ant	Josephus, Flavius, *Antiquities of the Jews*
Jos Api	Josephus, Flavius, *Against Apion*
Just	Justinus (Justin), Marcus Junianus, *Epitome of the Philippic History of Pompeius Trogus* (trans. Rev. J. S. Watson, Henry G. Bohn, London, 1853)
LiberM	*Liber de Morte, Concerning the Death and Testament of Alexander the Great*
Luc Alex	Lucian, *Alexander the False Prophet*
Luc Dial Dead	Lucian, *Dialogues of the Dead*
Luc Herod	Lucian, *Herodotus and Aetion*
Luc Slander	Lucian, *Slander*
Metz	Metz Epitome
Oxy	Oxyrhycus Papyri
Od	*Odyssey,* Homer
Paus	Pausanias, *Description of Greece*
Phot	Photius, *Bibliotheca*

Pind	Pindar, *Odes* (trans. Maurice Bowra, Penguin Classics, Harmondsworth 1982)
Pind Enc	Pindar, *Encomia*
Pind Pyth	Pindar, *Pythians*
Plato Gorg	Plato, *Gorgias*
Plato Rep	Plato, *The Republic*
Pliny	Pliny, *Natural History*
Plut Alex	Plutarch, *Age of Alexander* (trans. Scott-Kilvert, Ian, and Duff, Timothy E. [also contains *Lives of Artaxerxes, Pelopidas, Dion, Timoleon, Demosthenes, Phocion, Alexander, Eumenes, Demetrius, Pyrrhus*] Introductions and Notes, Duff, Timothy E., Penguin Books, London, 2011)
Plut Erot	Plutarch, *Erotikos (Dialogue on Love)*
Plut Age	Plutarch, *Life of Agesilaus*
Plut Alex	Plutarch, *Life of Alexander*
Plut Gal	Plutarch, *Life of Galba*
Plut Mor	Plutarch, *Moralia*
Plut Fort	Plutarch, *On the Fortune or the Virtue of Alexander*
Plut Pel	Plutarch, *Life of Pelopidas*
Plut Per	Plutarch, *Life of Pericles*
Plut Rom	Plutarch, *Life of Romulus*
Poll	Pollux, Julius, *Onomasticon* (pub. Imm. Bekker, Berlin, 1846)
Poly	Polyaenus, *Stratagems in War*
Polyb	Polybius, *The Histories*
Quint	Quintilian, *Institutes of Oratory*
Strabo	Strabo, *Geography*
Suda	Suda
Theo Phil	Theopompus, *Philippica*
Theo Hell	Theopompus, *Hellenica*
Val Max	Valerius Maximus, *Memorable Deeds and Sayings*
Virg Aen	Virgil, *Aeneid*

Vit	Vitruvius, *De Architectura*
Xen Cyr	Xenophon, *Cyropaedia*
Xen Anab	Xenophon, *Anabasis*
Xen Hip	Xenophon, *Hipparchicus* (On the Cavalry Commander)

MODERN SOURCES

Here is a selection from modern scholarship for the interested general reader. I am especially grateful for two invaluable compendiums—the *Oxford Classical Dictionary*, which contains in brief everything worth knowing about the Greek and Roman world, and Waldemar Heckel's *Who's Who in the Age of Alexander the Great* (for details of both, see below).

Arsuaga, Juan-Luis, and others. *The Lameness of King Philip II and Royal Tomb I at Vergina, Macedonia.* Washington, D.C.: National Academy of Science of the United States of America, vol. 112, no. 32, 2015.

Badian, Ernst. "Alexander's Mules." *New York Review of Books,* December 20, 1979.

———. *Collected Papers on Alexander the Great.* Abingdon Oxon: Routledge, Abingdon, Oxfordshire, 2012.

Bodson, Liliane. "Alexander the Great and the Scientific Exploration of the Oriental Part of His Empire: An Overview of the Background, Trends and Results." *Ancient Society* (published by the Katholieke Universiteit Leuven, Belgium), vol. 22 (1991), pp. 127–38.

Bosworth, A. B., *Conquest and Empire: The Reign of Alexander the Great.* Cambridge: Cambridge University Press, 1988.

Bosworth, A. B., and E. J. Baynham. *Alexander the Great in Fact and Fiction.* Oxford: Oxford University Press, 2000.

Briant, Pierre. *From Cyrus to Alexander: A History of the Persian Empire* (trans. Peter D. Daniels). Winona Lake, Ind.: Eisembrauns, 2002.

Brill's New Jacoby, Leiden, Netherlands, 2007.

Cambridge Ancient History, Volume 6, the Fourth Century B.C. Cambridge: Cambridge University Press, 1994.

Carney, Elizabeth. "Macedonians and Mutiny: Discipline and Indiscipline in the Army of Philip and Alexander." *Classical Philology,* vol. 91, no. 1 (January 1996), pp. 19–44.

———. *Olympias, Mother of Alexander the Great.* New York and Abingdon: Routledge, 2006.

———. *Women and Monarchy in Macedonia.* Norman: University of Oklahoma Press, 2000.

Ceccarelli, Paola. *Ancient Greek Letter Writing.* Oxford: Oxford University Press, 2013.

Chugg, Andrew. *Alexander's Lovers.* Raleigh, N.C.: Lulu.com, 2016.

Connolly, Peter. *Greece and Rome at War.* London: Greenhill Books, 1998.

————. *The Greek Armies.* London: Macdonald Educational, 1977.

Engels, Donald W. *Alexander the Great and the Logistics of the Macedonian Army.* Berkeley and Los Angeles: University of California Press, 1978.

————. "A Note on Alexander's Death." *Classical Philology,* vol. 73, no. 3 (July 1978), pp. 224–28.

Everitt, Anthony. *The Rise of Athens: The Story of the World's Greatest Civilization.* New York: Penguin Random House, 2016.

Everson, Tim. *Warfare in Ancient Greece: Arms and Armor from the Heroes of Homer to Alexander the Great.* Stroud, U.K.: Sutton Publishing, 2004.

Finkel, Irving L. "The Hanging Gardens of Babylon." In Peter A. Clayton and Martin J. Price, eds., *The Seven Wonders of the Ancient World.* London and New York: Routledge, 1988.

Forster, E. M. *Alexandria: A History and a Guide.* New York: Doubleday, 1961 (originally published 1922; Alexandria: Whitehead Morris Ltd.).

Fuller, Major-General J. F. C. *The Generalship of Alexander the Great.* London: Eyre and Spottiswoode, 1958.

Garland, Robert. *Daily Life of the Ancient Greeks.* Westport, Conn.: Greenwood Press, 1998.

Green, Peter. *Alexander of Macedon.* Harmondsworth: Pelican Books, 1974.

Hammond, N. G. L. *A History of Greece to 322 B.C.* Oxford, 1959.

Hammond, N. G. L., and G. T. Griffith. *A History of Macedonia,* vol. 2. Oxford: Clarendon Press, 1979.

Hammond, N. G. L., and F. W. Walbank. *A History of Macedonia,* vol. 3. Oxford: Clarendon Press, 1988.

Harding, Phillip, ed. and trans. *From the End of the Peloponnesian War to the Battle of Ipsus. Translated Documents of Greece and Rome.* Cambridge: Cambridge University Press, 1985.

Heckel, Waldemar. *The Conquests of Alexander the Great.* Cambridge: Cambridge University Press, 2008.

————. "Two Doctors from Kos?" *Mnemosyne* (4th ser.), vol. 34, fasc. 3/4 (1981), pp. 396–98.

————. *Who's Who in the Age of Alexander the Great.* Chichester, U.K.: Wiley-Blackwell, 2009.

Holt, Frank L. *Alexander the Great and Bactria.* Leiden, New York, and Köln: E. J. Brill, 1988.

Hornblower, Simon. *Mausolus.* Oxford: Clarendon Press, 1982.

———— and Antony Spawforth, eds., *The Oxford Classical Dictionary.* Oxford: Oxford University Press, 2003.

Jackson, Ralph. *Doctors and Diseases in the Roman Empire.* London: British Museum Press, 1998.

Jacoby, Felix. *Die Fragmente der griechischen Historiker.* Berlin: Brill, 1923 FGrH.

Lane Fox, Robin. *Alexander the Great.* London: Allen Lane in association with Longman, 1973.

Langdon, S. *Building Inscriptions of the Neo-Babylonian Empire I.* Paris: Ernest Leroux, 1905.

Lehmann, P. W. *Samothrace: A Guide to the Excavations and the Museum*. New York: NYU Institute of Fine Arts, 1975.

Llewellyn-Jones, Lloyd. *King and Court in Ancient Persia 559–331 B.C.E.* Edinburgh: Edinburgh University Press, 2013.

Marsden, E. W. *The Campaign of Gaugamela*. Liverpool: Liverpool University Press, 1964.

Merritt, B. D. *Hesperia 21,* American School of Classical Studies at Athens, Princeton 1952, pp. 355–59.

Montaigne, Michel de. *The Complete Essays*. Translated by M. A. Screech. Harmondsworth: Penguin, 1987.

Oates, Joan. *Babylon*. London: Thames & Hudson, 2008.

O'Brien, John Maxwell. *Alexander the Great: The Invisible Enemy*. London and New York: Routledge, 1992.

Oppenheim, A. Leo. *Ancient Mesopotamia: Portrait of a Dead Civilization*. Chicago and London: University of Chicago Press, 1964.

Pritchett, W. K. "Observations on Chaeronea." *American Journal of Archaeology,* vol. 62 (1992), pp. 307–11.

Reade, Julian. "Alexander the Great and the Hanging Gardens of Babylon." *Iraq,* vol. 62 (2000), pp. 195–217.

Renault, Mary. *The Nature of Alexander*. London: Allen Lane, 1975.

Roisman, Joseph, and Ian Worthington, eds. *A Companion to Ancient Macedonia*. Chichester, U.K.: Wiley-Blackwell, 2010.

Samuel, Alan E. "Philip and Alexander as Kings: Macedonian Monarchy and Merovingian Parallels." *American Historical Review,* vol. 93, no. 5 (December 1988), pp. 1270–86.

Schachermeyr, F. *Alexander in Babylon und die Reichsordnung nach seinem Tode*. Osterreichische Akademie der Wissenschaften: Philosophisch-Historische Klasse: Sitzungsberichte 268, Abhandlung 3, 1970.

———. *Alexander der Grosse: Das Problem seiner Personlichkeit und seine Wirkens*. Vienna: Verlag der Österreichischen Akademie der Wissenschaften, 1973.

Schuster, Angela M.H. "Not Philip II of Macedon." *Archaeology,* April 21, 2000, Online Features, https://archive.archaeology.org/online/features/macedon/.

Seltman, Charles. *Wine in the Ancient World*. London: Routledge & Kegan Paul, 1957).

Spawforth, Antony J. S. "The Pamphleteer Ephippus, King Alexander and the Persian Royal Hunt," *Histos,* vol. 6 (2012), pp. 169–213.

Stein, Sir Aurel. "Notes on Alexander's Crossing of the Tigris and the Battle of Arbela," *The Geographical Journal,* vol. 100, no. 4 (October 1942), pp. 155–64.

———. *On Alexander's Track to the Indus,* Macmillan and Co., 1929.

Stoneman, Richard, trans., *The Greek Alexander Romance*. Harmondsworth, U.K.: Penguin, 1991.

Tod, M. N. *A Selection of Greek Historical Inscriptions II*. Oxford: Oxford University Press, 1948.

Worthington, Ian. *By the Spear, Philip II, Alexander the Great and the Rise and Fall of the Macedonian Empire*. Oxford: Oxford University Press, 2014.

———. *Demosthenes of Athens and the Fall of Classical Greece*. Oxford: Oxford University Press, 2013.

NOTES

PREFACE: THE KING TAKES A HOLIDAY

xi *the deluxe metropolis of Babylon*   The remains of Babylon have not been fully excavated. The German archaeologist R. J. Koldewey worked on the site between 1899 and 1917, but much remains to be uncovered and explained. In my reconstruction of events in Babylon in June 323, especially the location of the Hanging Gardens and Alexander's movements, I rely on Reade.

xi *one of the Seven Wonders*   Some scholars doubt the existence of the Hanging Gardens, or locate them in the Assyrian capital of Nineveh. Archaeologists have failed to identify its remains in Babylon. However, rulers in Mesopotamia and the ancient Middle East were passionate lovers of gardens. To judge by the architectural sophistication of their city's monuments, the Babylonians were perfectly capable of building the kind of tiered structure described in the literary sources. All the other "Wonders," from the Pyramids at Gizeh to the temple of Artemis in Ephesus, were historical and there is no good reason to suppose the Hanging Gardens to have been an exception (see Oates, pp. 151 and 157, and Reade, *passim*).

xi *Two colossal palaces*   The following description of Babylon is indebted to Oates, pp. 144–49 and Reade, *passim*.

xii *summer palace*   It has proved difficult to determine Alexander's movements during his last illness against what we know of Babylon's layout and monuments. Schachermeyr (1970, 65–73) argues that he was transferred from the palace complex in the main city up the Euphrates to the "summer" palace. Reade shows, more convincingly, that it must have been the other way around—namely that the king was based in the summer palace, then transported south to the Hanging Gardens in the city and then back again. This reconstruction is necessarily speculative, but it fits known data.

xiii *to organize a banquet* The following account is based on a conflation of Arrian 7 23 6–8, 24–30, and Plut Alex 75–77. They quoted from a document often referred to as the Royal Journals (e.g., Arrian 725–28). According to some authorities, it is best to see them not as an official daybook but as a statement specially produced about five years after Alexander's death, probably by the king's secretary, Eumenes. It was designed to rebut claims that he had been poisoned. Although intended as propaganda, it probably gives an accurate description of Alexander's last days. It may have been based on some kind of court diary or other documents in the royal archives or even notes taken at the time by Eumenes or his staff. I discuss all these matters at greater length on pages 378–79, 401, and 414 below.

xiii *his play,* Andromeda Ath 12 537. A plausible anecdote, bearing in mind Alexander's reported enthusiasm for Euripides and the Attic dramatists.

xiii *"I gained glory, not without many trials."* Eur Andr 134 (Loeb).

xiv *"For sensible men"* Eubulus, Fragment 93, preserved in Athenaeus 2 37c, from a play about Semele and her son, Dionysus.

xiv *Alexander challenged a fellow guest* Ath 10 434a, quoting Ephippus, a contemporary of Alexander and author of *The Deaths of Alexander and Hephaestion*.

xiv *"as if he had been pierced by a spear"* Plut Alex 75 3.

xv *or in the royal tent* Curtius, at 10 5 8, places Alexander's newly dead body in the royal tent. It is perfectly possible that in his last days he felt more comfortable, or that it was deemed more appropriate, for him to lie among his soldiers.

xv *"I imagine some suspected"* Arrian 7 26 1.

xv *temple of a Babylonian deity* The sources say, perhaps anachronistically, that this was Sarapis, a novel Egyptian god of healing. Alternatively, they could have meant the chief Babylonian divinity, Bel-Marduk, sometimes referred to as Sarri-Rabu, "Great King." Either way there is no reason to doubt the historicity of the event.

xvi *On June 11* Plut Alex 76 4 says June 10, but a contemporary source, *Astronomical Diaries, The Omen Catalogue, British Museum,* compiled contemporaneously by Babylonian religious officials, dates the death to June 11.

xvi *"To whom do you leave the kingdom?"* For both quotations, see Diod 17 117 4; or ("To the best man") Curt 10 5 5. "When you yourselves": Curt 10 5 6. There was competition for the king's final message to the world. Readers may take their pick.

CHAPTER 1. GOAT KINGS

4 *"In the old days"* Her 8 137.

5 *"with a store of disorderly words."* Homer Il 2 211–77.

5 *"Lower your tunic a little"* Plut Mor 178 c–d.

5 *appointed by acclamation* Just 7 5 1.

5 *"kingship . . . is organized"* Ar Pol 1310b31.

6 *about fifty million inhabitants*   Fuller, p. 72.

7 *become an imperial province*   Macedonia may have been incorporated alongside Thrace into the larger satrapy of Skudra; see Hammond 2, p. 69f. The exact arrangements are unclear. In any case Amyntas was left on his throne as a client-king.

7 *took violent measures*   Herod, 5 20–21. The story is in a tradition of travesty killings. If it is apocryphal, as is possible, it may have been told to Herodotus by the inventive Alexander himself, who wanted to demonstrate that he had been secretly hostile to his Persian overlords until their removal.

7 *the Persian occupation*   Hammond 2, p. 64.

8 *Anyone who was not Greek*   See Hammond 2, p. 46 for a discussion of the Macedonian language.

8 *"frogs around a pond"*   Plato Phaedo 109b.

8 *"He strung an arrow"*   Herod 5 105 1–2.

9 *assembled an army*   Everitt, p. 147f.

9 *"When that monarch overspread"*   Just 7 4 1.

10 *"The greater part of the sentries"*   Herod 9 45 1.

10 *"Should you bring this war"*   Ibid., 45 3.

10 *"first fruit of spoils"*   Hammond 2 p.102. The Greeks used "Medes" interchangeably with "Persians." The Medes were an ancient people who lived in northwestern Iran and were an important part of the Persian empire.

11 *Macedonia had quadrupled*   Roisman, p. 47.

11 *"I will not rebuild a single one"*   Everitt, p. 193.

11 *"The Greeks who"*   Herod 522.

11 *"bold-scheming son of Amyntas"*   Pind Enc frag. 120.

12 *"It is right for the good to be hymned"*   Ibid., frag. 121.

12 *his death in 452*   Hammond 2, p.103f. for a discussion of the date of Alexander's death.

13 *"Springtime isn't the only beautiful season"*   Plut Mor 177a.

13 *Zeuxis to decorate his house*   Ael VH14 17.

13 *no luck with Socrates*   Ar Rhet 2 23 8.

13 *nine-day festival*   Diod 17 16 3.

13 *"Shall we, who are Greeks"*   Clem 6 1.

13 *When Plato died in 347*   Theo BNJ 115, frag. 294.

13 *"not only not Greek"*   Dem Phil 3 30–31.

14 *"had no claim to the throne"*   Plato Gorg 471 a and b; I take the following bloodthirsty anecdote from the *Gorgias*.

14 *a boyfriend called Craterus*   Ael 8 9. Or Crataeas.

15 *the royal family imploded*   Just 7 4 8, 7 5 4–7.

15 *"by her diligence"*   Plut Mor 14c. Some scholars assert that Eurydice's claimed affection for her children discredits the stories of her murderous ambition. Hardly so. Even third-rate politicians work to improve their public image.

15 *hostage among the Illyrians and then in Thebes*   Diod 16 2 1–5. Plut Pel 26 5.

15 *amorous commander*   Plut Erot 17.

16 *origin in the heroic age*   Connolly 1998, p. 50.

16 *"gave Philip fine opportunities"*   Just 7 5 3.

16 *trusted his little brother*   See Hammond 2, p. 207. There is some evidence that the brothers may have quarrelled and that in fact Philip was exiled to a royal estate in a loose form of "house" arrest. But Perdiccas knew the history of plots and assassinations in the royal family. If he had grounds for mistrusting his brother, he would surely have taken more severe measures.

17 *Philip was appointed regent*   Some argue that Philip was made king at once. I find it more likely that he was promoted after he had shown his mettle. Hammond 2, p. 208f.

18 *"In their swift advance"*   Il 3, 10–15.

18 *kings and aristocrats stood on chariots*   see Fuller, p. 39f, for development of Greek warfare.

19 *A hand and a leg*   Dem Crown 18 67.

19 *lost an eye*   Diod 16 34 5.

19 *"he did not cover over"*   Plut Mor 331b–c.

20 *remodeled the remains*   This section on the Macedonian army and Philip's reforms is indebted to Fuller, pp. 39–54, and Connolly 1997, *passim*. Also Poly 4 2 and Asclepiodotus, *passim*.

21 *replaced the throwing spears*   Connolly 1998, p. 51. It is possible that the Thebans used a two-handed pike to avoid the crumbling effect.

21 *"Wheeling was thus easier"*   Ascl 7 3.

22 *"we don't even allow"*   Poly 4 2 1.

22 *going for a drink*   Ael 14 49

22 *"Philip's court in Macedonia"*   Poly 8 9 1.

CHAPTER 2. THE APPRENTICE

25 *Here arcane rites*   Lehmann, *passim,* for an account of ancient Samothrace, its archaeology, and its religion.

26 *Polyxena acquired another name*   Carney, pp. 17, 93. It is possible that "Myrtale" was something in the nature of a nickname for everyday use and that "Polyxena" had a formal or official function.

26 *coming-of-age ceremony*   An analogy suggests itself with the Roman Catholic confirmation ceremony, at which the child participant chooses a new sacred name.

27 *"Here where I struck"*   Aeschyl Ag 1380f.

28 *"It was not for you"*   Medea 1354–60.

28 *An initiate of the transcendental Orphic religion*   Plut Alex 2 5–6.

28 *god of transcendence*   Carney, p. 98.

29 *"What sweetness is in the mountains"*   Eur Bacc 135–144, and for the following quotation as well.

29 *"to enter into these states"*   Plut Alex 2 6.

30 *"great serpents"*   Luc Alex 7.

30 *schooling in the Greek manner*   The stories about Alexander's childhood education derive from Plut Alex 4–6.

30 *A* paedogogus *was usually*   Ibid. 5 8 Lysimachus may have preceded rather than followed Leonidas in the nursery. See Heckel (2009), p. 153. Also Garland, p. 103.

30 *an excessive amount of frankincense*   Plut Alex 25 4–5, Plut Mor 179 e–f, Pliny Nat Hist 12 62.

31 *a tall, finely bred stallion*   For the story of Bucephalas, Plut Alex 6 1–5. For his age and that of Alexander, see the estimates in Green, pp. 43–44. Plut Alex 33 1 for Aristander and the eagle.

31 *black with a white blaze*   Arrian 5 19 5.

31 *thirteen talents*   The Attic or Athenian silver talent was equivalent to 6,000 drachmas, and one drachma was an infantryman's daily wage.

32 *"My boy, we'll have to find"*   Plut Alex 6 5.

32 *played music on the cithara*   Aesch Tim 6 5.

32 *"Aren't you ashamed"*   Plut Per 1 5.

33 *received them*   Plut Alex 5 1.

33 *Hanging Gardens of Babylon*   Ibid. Mor 342 b–c.

34 *very proud of their son*   This section relies heavily on Plut Alex 7–8.

34 *"the rudder's guidance"*   Plut Alex 7 2.

34 *Aristotle spoke with a lisp*   Diog Lae 5 1 1.

35 *"show you Aristotle's stone seats"*   Plut Alex 7 4–5.

35 *Isocrates came to hear*   See Isoc Alex. Also Merlan, pp. 60–63.

36 *"far smaller than some of the stars"*   Ar Met 1 3 339b.

36 *"When therefore either a whole family"*   Ar Pol 1288a15.

36 *"by nature some are free"*   Ibid., 1254b 32.

37 *"non-Greeks and slave"*   Ibid., 1252b 8.

37 *knowing the* Iliad *by heart*   Dio Chrys 4 39.

37 *"He is two things"*   Hom Il 3 179.

37 *"And now it was noon"*   Xen Anab 1 8 8.

38 *"He caught sight of the Great King"*   Ibid., 1 8 26.

39 *"An intelligent observer"*   Ibid., 1 5 9.

40 *"If any man makes war"*   Cyr 8 8 4–7.

40 *"Alexander the Great would not have become great"*   See Roisman, p. 352. Eunapius was a Greek sophist and historian of the fourth century A.D.

41 *"like a lion's mane"*   Plut Rom 1 13. This detail and others concerning Alexander's teeth, eyes, and movement derive from the often fantastical *Alexander Romance*. But some of the *Romance*'s information seems to originate in historical sources and is convincing.

41 *His voice was . . . high-pitched*   For this and the girlish appearance, see Green, p. 55 and p. 518, n. 36.

41 *"neck which was tilted slightly to the left"* and *"a certain melting look"*   Plut Alex 4 1–2.

41 *attractive prostitute from Thessaly*   Athen 10:435a.

42 *"his looks and boyishness"*   Just 12 12 11.

43 *"used to say that sleep and sex"*   Plut Alex 22 3.

43 *"Aeschylus [the tragic playwright]"*   Plato Symp 179e.

43 *regent of the kingdom*   Plut Alex 9 1.

44 *"I slept safely"*   Plut Mor 179b.

44 *thought well of his charge*   I say so because Antipater was an unhesitating supporter after Philip's death a few years later.

44 *tried to bribe some Macedonians*   Val Max 7 2, ext. 10.

44 *"gift-devouring lords"*   Hes WD, line 39.

45 *a population of 500,000*   Roisman, p. 477.

45 *"as from a watch-tower"*   Just 8 1.

45 *"an Iliad of woes"*   Dem 19 148.

46 *"like a ram"*   Poly 2 38 2.

46 *annual income of a thousand talents*   Ibid., 16 8 6.

46 *"I enlarged my kingdom"*   Ibid., 16 53 3.

46 *"He was the worst manager"*   Theo Phil FGrH 115 F 217.

47 *"With every campaign"*   Ath 13 557b.

47 *"You are your own best magic"*   Plut Mor 141b.

47 *When Nicesipolis died in childbirth*   Carney (2000), pp. 155–57.

47 *"violet-crowned"*   Pind frag. 76.

47 *The population of adult male citizens*   Everitt, p. 379f.

48 *"It is an Athenian"*   Theo Hell frag 213.

49 *"These then are the complaints"*   Dem 12 23.

49 *the small town of Chaeronea*   For my account of the battle, I rely on Hammond (1959). The sources have little to say and much is speculative, but Hammond is convincing and coherent.

51 *"On, on, on, to Macedonia"*   Poly 4 2 7. See the same source for the below remark of Philip.

51 *archaeologists excavated*   Pritchett, *passim.*

51 *"Death to those who suspect"*   Plut Pel 18 5.

52 *"extravagantly fond"*   Plut Alex 9 4.

CHAPTER 3. "THE BULL IS WREATHED"

54 *"the deification of renown"*   Cic Nat 2 24.

55 *toured the battlefield*   Plut Dem 20 3.

55 *"King, when fate"*   Diod 16 87 1–2.

55 *The king artfully avoided*   Just 9 4 1–4.

55 *"careful to manage Greek affairs"*   Plut Mor 177c 4.

55 *"By his kindness and moderation"*   Polyb 5 10 4.

55 *"Striving to save the sacred land"*   IG II² 5226.

56 *"common peace"*   A much used phrase in the fourth century B.C.; the ideal was honored more in the breach than in the observance.

56 *"I swear by Zeus"*   IG II² 236.

57 *All the oath-givers*   An analogy suggests itself with NATO, with the United States as *hegemon*.

57 *"if anyone revolts"*   Merritt, pp. 355–59.

58 *right to convene a Panhellenic army*   The text of the full treaty has not survived and we do not know exactly what such a right might consist in. Perhaps Philip was using his implicit authority rather than relying on a treaty clause.

58 *Isocrates has left helpful clues*   Isoc Phil 5 119ff.

59 *"The bull is wreathed. All is done."*   Diod 16 91 2.

60 *"The Athenians elect ten generals"*   Plut Mor 177c.

60 *Philip . . . fell in love*   Plut Alex 9 3–6, mainly, for the quarrel and reconciliation.

60 *"Now, for sure"*   Ath 13 557d–e.

60 *"Cretin, do you take me"*   Plut Alex 9 8.

61 *stayed with King Langarus*   For this sensible suggestion, see Green, p. 90.

61 *"Alexander is not my son"*   Just 11 11 3–5. This is the only source for this event and should be treated with caution. If the account is true, the episode must have taken place after mother and son's departure from Pella.

62 *Alexander as their king*   Plut Alex 9 3.

62 *plotting his overthrow*   Green, p. 90f.

63 *"These men flung away national prosperity"*   Dem 18 295.

63 *"Good for you to ask"*   For the intervention of Demaratus, Plut Alex 9 and Plut Mor 179c 5.

63 *the mother of the bride*   It is often assumed that Olympias remained in Epirus, but it seems more likely that she too was present at Aegae. If Philip wanted to present the image of a happy and united family, it would have been odd for her to have been absent.

64 *A handsome Royal Page*   For Pausanias's story, Diod 16 93–4 and Just 9 6–7.

65 *in touch with Pixodarus*   Plut Alex 10 1–5, the only source for this incident. Some commentators doubt the story on grounds of inherent improbability, but there is no reason to do so. Human beings must be allowed to behave foolishly and erratically.

65 *"reproached him for behaving"*   Ibid., 10 3.

66 *group of youthful followers*   Arrian 3 6 5.

66 *rumored to have been sired*   Paus 1 6 2.

66 *Harpalus, probably the nephew of*   Phila Ath 13 557c.

66 *a remarkable young woman*   Poly 8 60.

66 *wedding of the king*   Diod 16 4–5.

66 *the kingdom's old capital, Aegae*   See the Greek Ministry of Culture website http://odysseus.culture.gr/h/3/eh3540.jsp?obj_id=2362.

67 *popular Athenian actor*   Plut Mor 844f.

67 *"matchless in the power of his voice"*   Diod 16 92 3.

67 *"Your thoughts reach higher"*   Ibid.

68 *"worked with great artistry"*   Ibid., 92 5.

69 *an uneasy frame of mind*   Just 11 1.

69 *wearing a breastplate*   Stoneman, p. 57.

69 *"established his authority"*   Diod 17 2 2.

70 *plotting with the Athenians*   Diod 17 5 1, for the end of Attalus.

70 *sent a* hetairos, *or Companion*   Diod 17 2 4–5.

70 *"Greece was still gasping"*   Plut Mor 327c.

71 *a two-room tomb at Aegae*   This tomb, along with two others, was uncovered in 1977 and 1978. It contained the remains of a middle-aged male. After years of controversy, these have been firmly identified as those of Philip. This is because knee ankylosis and a hole through the knee tie perfectly with the penetrating wound and lameness known to have been suffered by Philip II. The tomb also contained, in the second chamber, the remains of a young woman about eighteen years of age and of an infant; these are very probably those of Philip's last wife, Cleopatra, and her infant daughter, Europa. We do not know whether the tomb was already built when Philip died. If not, then some time would have had to elapse before its occupants were housed.

71 *Cicero's famous test, Cui bono?*   Cic Rosc 84.

72 *"The father, bride, and bridegroom"*   Eur Med 288.

72 *the getaway horses*   Just 9 7, for Olympias's activities after the assassination.

72 *Philip's widow*   Paus 8 7 7.

73 *valued eunuchs highly*   Herod 8 105.

73 *"when at meals"*   Xen Cyr 7 5 59–60.

73 *"A eunuch in physical fact"*   Diod 17 5 3, for the Bagoas story.

74 *Darius once accepted a challenge*   Diod 17 6 1.

74 *tried to suborn Greek soldiers*   Curt 4 10 16.

74 *He seems to have heard of the assassination*   Renault, pp. 64–65.

74 *"overwhelmed by Persian gold"*   Plut Dem 14 2

74 *gave himself "prodigious airs"*   Aesch Ctes 160, and for Demosthenes' general reaction to Philip's death.

75 *he was past his best*   Hammond 1979, p. 691f.

CHAPTER 4. THE LONE WOLF

76 *Alexander's advisers urged caution*   Plut Alex 11 2.

77 *"immediately offered up sacrifices"*   Plut Dem 21 1–2.

77 *"keep watch over the omens"*   Aesch Ctes 160.

77 *"they had been only a little premature"*   Diod 17 4 3.

77 *Demosthenes was appointed*   Ibid., 17 4 7–8. Plut Dem 23 3.

78 *tiny city-state of Megara*   Plut Mor 826c–d.

78 *"I swear by Zeus"*   Tod 177.

78 *to meet Diogenes*   see Diog Lae 6, *passim,* for Diogenes.

78 *"Humans have complicated"*   Diog Lae 6 44.

79 *"a Socrates gone mad"*   Ibid., 6 54.

79 *extremely independent-minded*   Plut Alex 14 1–5 for the famous encounter between Diogenes and Alexander. Also Diog Lae 6.78 and 32.

79 *stubborn, implacable and self-absorbed*   I am indebted to Peter Green for this
insight. Green, p. 123.

79 *revolts in the north*   Arrian 1 4–6 11 for the Danube campaign.

79 *he called by at Delphi*   Plut Alex 14 5–7. The historicity of the encounter
with the Pythia is sometimes doubted, but this view rests on connoisseurship
rather than evidence.

80 *fifteen thousand highly trained Macedonians*   Bosworth 1988 p29.

83 *the ancient Greek word* pothos   Ibid., 1 3 5. Also 2 3 1, 3 1 5, and 7 2 2.

84 *"It is only between those who are good"*   Ar Nic Eth 8 3 6.

85 *"When he heard that Alexander wanted to know"*   Arrian 1 5 3.

86 *The fortified settlement of Pelium*   Ibid., 1 5 8–12, 6 1–8 for the episode. Also
Fuller, pp. 223–26, and Hammond (1988), pp. 39–48. I follow Hammond's interpretation and his identification of the battlefield.

87 *"He commanded total silence"*   Arrian 1 6 1–2.

88 *baggage train followed*   The sources do not make this explicitly clear, but it
must be inferred by the reference to catapults.

88 *"Alexander let them get close"*   Arrian 1 6 7–8.

90 *He always sent scouts out ahead*   Ibid., 1 12 7.

91 *"the feelings of all the cities"*   Just 11 2 9.

91 *"making play with the fine old words"*   Arrian 1 7 2.

91 *To abrogate unilaterally*   See Hammond (1988), pp. 62–64, for the consequences of abrogation.

92 *"Demosthenes called me a boy"*   Plut Alex 11 3.

92 *Cleopatra, and her little girl*   Just 9 7 12. Some argue that Cleopatra also had a
son, Caranus, but he is probably a fiction.

92 *As usual she overdid things*   Paus 8 7 7.

93 *furious with her*   Plut Alex 10 4.

93 *a place where male lovers worshipped*   Plut Erot 761d.

94 *The citadel was close*   For the capture of Thebes there are two versions, one
by Diod 17 9 1–6 and the other by Arrian 1 8 1–8. The former is a rhetorical
cocktail and the latter is to be preferred, although it makes sense that Alexander and P. agreed a plan of attack as Diodorus reports. The origin of the story
of P.'s premature assault is attributed to his personal enemy, Ptolemy. But this

is more likely to have been a disobliging report of something that happened than an invention. See Hammond (1980), pp. 60–63 (but also see Green, p. 529, n. 52).

95 *"There followed a furious slaughter"*   Arrian 1 8 8.
96 *That universal moralist, Isocrates*   Isoc Plat, *passim*.
96 *Theban musician Ismenias*   Alex Rom 1 27.
97 *"Creatures for a day!"*   Pind Pyth 8.
97 *house was left untouched*   Arrian 1 9 10.
97 *Some wolves were trying to surprise*   Aes 217.
98 *"Wolves tend to be man-eaters"*   Ar Anim 594 a–b.
98 *"may have trusted in his personal relationship"*   Plut Dem 23 6.

CHAPTER 5. FIRST BLOOD

For the visit to Troy, Plutarch (*Life of Alexander*) and Arrian are the main sources. The Battle of the Granicus is described in Plutarch 16, Arrian 1 13–16, and Diodorus 17 19–22.

99 *"while leaping foremost of the Achaeans"*   Il 2 702.
100 *"From the gods I accept Asia"*   Diod 17 17 2.
100 *"small and cheap"*   Strabo 13 1 25–26.
100 *"I don't care a jot for that lyre"*   Plut Alex 15 9.
100 *as great a poet as Homer*   Cic Arch 10 24.
101 *He assembled his expeditionary force*   Diod 17 16 3.
101 *a vast marquee*   Hammond (1980).
101 *"everything else suitable"*   Diod 17 16.
102 *a large number of men*   See Hammond (1980), pp. 67–68, Green, p.158, and Bosworth, pp. 35–38. Ancient historians were unhelpful with numbers. Either they did not have access to accurate data or they inflated them to make a powerful impression. Those proposed here are best estimates.
102 *Parmenion's advance force*   Poly 5 44 4. It is not altogether clear that the size of the advance force is to be added to that of the invasion army to reach a grand total. But the implication in the ancient sources is that it should and I agree.
103 *"You should spare your own property"*   Just 11 6.
103 *special interest in animals*   Bodson, pp. 136–38.
103 *When he saw peacocks*   Ael 15 21.
104 *"he gave orders to some thousands"*   Pliny 8 44.
104 *What was it like to be a soldier*   This section is indebted to Engels and Connolly (1977) and (1998).
106 *"though the pointed barbs"*   Il 4 213–19.
106 *A skeleton dating from about 300 B.C.*   Jackson, p. 68. The medical discussion in these paragraphs is indebted to Jackson, *passim*. Much of the information about ancient medicine dates from the first century A.D. or later, but we may suppose that much is relevant to Alexander's day.

107 *one modern estimate*   Ibid., p. 68.

107 *"confided to him"*   Plut Alex 3 3.

107 *Both Antipater at home and Parmenion*   Diod 17 16 2.

108 *"It would be a disgrace"*   Ibid.

108 *One of his daughters . . . was called Barsine*   For more on Barsine and her date of birth, see Barsine entry at Heckel (2009).

109 *the Persians mustered an estimated force*   The ancient sources disagree on the numbers. I offer a likely estimate.

110 *"Instead, they should march on"*   Arrian 1 12 9.

111 *"My inheritance from my father"*   Ibid., 7 9 6. Ancient historians often put into speeches sentiments appropriate to the occasion rather than what was actually said. However, a similar factual point is also made in Curt 10 2 24. Arrian's account is plausible.

111 *"When he had shared out or given away"*   Plut Alex 15 2–3.

112 *If one reads between the lines*   Green, 155–56.

112 *His omnipresent scouts warned*   Two main accounts of the Battle of the Granicus survive. That by Diodorus (17 17–21) can safely be ignored, for it is a rhetorical confection. He argues that Alexander did not fight the day he arrived on the scene, but crossed the river the following dawn, after which a conventional pitched battle took place. Except for the odd detail, he is best ignored. Arrian (1 13–16) is more objective, but leaves gaps. He has the battle take place without delay, but is not interested in its development as a whole; so we are told about activity on the right wing, where Alexander was in charge, but hear nothing of the Macedonian left, under Parmenion's command. Reference is made to the Macedonian right shifting to the right in Polyaenus (4 3 16), but without clear explanation. My reconstruction supposes that 1. The Persians were not in line of battle and did not have time to insert the Greek infantry into it. For this I have no evidence, except for want of a convincing alternative; 2. The consequence if not the purpose of the shift to the right was to thin the Persian line to assist Alexander's attack and for the Agrianians et al. to strike at the enemy flank. This is guesswork but is based on probabilistic fundamentals, even if they are not mentioned in the inadequate ancient sources. Much of my narrative is indebted to Badian, pp. 224–36.

112 *When the Granicus came into view*   The river today looks much as it did in Alexander's time and, to judge by an old Roman bridge nearby, has not significantly altered its course. There is a great deal of vegetation, which cannot have been present when the battle was fought and may be a result of modern irrigation.

114 *a habit of rejecting his advice*   For one example from many, see Green, p. 175.

114 *"It seems to me, sir"*   Arrian 1 13 3–5. There is no good reason for rejecting this story, as some have done who blame a later but purely putative campaign to ruin Parmenion's reputation.

115 *The center was occupied*   The composition of this assault force is somewhat

unclear. It may also have included an infantry company led by Ptolemy, son of Philip.

116 *was carrying the antique shield*   Diod 17 21 2.

116 *two blows on his breastplate*   Diod 17 21 2.

116 *"A fierce fight developed"*   Arrian 1 15 4.

117 *disheartened—albeit till now disengaged—enemy*   The sources tell us next to nothing of what Parmenion and his left wing did during the battle. I assume that they waited until the outcome of the special assault force's attack and then Alexander's charge became clear, and that the Persian cavalry opposite them did nothing. They then charged across the river. If anything outstanding occurred on the left, I assume we would have been told.

118 *"It was here that most"*   Plut Alex 16 7.

118 *"showed great care for the wounded"*   Arrian 1 16 5.

119 *"Alexander the son of Philip"*   Ibid., 1 16 7.

120 *no one rises so high*   Oliver Cromwell to Pomponne de Bellievre, as told to Cardinal de Retz in 1651. *Memoirs of Cardinal de Retz* (London and New York: Merrill and Baker, 1717?), p. 264.

CHAPTER 6. UNDOING THE KNOT

The major sources are Arrian and the sometimes unreliable Diodorus, with a slight contribution from Justin. Fuller offers convincing accounts of the sieges.

121 *Once upon a time in Phrygia*   The section on the Gordian knot derives from Arrian 2 3 1–8, Curtius 3 1 14–18, Plutarch *Life of Alexander* 18 1–2 and Justin 11 7 3–16. There are other versions of the rise of Midas; I have mainly followed Arrian.

122 *"It's undone now"*   Arrian 2 3 7. According to another version, he simply pulled out a bolt or pole pin, which released the pole.

123 *"in a position of honor"*   Ibid., 1 17 4.

124 *"prevented any further inquisitions"*   Ibid., 1 17 12.

124 *Strabo . . . recounts that the king*   Strabo 14 1 22–3.

124 *the famous artist Apelles*   For Apelles generally, Pliny NH 35 79–97, 7 125, and Ael VH 2 3. Although we have many descriptions of ancient Greek panel paintings, not a single one has survived the upheavals at the end of the Roman empire. However, some wall paintings have been discovered—for example, in the Macedonian royal tombs at Vergina.

124 *"sold for the price of a whole town"*   Pliny NH 35 50.

125 *One fine morning*   For the best-known account of the fall of Troy, see Virg, *Aen,* book 2. This section on siegecraft is much indebted to Connolly (1977), pp. 50, 64–69.

125 *great part of Miletus*   For the siege of Miletus, see Arrian 118 3–119 11.

125 *giant wooden horse*   It has been suggested that the wooden horse was really a

battering ram. The battering ram seems to have been invented by the Assyrians, but apparently was not used by the Greeks until the fifth century B.C.—see Connolly (1981), p. 276.

126 *"There is no citadel"*   Cic Att 16 (1 16) 12.

126 *impregnable from land*   Connolly (1981)., p. 289.

126 *a Thessalian called Diades*   Vit 7 Intros, 14, 10 13 3–8.

128 *one eternal substance*   Ar Meta 983 b6 8–11, 17–21.

128 *Aristotle regarded him as the first philosopher*   Ar Meta 983b18.

128 *"Go back at once inside the city"*   Ibid., 1 19 2.

129 *The Rhodian general*   Diod 17 22 1.

129 *"Where were the men with bodies like these"*   Plut Mor 180a.

130 *defeat the Persian navy from dry land*   Arrian 1 20 1.

130 *it stood on a barren peninsula*   For the siege of Halicarnassus, see Arrian 1 20 2–23 6 and Dio 17 23 4–27. For the Bodrum peninsula, see Engels, pp. 34–35.

130 *members of the same family: Hecatomnus*   For the story of the Hecatomnids, see Hornblower, *passim*.

131 *"It seems that the effeminacy of man"*   Strabo 14 2 16 [656].

131 *swallowed his ashes*   Aul Gell 10 18.

131 *"I do not need your chefs"*   Plut Alex 22 7–10.

132 *promised to be a challenge*   See Fuller, pp. 200–206, for an account of the siege.

133 *"came near to being captured"*   Arrian 1 21 3.

134 *"Alexander did not really know what to do"*   Diod 17 26 7.

135 *all fire-raisers to be put to death*   Diodorus 17 27 6 and Arrian 1 23 6 both report that that Alexander razed Halicarnassus to the ground. This is extremely unlikely, if he had ordered that the citizens should be well treated and that arsonists were to be executed. Perhaps the king destroyed some houses as firebreaks or to make space for siege equipment around one of the citadels occupied by the enemy (the other was an island).

135 *"News of the general's activity"*   Diod 17 29 3.

136 *five hundred talents for their costs*   Curt 3 1 20.

137 *"to some revolutionary purpose"*   Arrian 1 25 5.

140 *"You have no time for Philip's men"*   Curt 8 1 36. This was Cleitus, speaking in 328 at the drunken symposium he did not survive, in Curtius's plausible words.

140 *the advice of Isocrates*   Isoc 5 119–26.

140 *Chaeronea, fatal to liberty*   See John Milton, "To the Lady Margaret Ley," sl. 7.

140 *His tactics were as clear-cut as his strategy*   Marsden, pp. 4–5.

CHAPTER 7. THE EMPIRE STRIKES BACK

Arrian 2 1–13 predominates, with anecdotes by Plutarch and backup from Diodorus 17 29–39. Quintus Curtius 3 1–12 at last comes into play. The reconstruction of Issus is indebted to Fuller and to Hammond (1980). Polybius's attack on Callisthenes adds useful details.

142 *no mean city*   This famous phrase was spoken by St. Paul, Acts 21:39.

142 *"attack of cramp, violent fever"*   Arrian 2 4 7ff, Curt 3 5 1–15, 6 1–20, Diod 17 31 5–6, and Plut Alex 19 1–10. It was said that the river water into which the king dived was pure, cold, and crystalline. Modern evidence suggests that it was warm, brown, and sluggish.

142 *What was the matter with him?*   For this account of the cause of Alexander's illness, I depend on Engels (July 1978). Scholars disagree; Green (p. 220), for example, posits a bronchial event which the river dip translated rapidly into pneumonia. But local conditions and the recorded symptoms point to malaria.

143 *Cilicia would be a dangerous place*   Bosworth, p. 57.

144 *"Either to send generals"*   Diod 17 30 1–2. The account of Darius's two Council meetings is to be found in Diod 17 30 and Curt 3 8. The historicity of these episodes is uncertain, but the issues raised were real enough.

145 *It was perhaps 100,000 men*   The ancient sources differ on Persian numbers. Arrian (2 8 8) and Plutarch (Alex 18 4) estimate 600,000 Persian soldiers in total, while Diodorus (17 31 2) proposes 500,000, Justin (11 9 1) offers 400,000, and Quintus Curtius (3 9 1–6) 119,000. Modern scholars find these numbers unlikely. It would be very difficult to feed more than 100,000 soldiers in the given location. We will not go far wrong if we guess the total size of Darius's army at Issus to be no larger than 100,000, including 11,000 cavalry, 10,000 Persian Immortals, and 10,000 Greek mercenaries.

146 *"He will come and find you"*   Arrian 2 6 6.

146 *"In fact, he is probably already on his way"*   Plut Alex 20 3.

146 *42,000 and 5,000 horse*   Thus Callisthenes, Polyb 12 19 3.

146 *"If giving advice brings danger of death"*   Curt 3 8 6.

147 *"In [Parmenian's] view, it was imperative"*   Ibid., 3 7 9–10.

147 *"You, stranger, should eat"*   Arrian 2 5 4.

149 *"he then gave orders for the men to be taken around"*   Curt 3 8 15.

150 *eleven and a half miles away*   Poly 12 19 4.

150 *outrageously optimistic talk*   Arrian 2 7 3–9.

151 *a shallow river, the Pinarus*   The location of the Pinarus is uncertain. The two candidates are today's Payas and Deli Chai Rivers. I accept Engels (1978), who has chosen the Payas. He has carefully calculated that the Deli Chai is too far for the Macedonian army to have reached it in time for the battle before sunset.

151 *"wanted the battle to be decided"*   Curt 3 11 1.

153 *stood richly robed*   Ibid., 3 3 15–16.

154 *as late as half past four*   Engels (1978), p. 52.

155 *had placed the Euphrates*   Arrian 2 13 1.

156 *a long casualty list*   Fuller, p. 162.

156 *"I myself happened," he writes*   Plut Mor 341c.

156 *for more than twenty miles*   Diod 17 37 2.

156 *Ptolemy, one of his close friends*   Arrian 2 11 8.

156 *"Let's wash off"*   Plut Alex 20 7.

156 *"he saw that the basins and jugs"*   Ibid., 20 7–8.

157 *When Alexander sat down*   There is nothing against these stories and I regard them as historical; but I have to admit that they are almost too good to be true, illustrating as they do stereotypical Persian "unmanliness" and Alexander's perfect manners. If false, they are consistent with what we judge Macedonian attitudes to be and with Alexander's sexual coolness.

157 *sounds of women wailing . . . "Don't worry"*   Arrian 2 12 4–6; Plut Alex 21 1–7.

157 *The king consecrated three altars*   Ibid., 3 12 27.

157 *cremation of the fallen*   Ibid., 3 12 14.

158 *soldier as well as a general*   Curt 3 11 7.

159 *Amyntas with four other Greek defectors*   Arrian 2 13 2–3.

160 *"put an end to their labors"*   Just 11 9 6.

CHAPTER 8. IMMORTAL LONGINGS

Arrian 2 16–24 and Curtius 4 2–4 guide us through the siege of Tyre, with an anecdote from Plutarch, Alexander 24. Fuller (pp. 206–18) is helpful. For Alexander's visit to Siwah, Arrian 3 3 and 4, Curtius 4 7, Diodorus 17 48 2 to 51, and Justin 11 11.

161 *gusts of snow*   See Curt 3 13 for the collection of Darius's treasure.

162 *"From now onwards, like dogs"*   Plut Alex 24 3.

162 *oversight of lowland Syria*   Our sources do not make it clear exactly what Parmenion's responsibilities were.

163 *first woman he had sex with*   Ibid., 21 4.

163 *"of a gentle disposition"*   Ibid., 21 7.

164 *"These Persian women"*   Ibid., 21 10.

164 *"irritated their eyes"*   Herod 5 18.

164 *as little attention as if they were stone statues*   Plut Alex 21 11.

164 *strongly objected to the sexual trafficking*   For the three following anecdotes, see Plut Alex 22 1–4.

165 *"monarch to monarch"*   Arrian 2 14 3. Arrian's version of these letters may have been composed by the author, as the records of speeches are in ancient histories. They express what the author felt would have been appropriate, what should have been said. Books of Alexander's correspondence were published in antiquity, many of which are works of fiction and all of which are in any case lost. But Alexander's reply to Darius, intelligent, dry, impatient, and direct, leaves a powerful impression of authenticity, and I accept it as such.

165 *"I would accept those terms"*   Plut Alex 29 4. This famous exchange between Alexander and Parmenion may have been made in response to Darius's third

overture for peace, just before the Battle of Gaugamela (Diod 17 54 and Curt 4 10 18–34). It seems unlikely that the general would have objected at this very late stage, so I go with Arrian.

166 *"It is for you, then"*   Arrian 2 14 8–9.

166 *The man, dressed in rags*   Diod 17 47 1–6, Curt 4 1 16–26, Plut Mor 340d, Justin 11 10 7–9. There is no need to reject this magical tale, but it may well conceal a conventional bout of civil strife with a democrat taking over from an aristocratic or oligarchic ruler. The details are lost forever.

167 *perfume made from henna*   Poll 6 105.

168 *two and three quarter miles*   Pliny 5 17 76.

168 *Herodotus paid a visit*   Herod 2 44.

168 *"You say, Tyre, 'I am perfect in beauty.'"*   Ibid., 27:3–7.

169 *income in kind included*   Ezek 27, passim.

169 *"Your end will be sudden"*   Ibid., 27:36.

169 *preferred alliance to capitulation*   Curt 4 2 2.

169 *"pay his dues to Heracles"*   Just 11 10 10.

170 *"I will either enter your city"*   Ibid., 4 2 5.

170 *"Because they were doing Darius a good turn"*   Diod 17 40 3.

171 *"When we have conquered Egypt"*   Arrian 2 17 4.

172 *"famous fighters loaded down"*   Curt 4 2 20.

172 *women, children, and men*   Just 11 10 14; Diod 17 40 1.

173 *a ten-day campaign*   Plut Alex 24 6–8.

173 *protect his supply lines*   Engels pp. 55–57.

173 *"Trusting to his speed and agility"*   Plut Alex 24 12–13.

173 *"Laid about him with his sword"*   Il 10 483–484.

176 *"Under fire from all directions"*   Arrian 2 23 3.

176 *"The Macedonians stopped at nothing"*   Ibid., 2 24 3–4.

176 *Sidonian sailors saved many defenders*   Curt 4 4 15.

177 *Two thousand men of military age*   Diod 17 46 4.

177 *hit by a catapult bolt*   For this episode, see Arrian 2 27 1–2 and Curt 4 6 17–30.

178 *For a long time he remained*   Curt 4 6 19–20.

178 *a corpulent black eunuch*   FGrH 142 FS.

178 *the most testing of sieges*   The accounts of Arrian and Curtius do not fully agree, and Alexander's successful building of a mound could hardly have been achieved within the two-month duration of the siege. My reconstruction is as plausible as I can make it.

179 *a carrion bird dropped*   Arrian 2 26 4, Curt 4 6 10–13.

180 *October was a bad month*   For the description of the march to Pelusium, see Engels, p. 50.

181 *recognized as pharaoh*   Alex Rom 34.

182 *Setep en Ra, mery Amun*   Karnak F 377 (room **XXIX**) Beckerath, *Handbuch der ägyptischen Königsnamen* (1999), pp. 232–33.

182 *"The Lion, Great of Might"*   Pedestal from the temple of Alexander at the Bahariya Oasis. See Bosch-Puche, *The Egyptian Royal Titulary of Alexander*, JEA, 99, 138–39.

182 *"to treat the Greeks"*   Plut Mor 329b.

184 *"wanted to catch up with [Alexander]"*   Curt 4 8 7–8. Aristobulus has Alexander return from Siwah the way he came, whereas Ptolemy has him cross the desert for a second visit to Memphis (Arrian 3 4 5). The former version is preferable (see Engels, pp. 62–63), but Alexander may have made a return visit to Memphis after founding Alexandria. Hector could have died either on the journey north before the Siwah adventure, or after it, as Curtius has it.

184 *"an island in the rolling seas"*   Od 4 354–59.

185 *"she had conceived Alexander"*   Just 11 11 2–4.

186 *"an overwhelming desire"*   Curt 4 7 8.

186 *A severe wind storm blew up*   For the journey to Siwah, Engels, pp. 62–63.

187 *move involuntarily where it willed*   Rather like table-turning or the Ouija planchette.

187 *path to the shrine*   The temple's ruins still exist. They were excavated by Ahmad Fakhry in the mid-twentieth century; see his *Siwa Oasis* (Cairo: American University in Cairo Press, 1990).

187 *"[Zeus] is by nature the father of us all"*   Plut Mor 180d.

188 *"Once there [in Siwah]"*   Arrian 3 4 5.

188 *Parmenion's son Philotas wrote*   Curt 6 10 26–27.

188 *"We have lost Alexander"*   Ibid., 6 11 24.

189 *"He was seized with a passion"*   Arrian 3 1 5.

CHAPTER 9. AT THE HOUSE OF THE CAMEL

The chief sources for the Battle of Gaugamela are Arrian 3 1–15 and Curtius, with modern support from Marsden's brilliant monograph and Fuller (pp. 163–80). Plutarch *Life of Alexander* 31–34 contributes color. Some of the evidence is confused or wrong, but it is possible to put together a plausible and verisimilar narrative. We do not know exactly what happened, but enough to say what could have happened.

192 *Camel's House*   Plut Alex 31 6.

192 *September 30, 331 B.C.*   Or September 29, if those scholars are correct who argue that the battle was fought on September 30 rather than October 1, as usually believed.

192 *"agleam with the watch-fires"*   Plut Alex 31 10.

193 *"I will not steal my victory"*   Ibid., 31 12.

193 *worrying about his tactics*   Curtius and Arrian do not say so explicitly, but Alexander came near to losing his nerve. I assume that only when he had determined his remarkable battle plan did he stop worrying.

193 *grandest so far of his arts festivals*   For this arts festival, see Plut Alex 29.

195 *"If I conquer Laconia"*   Plut Mor 511a.

196 *"a certain degree of immunity"*   For this episode, see Jacoby FGrH 135 F2 and Aesch Ctes 162.

196 *was on a confidential mission*   Green, p. 281.

197 *logistical planning*   For Alexander's march from Tyre to Gaugamela, see Engels, pp. 64–70.

197 *an estimated five days*   Ibid., p. 66.

197 *the Tigris in September*   Arrian 3 7 5 and Curtius 4 9 18–21 wrongly describe a deep and fast current.

198 *nearly total lunar eclipse*   The fact and date of the eclipse have been computed in modern times and by the Babylonians (see, for example, Bert van der Spek, "Darius III, Alexander the Great and Babylonian Scholarship," *Achaemenid History,* vol. 13 (2003), pp. 289–346).

198 *"Sunset to moonrise"*   2 9th ahû tablet of Enûma Anu Enlil; obv. 59–61.

199 *"for eight years he will exercise kingship"*   Ibid. An inexplicably accurate prophecy, as we shall see later.

200 *death of Darius's wife, Stateira*   Curt 4 10 18–34.

200 *the unlikely story*   Plut Alex 30 1.

200 *the traditional Persian manner*   It is not certain what this might be. According to Zoroastrian practice, dead bodies were pollutants and should not be buried in the ground. They were exposed on high towers where they decomposed and were eaten by birds. Their bones were then collected and kept. Achaemenid kings were buried in rock tombs; the founder of the dynasty, Cyrus the Great, was laid in a small stone mausoleum.

200 *a third peace initiative*   Diodorus 17 54 1–6 and Curtius 4 11 place this before they mention Stateira's death, but Justin 11 12 7–16 makes it follow after. As a late source, he is not usually to be preferred, but this is an exception. The initiative is too close to the battle to be credible. It was so generous in its offer that it is more psychologically plausible to regard it as a consequence of the Great King's emotion at bereavement and his gratitude to Alexander for his respectful behavior. However, the point is a fine one. See Green, p. 287.

200 *The Great King agreed*   The deal Darius proposed recalls the Treaty of Troyes, under which the victorious Henry V of England married the French king's daughter and became his heir.

201 *how two suns could occupy*   Diod 17 54 5.

203 *about 44,000 infantry*   I have taken my Macedonian numbers from Marsden (*passim*). Other modern scholars offer similar estimates.

205 *wearing his armor*   Plut Alex 32 8–11.

205 *quite a sight on the battlefield*   Alexander's carelessness of his safety prefigures that of Nelson wearing all his decorations at the Battle of Trafalgar.

206 *if he really was the son of Zeus*   Plut Alex 33 1.

207 *backed by the veteran mercenaries*   Some modern opinion supposes that they were on horseback. This is a mistake.

207 *"If he has got some infantry"*   Xen Hip 5 13, 8 19.

207 *force of a hundred chariots*   We are not told what happened to the other chariots, but presumably they met the same fate as those facing the Companions.

208 *"The cavalry sent out to engage"*   Arrian 3 14 2.

209 *Mazaeus on the right*   Diod 17 59 5. The literary sources describe two separate incidents—an outflanking gallop to the Macedonian camp to retrieve the imperial women, and the Persian and Indian cavalry pouring through a gap in the phalanx to the baggage deposit area. There is some confusion of identity, but no good reason for conflating them, as some suppose.

209 *no difficulty breaking in*   Ibid., 59 7; Curt 4 15 10–11.

209 *"retained her former demeanor"*   Curt 4 15 11.

209 *Persian and Indian cavalry*   Fuller, p. 176.

209 *"The commanders of the infantry reserve"*   Arrian 3 14 6.

210 *Parmenion sent off a dispatch rider*   I follow Marsden, pp. 61–62.

211 *"what ensued"*   Arrian 3 15 2.

211 *Implausibly high estimates*   Arrian 3 15 6.

211 *best guess for Macedonian losses*   Oxy XV 1798.

212 *"Once the battle"*   Plut Alex 24 1.

CHAPTER 10. "PASSING BRAVE TO BE A KING"

214 *"Passing brave"*   Christopher Marlowe, *Tamburlaine the Great, Part,* Act 2, sc. 5: "Is it not passing brave to be a King, / And ride in triumph through Persepolis?"

214 *"Alexander was proclaimed"*   Plut Alex 34 1.

215 *The enemy corpses on the battlefield*   Curt 5 1 11.

215 *the high walls of Babylon*   See Curt 5 1 17–23 for the arrival in Babylon.

217 *Xerxes is reported*   Arr 3 16 4. But Herodotus in the fifth century, after Xerxes, saw it intact (1 181–82).

217 *sent Aristotle a list*   Ar Cael 2 12.

218 *"The moral corruption there"*   Curt 5 1 36–38. It is difficult to sort out fact from fiction in Curtius's and Herodotus's accounts. But there is no evidence to rebut them.

219 *"There is a great multitude of women"*   Herod 1 198 2–4.

219 *advance information on roads*   See Engels, pp. 71–72 for the change in Alexander's supply situation.

220 *joined by Amyntas*   Curt 5 1 40, Arrian 3 16 10.

221 *potentially very bad news*   I follow the drift of Badian, pp. 153–73.

221 *"Alexander had withdrawn"*   Aesch Ctes 165.

222 *battle outside Megalopolis*   Diod 17 62 1–4, Curt 6 1–21.

222 *"gave orders that he be put down"*   Curt 6 1 13.

222 *"It would seem, my men"*   Plut Age 15 4.

223 *An inscription . . . reveals*   GHI, pp. 36–37.

224 *sex with a good-looking man*   Plut Mor 818b–c.

224 *"by a flame's radiance"*   Plut Alex 35 2; for the petroleum incident, see the entire chapter.

225 *"Susa, the great holy city"*   Persians: Masters of Empire (Lost Civilizations), ed. Brown, Dale, Time Life (UK); Fairfax, Virginia, and New York, 1996, pp. 7–8.

225 *the staggering sum*   Diod 17 66 1.

225 *"fabulous royal palace"*   Ibid., 17 65 5.

225 *a daily bill of fare*   Poly 4 3.

226 *a golden vine*   Ath 12 514 6f.

226 *objets d'art together weighing*   Diod 19 48 6.

226 *seated himself*   Diod 17 66 3–6.

226 *"Don't do that, Sir"*   Curt 5 2.

226 *Demaratus, the aged fixer*   Plut Mor 329d.

226 *A cloud briefly spoiled*   Curt 5 2 12.

226 *teach them the Greek language*   Diod 17 67 1.

227 *the journey to Persepolis*   Arrian 3 18 1–9, Curt 5 31-3-4, and Diod 17 67–68. But their accounts differ somewhat and it is wisest to follow Arrian.

227 *"sparse and rugged"*   Herod 9 122.

228 *"pay them what was owing"*   Arrian 3 17 2.

229 *some prisoners of war*   Or perhaps a local shepherd (suspiciously echoing, however, the one who showed Xerxes how to turn the Greek position at Thermopylae), Diod 17 68 5 and Plut Alex 37 1.

230 *Persepolis . . . was invented*   Loose modern analogies can be drawn with Brasilia, Islamabad, and the shiny new capital of Burma.

231 *"I am Xerxes, the great king"*   XPf ("Harem Inscription"), Achaemenid Royal Inscriptions. See https://www.livius.org/sources/content/achaemenid-royal -inscriptions/xpf/

231 *"He stopped and spoke to it"*   Plut Alex 37 5.

232 *"because he thought that would help"*   Ibid., 37 3.

232 *"giddy with wine"*   Ibid.

232 *let them stage a komos*   Diod 17 b72 1.

233 *restated the obsolete war aim*   Curt 5 6 1.

233 *"a tour of conquest"*   Arrian 3 18 11.

234 *Darius's personal authority*   For this paragraph, see Briant, p. 865.

234 *to have had second thoughts*   Plut Alex 38, Curt 5 7 11.

CHAPTER 11. TREASON!

Arrian and Curtius, with a little aid from Plutarch, dominate as usual. Curtius's account of the betrayal and death of Darius is politically and psychologically convincing.

236 *Curtius, always well-informed*   Engels, *passim,* quotes from modern (nineteenth and early twentieth centuries) sources that confirm Curtius's descriptions, even if they tend to the overrhetorical. Engels writes: "It is difficult not

to be impressed by Curtius's remarkable geographical knowledge of Alexander's route" (p. 84).

236 *"jumped from his horse"*   Curt 5 6 14.

236 *catch up on his correspondence*   Collections of Alexander's letters were published after his death, as already noted. Unfortunately, fictional anthologies also appeared. We have to trust the good judgment of the ancient writers—especially Plutarch and Arrian. Almost no complete and genuine letters have survived and we must make do with excerpts.

236 *It is astonishing that*   Plut Alex 421.

237 *"the people should decide"*   GHI 17 136.

238 *urged her son to buy a slave of hers*   Ath 14 359f.

238 *"Stop quarrelling with us"*   Diod 17 114 3.

238 *"so much as to tell him"*   Plut Alex 39 5. For the epistolary anecdotes in this section, see Ibid., 41–42.

240 *"We shall follow our king into battle"*   Curt 5 9 1. So Curtius has it, perhaps fictionally. The sentiments are correct.

240 *"They reasoned that if Alexander"*   Ibid., 5 9 2.

240 *"Temporarily transfer your authority"*   Ibid., 5 9 4.

243 *"Its walls are of great size and strength"*   Herod 1 98–99.

244 *"Alexander was by nature"*   Plut Alex 39 1.

245 *"I wish you would find other ways"*   Ibid., 39 7.

245 *He was brave, hardworking, and true*   For Leonnatus's expensive tastes, see ibid., 40 1, and Arrian Succ 12.

245 *"How can a man look after his horse"*   Plut Alex 40 3.

245 *"[the king's] friends"*   Ibid., 41 1.

246 *an ancient highway*   In a later age it became part of the Silk Road.

247 *"inclined Alexander to trust him"*   Arrian 3 20 7.

248 *"they had no one else to follow"*   Curt 5 12 19.

249 *"Through you, I give him my hand"*   Plut Alex 43 4. Plutarch gives Darius a parting speech, which we can safely ignore, but the narrative of the king's last days, the guilt-ridden conspirators and the hectic Alexander have the untidiness of truth. Diodorus 17 73 unconvincingly has the two kings meet and talk.

249 *Darius has been portrayed*   This assessment of Darius is indebted to Badian, pp. 457ff.

249 *"a consummate coward"*   Arrian 3 22 2.

252 *"Hephaestion who approved"*   Plut Alex 47 9–11 and Plut Mor 181D.

252 *"The soldiers scattered to their tents"*   Ibid., 6 2 15–16. Arrian does not mention this episode, but his favorite sources tend to ignore or downplay opposition to Alexander.

253 *A general assembly was called*   Ibid., 6 3. As is usual among ancient historians, Alexander's speech probably set out what he should or would have said, rather than what he did say. But Curtius's confection, assisted by Plutarch, is plausible.

253 *"The moment our backs are turned"*   Curt 6 3 9.

253 *"as if they were so many women"*   Plut Alex 47 1.

253 *In a dispatch to Antipater*   Ibid., 47 3.

253 *regularly providing lavish feasts*   Just 12 3 11–4 6.

254 *"Maintenance was provided for the boys"*   Ibid., 12 4 10.

254 *Dimnus was infatuated*   The main sources for the Philotas affair are Curt 6 7–11, Arrian 3 26–27, and Plut Alex 48–49.

254 *A member of the Companion cavalry*   Diod 17 79 1.

255 *Cebalinus, upset and anxious*   According to Plut Alex 49 4, Cebalinus simply told Philotas about a matter of great importance and did not mention a plot. If so, it is incomprehensible that Philotas failed to insist on further and better particulars if he was to trouble Alexander with the affair.

256 *stabbed himself with a sword*   Plutarch has Dimnus killed when resisting arrest—Plut Alex 49 7.

256 *"a quarrel between a male prostitute"*   Curt 6 7 33.

256 *"also displayed an arrogance"*   Ibid., 48 3.

257 *Olympias, no slouch*   Curt 7 1 11.

257 *"Son, don't make"*   Plut Alex 48 4.

257 *Sailing to Samothrace for the Mysteries*   Plut Mor 339e–f.

257 *He tended to discount carping*   Curt 7 1 12.

258 *"The enemies we are about to pursue"*   Curt 6 8 9.

258 *a direct lie*   For example, Badian, pp. 427–30.

259 *"Unfortunately for me"*   Curt 6 10 16.

260 *some say he listened in*   Plut Alex 49 11.

260 *"Why hurt me?"*   Curt 6 11 14.

260 *"fire and beatings"*   Ibid. 6 11 16.

260 *"With Darius still alive, Parmenion"*   Ibid., 6 11 29.

261 *stoned to death*   According to Arrian 3 26 3, they were killed with javelins; but stoning was the traditional penalty.

261 *"it would be too dangerous to let him survive"*   Arrian 3 26 4.

262 *the hapless Alexander of Lyncestis*   Diod 17 80 2; Curt 7 1 5–9.

262 *"Although he had had all of three years"*   Curt 7 1 8.

262 *bring back Polemon*   Arrian 3 27 2–3. For a slightly different version, see Curt 7 2 1–7.

265 *"While we should perhaps give Alexander"*   Polyb 8 10 8–9.

266 *He divided the command*   Arrian 3 27 4.

266 *Letters sent home to family*   Curt 7 2 36–38; Diod 17 80 4.

266 *"If Parmenion plotted"*   Plut Mor 183f.

CHAPTER 12. WAR WITHOUT END

Arrian and Curtius with some Plutarch, as usual. Fuller helps disentangle the years of guerrilla fighting. For Alexander's travels, Engels is essential.

267 *twenty thousand foot and three thousand horse*   Plut Alex 47 1.

267 *it is tropically fertile*   Curtius's description, at 6 4 20–22, is not fantasy and is confirmed by modern observation—see Engels, p. 84.

268 *"in the flower of his youth"*   Curt 6 5 23.

268 *his emasculation*   Chugg, p. 147.

268 *acquired a sinister reputation*   For a friendly account, see Mary Renault's *The Persian Boy* (London: Longmans, 1972).

269 *"a culturally backward race"*   Curt 6 5 11.

269 *eight thousand capable warriors*   Diod 17 76 4.

269 *he would not let anyone*   Curt 6 5 18–21.

269 *sent an interpreter*   Plut Alex 44 4.

269 *Alexander returned to his camp*   It was about now that some ancient writers record the visit to Alexander's camp of the completely fictional queen of the Amazons, Thalestris, together with three hundred women fighters. Plutarch (Alex 46) did not believe the tale, nor do I.

270 *his sight began to fail*   Plut Mor 341b.

271 *on a large flat-topped mountain*   Engels, pp. 87ff, identifies this "Gibraltar" of Persia with Kalat-i-Nadiri.

271 *the novel art of guerrilla*   Unfortunately the ancient sources fail to address this factor directly, and much detail is missing.

271 *swimming in the sea of the people*   Mao Zedong, *On Guerrilla Warfare, Ch. 6: The Political Problems of Guerrilla Warfare.*

271 *Lake Seistan, the land*   See Engels, pp. 91–92.

272 *"The barbarian threw his spear"*   Curt 7 4 36–37.

273 *another garrison town*   Today's Kandahar.

273 *harsh treeless highlands*   Curtius's description is confirmed by modern accounts; see Engels, p. 94.

273 *The numbing cold*   Curt 7 3 13.

273 *Prometheus, one of the old gods*   Diod 17 83 1.

274 *seven thousand local people*   Diod 17 83 2. The garrison town was near Kabul.

274 *"but still they came on and on"*   Arrian 3 28 9.

275 *the cause of Artaxerxes V*   The details in the ancient accounts vary; I favor Arrian 3 29 6-7–3 30 1–5 and 4 7 3–4.

275 *Ptolemy, a Macedonian friend from his teens*   After Alexander's death, Ptolemy went on to become pharaoh of Egypt and to found a dynasty which ended with Cleopatra in the first century B.C.

276 *the royal insignia*   Metz 2.

276 *impalement up the anus*   Metz 14.

276 *"For my part, I cannot approve"*   Arrian 4 7 4.

277 *a small town in Sogdiana*   Curt 7 5 28–35. Some argue that this event never took place. But the broad outline of the story seems convincing enough. See N. G. L. Hammond, "The Branchidae at Didyma and in Sogdiana," *The Clas-*

sical Quarterly, vol. 48, no. 2 (1998), pp. 339–44; and H. W. Parke, "Massacre of the Branchidae," *The Journal of Hellenic Studies,* vol. 105 (1985), pp. 59–68.

278 *"Neither community of language"*   Curt 7 5 33.

280 *"I would rather face"*   Arrian 4 4 3.

281 *the ever-circling enemy horsemen*   Arrian's account is obscure. Fuller, pp. 239ff, has devised a convincing reconstruction.

282 *"grasped the conditions"*   Fuller, p. 241.

282 *Pharnuches formed his troops into a square*   My version follows Arrian 4 5 2–9. Curtius 7 9 10–13 tells a different story about an ambush. The upshot was the same.

283 *19,400 infantry and 2,600 cavalry*   Curt 7 10 12.

284 *"with India subdued"*   Arrian 4 15 6.

284 *"pursued their own line of invasion"*   Ibid., 4 16 3.

285 *"issued orders for the animals"*   Curt 8 1 13–14.

286 *A consignment of Greek fruit*   Plut Alex 50 3. The three main accounts (by Plutarch, *Life of Alexander* 50–52, Arrian 4 8–9ff, and Curtius 8 1 22ff) are broadly similar but differ in detail. They include references to evil dreams, mistaken sacrifices, and angry gods, which read like attempts to blame destiny rather than Alexander for what took place that day. These I ignore and otherwise offer what I hope is a reasonable conflation.

288 *"There is a bad custom which now obtains in Hellas"*   Eur Androm ll. 695ff. See below for the further lines.

289 *"neglected all other bodily needs"*   Arrian 4 9 4.

289 *"lying on the floor weeping"*   Plut Alex 52 5.

290 *"had no notion of moderation"*   Athen 120d–e.

290 *"old, easy relationship"*   Arrian 7 8 3.

291 *These divisions were replicated*   Plut Alex 47 9.

291 *"Alexander had some great natural gifts"*   Curt 5 7 1.

292 *"The impression that he was a heavy drinker"*   Plut Alex 23 1.

293 *a domestic twist*   Curt 8 3 1ff.

293 *"You'll need soldiers with wings"*   Arrian 4 18 5.

293 *large number of rebellious Sogdians*   Curt 7 11 1. Curtius estimates thirty thousand, which seems far too large a number.

294 *"fixing their pegs where they could"*   Arrian 4 19 1–3.

295 *an attractive sixteen-year-old*   Arrian 4 19 5–20 3 and Curtius 8 4 23–30 disagree about the story of Rhoxane. Arrian places the first encounter with Alexander after the siege of the Sogdian Rock. Although he makes the king's behavior to be respectful, he probably chose her as a victors' sex prize. Curtius has the couple meet at a banquet after the siege of the Rock of Chorienes a little later on. I prefer Arrian for plausible detail, but see no reason entirely to reject Curtius's banquet.

295 *Achilles and Briseis in the* Iliad   Curt 8 4 26.

295 *"a banquet of typically barbaric extravagance"* Ibid., 8 4 22.
297 *thirty thousand local boys* Plut Alex 47 5–6, Arrian 7 6 1.

CHAPTER 13. A PASSAGE TO INDIA

298 *"When the Persians meet one another"* Herod 1 134.
299 *An experiment was arranged* Curtius and Arrian write of the banquet described here as well as of a public symposium at which elaborate speeches for and against were delivered. Alexander did not need to be told twice that *proskynesis* was a nonstarter and the symposium was probably invented to allow rhetorical displays.
300 *"Single is the race, single"* Pind Nem 6 1–5.
301 *"held out to me the title of son"* Curt 8 8 15.
301 *"What you see flowing, my friends, is blood not 'ichor' "* Plut Alex 28, quoting the *Iliad,* book 5, line 340.
301 *hardly ever mentioned his godhead* Plut Alex 28 1.
301 *"not at all vain or deluded"* Ibid.
302 *"The gods always give good advice"* Curt 8 6 17.
303 *"You ask as if you didn't know"* Curt 8 7 1.
304 *"I am foisting Persian habits"* Curt 8 8 13.
304 *"Not one of Hermolaus' accomplices"* Plut Alex 55 5–6
305 *"The youths were stoned to death"* Ibid., 55 7.
305 *Various versions of his fate* Ibid., 55 9; Arrian 4 14 3; Plut Sulla 36; Suda K 240.
306 *They knew very little* Tall tales about India can be found in Herodotus 3 98–106.
306 *Gods visited* The Greeks were syncretists and equated others' gods to their own. It is not inconceivable that advisers like Aristander invented connections for reasons of propaganda.
306 *India was the most populous nation* Herod 3 94.
306 *"The extravagance of [the Indians'] royalty"* Curt 8 9 23–26.
307 *Darius I had taken the boundary* Herod 4 44.
307 *Unwilling to be outdone* Curt 8 5 4, and also for the figure of 120,000 soldiers.
308 *not more than sixty thousand* See Heckel (2008), pp. 160–61.
308 *recruitment of thirty thousand men* Curt 8 5 1.
308 *Taxiles, the king of Taxila* Taxiles was a regnal name, not a personal one, and was also adopted by his son.
308 *"If I possess more than you"* Plut Alex 59 3.
308 *"At least in India"* Curt 8 12 17–18.
309 *an arrow pierced his breastplate* Arrian 4 23 3.
309 *"pulled out the barb"* Curt 8 10 28–29.

310 *she was good-looking*   Ibid., 8 10 35–36.

310 *a case of cruel necessity*   Fuller, p. 126, n. 2.

310 *Cradled in a bend*   See Stein, chapters 19 and 20, for this section. His identification of Aornos with Pir-Sar is convincing.

311 *a bridge or causeway*   Arrian 4 29 7 reports that the Macedonians built a ramp, but this would have taken too long to complete. It must have been some sort of bridge.

311 *early American railroad trestle bridge*   Green, p. 385.

312 *"Alexander was now master of the rock"*   Arrian 4 30 4.

312 *The king was modest enough*   Plut Mor 181d.

312 *The army was acting very oddly*   There is no reason to deny the historicity of this event, but it does look as if Alexander had the wool pulled over his eyes.

312 *women from the baggage train*   Women are not mentioned in the sources, but were known to participate in similar orgies—see *The Bacchae* of Euripides, which premiered in Pella.

312 *"He spent all his time"*   Hom Hymns 26.

313 *"became possessed by Dionysus"*   Arrian 5 2 7.

314 *Indian king Porus*   Ancient accounts of the Battle of the Hydaspes are flawed. The best is Arrian (5 8 4– 5 19 3). I have relied on Fuller—except that I take it that Coenus took his cavalry to Porus's left wing *behind* his infantry, not in front of it. See Green, p. 397 and note 87 on p. 554.

314 *"rode an elephant"*   Curt 8 13 7.

314 *but a rational guess posits*   For the differing numbers, see Arrian 5 15 4; Diod 17 87 2; Curt 8 13 6.

315 *"With his boats plying up and down"*   Arrian 5 9 3.

317 *"But if Porus takes part of his army"*   Ibid., 5 11 4. This may be a quotation from the king's written orders.

318 *between eighty-five and two hundred elephants*   Arrian 5 15 5 suggests two hundred elephants, implying a front six kilometers long. Curtius proposes only eighty-five, and Polyaenus has them spaced at thirteen-meter intervals, producing a front of only one kilometer. The Macedonian phalanx of six thousand men would have a front of .75 kilometer.

318 *"His whole array"*   Diod 17 87 5

319 *With Coenus's arrival*   The observant reader will be asking what happened to the chariots on Porus's right wing. Our sources do not say. We must presume that Coenus simply brushed them aside. It seems unlikely that these cumbersome vehicles accompanied the cavalry all the way to Porus's right.

320 *Crowded now*   Arrian 5 17 5–6.

320 *The phalanx recovered its élan*   Arrian's account loses focus. It is unclear how the Macedonian cavalry were able to encircle Porus's long infantry battle line. But the destruction of the Indian cavalry decided the battle.

320 *twenty thousand Indian infantry and three thousand cavalry*   Arrian 5 18 3. As

usual the sources disagree on numbers. Diodorus 17 89 3 has Macedonian losses of 280 cavalry and more than seven hundred infantry.

322 *"Like a king"*   Ibid., 5 19 1–3.

323 *Seventeen thousand Indians*   Ibid., 5 24 5.

323 *"This act greatly damaged his reputation"*   Poly 4 3 30.

324 *cities of Nicaea and Bucephala*   Diod 17 95 5.

324 *two hundred thousand infantry*   Diod 17 93 2.

324 *confronted by an enigma*   This section is indebted to the discussion in Heckel, pp. 120–25.

325 *Soldiers' wives were granted monthly rations*   Diod 17 94 4.

325 *gave them a pep talk*   Arrian and Curtius composed versions of the king's and Coenus's speeches. These were not records of what was actually said, but reflect what their authors thought could or should have been said. They do reflect the relevant issues and the situation of the parties, so they are worth citing.

325 *"All this land is yours"*   Arrian 5 26 8.

325 *"I must have hurt you in some way"*   Curt 9 2 31.

325 *"You should not now lead forward"*   Arrian 5 27 7.

CHAPTER 14. SHOW ME THE WAY TO GO HOME

Arrian, including his *Indica,* and Curtius predominate.

328 *nearly two thousand vessels*   Arrian 6 2 4. Arrian disagrees with himself, for in the *Indica* he estimates only eight hundred vessels. The difference may mean that the Indian craft were counted in on the first occasion. Diod 17 94 5 and Curt 9 3 22 claims one thousand vessels.

329 *"One of the falsities"*   Ibid., 6 2 3.

329 *"The noise of the simultaneous rowing"*   Arrian 6 3 3–4. Readers may recall Thucydides' evocation (6 30–32) of the Athenian fleet as it left for Sicily in 415 B.C. A model, perhaps, for Arrian.

330 *"They did not rise so high"*   Ibid. 6 5 2–3.

330 *"except to the nerves"*   Arrian 6 5 2.

330 *they actually drew swords*   Plut Alex 47 11–12, including the quoted oath below.

331 *one more hard-fought campaign*   For the Mallian episode, see Arrian 6 8–11; Diodorus 17 98–99; Plut Alex 63; Curt 9 4 26–9 5 18.

332 *"the blood escaping from the wound"*   Arrian 6 10 1.

333 *surgeon on hand*   Curtius 9 5 attributes the extraction to a skillful surgeon, Critobulus.

333 *Perdiccas, cut round the wound*   Ibid., 6 11 1. Arrian attributes the surgery either to one of his generals, Perdiccas, or to a doctor from Cos, Critodemus or Critobulus (see also Curt 9 5 25). It seems marginally more likely that Perdiccas removed the arrow in the field without waiting for an army doctor to appear.

333 *splintered rib*   Renault, p. 187. I make use of the analysis.

334 *"I would guess that Alexander's annoyance"*   Ibid., 6 13 4.

335 *"When they came to the point"*   Ibid., 6 18 5.

335 *The next stage of Alexander's journey*   Engels, pp. 110–18 is by far the soundest guide to this enigmatic and disastrous episode in Alexander's career.

335 *"Chiefly a barren repetition"*   Encyclopedia Britannica (1911 ed.), vol. 17, p. 452.

337 *Estimates of his numbers*   See, e.g., Heckel (2008), pp. 162–63, or *contra* Engels, Appendix 5.

337 *He sent out fast-riding messengers*   Diod 17 105 7.

337 *"living in stifling huts"*   Arrian 6 23 3.

338 *"One factor was the depth of the sand"*   Arrian 6 24 4.

338 *"All along the route"*   Ibid., 6 25 3.

339 *Once a party of soldiers*   Ibid., 6 26 1–3.

339 *"The effect on the morale"*   Ibid., 6 26 3/.

339 *The agony had lasted sixty days*   Ibid., 66 7.

339 *a quarter of the army's fighting force*   Ibid., 66 2.

339 *"Diseases, wretched food"*   Ibid.

340 *he loosened the bonds of discipline*   Arrian 6 28 1–2; Curt 9 10 24–29. Arrian and some moderns disbelieve this story. There seems no good reason why.

340 *"Alexander himself feasted continually"*   Plut Alex 67 1–3.

341 *"such was the great change in their appearance"*   Arr Ind 34 7.

341 *"Sir, your ships"*   Ibid., 35 6–7.

341 *Bagoas, the lovely eunuch*   Plut Alex 67 7–8.

342 *A famous work of art*   This discussion of Aetion's painting is indebted to Chugg, pp. 80–81, and his clever identification of Bagoas.

342 *the scene was a very beautiful bedroom*   Lucian Herod 4 7. The description is so detailed that the Renaissance artist Giovanni Antonio Bazzi, known as Il Sodoma, was able to paint a version that cannot have differed very greatly from the original.

343 *"Mortal, I am Cyrus"*   Arrian 6 29 8.

343 *descendant of Cyrus himself was responsible*   Plutarch blames a Macedonian, Polymachus. It is perfectly plausible that he and Orxines were partners in crime. Plutarch might have been more shocked by a Macedonian behaving badly and ignored the typical "Oriental."

343 *According to Curtius, he paid his respects*   Curt 10 1 30–39. The historian does his best to blacken Bagoas's name and exonerate Orxines. He tries too hard and his efforts are counterproductive. Arrian 6 29 9-11–30 2 gives the sounder account. It seems clear that Orxines plundered Cyrus's tomb, although this is not explicitly stated.

344 *many newly appointed satraps*   For a harsher verdict on the purge of the satraps in the sections that follow, see Badian pp. 58–95, "Harpalus." Badian compares

the unspecified fate of Coenus (p. 62) with the forced suicide of Rommel in the Second World War, a judgment resting entirely on supposition.

344 *Even at home, Olympias*   Plut Alex 68 4.

345 *"this could not compensate"*   Curt 10 1 2–3.

345 *"oppression of the ruled"*   Arrian 6 27 5.

345 *He wrote to all his satraps*   Diod 17 106 3.

346 *"King Alexander to the exiles"*   Ibid., 18 8 4.

347 *"become more inclined to accept"*   Arrian 7 4 3.

347 *"his degeneration from his former self"*   Curt 10 1 42.

348 *"In the middle of the tent"*   Ath 13 539d–f.

348 *"trebly a slave"*   Ibid., 595a–c.

349 *"Harpalus was exceptionally shrewd"*   Plut Dem 25 5.

350 *Brahmins, a priestly aristocratic class*   See Arrian 6 16 5; 6 17 1–2; 7 5–6; 7 2–4.

350 *the sage told him a parable*   Plut Alex 65 6–8.

352 *suffered from a disease of the intestine*   For Calanus's suicide, see Arrian 7 3 1–6; Plut Alex 69 6–9; Diod 17 107 1–6.

351 *"Drink deep with the king"*   Plut Alex 69 7.

351 *"He believed that he came"*   Plut Mor 329 c–d.

352 *The celebrations took place*   Ath 12 538b–f; Arrian 7 4–8; Plut Alex 70 3. Chares and Arrian are not altogether clear; my reconstruction of the mass wedding ceremony is consistent with the sources.

354 *"deeply resented all this"*   Arrian 7 6 5.

354 *the king called an assembly*   For the Otis mutiny, see Arrian 7 8–12; Curt 10 2 12–4; Dios 17 109 2.

355 *"He had become by that time quicker"*   Arrian 7 8 3.

356 *"you are all my kinsmen"*   Ibid., 7 11 7.

356 *"hero, friend, soldiers' father"*   Schachermeyr, p. 232.

357 *"was charging a high rent"*   Arrian 7 12 6.

357 *"Antipater does not understand"*   Plut Alex 39 13.

357 *"On the outside, Antipater"*   Plut Mor 180E.

358 *"We hear of nothing"*   Arrian 7 12 7.

CHAPTER 15. LAST THINGS

Arrian and Plutarch are the essential texts for the end of the reign. Also the *Alexander Romance* and the *Liber Mortis,* usually unreliable but with important, apparently correct details.

359 *"On the fifth day of the month of Dius"*   Ael VH 3 23.. The Royal Journal is lost, but some quotations (or paraphrases) appear in the literary sources. See page 461 for further information

360 *The exact nature of Hephaestions's illness*   See Chugg, pp. 111–12.

360 *"I believe he would rather have been the first"*   Arrian 7 16 8.

361 *"As a token of mourning"*   Plut Alex 72 2.

361 *ten thousand or more talents*   Just 12 12 12 and Diod 17 115 5 give twelve thousand talents; Plut Alex 72 3 and Arrian 7:14.8, ten thousand.

361 *"Alexander collected artisans"*   Diod 17 115 1–2. There is some confusion in the sources between a funeral pyre and a funerary monument. My assumption is that the king intended a pyre on which Hephaestion's remains would be cremated. The archaeologist R. Koldewey found a possible site for the pyre at a scorched platform below a pile of brick rubble in Babylon. See R. Koldewey, *The Excavations at Babylon* (London: Macmillan, 1914), pp. 310–11.

361 *quench temple fires*   Diod 17 114 4.

362 *"a sacrifice to the spirit"*   Plut Alex 72 4 and Il 23 175ff.

362 *"ruled by Hephaestion's thighs"*   A quotation from a collection of letters wrongly attributed to Diogenes and probably published in the first century A.D.

362 *the couple were coeval*   Curtius 3 12 16.

363 *"If I find the temples"*   Arrian 7 23 8.

363 *"Alexander used to wear even the sacred vestments"*   Ath 12 537g–f. This is a quotation from Ephippus, contemporary author of *The Deaths of Alexander and Hephaestion.*

365 *"The delegates wore ceremonial wreaths"*   Arrian 7 23 2.

365 *"The practices which even now"*   Hyp Fun 21.

365 *"Alexander might be the son of Zeus"*   Hyp Dem 7.

365 *"Alexander wants to be a god"*   Plut Mor 219e–f.

366 *a multitude of embassies*   Arrian 7 15 1–5.

367 *the king's contemporary, Cleitarchus*   Pliny 3 57.

367 *the moment "when Alexander himself"*   Arrian 7 15 4–5.

368 *Alexander set out his strategy*   Diod 18 4 4–6. Diodorus provides a long list of Alexander's *grands projets,* on which some have cast doubt. There seems to be no good reason to challenge the authenticity of the items on Diodorus's list, for they develop naturally from the king's known policies and achievements.

369 *establish cities*   Ibid.

369 *"dangerous for him"*   Arrian 7 16 5.

369 *"exercise kingship"*   29th ahû tablet of *Enûma Anu Enlil,* obv. 59–61. British Museum.

369 *Callisthenes had been given access*   http://www.livius.org/articles/person/callisthenes-of-olynthus/

369 *"The best of prophets"*   Fragment 963 Nuack.

370 *one of the king's Companions, Apollodorus*   Arrian 7 18 1–5. Aristobulus reports that he heard this anecdote from Peithagoras himself.

371 *He sailed through a swamp*   Arrian 7 22 1–5, Diod 17 112 5–7, Strabo 16 1 11.

371 *lèse-majesté at its worst*   Ibid., 7 22 4.

372 *"Alexander had become overwrought"*   Plut Alex 75 1.

373 *"Alexander dead?"*   Plut Phoc 22.

373 *When the dowager queen, Sisygambis*   Curt 105 19–25.

373 *The royal helmsman, Onesicritus*   LiberM 97.

373 *the rumor mill only began*   Plut Alex 77 1.

374 *the greatest philosopher of the age*   Plut Alex 77 3; Arrian 7 27 1.

374 *with a stick*   Alex Rom 3 31.

374 *consisted of ice-cold water*   Ibid., 77 4. The *Alexander Romance* 3 31 proposes a less exotic container; it says that the poison would shatter bronze, glass, or clay, but was stored safely in a lead container inside an iron container.

374 *Cassander handed the poison*   Alex Rom 3 31. Also for Tolaus's grudge.

374 *whose drinking party*   The names of those attending the party are listed in usually unreliable late texts (see the *Alexander Romance* 3 31, p. 150, and the Liber de Morte 97 and 98). But it is a convincing list. Those we recognize are exactly the kind of person we would have expected as the king's drinking companions.

375 *Iolaus slipped the poison*   LiberM 99.

375 *a mysterious end*   Alex Rom 3 32.

375 *The king's health gradually improved*   Ibid., 110.

375 *"the business is concluded"*   Ibid.

377 *"It could well be that Antipater's recall"*   Arrian 7 12 6.

378 *There is no known liquid*   That said, there has been talk of a highly toxic anti-tumor antibiotic, calicheamicin, which can subsist in limestone—as, for example in the river Styx, today's Mavroneri, in the Peloponnese. See Adrienne Mayor and Antoinette Hayes, "The Deadly Styx River and the Death of Alexander" (Princeton/Stanford Working Papers in Classics, 2011; available online at http://www.princeton.edu/~pswpc/pdfs/mayor/051101.pdf). The bacterium has been found in Texas. The hypothesis that the water of Mavroneri is poisonous remains a hypothesis. It has been reported that contemporary locals and visitors have tasted the Stygian water with no deleterious effect (http://www.ellieismailidou.com/2011/09/river-styx-dont-sip-from-immortal.html).

378 *"Nobody had any suspicion"*   Plut Alex 77 1.

378 *she acted with her usual fury*   Diod 19 11 4–9

378 *honored for his role in the assassination*   Plut Mor 849f.

378 *Alexander's decline and death*   *Alexander Romance* 3 31, 32 has the king survive three days after being poisoned, which is still too long for him to survive most poisons.

379 *strychnine administered in unmixed wine*   This section on the cause of Alexander's death is indebted to Engels (July 1978), who has settled the matter.

379 *"most authorities consider"*   Plut Alex 77 5.

380 *the many wounds*   Here is a detailed list of injuries:

    i.   335 B.C. Struck on the head by a stone while fighting Illyrians

    ii.   335 B.C. Struck on the neck by an iron mace while fighting the Illyrians

    iii.   334 B.C. ". . . my head was . . . gashed with a barbarian scimitar" at the Battle of the Granicus

   iv.   333 B.C. ". . . run through the thigh with a sword" at the Battle of Issus

   v.   332 B.C. ". . . shot in the ankle with a dart" during the siege of Gaza

   vi.   ?* Dislocated shoulder after falling from his horse

   vii.   ?** Shinbone split by a Maracadartean arrow

   viii.   327 B.C. ". . . shot through the shoulder" by an Assacanian arrow

   ix.   ? Wounded in the thigh by the Gandridae

   x.   326 B.C. Shot in the breast by an arrow fired by "one of the Mallotes" (i.e., Mallians)

   xi.   325 B.C. Received a blow to the neck while fighting the Mallians

380 *especially common in June or July*   Engels (July 1978), p. 225.

CHAPTER 16. FUNERAL GAMES

Diodorus leads, with a little help from Forster and Tennyson.

381 *the blinded Cyclops*   Plut Gal 1 4.

382 *"our expected hope"*   Phot 92 2 (from Arrian *The Successors,* book 1).

382 *"Nowhere are more searing temperatures"*   Curt 10 10 10–12.

383 *In 1850 . . . a dragoman*   Forster, pp. 112–13.

386 *"When he asked the man"*   Aug 444.

387 *"Alexander . . . taught the Gedrosians"*   Plut Mor 328C–329D.

388 *"To sail beyond the sunset"*   Tennyson, "Ulysses," ll. 60–61.

BACKGROUND AND SOURCES

402 *"brilliantly ingenious"*   Quint 10 1 74.

INDEX

ANTHONY EVERITT is a former visiting professor in the visual and performing arts at Nottingham Trent University. He has written extensively on European culture and is the author of *Cicero, Augustus, Hadrian and the Triumph of Rome, The Rise of Rome,* and *The Rise of Athens.* He has served as secretary general of the Arts Council for Great Britain. Everitt lives near Colchester, England's first recorded town, founded by the Romans.

ABOUT THE TYPE

———

This book was set in Bembo, a typeface based on an old-style
Roman face that was used for Cardinal Pietro Bembo's tract *De
Aetna* in 1495. Bembo was cut by Francesco Griffo (1450–1518) in
the early sixteenth century for Italian Renaissance printer and
publisher Aldus Manutius (1449–1515). The Lanston Monotype
Company of Philadelphia brought the well-proportioned letter-
forms of Bembo to the United States in the 1930s.